Toll
Plar……g

Tolley's Equine Tax Planning

Julie Butler (Butler & Co)

with contributions by

Allison Broadey (The VAT Consultancy)
Mark Charter (White & Bowker)
Guy Hurst (Withers[LLP])
Andrew Miles (Thomson's Group plc)

LexisNexis™ UK

Members of the LexisNexis Group worldwide

United Kingdom	LexisNexis UK, a Division of Reed Elsevier (UK) Ltd, Halsbury House, 35 Chancery Lane, London, WC2A 1EL, and 4 Hill Street, Edinburgh EH2 3JZ
Argentina	LexisNexis Argentina, Buenos Aires
Australia	LexisNexis Butterworths, Chatswood, New South Wales
Austria	LexisNexis Verlag ARD Orac GmbH & Co KG, Vienna
Canada	LexisNexis Butterworths, Markham, Ontario
Chile	LexisNexis Chile Ltda, Santiago de Chile
Czech Republic	Nakladatelství Orac sro, Prague
France	Editions du Juris-Classeur SA, Paris
Germany	LexisNexis Deutschland GmbH, Frankfurt and Munster
Hong Kong	LexisNexis Butterworths, Hong Kong
Hungary	HVG-Orac, Budapest
India	LexisNexis Butterworths, New Delhi
Ireland	LexisNexis, Dublin
Italy	Giuffrè Editore, Milan
Malaysia	Malayan Law Journal Sdn Bhd, Kuala Lumpur
New Zealand	LexisNexis Butterworths, Wellington
Poland	Wydawnictwo Prawnicze LexisNexis, Warsaw
Singapore	LexisNexis Butterworths, Singapore
South Africa	LexisNexis Butterworths, Durban
Switzerland	Stämpfli Verlag AG, Berne
USA	LexisNexis, Dayton, Ohio

A CIP Catalogue record for this book is available from the British Library.

ISBN 0 406 966540

Typeset by Phoenix Photosetting, Chatham, Kent
Printed and bound in Great Britain by Antony Rowe Ltd, Chippenham, Wilts

Visit LexisNexis UK at www.lexisnexis.co.uk

Foreword

The racing industry as a whole has been crying out for a book like this, written in understandable layman's terms for every professional in the business. This book can genuinely save you money, as it recommends ways in which any stud owner, racehorse owner, trainer and jockey can achieve maximum tax efficiency.

Equine Tax Planning accepts that the equine world is very complex. The very different areas of stud farming, owning racehorses, training, breeding and standing stallions at stud are all linked together and they all have very different tax and VAT treatments which need careful examination.

Julie Butler has joined forces with Withers LLP, the solicitors, and Mark Charter of White & Bowker solicitors to present the need for tax planning with the joint resources of the legal and accountancy professions. Throughout the book there are references to the need for legal protection and the drafting of good legal agreements. One of the largest concerns of those owning horses and being in business with horses is that of VAT registration, claiming VAT and having to charge VAT. Allison Broadey of The VAT Consultancy devotes a whole chapter to this subject. In addition this book embraces the consideration that tax planning can be enhanced through the financial services sector. The author has invited Thomson's Group plc to explain the benefits of tax planning using the tools of their industry.

Current debates in the racing industry focus on the levels of prize money and emphasise the need of every owner and trainer to become more commercial. Of utmost concern is the role of the stable staff and the need to try and put together a remuneration package in a tax efficient manner.

Many tax practitioners, particularly those in urban or suburban environments, might consider that their clients are unaffected by the current growth of the equine industry and the collapse of the farming industry. However, many of their clients own racehorses or have family members who enjoy equine sports. These have evolved into activities which might either require disclosure to the Inland Revenue or be capable of achieving very beneficial tax reliefs. At the very least, these activities require communication between taxpayer and tax adviser in the interests of planning and protection.

This book will enable you to learn the rules and get the best out of the system. It is a must for those who are investing money in racing and not getting their due returns. Read it and start saving money.

Clare Balding
Sports presenter and journalist

Author Biography

Julie Butler qualified as a Chartered Accountant in 1980 with first time passes in all her exams, and in 1990 she became a Fellow of the Institute of Chartered Accountants. She formed her own practice, Butler & Co, in 1986, which specialises in agriculture, land and equine matters. It was initially based at her farmhouse in Hampshire with offices then opening in Alresford, Bishops Waltham and Fareham. Julie is managing partner at Butler & Co.

Julie lives on a farm and her family is very integrated into the farming way of life. She acts for a large number of farming and equestrian clients and has strong roots with the countryside. Julie has lectured extensively on proactive tax planning for farmers, landowners and the equine industry. Julie is a master of foxhounds and owns a number of point-to-pointers and shares in racehorses giving her a first hand understanding of the needs of the equine and racing community and the problems they face.

Julie has ridden Point to Point winners, including one when she was in her early forties. However, the doctors stopped this avenue of pleasure, and so she transferred her energy and enthusiasm into writing.

Julie has started various newsletters and periodicals and has written for a large number of the tax and farming journals. Her views on the countryside and the surrounding tax planning issues have been featured in newspapers such as *The Daily Telegraph, The Times* and the *Financial Times.*

Contributor Biographies

Allison Broadey

Allison Broadey has over 16 years' experience as a VAT practitioner, initially as a VAT Inspector with HM Customs & Excise, and then as 'gamekeeper turned poacher' in commercial practice. Having qualified as a Chartered Tax Adviser specialising in VAT with Coopers & Lybrand, she is now a Senior Consultant with The VAT Consultancy. She has a diverse range of clients in the farming and private sector and specialises in planning for land and property. She lectures to associations, practitioners and private businesses on all VAT matters. Allison Broadey and The VAT Consultancy can be contacted via www.thevatconsultancy.com or allison.broadey@thevatconsultancy.com.

Mark Charter

White & Bowker partner Mark Charter is a property specialist and is particularly involved in the sale and acquisition of equine, agricultural and rural property, and property work associated with tax and estate planning arrangements. Mark is also involved in advising clients on business structures for rural businesses, landlord and tenant issues, countryside issues (for example, rights of way and sporting rights) and Town and Country Planning matters. He is also a member of the Equine Lawyers Association and the Agricultural Lawyers Association, and Assistant Deputy Coroner for Hampshire Central. Mark enthusiastically rides, shoots and fishes, but says that despite nearly 40 years of doing so he doesn't get any better at any of them!

Guy Hurst

Guy Hurst is a Senior Assistant solicitor in the Landed Estates Group of Withers LLP, where he deals exclusively in the sale, purchase and management of rural estates throughout the country. He is also a qualified chartered surveyor. He has had his own stud of ponies for thirty years and is a keen follower of hounds in Hampshire where he lives with his wife and four young children. He is a member of council of the Royal Agricultural Society of England and is Chief Horse Steward at the Royal Show.

Andrew Miles

Andrew Miles is head of the research department at Thomson's Group plc, providing a dedicated technical resource to Thomson's specialist private client and employee benefit advisers. Since 1969 Thomson's has dedicated itself to developing working relationships with other professionals and has many long-standing relationships, providing independent advice to mutual clients. Few would doubt the wisdom of planning financially for the future. Financial services can provide practical, and sometimes innovative, solutions. Hailing from Cheltenham, Andrew is a keen (and occasionally successful) follower of the National Hunt.

Contents

Abbreviations

ABA = Agricultural Building Allowance
ABB = Association of British Bookmakers
ABI = Association of British Insurers
AJA = Amateur Jockeys Association
AIM = Alternative Investments Market
APR = Agricultural Property Relief
AONB = Areas of Outstanding Natural Beauty
ASLI = Areas of Special Landscape Importance
BATR = Business Asset Taper Relief
BEN = Business Economic Note
BEVA = British Equine Veterinary Association
BHB = British Horseracing Board
BHTB = British Horseracing Training Board
BHS = British Horse Society
BPR = Business Property Relief
CAP = Common Agricultural Policy
CGAS = Capital Goods Adjustment Scheme
CGT = Capital Gains Tax
CIR = Commission of Inland Revenue
CLA = Country Land and Business Association
CPRE = Council for the Protection of Rural England
CROW = Countryside and Rights Of Way Act
CTO = Capital Taxes Office
DEFRA = Department of the Environment, Food and Rural Affairs
DIY = Do It Yourself
DV = District Valuer
EIS = Enterprise Investment Scheme
ERDP = England Rural Development Programme
ESA = Environmentally Sensitive Areas
ESOP = Employees Share Option Plan
EZT = Enterprise Zone Trust
FBA – Federation of Bloodstock Agents
FBT = Farm Business Tenancy
FEU = Foreign Entertainers Unit
FHL = Furnished Holiday Let
FMD = Foot and Mouth Disease
FTS = Fiscally Transparent Syndicate
FURBS = Funded Unapproved Retirement Benefit Scheme
FYA = First Year Allowance
GTP = Green Transport Plan
GROB = Gift With Reservation of Benefit
HBLB = Horserace Betting Levy Board
HDC = Horticultural Development Council

HFL	=	Horseracing Forensic Laboratory
HSA	=	Horseracing Sponsors Association
HTB	=	Horserace Totalisator Board
IAS	=	International Accounting Standard
IBA	=	Industrial Building Allowance
ICHL	=	Industry Committee (Horseracing) Limited
IFA	=	Independent Financial Advisor
IHT	=	Inheritance Tax
IHTA	=	Inheritance Tax Act
ILPH	=	International League for Protection of Horses
IRC	=	Inland Revenue Commisioners
ITBA	=	Irish Thoroughbred Breeders Association
JAGB	=	Jockeys Association of Great Britain
JC	=	Jockey Club
LFA	=	Less Favoured Areas
LLP	=	Limited Liability Partnership
LPA	=	Local Planning Authority
MFH	=	Master of Foxhounds
MFHA	=	Masters of Foxhounds Association
MP	=	Member of Parliament
NAB	=	National Association of Bookmakers
NFU	=	National Farmers Union
NIC	=	National Insurance Contributions
NICO	=	National Insurance Contributions Office
NJPC	=	National Joint Pitch Council
NTF	=	National Trainers Federation
OEIC	=	Open Ended Investment Company
PAYE	=	Pay As You Earn
PET	=	Potentially Exempt Transfer
PMG	=	Processing and Marketing Grant
PPG	=	Planning Policy Guidance Notes
PPP	=	Personal Pension Plan
PPORA	=	Point-to-Point Owners and Riders Association
PPR	=	Principal Private Residence
PPSA	=	Point-to-Point Secretaries Association
PR	=	Public Relations
PRIS	=	Professional Riders Insurance Scheme
PTA	=	Permit Trainers Association
RBA	=	Rails Bookmakers Association
RCA	=	Racecourse Association
RES	=	Rural Enterprise Scheme
RHT	=	Racecourse Holdings Trust
RIBA	=	Royal Institute of British Architects
RICS	=	Royal Institute of Chartered Surveyors
ROA	=	Racehorse Owners Association
RSPCA	=	Royal Society for Prevention of Cruelty to Animals

RTA = Racehorse Transporters Association
RTPA = Royal Town Planning Institute
SIPP = Self-Invested Personal Pension
SLA = Stable Lads Association
SpC = Special Commissioners
SSAP = Statement of Standard Accounting Practice
SSAS = Small Self-Administered Scheme
SSSI = Sites of Special Scientific Interest
SVD = Share Valuation Division
TBA = Thoroughbred Breeders Association
TMA = Taxes Management Act
TOGC = Transfer of a Going Concern
VCT = Venture Capital Trust
VOA = Valuation Office Agency
VTS = Vocational Training Scheme
WDV = Written Down Value
WGS = Woodland Grant Scheme

Table of Statutes

Paragraph number in bold type indicate where the legislation is set out in part or in full.

Table of Statutory Instruments

1987/530 Income Tax (Entertainers and Sportsmen) Regulations 1987	8.18
1987/790 Infectious Diseases of Horses Order 1987	19.3
1989/2261 Non-Domestic Rating (Unoccupied Property) Regulations 1989	18.30
1995/549 Non-Domestic Rating (Unoccupied Property) (Amendment) Regulations 1995	18.30
1995/1755 Equine Viral Arteritis Order 1995	19.3
1995/2518 Value Added Tax Regulations 1995	17.25
1997/1480 Welfare of Animals (Transport) Order 1997	19.1
2001/2585 Non-Domestic Rating (Former Agricultural Premises) (England) Order 2001	18.37
2001/2586 Non-Domestic Rating (Stud Farms) (England) Order 2001	18.36
2001/117 Personal Pension Schemes (Restriction on Discretion to Approve) (Permitted Investments) Regulations 2001	20.11
2002/3045 Sale and Supply of Goods to Consumers Regulations 2002	
reg 4	5.2

Table of cases

J

K

L

M

T

W

Y

The Equine Industry 1

The growth of the equestrian industry

1.1 The last year has seen significant growth in the UK racing industry. The 2002 Report Summary of the British Horseracing Board (BHB) showed an increase in racing prize money from £72m to £84m in 2002 with a projected £100m in 2003. In 2002 racecourse attendance exceeded 5.5 million customers, surpassing all records since 1959. The racing industry is, however, going through tremendous change. At the time of writing, owners are 'striking' due to the very harsh cut back of £6m prize money. It has been said that the decisions made in the year ahead will shape racing for the next generation. Whilst there is a mixture of radical change and enormous potential, it is an excellent opportunity for the racing industry to take a radical view about the tax planning and the commercial approach. The tax man can help and this book attempts to show how.

Many areas of equine activity are increasing in popularity and there are clear signs of commercial growth. There is also increased interest in the 'pony-paddock' culture whilst the need for farm diversification is also having an effect in this area. A recent tax case *Longson v Baker (2001) 73 TC 415* (see **2.5** below) considered whether or not stables, a paddock and related facilities could be regarded as part of a principal private residence for a capital gains tax purposes. Unfortunately the High Court ruled that it was not necessary to take into account the 'equestrian' aspect of the dwelling house saying, 'it is not objectively required, ie necessary to keep horses at a house in order to enjoy it as a residence' (see **2.34** below).

This case has been a cause of some dismay to equine enthusiasts, suggesting as it does, a total misunderstanding of the horse world amongst the tax and legal professions. The horse population is growing and it has to live somewhere.

Some areas of the equestrian industry (riding schools and livery yards within riding schools) are in decline as a result of the high cost of regulation and rates. The British Riding School Association reported that in 1999, almost 10% of Britain's 2,400 riding schools closed. On the other hand, it is arguable at least that the equestrian industry is an ideal area for further agricultural diversification:

- it is not damaging to the rural environment;
- uses existing farm buildings; and
- it opens up the countryside to those from rural and urban areas.

The present Government has effectively neglected equestrian centres, merely issuing a consultation document with what are in effect diluted and recycled proposals which do little to assist this important industry. The value that riding schools can add to the social and educational infrastructure of the UK is considered by many to be outstanding and worthy of greater consideration.

This book questions how the growth in numbers involved in this area of activity and its evident popularity can be treated tax efficiently by the commercial businesses involved in the sport. It also sets out the tax 'pitfalls' to the tax adviser and equine participant.

Are horses agriculture?

1.2 Stud farming is 'farming' for tax purposes. The ordinary meaning of farming is considered to be husbandry, ie the raising of livestock. Guidance as to the definition of agricultural property or 'farmland' is given in the Income and Corporation Taxes Act 1988 s 832(1) and the Inheritance Tax Act 1984 s 115(2). This can contradict with business rates rulings (see **18.15** to **18.37**)

There are many people involved in the industries of farming, equestrian activities and land management/ownership who consider that the definition of agriculture should be reviewed. There are also those who consider that the definition of the horse as 'agricultural' or 'non-agricultural' should be given greater clarity and consistency. There are contradictions of definition between the UK and Europe and between the tax authorities and the rating authorities.

In the tax case of *Wheatly v IRC [1988] STC (SCD) 60* it was accepted that a meadow constituted pasture for the purposes of inheritance tax. However, since the horses in question were used for leisure pursuits they could not be said to be 'connected with agricultural activity or with stud farming' and they were not, therefore, involved in agriculture. This judgment is, however, at odds with the accepted tax principle that the activity of growing grass, which can properly be regarded as a 'crop', can be regarded as an act of husbandry and grass lettings are currently taxed as farming income, provided the 'landlord' meets certain criteria and can generally gain vacant possession within 12 months. Thus, it is surely arguable that such property ought to be regarded as within the definition of agricultural property irrespective of the way in which the crop is exploited or utilised, ie grazed by horses.

Equestrian business rates

1.3 This is an important element in the development of an equine business and therefore it is covered in detail in CHAPTER **18**. The treatment of equestrian buildings for the purposes of business rating is currently inconsistent among different types and inconsistent with inheritance tax rules mentioned at **1.2** above. Whilst a shed holding heavy horses for farming is classed as an agricultural building and does not attract business rates, a House of Lords ruling in 1987 decided that a shed holding light horses for riding does attract business rates because it is not involved in 'agricultural' activities.

The role of the Country and Land Business Association

1.4 The Country Land and Business Association (CLA) has a dedicated tax department to offer tax advice to its members or their professional advisers. The advisory service is free of charge but is limited to answering questions arising from the ownership of land in England and Wales.

A large number of equine tax problems faced by landowners fall within the scope of this advisory service. The current Chief Taxation Adviser, Adrian Baird, is also a co-author of *Stanley: Taxation of Farmers and Landowners* (LexisNexis Butterworths Tolley). It is sufficient for CLA members to quote their membership number when seeking advice (or for their professional advisers to quote it when making use of the service on behalf of clients who are CLA members).

More access to the countryside

1.5 All horse owners must worry about what would happen if their beloved animal should escape and cause damage, even if they have taken every precaution to prevent this.

The Countryside and Rights of Way Act 2000 (CROW) plans to open up four million acres for the 'enjoyment of all'. Such increased public access brings significant increased concerns over public safety and the financial implications this may bring for all livestock owners. By definition, there are likely to be more gates left open, more dogs straying and more bright-coloured walking attire, all of which have potential impacts on livestock.

A recent legal case has highlighted the need for horse owners to protect themselves against potential litigation. The whole area of legal responsibility is dealt with in **CHAPTER 5: ESCAPE OR STRAYING BY HORSES**. This section attempts to set out the preventative action that can be taken.

In *Mirvahedy v Henley [2003] 2 All ER 401* the defendants kept three horses in a field. As a result of some unidentified disturbance the horses broke out of their field, first through an electric fence and then a barbed wire fence through undergrowth and onto a dual carriageway road. One of the horses collided with the claimant's vehicle resulting in the death of the horse and serious injuries to the claimant. In a controversial decision, the Court of Appeal held the defendants liable under the 'second limb' Animals Act 1971 s 2(2). The reason given was that, the horses had displayed behavioural characteristics (ie fleeing in panic from danger) which might be expected from horses placed in particular circumstances when they had been terrified by something. Thus, this was a predictable response to stimulus which the owners ought to have foreseen and taken precautions to prevent.

So what action can horse owners take to protect themselves? Obvious ideas would be to have adequate insurance, and double-check fencing and security precautions. A landowner must also obtain copies of the countryside 'agency map' to ascertain how it affects them.

Some horses are simply known as 'mad, bad and dangerous' and the increased risks of keeping this type of horse should probably be reviewed.

The problems of employing staff

1.6 One of the biggest problems facing any equestrian employer is finding and keeping staff. The problems can be helped by good tax planning to ensure that the remuneration package is as tax efficient as possible. It has been suggested that the way to keep good staff is by holding out the promise of future rides in races or competitions. Employee tax planning must be tailor made to the trainer and employee circumstances and facts.

This topic is covered in detail in **CHAPTER 12: EMPLOYMENT ISSUES**.

The proposed 'hunting ban'

1.7 With the recent [2003] vote by Members of Parliament on the proposed banning of hunting with dogs it is appropriate to consider what commercial effect this may have on the equine industry. There are a large number of people who 'ride to hounds' who would probably not otherwise ride a horse. There can be little doubt that a hunting ban would reduce the demand for horses and the industries that support them.

Each hunt generally also organises a large number of other local equine events, such as point to point racing, horse shows, hunter trials, sponsored rides etc. It is their enthusiasm and passion for the sport of hunting that encourages them to give up their time to organise such events. Generally, those associated with these activities give their time or facilities for free thus enabling them to remain viable.

There is no doubt that the hunting world provides an excellent home for retired racehorses. In addition there are a number of businesses totally dedicated to hunting such as hunter livery yards etc.

If the hunting ban goes ahead this will question the entire future commercial viability of the whole equestrian world.

The riding school

1.8 Riding schools generally offer a wide range of equine-related activities and training, including lessons at all levels, holiday accommodation, trekking and hacking, show jumping tuition, dressage, etc. They may also offer ancillary facilities such as all-weather or indoor sand schools, full, part or do-it-yourself livery, holiday accommodation and tack and equine supplies. Some riding schools are small-scale and offer only basic facilities, whilst at the other extreme, they may have a whole team of British Horse Society (BHS) qualified instructors and quality horses/ponies. Once the VAT registration limit has been exceeded, however, the VAT-registered business will often have to charge VAT inclusive prices roughly equal to its non-registered competitors. This means that margins are often reduced, with the effect that larger organisations often have a lower gross profit than smaller ones. Apart from the relatively few cases where a customer is VAT registered and can recover the extra money, prices have to remain competitive.

Proprietors of such businesses often have to be willing to work long hours, since many people, particularly in spring/summer, prefer to take their riding lessons in the evenings. Whilst courses of lessons may be paid for by cheque, individual lessons are usually paid for in cash, making this business an ideal target for the Inland Revenue's compliance teams who historically mistrust 'mainly cash' businesses.

Any riding school will come under the BHS licensing provisions.

Historically, most livery operations did not come within the operation of the licensing provisions of riding schools but are now being encouraged to join the scheme set out at **1.22** below.

The chief objective of the licensing provisions is to ensure that horses are properly fed, accommodated and cared for. However, there are also provisions about the supervision by responsible persons of horses which are hired out for riding unless a rider is competent to ride without supervision. The licence holder must hold an insurance policy covering him for liability for injury suffered by persons hiring horses for riding. The licence holder must also keep a register of all horses up to the age of three which are kept on the premises, and these horses must not be hired out for riding or used for riding instruction on payment.

The combination of the costs of the compliance with the BHS licensing provisions, business rates and the insurance costs associated with protecting against risk have caused a decline in the traditional riding school. Many have been making a loss and are unable to compete on price with the smaller unlicensed operations.

The structure of the equine business world has moved away from riding schools over the last 30 years. The casual rider has almost disappeared as there are so many other forms of leisure activities available. There has been a growth in general ownership, with many horses being kept at home or at a small livery yard. Lessons are now often given by freelance instructors and generally everything is dealt with below the VAT-registration limit. The collapse of farming has resulted in paddocks being sold at high prices to large houses in order to facilitate the keeping of horses. Small farms have been sold as potential equine establishments.

In short, the riding school is not necessarily where the pupils learn to ride. There has been a restructuring of the industry.

A racehorse trainer does not just train racehorses

1.9 A racehorse trainer does not just train horses. A racehorse trainer needs a skill base at least equal to and arguably greater than the average small business owner. So what skills are required for training?

Marketing:	Attracting owners (requiring charm and confidence); previous winners and entertaining are essential.
Public relations:	Keeping owners happy. Having a positive profile together with press and possibly TV coverage. Role models such as Jenny Pitman come to mind.
Debt collection:	Historically, owners do not pay bills unless subjected to heavy persuasion. Positive debt collection can conflict with good marketing skills.

Financial controller:	Budgets, forecasts, keeping bank managers happy and trying to cover excessive overheads are an everyday need.
Bloodstock historian:	The thoroughbred's antecedents and potential must be known in detail (ie its progeny and form) by the trainer. Reference to any form of reference book can be seen as a weakness.
Fitness expert:	A total understanding of equine fitness, build-up, recovery and responses to pressure.
Handicap expert:	Total understanding of all handicaps and maximising benefits for the owners.
Choosing the right race:	Placing the horse and finding the 'right race' are a necessity. This requires a total understanding of the whole racing calendar by the trainer.
Motor vehicle buyer:	The business miles required of the average race-horse trainer can easily exceed a motivated sales representative. There is a need to combine speed with durability and the safety of livestock.
Geography:	The trainer must have a total knowledge of the location of all racecourses, combining visits to prospective owners, current and past owners.
Human resources:	Staff. Racing is labour intensive. The trainer probably needs the skills and expertise of a psychologist, team motivator, employment law specialist and even, on occasion, a marriage counsellor!
Bloodstock buyer:	Ability to have full 'crystal ball' facilities to buy right and be able to judge the right stamp. The trainer needs an 'Alex Ferguson' knack for introducing young raw talent.
Bloodstock seller:	Ability to always sell at a profit and at the right time, ideally foreseeing all future injuries.
Veterinary skills:	Many trainers would claim that they are expected to know more than a qualified vet but are unable to charge for this skill.
Catering supremo:	Owners expect full English breakfast after watching horses work and various forms of amazing entertaining all included in their standard training fees.
Post race analyst:	Stating 'he/she will win a race' with confidence is not sufficient. Winning a race will be necessary. Each owner requires explanations, charm, drinks in the bar and positive observations on actual and future performance. This generally has to be conducted whilst saddling the next three runners or when the trainer arrives home wanting to collapse in peace and quiet.

24-hour chemist:	One national newspaper is quoted as saying that trainers would all need chemists on a 24-hour shift to analyse all the ingredients that go to making a horse fit. They also state 'one wonders how trainers can sleep at night'. The responsibility they must take for the welfare of their charges is constantly being undermined by developments beyond their control.

Larger trainers have more financial resources to provide the above infrastructure. Perhaps financial training and serious profit projections before commencing would be a positive direction as opposed to just introducing some lower quality races.

Survival of the small racehorse trainer

1.10 Whilst there are problems with the prize money it is argued that the trainers do not always go for the high prize money but for the wins. Michael Osborne, representing Sheikh Mohammed at the Gimcrack dinner, described prize money in Great Britain as being 'on the pathetic side of poor'.

The problems are deep rooted. Just because a jockey has exceptional riding talents does not mean that he or she will make a good trainer. David Beckham will not necessarily make a great trainer and Arsene Wenger and Alex Ferguson were not necessarily the best footballers. In the same way that a football manager requires a greater base of skills than a coach, a trainer requires a very full set of managerial and financial skills (see **1.9** above).

A way forward could be to provide a management helpline infrastructure for small trainers with advice on financial management. The emphasis could be on commerciality. It is hoped that this book helps put the focus on tax and financial planning.

The racehorse owner – the costs and the prize money

1.11 For most tax advisers, interaction with the equestrian business is through their client's ownership of racehorses.

At the time of writing the registration costs for a sole owner of a two- or three-year-old racehorse is estimated to be approximately £200. This includes naming, re-issue of passport, registration of the owner, colours and authority to act. It should be noted the registration of colours and authority to act have to be carried out annually.

Some relief for owners has come as a result of the BHB's decision not to increase registration and renewal charges this year. However, the Racehorse Owners Association (ROA) believes the registration system remains too complicated and are currently involved in discussions with the BHB and Weatherbys (the company which deals with the payments to owners and remuneration to jockeys in the UK), about how the system could be simplified.

The BHB and Weatherbys have also acceded to the ROA's request that owners' statements with Weatherbys should include details of the amounts deducted from the prize money for trainer's fees, jockeys and stable staff. These amounts will in future be shown in full on Weatherbys' statements, ie not just a net amount but full disclosure.

Of course, by far the biggest cost to owners relates to training fees. Recent discussions on increased pay awards to stable lads will inevitably be reflected in higher training fees, although it is felt that that the vast majority of owners do not begrudge paying more to stable staff.

The recent impressive increase in prize monies (2001: £72m; 2002: £84m) inevitably draws some racing commentators to the conclusion that owners are now better off, but much of this increase will have been eroded by higher costs.

If Sheikh Mohammed's comment (see **1.10** above) about UK prize money is accurate then it is obvious why the Inland Revenue wants to keep racing 'tax-free' for the owner. The Inland Revenue's traditional reluctance to provide tax loss relief for the owner is unlikely to change. However, owners contend that they are funding an industry which provides significant employment and consequently tax revenue for the Government. Therefore, in general, racehorse owners feel justified at lobbying hard to achieve maximum tax relief from all areas of racing.

Levy income for 2002/03 has fallen short of expectations but owners are still better able to contribute towards a better deal for staff than at any time in the recent past.

It is likely that the entry of most taxpayers into the equine industry is in the capacity as owner. We look here specifically at the racing industry. It could be that some owners just stay owners and perhaps wisely never try to move into the other more financially problematical areas of breeding, training or stud farming.

Background of the small breeder

1.12 The Thoroughbred Breeders Association's (TBA) statistics show that the average breeder only has a couple of mares or, perhaps, one stallion. Most horses racing on the flat are fillies or colts that will have some life after they have finished their time on the racetrack. Some horses will retire to stud at their prime before there can be possible loss of value. The problem is that a breeder who does not occupy a stud farm may find it more difficult to convince the Inspector of Taxes that he is operating a bona-fide trade.

For most tax advisers the biggest possible impact on their client base is the entry into horse ownership and/or breeding by a client. This activity is often viewed by client and tax adviser alike as tax-free and therefore irrelevant. However, it is suggested that all practitioners need to be fully aware of their client's racing/equine interests, especially with regard to tax planning or during any future Revenue enquiry into their clients' affairs generally. The whole question of late registration of a taxable 'business' is dealt with later in this book (see **3.13** below).

Stallions and broodmares

1.13 Stallions feature throughout this book as they integrate with every angle of tax planning. It is stallions which normally provide the greatest financial rewards for owners since they will generate fees for nominations, ie the right of owners to have their mares covered by the stallion. A stallion will normally cover at least forty mares in a season. For this reason, stallion syndicates are often established in which each syndicate member (usually a mare owner) owns a one-fortieth interest, which gives the right to nominate at least one mare each year to the stallion.

Broodmares do not generate income until they produce progeny. Before they can do this they require a nomination, which can cost tens of thousands of pounds for the right to visit a successful stallion. This is a very high-risk investment, since there is no guarantee that the mare will conceive, and even when she does, it may take up to five years before the owner knows whether he has a profitable animal on his hands, or just an expensive pet! For progeny bred for national hunt racing this period may be even longer.

The thoroughbred and the non-thoroughbred

1.14 The UK thoroughbred horse is registered with Weatherbys. Only thoroughbreds can race. The term 'bloodstock' refers to the thoroughbred racehorse. Many tax cases, particularly those dealing with stud farming, refer to the thoroughbred. The Inland Revenue Inspector's Manuals on such subjects as Agricultural Property Relief (APR) for inheritance tax (IHT) refer to horses as opposed to thoroughbred horses. It is assumed that the tax principles relate to thoroughbred and non-thoroughbred equally, although again, each case must be tested on its own merits. This is looked at further at **2.29** and **7.15** below.

Age classification of racehorses

1.15 For the purpose of racing, horses are classified as two- and three-year-olds, etc and all horses are deemed to have their birthday on 1 January. Therefore, a foal becomes a yearling on 1 January following its birth, regardless of the time of year when it was born. It is obviously preferable for the foal to be born early in the year so that it has the maximum period for growth before it races as a two-year-old. The gestation period of a mare is eleven months and, therefore, in order to allow for the possibility of a premature foaling, the breeding season commences on 15 February and lasts until 15 July.

The owner of a filly retiring from racing in 2003 will seek a nomination for the 2004 season. Assuming that the mare then foals in 2005, the foal will become a yearling on 1 January 2006 and begin racing as a two-year-old in 2007. It may not be until the horse is racing as a three-year-old, in 2008, that the owner can really judge whether the choice of stallion has been a successful one. In the intervening five year period, nomination fees are likely to have been paid each year in respect of the mare. Accordingly, it can be seen that there is a considerable investment requirement before the commercial viability of the mare can be established.

Breeding and commerciality

1.16 Keeping mares is clearly a higher risk, and longer term activity, than investment in stallions. Stallions often produce a profit, while mares generate no income directly. This explains why the Inland Revenue has been eager in the past to treat stallions as a taxable activity and mares as merely a hobby of the owner. Similarly, the Inland Revenue does not seek to tax prize money from racing, since the vast majority of racehorses never earn sufficient prize money to recover the expenditure which is required to keep and train them. If racing were treated as a taxable activity, the Inland Revenue would be handling loss claims in excess of the profits being taxed. See **4.1** to **4.7** below for tax efficiency of racehorse ownership. The possibility of a large tax-free prize or tax-free gain on the sale of a racehorse, no doubt encourages many owners to sustain the high cost of training a horse, despite the fact that they are unlikely to obtain tax relief for such expenditure (see **2.7** below).

There are normally two types of bloodstock breeder, the one who owns horses and owns or leases a stud farm (see CHAPTER 7: THE STUD FARM) and the one who owns horses but not the stud farm itself and so keeps his horse at a public stud.

The racing and breeding cycle

1.17 As the breeding cycle often involves a transfer of the yearling from the stud into racing, and its return to the stud after its racing career to produce bloodstock of its own, there is considerable merit in the view that that racing is actually an integral part of a stud farm's activities and ought to be included as part of the taxable trading activity.

The racing activity can arguably be regarded as an essential part of the breeding process as a horse will need to be tested through its success in racing for its speed, stamina and courage in order to determine whether it is likely to have a successful breeding career. If a breeder's racing activities were to be regarded as an integral part of his breeding trade, then the expenses of racing would be an allowable deduction for tax purposes and any winnings would be taxable.

In order for any activity to be treated as a taxable trade under Schedule D Case 1, it must be managed on a commercial basis with a view to the realisation of profits. As far as racing is concerned, the majority of horses are not profitable as only a small number win more than the cost of training. **Chapter 3** deals with the 'trade or hobby?' problem in more detail.

Combining racing and breeding

1.18 In general, the Inland Revenue currently regards the prospect of profits from horse-racing to be too remote and so do not accept that it is a taxable trade. It is regarded as a hobby or recreational activity or, in the case of a company, a non-taxable activity. This means that the costs of training are not tax deductible but, conversely, any winnings and capital profit are tax-free. Nonetheless, there have been cases where the taxpayer (normally a company or a breeder who personally trains and races progeny) has been treated as carrying on a taxable activity but these have been extremely rare.

There is one other occasion when the Inland Revenue may attempt to combine the breeding and racing activities. This is when they consider the breeding of horses to be a hobby, and merely ancillary to the racing activity. In this situation, they would not allow relief for the breeding expenses since these expenses would be considered to have arisen from a non-taxable activity. Although the hobby breeder is not trading, the taxpayer may, in certain circumstances, still need to consider declaration of the occasional profit which he may make. The Inland Revenue does not need to establish that there is any continuity of trade in order to do so. If a hobby breeder achieves a very successful sale, there is a fair chance that he will be able to persuade the Inspector of Taxes that his losses from the past years should be taken into account, in which case, the amount of income tax payable will be reduced or eliminated. (Again the hobby element is looked at in **CHAPTER 3**).

The tax adviser must encourage clients to advise them of large one-off profits so they can determine what correspondence with the Inland Revenue should take place.

The shortage of professional jockeys

1.19 The question of professional horsemen is dealt with in **CHAPTER 8**.

This section of the chapter is taken from various equestrian magazines so as to give the necessary background. One such source is the 'Owner' magazine of the ROA, which contains very interesting insights into the commercial reality of ownership.

In 1993 there were 139 licensed professionals jump jockeys and 158 conditionals. By 2002 this number had fallen to only 82 and 89 respectively – falls of 41% and 43%. Yet riding levels on the flat have remained comparatively consistent. The number of professional flat jockeys in 2002 was 109, compared to 104 in 1993, and there were only four fewer apprentices (147) than there were ten years ago.

This issue has attracted the concern, in particular, of the National Trainers' Federation (NTF), which warned in a recent report that: 'The number of licensed professional National Hunt jockeys has fallen to a figure where supply is insufficient to meet demand. This is particularly evident during holiday periods and on Saturdays with multiple fixtures'. The NFT stated that:

> 'whilst we have no desire to see the numbers rise dramatically, we believe that with an expanding fixture list, the current figure is not sufficient to service future needs'.

Suggestions from the National Trainers' Federation

1.20 Example suggestions by the NTF to increase the number of jockeys are as follows:

- reducing the number of 'free' rides for amateurs to 50;
- introducing a new allowance system for jockeys switching from the flat to jumping, so that their previous wins do not count in their claim;
- extending the period to 48 months in which a conditional can remain professional before reverting to amateur status;
- introducing a greater number of women-only conditional/amateur races and giving consideration to women receiving a 3lb allowance when they ride against men;

- the NTF sees no reason why female jockeys should not make it through to the ranks of experienced professionals. The reason why so few do, they suggest, is probably down to a bias from trainers and this should be addressed.

Livery yards

1.21 In the UK over the last ten years there has been a large increase in the number of livery/DIY yards for horses as a consequence of an expanding equine leisure industry. The recent need for agricultural diversification will probably increase the number of new livery yards even further. The legal and tax angles of livery yards feature throughout the book.

At present, all cat and dog boarding kennels have to be inspected and licensed by law as do riding schools, whilst livery yards fall outside the licensing requirements. There is currently no control over the standards of care offered or the experience of the staff in charge of these yards.

It is of concern to the British Equine Veterinary Association (BEVA) that if there is no registration system for livery yards and no control over the standards of care then the ability to maintain proper disease control within the horse population in the UK is inadequate.

The legal angles are dealt with at **5.1** below, the VAT angles at **17.23**, and the tax considerations at **18.1** and **18.2**.

A new BHS Livery Approval Scheme

1.22 An increasing awareness of this situation and concern for the welfare of the horses kept in livery yards has prompted the formation of a working party from within the horse industry.

This group consists of the British Equine Veterinary Association (BEVA), the British Horse Society (BHS), the International League for the Protection of Horses (ILPH) and the Royal Society for the Prevention of Cruelty to Animals (RSPCA), which together with the Department for Environment Food and Rural Affairs (DEFRA) have drawn up a Code of Practice of minimum standards required of livery yards. This code has been used as an achievable baseline for the design of the new Livery Approval Scheme, which is to be co-ordinated and run by the BHS.

The aims of the scheme are to:

- ensure that the standard of care and facilities provided in livery yards are of an acceptable level;
- provide guidelines for new yards opening up; and
- enable improved disease surveillance in the horse.

This approval scheme in the UK will therefore raise welfare standards for horses all over Britain. The scheme will also give reassurance to the first-time horse owner that their animal is in the care of experienced, knowledgeable persons with adequate facilities.

If livery yard licensing becomes mandatory as a result of the current review of equine welfare legislation, this scheme will have provided much of the necessary groundwork. The working group fully encourages livery yards to join this scheme and to work towards achieving the green BHS plaque of Livery Yard Approval.

The following details are taken direct from the RSPCA:

> 'The RSPCA has been involved in the development of this scheme from its inception, and is pleased to welcome and support its introduction. It sets out reasonable standards of horse care and management, which should be within reach of most yards.
>
> For many years the Society has had concerns about the standards of welfare in many, though not all, livery yards. This scheme will enable those yards with good management and welfare standards to proclaim their achievements, and at the same time allow the responsible owner to choose a yard which has reached at least a basic, but acceptable standard of good horse care.
>
> The RSPCA welcomes this scheme which has been produced by the British Horse Society in consultation with the BEVA, and the ILPH.

It might well be that the livery yard wants to let out grazing to other horse owners or, indeed, is the tenant of an equestrian establishment. CHAPTER **15**: THE EQUESTRIAN LANDLORD deals with all such arrangements. There is also a section on business tenancies of stables – see **15.6** below.

Many businesses will start life as a livery yard. All such yards should seek approval and regulation from the BHS.

The ILPH believes that those running a business, such as a livery yard based around the care of horses, should exhibit and should be responsible for ensuring a good level of husbandry.

Riding establishments are licensed. There appears to be no logical reason why other similar businesses should be excluded from such a requirement. With the Government currently encouraging farmers to diversify into the horse industry and an increase in 'new' horse owners using livery facilities, there is the potential for considerable increases in welfare problems for horses which will need to be addressed.

Some of the most surprising and disturbing welfare complaints received by the ILPH have related to horses kept at DIY livery yards.

These have even included horses found dead and dying at the worst establishments.

The ILPH believes that livery yards should be regulated and has, alongside DEFRA, the BEVA, the BHS and the RSPCA been looking at ways to move proposals forward.

The working group of the ILPH, BEVA, BHS and RSPCA, realising that legislative change was not imminent, have designed an excellent approval scheme and draft contract for livery yards which sets sensible achievable standards for those yards who wish to demonstrate a verified level of husbandry.

The following information is taken direct from the BHS:

> 'Livery facilities are crucial to equestrian life in this country, and it is essential that the facilities available are equal to the rising standards of horse mastership equitation among horse owners generally.
>
> It was this, and the concern expressed by the veterinary profession about equine welfare, which encouraged the BHS, together with the BEVA, ILPH and the RSPCA to start work on this scheme.
>
> The British Horse Society Livery Yard Approval Scheme is dependent on voluntary involvement by livery proprietors, but when we set up the Riding Schools Approvals Scheme 37 years ago, the same conditions were involved, and that has been an outstanding success. We have no doubts that once again proprietors will acknowledge their responsibilities and choose to register.
>
> A constant set of standards countrywide, together with annual inspection, can only be welcomed, in particular by horse owners who will now have access to a comprehensive list of member establishments, thus simplifying their search for adequate facilities with responsible people who realise their responsibilities to welfare requirements as well as business.
>
> There will be other benefits, particularly for proprietors. It could, for instance, help them to find business, and it will most certainly help them to keep up to date with advances and developments on the welfare and business fronts. Our insurers, too, will be able to offer help and advice, especially in the thorny area of public liability.
>
> The scheme will also be of interest to, for instance, farmers seeking to diversify. The information pack which goes to every applicant will contain a wealth of information and, as a by-product,

provide a blueprint for new businesses. And of course, the input by the four organisations involved may well be useful to DEFRA if it chooses to look at legislation demanding that livery yards be licensed.'

Polo

1.23 Polo is currently a growth industry. It has benefited from exceptionally good marketing and PR aimed at the 'glamour' market, not necessarily just those traditionally involved in equine pursuits themselves. Many supporters and participants might be categorised as those who attend Royal Ascot – they enjoy the glamour, the clamour and the entertaining.

As a result of this, the leading polo organisations seem to have attracted excellent sponsorship deals and have television coverage of all the big games on the Sky television sports channel.

The sport has also concentrated on its grass roots, ie encouraging a revival of pony club polo and a big interest in club level polo, encouraging courses for beginners and a significant social element to activities. Polo club houses are positively booming with the same sort of atmosphere at a golf club or yacht club, all of which helps to fund the sport.

Every player has a handicap starting at –2 and going up to 10. Generally, most of the players rated 10 originate from Argentina, whilst there are many UK professionals with handicaps of only 3 or 4 goals. The handicap system works so that when two teams of four line up against each other, the handicaps of each player in each team are added together so that the teams can be balanced by the aggregate handicap of the whole team.

There are expressions such as 'low goal' and 'high goal' polo and this is based on the aggregate handicaps of the teams. A low goal team is one which by definition has a relatively low goal handicap. A new professional polo player with a low goal rating can be very attractive to a team wishing to keep their handicap down.

The polo industry creates a large number of businesses and associated tax problems. There has been a trend for polo clubs to be owned by individuals with a passion for polo but sometimes coming from very commercial backgrounds and who operate these activities in a very commercial manner. There are a number of polo schools which offer tuition for people wanting to be introduced into the game of polo and there are a number of polo livery yards which will keep polo ponies for their customers. Many of these polo livery yards will also buy and sell polo ponies and also hire polo ponies for those players who do not want the all-year round responsibility, but nevertheless enjoy the game. This can also be very useful for those who have injured ponies etc.

In order for the UK professional polo player to survive, it has been said that they 'need a very large trust fund income'. However, there are those who can make a living from the sport and in addition to appearance fees and fees for playing certain teams, they generally support their income through buying and selling polo ponies and also 'making' a polo pony which will often involve re-schooling a small failed racehorse or breeding their own polo ponies which in turn leaves them operating stud farms.

A lot of the stud farms that produce polo ponies are based in Argentina, Ireland and other countries but there has recently been a growth of the UK polo pony stud. Tax planning in relation to these activities is covered in **CHAPTER 7: TAX PLANNING FOR STUD FARMS.**

Show jumping

1.24 To those not involved in the industry of show jumping it might appear to be an industry in decline. It is a long time since the UK had any Olympic or World Cup success such as was enjoyed years ago and a long time since the likes of Harvey Smith graced television with almost prime time viewing.

However, at grass roots this remains a buoyant industry. Everyone who learns to ride wants to progress by trotting over a coloured pole and then jumping a coloured pole and then entering a show jumping class at the local show, and enthusiasm for this does not seem to have diminished in any way.

As the standard of show jumping improves so the cost of an experienced show jumper increases dramatically and, despite relatively small prize money, the horses command very high prices. Many tax advisers see this as merely a way for their successful clients to indulge the interests of their sons and daughters, but there are still some very important tax and commercial angles which ought to be considered.

In particular, there are important questions to be considered regarding the tax status of sponsorship payments, competition yards and the boundary line between a commercial business and a hobby (see further **CHAPTER 3**). There are also a large number of professional show jumpers who buy and sell horses to support their profession and also give freelance instruction.

Eventing

1.25 The eventing industry can probably be seen as possibly the least commercial of all equestrian disciplines. Competitors require all three skills of dressage, show jumping and cross country. They need to possess boldness to ride cross country, technical competence to perform dressage and superior technical riding skills and judgment for show jumping. Likewise, the horse needs to have all these skills. A good eventing horse commands a considerable price premium in the same way that a good polo pony or show jumper does. Eventing still achieves some television coverage at Badminton and Burghley Horse Trials and the attendance figures for spectators at three-day events, such as Badminton, Blenheim or Gatcombe, remain very strong.

Eventing also provides a commercial outlet for a large number of other related businesses such as equine clothing retailers and refreshment providers.

Eventing does not have the benefit of the glamour and, therefore, does not attract the valuable sponsorship deals seen in polo or the horse racing world. As a result, it is extremely difficult for a professional 'eventer' to survive commercially and again they frequently have to involve themselves in other equestrian activities, such as developing and selling young event horses in addition to giving instruction and trying to attract suitable sponsorship deals.

The industry does, however, have a commercial infrastructure with successful eventing yards, and freelance eventing instructors etc.

The recent success of the British team in the European Eventing Championships at Punchestown, and Pippa Funnell's momentous Burghley victory, should create strong commercial opportunities. However, sparse coverage in the mainstream media (especially in contrast to Henman and Beckham mania) restrict serious commercial development of the sport.

Dressage

1.26 The dressage industry is another area of growth and, like polo, attracts glamour and sometimes sponsorship. It is, perhaps, rather cynically perceived by the outside world as just a beautiful and elegant way to spend a lot of money on a hobby activity. However, there are some core elements of commerciality with top horses being sold for large sums. There are strong commercial aspects involved in being able to either breed or produce a top dressage horse and success in the competitive world of dressage goes hand in hand with this.

As a result, there are studs which focus purely on breeding dressage horses and there are some studs which breed horses for the dual disciplines of, say, dressage or eventing or show jumping. There are a relatively large number of good freelance dressage instructors, there are dressage livery yards and the sport has a very dedicated and committed support structure.

Point to Point

1.27 The Point to Point industry is amateur racing which runs from January to June annually and is another very thriving and popular sport. All the riders have to be amateur jockeys, although they can earn their living from other equestrian pursuits (there was a time when they had to be entirely amateur) and each Point to Point is, in the main, run by a local hunt.

Each Point to Point horse has to have been fairly and regularly hunted with a local pack of hounds (which does include bloodhounds and draghounds). Prize money is very small whilst enthusiasm levels can be exceptionally large.

The sport includes a large number of activities, not only fund raising for local hunts but offering a second chance for retired racehorses that are perhaps no longer good enough to support full training fees in a proper training yard, but can provide a keen amateur with a lot of fun. Point to Point also offers an alternative for young racehorses to race without too much financial outlay. There have been many successful Cheltenham Gold Cup or Grand National winners who have originated from the world of Point to Pointing.

Those who own and ride Point to Pointers find it an exceptionally enjoyable and thrilling way to spend their hard-earned money. When compared to keeping a racehorse in training or some of the other equestrian disciplines, it is also relatively cost-effective. The average Point to Point yard will only charge £120 per week livery, whereas a jump racehorse in training would be in excess of £250 per week at the time of writing.

Point to Points also attracts a large number of spectators and, within its structure, it supports a large number of equine businesses, such as Point to Point livery yards (which often double as hunter livery yards) and small training yards.

Point to Point horses can only cost around £2,000 to purchase. A good place to purchase potential Point to Pointers will be Ascot bloodstock sales or direct from the trainers. The jump trainers who love their racehorses and want to see them going to good homes are very keen to try and sell them to a good Point to Point yard for relatively small sums, which they could probably justify under the heading 'equine welfare' rather then 'commercial reality'.

Other equestrian activities

1.28 There are a large number of other equestrian disciplines which are also currently thriving, such as endurance riding, showing and the whole area of the sports horse generally.

The decline in the farming industry has meant the sale of a large number of paddocks to houses which has the combined benefit of increasing the value of the house and letting the farmer command a very commercial price for a small area of agricultural land. It is for this reason that there are so many ponies to be seen in paddocks around the countryside whilst there has been a big move away from the riding school.

There is a sports horse society and also a society for each breed of horse in the UK and they all tend to have a very enthusiastic following.

All these activities have created a large number of equestrian businesses such as show yards, the buying and selling of show horses and competition horses. To support all of this, there are a large number of freelance instructors, farriers and saddlers etc, which, all together, present a picture of a thriving equine industry.

Taxation and the Equine Industry 2

Tax planning for a passion

2.1 The current UK tax regime offers a large number of beneficial tax reliefs to the equine industry. The aim of this book is to highlight the benefits and help avoid the pitfalls.

In the author's experience, most practitioners and taxpayers ignore the equine elements of theirs and their clients' affairs as 'tax-free' and of no consequence for the tax return or tax planning. There are many examples where this is not the case and where it will be necessary to consider either tax compliance or planning aspects. For example:

- breeding and stud activities could be a taxable trade. There is also the potential for income tax relief on any losses and the protection of valuable inheritance and capital gains tax reliefs on stud property;
- stallion nomination fee income can be taxable;
- leasing income received in respect of a racehorse can be taxable;
- owning a racehorse can have tax advantages through the specific VAT scheme and where it is carried on as a genuine business activity;
- gambling – not normally regarded as a taxable activity, but involvement may 'colour' the attitude of the tax inspector to the taxpayer's disclosed income.

CHAPTER 3: BUSINESS OR HOBBY? is devoted to trying to differentiate between business and hobby activities and to the task of defining the business element.

Stud farming will normally be regarded as farming and should, therefore, qualify for all the beneficial tax advantages currently associated with farming. The tax planner can also encounter some pitfalls here – see CHAPTER 7: TAX PLANNING FOR STUD FARMS.

The tax affairs of those involved in the equine industry can become complex as a direct result of the tendency of those involved to allow their passion for the sport to lead them into its many different areas, such that a small initial interest can expand considerably and cause unexpected complexity.

Some specific tax points are as follows:

- stud farming is classed as farming (ICTA 1988 s 53(1)) (IM2350b);
- racing itself is generally tax-free – it is *not* a taxable activity (IM2350b);
- stud farm losses attract special loss relief treatment. A qualifying stud will mean that the provisions of ICTA 1988 s 397 only come into play after the eleventh year, not the fifth as for ordinary farmers;
- stallion nomination fees are assessed under Schedule D Case VI unless the stallion is integrated in a stud farm – *Malcolm v Lockhart (Surveyor of Taxes) (1919) 7 TC 99*;
- a stallion is *not* plant and machinery;
- horses are not subject to capital gains tax;
- when horses move from stud to racing or racing to stud they are transferred at market value – *Sharkey v Wernher (1955) 36 TC 275;*
- stock is valued at the lower of cost and net realisable value on an item-by-item basis;
- stallion syndicates are divided into 40 shares;
- stallion nomination fees are 'tax-free' in Ireland but be aware of the UK residence position;
- gambling is tax-free, ie not assessable to income tax;
- the special 'Weatherby VAT' scheme for racehorse owners allows owners to claim back their input VAT;
- there can be VAT on DIY liveries.

Stud farming is farming

2.2 Some specific guidance can be found in the Inland Revenue's Inspector's Manual IM2350b:

> 'Stud farming, which in these paragraphs is taken to mean the occupation of land for the purpose of breeding thoroughbred horses, is a very expensive and high-risk activity. In some cases it may be carried on by wealthy individuals essentially as an adjunct to their racing activities. Nevertheless, for tax purposes it is treated as farming and thus, by virtue of section 53(1), Taxes Act 1988, as the carrying on of a trade regardless of its commercial viability.'

Therefore, the stud farm as a business attracts all the benefits of the special reliefs for capital gains tax and inheritance tax which will include in some cases the farmhouse, and so is worth looking at in detail. **CHAPTER 7: TAX PLANNING FOR STUD FARMS** covers the tax benefits and pitfalls for the taxpayer.

A horse will therefore be an agricultural animal if it is used for breeding, regardless of the ultimate use of the progeny. A horse is also an agricultural animal if it is intended for human consumption or to work as a draught horse.

11-year loss rule for stud farms and equine losses

2.3 The subject of losses and how to maximise tax relief is always a subject of great interest to tax adviser and taxpayer alike. **CHAPTER 11: PLANNING FOR LOSSES** devotes itself entirely to this subject. As part of the introduction it is important to highlight the 11-year loss rule for studs and also a specific 'sting in the tail' which can be found within the 11-year loss rule.

As with any trading loss, the tax loss arising from a stud farm can be offset against an individual's total income under ICTA 1988 ss 380 and 381. Thus, losses can be offset against dividends, employment income and profits from a trade. Losses can also be offset against capital gains under FA 1991 s 72. The difference between a stud farm and a farm is the ability to claim tax relief for losses for the first 11 years and this is dealt with in **CHAPTER 11**.

Many equine businesses trade at a loss. Horses are expensive to keep and costs such as compliance with riding school regulations and employment law can turn a potential profit into a loss.

Protection of land and buildings from capital gains tax

2.4 To undertake equestrian activities generally requires the ownership of land and/or buildings. With the recently steep increase in property values it will be essential to ensure that any capital gains tax relief that may be available on an eventual disposal are preserved. **CHAPTER 7** sets out how this specifically applies to the stud farms. The question of Business Asset Taper Relief (BATR) and how to avoid 'tainted taper' is dealt with in **CHAPTER 13: BUYING AND SELLING EQUESTRIAN PROPERTY – TAX PLANNING** on property disposals.

The problems of the loss of BATR in the limited company are looked at in depth in **CHAPTER 10: OVERVIEW OF EQUINE BUSINESS TAXATION**, whilst **CHAPTER 9: THE EQUINE BUSINESS STRUCTURE**, deals with the subject of incorporation.

Many equestrian activities might be enjoyed with a passion whilst incurring early losses. However, if the owners do not recognise that they may be able to achieve trading status they will forego the advantages of all the tax reliefs, notably loss relief. Late registration of a taxable business is dealt with in detail in CHAPTER **3** and represents a 'minefield' of alternatives for the tax adviser. If registration of a business takes place then the assets used in the business, such as the land, buildings and stud house will have 'mixed used' for business asset taper relief and tax planning should take this into account.

It may be worth going back to 6 April 1998 and having a business registered for tax purposes from that earlier date in order to maximise available BATR from CGT. Consideration must be given to the interest and penalties which can arise on a late registration as well as the need to revise tax returns and the ability to make timely claims for loss relief etc. In some cases, the time limits will have been exceeded but there will still be scope to carry forward losses under ICTA 1988 s 385.

In some cases it may be worthwhile restructuring the ownership of valuable assets in order to 'restart' the taper relief clock. Where development gains are in prospect this may be of even more importance.

The loss of BATR is a real worry if the landowner/livery provider is not carrying out a trade. In *Powell and another (personal representatives of the Pearce, deceased) v IRC [1997] STC (SCD) 181* it was held that the Revenue will not be bound by an Inspector having accepted Schedule D Case I treatment for income tax, where another tax is being considered.

The equine house

2.5 The inheritance tax advantages of farming have always been that the farmhouse and farm cottages are potentially business assets and eligible for Agricultural Property Relief (APR) for inheritance tax as well as the stud land and buildings.

Some recent tax cases have, however, considerably revised the court's attitudes to farmhouses and their APR eligibility. In general, APR on a farmhouse is no longer taken for granted by the tax profession in perhaps quite the same way it was in earlier years.

The tax status of a farmhouse can thus be a very complex issue for the adviser. Care must be taken to ensure that, for capital gains tax purposes, optimum use is made of the principal private residence relief (PPR), whilst trying to ensure that the farmhouse does, potentially, qualify for APR (see **13.1** below).

Although for APR purposes this only applies to studs, the ability to claim 'the equine house' as a business asset for inheritance tax relief should not be overlooked. This is looked at in detail in CHAPTER **7**: THE STUD HOUSE. The income tax implications are also looked at in detail in CHAPTER **8**: THE TRAINER'S HOUSE.

For income tax purposes, expenditure on an equine house may be apportioned rather similarly to the method commonly used for farmhouses. The claim for expenses will be proportionate to the scale and nature of the business, for example:

- does it provide holiday accommodation for those on riding holidays;
- does it include an office, staff accommodation;
- does it include a place for staff and client meetings etc?

As mentioned in **1.1** above, the CGT position of houses with stables, particularly in relation to private residence exemption, was looked at in *Longson v Baker [2001] STC 6, 73 TC 415* (see **2.34** below).

Equine cottages – Farmer (Farmer's Executors) v IRC

2.6 Most stud farms employ staff who need accommodation on the premises so that they can deal with problems 'on site'. The case of *Farmer (Farmer's Executors) v IRC [1999] STC (SCD) 321* has given some hope for stud cottages, which were previously part of the stud operation and now let out. Some of the disputed accommodation was in converted buildings and the guidance given by this case cannot be overlooked. However, the capital gains tax eligibility of each property has to be looked at on a property-by-property basis.

Horse racing is tax-free – are other equine activities?

2.7 On the principle that the Inland Revenue have sought to collect tax on profitable activities whilst simultaneously attempting to deny relief on those that are loss making, the Inland Revenue has traditionally viewed the ownership of racehorses and associated activities as 'tax-free'. This was first looked at in **1.16** above.

Guidance is given in the Inland Revenue's Inspector's Manual at IM2350b which states:

> 'Horse racing, however, is not a taxable activity. Where, as is often the case, a stud farmer also races horses, considerable care may therefore be needed to ensure that the division between the two activities has been correctly made.
>
> In particular, attention should be given to any transfers of animals from the stud farm to training (that is, being kept for the purpose of racing) or vice versa. As racing is not taxable the prize

money is also not taxable and therefore racing expenses are not allowable.'

Clearly, this means that the taxpayer cannot claim tax relief (in principle) on the losses or the cost of owning a racehorse.

A frequently asked question is can the tax-free status of racing be extended to other equine pursuits, particularly where carried on by the same individual? For example, is the ownership of dressage, show jumping, show and general competition horses also tax-free? The answer is that it depends on the particular circumstances of a case. The motive behind ownership has to be looked at. Clearly, a professional trainer of horses is trading and will exhibit the commercial badges of trading.

Integrated studs and racing

2.8 Problems may arise when a stud owner also races horses. What is the taxable element and what is the tax-free element? The tax advice is complex.

Some comment on this is given in the Inland Revenue's Inspector's Manual at IM2350e:

> '• The stud farm accounts should be credited when animals are transferred to training with the then market value of the transferred animals, as if they had been sold at that value (*Sharkey v Wernher (1955) 36 TC 275*).
> • When animals return to the stud farm after racing, the stud farm accounts should be debited with their market value, at the time of return, as if they had been purchased at that value.
> • If an animal purchased and not bred on the stud farm is brought into the stud after racing by the occupier, the stud farm accounts should similarly be debited with the then market value of the animal, as if it had then been purchased at that value.
>
> The same treatment should be applied to a person who is assessable under Schedule D on the profits of dealing in thoroughbred animals bred by him, but on a stud farm occupied by some other person.'

One of the key practical tax planning points here is to encourage the taxpayer/stud owner to keep records which differentiate between the activity of racing and stud ownership to help the correct recording and apportionment of cost information.

If a breeder transfers an animal to training which is then subsequently returned to stud at a higher value after a successful racing career, the uplift in the market value achieved whilst it was in training is effectively enjoyed tax-free.

Furthermore, the value at which the animal is returned to stud is relieved over the rest of its life. The valuations of animals at the dates of transfer to or from training are, therefore, significant.

The whole subject of integrated equine activities features throughout the industry. The equine taxpayer rarely just owns a horse or trains or competes or breeds. They normally undertake all these disciplines at the same time.

Trading as a limited company

2.9 Many equine businesses might look to the protection of limited liability in view of the high-risk nature of the equine and stud industry. The problems are that losses can be trapped inside a limited company for tax purposes and not otherwise relievable and, similarly, stud land and buildings held in the limited company will not qualify for BATR.

The current Government has, in effect, made the small limited company very attractive to the entrepreneurial small business (see **9.4**, **10.5** and **10.6** below).

The implications of inheritance tax and the tax treatment of shareholders must also be considered.

For inheritance purposes only, controlling interests qualify for APR (IHTA 1984 s 122), although a minority interest may attract Business Property Relief (BPR). If a company does not qualify as a trading company but as an investment company, then BPR will not apply. Likewise, a subsidiary company does not qualify for APR but might qualify for BPR if the conditions are right. Every equine shareholding should be reviewed for eligibility for APR/BPR.

Stock valuation

2.10 Stud Stock is valued at the lower of cost and net realisable value on an individual basis. The herd basis can be used – see CHAPTER 7: TAX PLANNING FOR STUD FARMS.

In some circumstances a working horse may possibly be defined as apparatus and therefore capital allowances could perhaps be claimed, although generally the Inland Revenue is reluctant to accept such claims except in exceptional cases. This is dealt with in more detail in CHAPTER **10**.

VAT registration

2.11 The question of VAT is complex and warrants its own chapter (CHAPTER **17**: PLANNING FOR VAT). Sooner or later the equestrian taxpayer will have to consider whether or not they can register for VAT and, if so, should they register?

HM Customs and Excise give the following direction on acceptance for VAT registration in respect of stud farms:

> 'Breeding is a long-term activity. A mare will not produce a foal every year, and the average may not be better than one in every two years. A breeder therefore will normally need to own several mares before supplies (sale of offspring) can be made with any degree of regularity. However, there will be exceptions to this, eg it is becoming more common to acquire one or two well bred mares, cover them by an expensive stallion and sell the offspring for considerable amounts of money. In these circumstances we would accept there was a business activity and registration may be permitted. In cases of doubt the trader should be requested to submit written details of their business intentions. Where subsequently a trader is registered it should be as an intending trader.'

In order to achieve VAT registration, however, there must again be the clear 'intention' of making a profit – it *must* be a business. In *C & E v Lord Fisher, QB [1981] STC 238,* the courts set down the the principle that an activity pursued for pleasure and social enjoyment is not business even if undertaken in an efficient and business-like manner. The *Turnbull* case (*Turnbull v Foster (Surveyor of Taxes) (1904) 6 TC 206*) ruled that although there was an element of hobby there was the simple commercial objective of achieving a good bloodline, which could produce profit, and was therefore a business.

In order to claim input VAT, the goods or services would have to have been purchased in the course, or furthering, of the business of stud farming.

There must be a business. There must be an intention of making a profit.

Stallion fees and other equine income missing from the tax return

2.12 As has already been stressed, horse-racing is generally treated as tax-free so that the Inland Revenue can deny tax relief for activities which are habitually loss making. They will, however, seek to collect tax on profitable activities such as the breeding of stallions, one-off breeding successes, successful horse dealing etc.

Owning a racehorse can be viewed as 'chasing a dream' but, generally, if a horse is successful enough to stand as a stallion it may be argued that it must be potentially financially rewarding and thus a profit making venture. A large number of taxpayers omit this source of income from the information supplied to their accountant. Generally, stallion fee income is taxable under Schedule D Case VI but if integrated with a stud farm will be regarded as Schedule D Case I. Losses of the stud are offset against the income as an integral part of the stud.

The Inland Revenue will, therefore, try to tax success and not give relief on the failures. It is for this reason that the racehorses tax status changes on becoming a stallion. In broad terms, it changes from being tax-free to taxable.

Enterprise Investment Scheme and the equine activity

2.13 The Enterprise Investment Scheme (EIS) is a specific tax investment scheme aimed at entrepreneurs willing to risk their own funds in what are regarded as higher risk commercial companies. The conditions for obtaining the relief are often complex and are generally beyond the scope of this book. However, the EIS can be incorporated into equine tax planning subject to the relevant conditions applying. Farming is specifically an excluded trade for the purposes of the EIS and, as stud farms are deemed to be farming for APR for inheritance tax, it is unlikely that they can qualify for this status. However, whilst a stud farm is treated as agricultural activity and hence within the definition of 'farming', some sections of the stud farming activity may perhaps escape the definition of farming for this purpose. Likewise, other equestrian activities which are neither studs nor farms may qualify for the tax relief.

EIS is available on an investment in shares in a qualifying unquoted trading company. Up-front income tax relief at 20% on the net amount invested in qualifying shares is available and, in some cases, there may also be the chance of CGT deferral in respect of other capital gains arising in the same or an earlier tax year. The subject is given more coverage in CHAPTER 7. See also **13.4** below which deals with the available form of deferral relief.

If the EIS investment is held for more than three years the gain will be tax-free.

With the move away from farm subsidies by Europe and the apparent efforts to revive the rural economy, it is perhaps arguable that there should be more encouragement to convert traditional farms to equestrian activities. However, there can be planning permission problems in providing quality accommodation for staff and where the conversion of traditional farm buildings to equine buildings is essential to such a project and so it would be encouraging if such applications could be met favourably by the planning authorities. The engagement of good planning consultants here should help greatly to achieve the aim.

Whilst there will be problems, a combination of the available tax reliefs and the efficiency that the share structure it offers could mean that the EIS may represent a useful means of funding the capital requirement of developing equine projects.

The equestrian landlord and grazing rights

2.14 The whole subject of owning an equestrian property and letting out premises tax efficiently is dealt with in **CHAPTER 15: THE EQUESTRIAN LANDLORD – TAX PLANNING.**

It is essential that a graziers agreement is properly drafted. The key point is that the landlord must remain the paramount occupier with regard to grazing rights granted to the equine business. Only in this manner will entitlement to valuable capital taxation reliefs be retained by the landowner. A well drafted grazing arrangement which is properly constructed will give the landowner the ability to show that he is the paramount occupier and therefore bring him within IHTA 1984 s 117(a). The result is that the minimum period of occupation or ownership required to be eligible for agricultural property relief is two years rather than seven years.

The following functions will have to be carried out to qualify as correctly drafted grazing arrangements:

- the owner cultivates, sows and establishes the grass crop;
- the owner harrows and rolls the grass as necessary;
- the owner fertilizes the grass crop in spring and through the season as necessary;
- it is important that the owner should cut or spray all weeds to prevent seeding and the owner must do any mowing that may be required for whatever reason.

The grazier must also covenant not to mow or cut the grass and the owner must maintain any hedging, fencing and ditching needed and any other work of a proprietary nature.

If the landowner manages to achieve the above, he should then be deemed to be a Schedule D taxpayer with paramount occupancy and, therefore, eligible for not only the APR on the land, but also the APR on the farmhouse – see **CHAPTER 7**. The period of occupancy could then be reduced whilst greater potential to claim business expenses and qualify for capital gains tax relief will rise.

Finance Act 2003

2.15 In the Chancellor's seventh Budget speech he identified enterprise, innovation and flexibility as the 'engines of growth'. He argued that the fortunes of the nation hinge on sustained investment. More businesses will qualify for 100% first year capital allowances for investment in IT made before April 2004 and there has been an extension of the Small Firms Loan Guarantee scheme.

The threshold for businesses to become eligible for the 40% initial capital allowance will be raised to £20m in the summer of 2003, while VAT registration threshold increases to £56,000 after 10 April 2003. Further VAT reforms should also reduce paperwork, while many more firms will avoid automatic fines for late payment.

The freezing of vehicle excise duty on lorries and the postponement of any duty-driven increase in fuel costs will be welcomed throughout the commercial sector. Corporation tax, capital gains tax, and insurance premium tax rates and the climate change levy are unchanged, although the landfill tax will rise from £14 per tonne in 2003/04 to £15 in 2004/05 and to £18 per tonne in 2005/06.

Mr Brown signalled an intensification of the war on red tape, enlisting the Confederation of British Industry (CBI) and Institute of Directors to help identify unnecessary regulation. He also promised to improve smaller firms' ability to compete for Government contracts. The Government will also contribute to costs where employers allow time off for training and study.

Such developments can only be of positive benefit to equine businesses.

The Chancellor also introduced a range of measures designed to boost the creation of small businesses throughout the country, including 2,000 designated enterprise areas.

Equine activities can take place in unfashionable industrial locations so this may be a development which may offer opportunities for new venture start-ups.

There is no doubt that the majority of equine businesses are 'small'. They may be high-profile in some cases and some may generate high individual profits or asset values, but in the main they benefit from small business company reliefs and they should also be able to take advantage of the small business reliefs that are promised.

Equine businesses employ staff, provide exports and assist with many linked areas of the UK economy. For example, stud farms help with looking after the landscape which assists the UK tourist industry, riding schools help with education and learning, whilst the racing industry has its own 'life form', which helps feed the betting industry and which in the main is served by small businesses.

Protecting future IHT and CGT reliefs

2.16 The principal short-term approach to tax planning in the equine industry is the concern to maximise income tax relief and claim maximum relief for VAT. In concentrating on these important aspects, however, the CGT and IHT positions can sometimes be overlooked. It is imperative to understand the principle benefits of all the available tax reliefs.

Similarly, the desire to claim immediate income tax losses and input VAT must not be undertaken without full consideration of the CGT and IHT benefits.

CGT is chargeable on the disposals of assets and is generally based on the difference between sale proceeds and the original cost of the asset or its March 1982 market value if this produces a smaller gain or loss. For the period from March 1982 to April 1998, individuals and trusts benefit from compensation for inflation provided by an indexation allowance on the cost of the asset. Companies continue to attract indexation after this 1998 date. Where the asset is accepted as having been used for the purpose of the business, certain reliefs are available, such as roll-over relief, tapering relief at the higher rate, and hold-over relief. These reliefs have their own inherent complications and suitable professional advice needs to be sought when contemplating the use thereof. Companies do not qualify for the taper relief.

Recently, the advantage of business status has enhanced the capital gains relief. These reliefs enable a large amount of increase in value in the land and buildings to either escape tax or achieve minimum penalty to tax.

The genuine equine business may perhaps also be used as a means of sheltering future development profits. Most equine businesses incorporate the use of business land and buildings which at some time might be developed for residential or other use with a large potential capital gain.

Are stallions farming?

2.17 This chapter has already looked at how easy it may be to omit stallion fees from a tax return. Every equine client is different and tax planning must be tailor-made to their needs. The advantage of operating an activity as a 'trade' and, in particular, achieving qualifying status as a 'farm', is the availability of the business tax reliefs flowing from the ownership of the land and buildings where the stallion stands. This subject is looked at in more detail at **6.8** below.

Stud farms in the past have caused difficulties. As long ago as 1933, the House of Lords held that stud fees were taxable as farming profits (see *Lord Glanely v Wightman (Inspector of Taxes) (1933) 17 TC 634*) and the provision was restricted to animals used on the farm.

However, the case of *Malcolm v Lockhart [1919] AC 463, 7 TC 99* held that stallion fees should be taxed under the rules of Schedule D Case VI. This highlighted the fact that every equine establishment and every equine taxpayer will be unique. For inheritance tax, this decision may not be of relevance because of a specific statutory direction in IHTA 1984 s 115(4) that:

> 'The breeding and rearing of horses on a stud farm and the grazing of horses in connection with those activities shall be taken to be agriculture and any buildings used in connection with those activities to be farm buildings.'

The recent case of *Wheatly v IRC [1998] STC SCD 60* before the Special Commissioners decided that the grazing of land by horses is not an agricultural activity, unless the horses have been used for the purpose of agriculture or are held as part of a stud farm business. This has important implications, not only for landowners who grant profit a prendre agreements for grazing, but also for landlords who grant farm business tenancies (FBT) permitting grazing by horses (see **7.23** below).

The maximum rate of agricultural property relief is 100% and it generally applies where the transferor has the vacant possession of land, or is able to obtain it within 24 months, or the land is let on tenancy beginning on or after 1 September 1995. The FBT is looked at in more detail at **15.8** below.

The tax efficient trading vehicle and property ownership

2.18 One of the most common tax problems encountered by the author is where the ownership of the equine property is not 'married' for tax purposes to the equine trading vehicle, ie the owner of the equine establishment is not the same as the trading activity. If the owner of the land is not the same as the trading vehicle, then ideally there should be some formal lease between the two and this may, in some cases, result in a loss of tax eligibility. There are important IHT and CGT reliefs at risk. This subject is covered in CHAPTER **15**: THE EQUESTRIAN LANDLORD – TAX PLANNING and also CHAPTER **9**: THE EQUINE BUSINESS STRUCTURE.

APR

General rules

2.19 As stud farms should qualify as agricultural farms they can benefit from the tax advantages of APR for inheritance tax.

To attract the relief two conditions must be satisfied:

- the land must be 'occupied for the purpose of agriculture' – this incorporates general farming, rearing of animals (including horses on a stud farm), and using land for grazing, providing the owner is responsible for the upkeep of the land; and
- it must be 'agricultural property' as defined by the IHTA 1984 s 115(2).

Agricultural property includes UK land, buildings used as farm buildings and cottages and farmhouses of a character appropriate to the land. Land outside the UK will not attract the relief but should be eligible for BPR. The availability of the APR on farmhouses can be complex (see **CHAPTER 7**).

An owner of 'let' agricultural property in use for the purposes of agriculture can claim up to 100% relief against the agricultural value provided any of the conditions below are satisfied:

- the owner has the right to vacant possession within 12 months (an Extra-Statutory Concession (ESC F17) extends this period to 24 months for land under tenancy, but not a license); or
- the property is let on an agricultural tenancy beginning on or after 1 September 1995 FBT (see **15.8** below); or
- if the owner has been beneficially entitled to the interest in the land since March 1981, and had he made a transfer of value before that time, would have attached the full relief under the old 'working farmer' rules. The owner must also not have had rights to vacant possession within 12 months.

Transfers of any other agricultural property are generally eligible for relief at 50% only (IHTA 1984 s 116(2)).

This is looked at in more detail in chapter 13 of Butler, J, *Tax Planning for Farm and Land Diversification* (2002, LexisNexis UK).

APR: how long will it stay?

2.20 With IHT relief of such potential value to a stud farm, the tax planner might seek to consider the history and origins of APR.

The measure exempting agricultural property from inheritance tax was described in the course of the 1992 Budget debate as an important and historic decision. APR, at its current rate, represents an attempt to accommodate the special economic problems of business and landowners whose enterprises are vulnerable to death duties. It supplements BPR and replaces full-time working farmer relief. It is applicable (at its current rates of 100% and 50%) to transfers of value made on or after 10 March 1992 and charges or further charges arising on a death on or after 10 March 1992 in respect of a transfer of value made before that date. In the past, a number of reasons had been given for the relief, eg that capital transfer tax had been holding back the supply of land for new entrants to the farming industry, and that it was important to maintain a proper balance between owner-occupied and tenanted land, allowing for their different values.

Cynics argue that the current Government's apparent unwillingness to revise agricultural property relief is a direct consequence of the current decline in UK farming, rather than any specific interest in the tax breaks the industry ought to attract on its own merits.

APR: agricultural value – the period of ownership

2.21 APR is available only against the agricultural value of the property, which in many cases, especially farmhouses, can be different to open market value. The value of agricultural property is often lower than the open market value as the agricultural value assumes use is restricted to agricultural occupancy only.

'Agricultural value' is set out in IHTA 1984 s 115(3) as:

> 'the value which would be the value of the property if the property were subjected to a perpetual covenant prohibiting its use otherwise than as agricultural property'.

This subject is an important tax planning consideration for equine stud farms with very high values.

Many equine tax advisers trying to protect the future inheritance tax liabilities of their clients might look to the ownership of a stud for IHT protection but what is the minimum period of ownership?

To obtain APR the property must be held for a minimum period. There are two periods of ownership relevant to the 100% relief:

- a minimum two-year period for the owner farmer; or
- a seven-year period for the owner of the property let out on tenancy.

The period required to qualify for full relief differs in certain circumstances where property is received on death and subsequently transferred, or when an individual who has recently received an agricultural property by gift or inheritance dies.

Importance of a structured will

2.22 If a will is not structured correctly and does not specify to whom the business property is to be left, this will cause problems. An example of this would be a trainer. There is often a batch of assets which could be divided between the children, eg the training yard, the gallop and the house, and it would be a big problem if these were just divided between children as opposed to allocated between the family in a business-friendly manner as well as with an eye on the tax position.

The 100% relief on the assets will be spread over the whole estate in whatever proportion the property is split, regardless of whether part of the estate is exempt. For example, if the relief was apportioned onto assets passing to the spouse the relief would be wasted, as the transfer would already be exempt.

Will planning (like all forms of tax planning) has to be tailor-made to suit the asset and the desires of the will maker. This is beyond the scope of this book – see by the same author, Butler J, *Tax Planning for Farm and Land Diversification* (2002) LexisNexis UK which has a whole chapter devoted to will planning.

Will planning – Deed of Variation

2.23 Whether or not lifetime planning has been implemented, there are opportunities to structure the will tax efficiently. If the will is not tax efficient, the executors and beneficiaries may consider using a 'Deed of Variation' to rewrite the will.

Will variation provides a useful mechanism for deferring and in many cases mitigating the inheritance tax liability arising on death.

As the law currently stands, it is open to any adult beneficiary under a will to vary the terms of the gift to that beneficiary. Such a variation can be made up to two years after the date of death of the person who made the will provided all the other beneficiaries agree. Failing this, a beneficiary may 'disclaim' their individual bequest, in which case, the assets simply fall back into the residue of the estate of the deceased.

The two most common forms of variation are to either effect a redirection of the gift to the beneficiary's children (which will avoid inheritance tax on the beneficiary's death), or to redirect the gift to the surviving spouse. The surviving spouse may then make subsequent lifetime gifts, which benefit from tax relief as Potentially Exempt Transfers, (ie exempt so long as the donor survives seven years from making the gift). Furthermore, the redirection of gifts to registered charities will avoid tax altogether.

Post-death will variation is effective by means of a formal Deed of Variation, which must be executed within two years of the date of death. It is perhaps surprising that the Government has so far overlooked this useful mechanism for avoiding or mitigating liability to inheritance tax and the benefits of using a Deed of Variation should always be considered.

Will planning – identifying tax efficient assets

2.24 Will planning should help the owner to verify the tax efficiency of his/her assets. Does the equestrian business qualify for BPR? Where there is a mix of taxable and exempt equestrian activities it will be important to take account of the interaction of the £nil rate band, surviving spouse exemption and business relief.

Ideally, any individual holding agricultural land that qualifies for APR or a business which qualifies for BPR should ensure his will takes advantage of APR and BPR and that the benefit of these valuable reliefs are not wasted by passing those assets qualifying for the relief to the exempt surviving spouse.

The surviving spouse may wish to control the business after the death of his or her partner. Instead of leaving assets direct to the spouse, those attracting APR could perhaps be bequeathed to a nil rate band discretionary will trust, from which the spouse can benefit.

Tax planning and the equine loan

2.25 Most equestrian businesses are generally asset-based and, more particularly, property-based and generally rely on some form of loan or mortgage secured thereon.

Financial arrangements need to be well structured to optimise the available tax reliefs.

In order to maximise APR and/or BPR, any loans required should not be secured against any property attracting the relief as this will reduce their value and waste the relief. Loans should wherever possible (and provided the lender can be persuaded that their security is adequate), be secured against non-qualifying property, thereby reducing the value chargeable to IHT and hence the tax payable.

The requirements for tax relief on interest must also be considered carefully.

Making lifetime gifts of equestrian businesses

2.26 Some high profile trainers have recently attracted publicity by passing on their businesses to the next generation via lifetime gifts. This can bring significant IHT advantages.

Where assets which do not qualify for business or agricultural reliefs are concerned, it will also be important to ensure that gifts are made without a 'reservation of benefit' (GROB).

If 100% APR or BPR is expected on the agricultural or business property on the death of an individual, a simple planning strategy might, of course, be to retain the property, ensuring it remains under current qualifying conditions. No tax should arise on death and the beneficiaries would inherit at market value.

On the other hand, there are also those who consider that the favourable relief will not last for ever and that action should be taken now (or at least before death).

Additionally, it is not inconceivable that the current benign regime for APR and BPR might change, and perhaps become more restrictive. A lifetime gift may, therefore, be desirable to take advantage of the 100% exemption. The capital gains tax consequences of any gift must not be ignored but with CGT taper relief and also the possibility of roll-over relief there are strong incentives to consider lifetime transfer.

Also, practically it may be impossible to hold the property under the same conditions to ensure the relief is available. For example, where the trainer, farmer or stud owner are becoming old and are unable to work there may be strong consideration to pass the business down a generation. Other owners may just want the next generation to have the 'pleasure of the responsibility' now!

Potentially exempt transfers

2.27 Problems arise where the person making the transfer of the equine business does not survive the seven-year period and the availability of APR/BPR becomes important. Where gifts are made during the lifetime into a discretionary trust, such a transfer would be a 'chargeable transfer' and tax would be calculated and payable at the time the gift was made. Provided the gift attracts 100% APR/BPR, no tax will be payable at the time of the gift and the chargeable value of the gift, ie nil (after 100% APR/BPR) will be fixed for the purpose of calculating the cumulative value of gifts made before death.

Should the APR/BPR not be available at the date of death, the tax would still be payable on the gift made under the claw-back rules. The only difference between a chargeable transfer and potentially exempt transfer (PET) in these circumstances is the fixing of the value of the gift.

The value of the gift (even with 100% APR/BPR) is of great importance in the hands of the recipient. This is the base cost for CGT for the recipient. If 100% APR/BPR is to be achieved there are strong arguments to say that the value should be as high as possible. But what value will the District Valuer accept? What are the tax consequences if the gift fails as a PET?

Tax payable upon death is calculated by reference to the cumulative value of transfers made within seven years of death. This is looked at in more detail at **10.15** below.

Reinvestment into new qualifying asset

2.28 When a lifetime equine business gift reinvested (or replaced) into another qualifying business asset is to take place then it must take place within three years of the sale of the original asset. The reinvestment can be made in stages provided all purchases fall within the three-year period of sale and all the proceeds are invested. If anything less than the whole of the proceeds are reinvested, the whole of the APR/BPR will be clawed back. Also, only one rollover of the proceeds is allowed and the replacement asset must be held at the death of the transferor to attract the relief. These conditions are often totally overlooked by those making gifts of equine business assets.

A little known fact is that it may be possible to reinvest the proceeds in an asset qualifying for BPR instead of APR and effectively swap the APR on the original gift for BPR. This is provided the original agricultural asset would have attracted BPR in its own right, due to it being a business asset. APR is always given in priority over BPR if both reliefs are available.

BPR is available for trading businesses only. Where land is held as an investment and taxable under Schedule A, BPR in general is not available. This would apply to tenanted land. See **CHAPTER 1: THE EQUINE INDUSTRY**.

It could be, therefore, that a farm or stud is gifted to the next generation. If they wish to re-invest the proceeds into a dedicated equestrian business that qualifies for BPR, then the replacement of business asset rules must be taken into consideration.

See *Stanley: Taxation of Farmers and Landowners* (1995) LexisNexis UK for an in-depth review of all areas of agricultural property ownership. Likewise, Toby Harris, *Tolley's Business and Agricultural Property Relief* (3rd edn, 2002) LexisNexis UK and the author's (Butler, J) *Tax Planning for Farm and Land Diversification* (2002) LexisNexis UK (see **2.22** above) give very detailed reviews of the subject.

Thoroughbred and non-thoroughbred studs

2.29 This was first looked at in **1.14** above.

There are no reasons to assume that the non-thoroughbred stud or other equestrian activity will be treated any differently to thoroughbred studs for tax purposes. Inland Revenue Booklet Guide IHT17 refers to the breeding and rearing of horses with no discrimination to the thoroughbred. The same principle for all taxes should therefore apply. It is assumed that in view of the fact that racing came before other activities such as eventing and show jumping it has priority. Racing has been involved with high financial rewards and, therefore, high-value tax liabilities are at stake. It has been the focus of many cases.

The Inspector's Manual quoted do refer throughout to thoroughbred horses, especially the 11-year rule principle that was agreed with the TBA in 1982. It can probably be safely assumed, however, that the tax principles are very similar for all activities, eg the stud is a farm, stock is valued at the lower of cost and net realisable value and the 11-year loss rule for studs also applies.

As with all tax problems, it is the facts of the case that are important and great store will rest on demonstrating and providing evidence of the commerciality and bona fide trading motives of a business activity and proof of commercial inspiration. It is worth quoting direct from the Inland Revenue Booklet Guide IHT17 to the inheritance tax relief on business property and agricultural property relief. This guidance can be found on the Inland Revenue website which states: 'Stud farms engaged in the breeding and rearing of horses and to land used for grazing associated with those activities (IHTA s 115(4))'. Note that no reference is made to the thoroughbred at all here. There is no exclusivity. This guide refers to the horse and not just the thoroughbred horse and should be the basis for treating thoroughbred and non-thoroughbred equally for tax. This is looked at further in **7.15** below. See the impact of transfer to equestrian sport at **2.31** below.

Commercial or hobby

2.30 The question of whether participation in a sport is to be regarded as a taxable activity will depend largely on what the individual's motives are. Is it amateur or professional? Is it commercial or hobby? Guidance can be given from points raised in **CHAPTER 3**. Each case will have to be looked at on its own merits. (The cynic will simply point out that, to the Inland Revenue, a hobby becomes a taxable trade when it turns from loss into profit!)

It must be remembered that it is only the owning and racing of racehorses that is generally regarded as tax-free by the Inland Revenue.

If a professional horseman (see **CHAPTER 8**) (including the trainer) approaches their business with commerciality and all the 'badges of trade' (see **3.3** below), the Inland Revenue will claim that the business is taxable. As mentioned at **2.7** above on the principle that the Inland Revenue have sought to collect tax on profitable activities whilst at the same time attempting to deny relief on any activity that can be deemed loss making, all those in the industry must be prepared for a challenge from the Revenue.

Stock transferred to 'equestrian sport'

2.31 As set out in the Inland Revenue's Inspector's Manual IM2350, where stock is transferred by an owner to carry out sporting activities, this must be effected for book and tax purposes at open market value. The leading case here is *Sharkey v Wernher (1955) 36 TC 275.* Lady Zina Wernher undertook a variety of activities away from her stud farm. The judge said that such 'other activities', namely, those of racing and training horses 'are neither farming nor any other kind of trading but are purely recreational in character, not giving rise to any liability to tax'.

The important issue therefore, is whether or not equestrian sport is recreation or commercial? 'Is it business or pleasure?' If the sport is an integral part of the stud then problems over market value need not be apparent. There are those cynics who argue that the tax adviser to the non-thoroughbred horse activity is the best placed of all. The tax adviser can use the racing/thoroughbred rules when it benefits the client and adjust as appropriate provided that the decision is consistent based on facts and capable of being argued with the Inland Revenue. Where circumstances are unique, complex or the taxpayer foresees problems with the Revenue, the practical approach may be to seek to obtain a ruling from the Inland Revenue.

Retiring from the equestrian business

2.32 Some see equestrian businesses as something that clients retire into, not from, whilst others may consider that once the equine passion enters the bloodstream there is no escape and no retirement. Many elements of the equine world can be enjoyed beyond standard retirement age and potential inheritance tax reliefs can be looked forward to in future years.

Irish stud fees tax-free

2.33 The position of Irish stud fees and their 'tax-free' status is dealt with in **CHAPTER 6: TAX PLANNING FOR THE BREEDER AND THE STALLION OWNER.**

The UK tax adviser must be very cautious about excluding such fees from a client's UK tax return. Exemption from the Irish tax return does not mean automatic exemption from the UK tax return. Is there a 'bridge' between Irish income and UK ownership? Can those of Irish domicile or residence be caught under ICTA 1988 s 68. The Irish tax exempt position may not always be as beneficial as it seems. (See **6.10** below).

Principal private residence – Longson v Baker

2.34 The subject of PPR was introduced at **1.1** and **2.5** above.

It would be impossible for an equine tax book to ignore the case of *Longson v Baker (HM Inspector of Taxes) [2001] STC 6, 73 TC 415.* Many equine enthusiasts would dispute the judge's key statement:

'it is not objectively required, ie necessary, to keep horses at a house in order to enjoy it as a residence'.

A review of the case will be essential to the reader's understanding of its implications.

From 1979, Longson ('L') and his wife owned, and occupied as their only or main residence a property ('VF'). VF comprised a Grade II listed, five bedroom, dwelling-house, with a range of stables, sufficient for 12 or 13 horses, and an enclosed exercise yard. The land comprised 7.56 hectares and included grazing sufficient for eight horses. L's family was interested in horses and further developed the site of the house for that purpose.

In 1990 L moved out of VF following the failure of the marriage. As a consequence of divorce proceedings, L made a disposal of his interest in VF. Under an Extra-Statutory Concession (ESC D6), L was treated as having resided at VF until 15 December 1995, the date of the disposal. L was, however, assessed to capital gains tax on the footing that only 1.054 hectares was, with regard being had to the size and character of the dwelling-house, required for the 'reasonable enjoyment' of it as a residence within the Taxation of Chargeable Gains Act 1992 s 222(3). L appealed on the grounds that the whole 7.56 hectares were so required. The Special Commissioners (SpC0238) dismissed the appeal. L appealed.

Held, in the Chancery Division, dismissing L's appeal, that the Commissioners had not erred in law in failing to take into account the equestrian aspect of the dwelling-house; to have done so would have been to disregard the inclusion in s 222(3) of the words 'as a residence' in 'regard being had to the size and character of the dwelling-house, that area is required for the reasonable enjoyment of it ... as a residence', the test under s 222(3) is an objective test; it is not objectively required, ie necessary, to keep horses at a house in order to enjoy it as a residence; the Commissioners had been engaged in an enquiry as to fact and their conclusion was not reviewable on appeal.

The tax adviser will often be asked for an opinion on the availability of the relief for principal private residence from CGT (PPR) and this will clearly henceforward represent a problem where the property has adjacent to it large 'equestrian garden or grounds'. This problem is further considered at **13.1** below.

Business or Hobby? 3

Business or Pleasure – The Fine Line

3.1 This subject was first considered at **2.30** above.

This chapter aims to lead the reader through all kinds of equine tax planning from the tax position of the owner to the stud farm, training, breeding etc. The utilisation of losses will be considered, as will the business advantages of owning business assets for capital gains tax and inheritance tax purposes.

Many equine businesses have become businesses from a simple leisure pursuit by a process of evolution rather than being planned as such from the outset. Because many proprietors' perception is of 'racing as being non-taxable' one frequently encounters 'businesses' which have not been registered with the tax authorities as such at the proper time or, more pertinently, at the best time. The carrying on of a business with a view to profits is not recreation; it is a taxable activity. There will, of course, frequently be cases in which some elements of the business, eg the stud (as to which see CHAPTER 7) are a properly taxable activity whilst others are not.

Sharkey (HM Inspector of Taxes) v Wernher (1955) 36 TC 275 demonstrates quite clearly that Lady Wernher's equine activities were similar to those seen in many other establishments and were indeed, a mixture of business and pleasure. Although this case was about horses being transferred to stud at market value, it also deals with many equine activities that exist today and the court had to consider what were business activities and what were recreational activities. The key question for the tax adviser to address will be when should a taxable business be registered with the tax authorities? Very often the answer here lies in encouraging the provision of better information transfer between taxpayer and tax adviser.

Defining the taxable moment

3.2 Many people enter the equine world without realising that certain events are taxable or at least require disclosure to their accountant.

Examples here could be where:

- a valuable racehorse becomes a stallion and stands at stud producing a very valuable income stream. Although there may be large pre-existing racing losses which absorb this profit in reality, from the Inland Revenue's viewpoint, one is a taxable profit and the other is not a tax deductible amount. The receipt of stallion fees therefore needs careful planning (see **CHAPTER 6**);
- a property is purchased to house some of the racing activities. There is already a principal private residence (PPR) election in place. The property is sold at a gain. The taxpayer assumes that it is all part of the 'racing is tax-free' mentality;
- a show jumping horse is sold at a very large profit. This involves extensive training expertise. No previous disclosure was made to the Inland Revenue as costs had been exceeding the income.

Commerciality – badges of trade

3.3 Throughout this book considerable emphasis has been placed on the need to demonstrate that activities carried on within the equine industry are commercial business activities and that the so-called 'badges of trade' exist. This is crucial to obtaining tax benefits and trading tax status.

If an equine activity is proved to be commercial this will establish business status for assets used in that business. The benefits of BATR and rollover relief for CGT and BPR/APR for IHT can only be enjoyed by the taxpayer if the equine business is commercial and accepted as such by the Inland Revenue. The capital gains tax considerations are looked at in more detail in **CHAPTER 13: BUYING AND SELLING EQUESTRIAN PROPERTY – TAX PLANNING**.

The subject of the 'reluctant farmer' is also reviewed in detail in the author's (Butler, J) *Tax Planning for Farm and Land Diversification* (2002) LexisNexis UK, in Chapter 10. Some equine enthusiasts will inevitably become reluctant registrants for their businesses in order to protect CGT and IHT reliefs.

If the Inland Revenue is not satisfied with the commerciality of a business then it will not tax it as a trade under Case I of Schedule D but will treat it as a hobby. This will lead to a denial of tax relief, particularly if losses arise, although the Inland Revenue may still pursue tax on profits eventually. Income tax losses are restricted to being carried forward if commercial inspiration cannot be proven. Thus, if a large profit appears in one year there may be a problem. A bloodstock breeder who does not occupy a stud farm may find it more difficult to convince the Inspector of Taxes that he is operating a bona fide trade. However, each case must be judged on its own merits and if, in fact, the relevant criteria have been satisfied then the breeder should meet with success.

Although bloodstock breeding, racing and other equine activities are a somewhat specialised industry, the well-known 'badges of trade' are equally applicable here and should be referred to in any case where it is necessary to convince the Inspector of Taxes that an activity is a taxable trade.

Asset of the trade or personal enjoyment?

3.4 While any form of tangible property can be traded, most commercial 'commodities' are rarely held as an investment – they offer the holder no 'pride of possession'. Property, which does not produce income simply by being held or offer the owner any personal enjoyment, is more likely to be held for the purposes of trade. As the stallion or share in a syndicated stallion can be a good income-producing asset, it is conceivable that the Inland Revenue could argue that it is being held as an investment and not trading stock. Similarly, as an owner of a racehorse is likely to derive personal enjoyment from the activity, but is unlikely to realise profits, the Inland Revenue tend to argue that racing is a hobby and not a taxable trade.

However, in such cases it can be important to stress to the Inland Revenue that commerciality does not preclude personal enjoyment. In the case of any equine business, are the horses held as an investment, for recreation or realisation at a profit? Likewise, with the ownership of equine property, is it held for investment, recreation or to house a business as part of a genuine trading activity?

Length of the period of ownership – an investment?

3.5 Property, which is to be traded, will commonly be held for a relatively short term whereas an investment is normally acquired for long-term income and capital growth. The Inland Revenue accept that bloodstock breeding is a high risk, long-term trade and cannot be assessed on the results of the first few years.

The disposal of some horses at a profit after being held for a relatively short time will obviously enhance arguments of commerciality. This does not mean the business has to involve instant dealing or 'pinhooking' (the purchase of young stock to bring on to the next stage of racing).

Frequency of transactions

3.6 A key consideration to determine commerciality will be the frequency or number of similar transactions by the taxpayer. The larger the bloodstock herd, the more likely it is that the tax adviser can convince the Inspector of Taxes that a trade is being carried on. If only one broodmare is owned, then the Inspector is likely to argue that a hobby is being enjoyed. Whereas if the investment encompasses a number of mares and stallion shares, then the Inspector is more likely to be convinced that there is a bona fide trade.

However, it is important to note here that the average number of horses held by members of the TBA is currently only two. Thus, it will be important to stress that commerciality is linked to motive not dependent upon volume.

Supplementary work

3.7 Supplementary work is any work undertaken in connection with the assets. For a genuine bloodstock breeder, the broodmare will need constant attention and the breeder will normally (but not always) own his own stud farm so that he is carrying out work on the mare, ie improving it, if possible, from its acquisition until it produces progeny. The ownership of a share of a stallion, for example, which is not kept at the breeder's premises, may not involve him in any supplementary work during its period of ownership, although he may be liable for his share of its upkeep. This could result in the stallion being classed as an investment as opposed to treatment as a trading asset. If a stallion is only being held for its income from nomination fees, rather than to enable the owner to send his own broodmares to the stallion, then the Inspector of Taxes may regard the stallion as an investment rather than trading stock, ie an investment rather than a trade.

If other equestrian activities are carried out in addition to breeding, this may provide evidence of an overall commercial entity being in existence, eg breaking and schooling. On the other hand, it has to be recognised that such activities might be classed as merely feeding and improving the animals' 'condition', which might not be considered a trade.

Circumstances of ownership

3.8 Certain assets can either be held as an investment or as trading stock of businesses. Syndicate shares in a stallion or a freehold building are two such examples. The length of ownership is often an important factor in the view of the courts and the Inland Revenue.

For example, the owner of a freehold building who sells at a large gain after two years is more likely to be held to be dealing in property than a similar property held for, say, ten years. However, the owner may have originally intended to hold the asset as a long-term investment but be faced with an urgent need for emergency finance which leads to the sale of the building after only two years. If the changed circumstances can be evidenced to the Inspector of Taxes, then he is likely to accept that the asset was acquired as an investment and not stock. If a stallion or a share in a syndicated stallion was, in reality, acquired as an investment, then its sale in the short term to raise finance for an emergency should not affect the nature of the asset when it was acquired. It is the circumstances surrounding ownership and trading activity, which is the key issue together with the original motives behind the acquisition of the asset.

Motive of the equine business

3.9 There are many who consider motive to be the most important badge of trade. In some cases, it will be clear that the motive of the owner was to trade or alternatively hold the horse as an investment. However, there will be many cases in which the distinction is not so clear cut. Here, evidence of the motive of the owner when he acquired the horse will be extremely important. For example, if it can be shown that a share in a syndicated stallion was acquired with a view to covering a broodmare at the stud farm and that arrangements were made for the broodmare to visit the stallion, then the Inland Revenue may well have to accept that it is stock, ie part of a trade, even though, for some reason, the broodmare was unable to visit the stallion. It is intention and motive, together with the supporting evidence at the time of the original transaction, which are important in deciding tax status.

What is absolutely crucial here is the primary purpose behind the activity. If this can be shown to have been commercially inspired, the fact that a proprietor derives some incidental personal benefits or pleasure from the ownership aspects of the activity should not detract from the acceptance of the activity as a genuine trade. However, if the pleasures of ownership were the original inspiration for the activity (often, in the Inland Revenue's view, evidenced by the proprietor's long-standing prior involvement in this sort of activity in general), then the Inland Revenue will seek to refuse the owner the bonus of qualifying tax relief status which would, in effect, be to subsidise the owner's personal hobby from the public purse.

The tax case of *McKnight v Sheppard [1999] STC 669* is useful in that it was held that the object of a taxpayer in making expenditure had to be distinguished from the effect of the expenditure.

VAT registration

3.10 VAT registration is dealt with in **CHAPTER 17: PLANNING FOR VAT** at **17.4** below. With the VAT threshold (following the 2003 Budget speech) at £56,000, there could be many equine disposals which would qualify as a VAT supply and require compulsory registration. This could be different from registration under the Racehorse Owners Scheme.

The 'business question' is looked at in **CHAPTER 17** and VAT cases which focus on business or hobby are listed. When looking at any case of business status in the 'round', VAT registration must be considered.

Transfer at market value from the stud

3.11 *Sharkey (Inspector of Taxes) v Wernher (1955) 36 TC 275* established the principle that transfers from a stud to racing are at market value. This was first looked at in **2.8** above.

In that case, Lady Zia Wernher, the wife of the respondent carried on a stud farm, the profits of which were agreed to be chargeable to income tax under Case I of Schedule D. She also carried on the activities of horse racing and training, which were agreed not to constitute trading. Five horses were transferred from the stud farm to the racing stables. The cost of breeding these horses had been debited in the stud farm accounts. On the question of the amount to be credited as a receipt, Lady Wernher contended before the Special Commissioners that the proper figure to be brought in respect of the transferred horses was the cost of breeding.

The Crown contended that the market value of the animals, which was considerably higher, was the proper figure.

It was held that the figure that should be credited was the market value.

Integration of stallions taxable and non-taxable

3.12 The case of *Sharkey v Wernher* shows the complex situation of stallions as integrated with other income. The facts of that case also show the recreational activity of breeding for own stables as opposed to the public.

Lady Wernher's activity of letting out the services of stallions at the stud farm for fees was separable from the general activity of breeding at the farm for her own stables. This latter activity was a recreational one, not attracting liability to tax, and consequently no profit or loss arising out of the breeding at the farm for her own stables fell to be taken into account in the assessment to income tax.

Late registration of an equine activity

3.13 The lack of clarity between business and hobby status, together with lack of clarity over trading stock and investment stock, can cause a genuine business to be registered late for tax purposes.

A stud or general equine business might develop slowly from owning a few shares in a racehorse to breeding from a favourite mare to a significant activity. The taxpayer might consider this a 'leisure activity'. It might cost a lot to run with outgoings exceeding incomings and every now and then there might be a valuable sale, but generating no profits as the costs already incurred exceed the sale price. The owner might want to proceed commercially. All these matters must be given consideration and clients must be encouraged to disclose the information to their tax adviser fully. This will be essential, not just to facilitate planning, but also to that ensure all compliance issues are considered.

In relation to the late registration of an equine trading activity or stud, some questions that could be raised between tax adviser and taxpayer are as follows.

- Are there more VAT implications than the Weatherbys' Racehorse Owners Scheme? Should normal trading registration be considered?
- Could the activities be considered trading and if so what are the compliance and planning considerations?
- Could the activity seek protection of IHT and CGT relief from the business status that would be accorded to business assets?
- Can losses be claimed and, if so, what are the time limits?
- Are there any other problems with late registration?

The importance of communication between client and tax adviser at an early stage is very clear.

When to register the equine business with the tax authorities

3.14 Once it has been decided that there is indeed a business in existence and it is established that some or all of the 'badges of trade' can be seen to be in place, the Inspector of Taxes should be presented with a positive business plan showing commercial inspiration and the carrying on of the activity with a view to a profit. The important decisions at this stage will be to choose a start date which will be accepted by the Inland Revenue. Clearly, if losses have arisen, the earlier the better from an income and CGT viewpoint, as this will limit future exposure to tax liabilities because the losses brought forward can be used to offset current and future taxable profits.

6 April 1998 as start date

3.15 There could be some considerable advantages if a trade could be shown to have been in existence from the start of taper relief. This could be of advantage when trying to avoid 'tainted' taper relief for Business Asset Taper Relief (BATR) – see CHAPTER **13**. Time limits would, however, have been exceeded for claims for income tax loss relief and therefore any losses would only be capable of being carried forward under ICTA 1988 s 385. There would also be the need to submit revised self-assessment tax returns and, possibly, late registration penalties with the National Insurance Contributions Office (NICO), although if losses have arisen these will not be imposed as the income will have been below the Small Earnings Exceptions limits for those periods. Furthermore, the ability to submit loss relief claims under ICTA 1988 s 381 will have been lost.

6 April 2003 as start date

3.16 If the last tax return submitted was up to 5 April 2003, then a start date of 6 April 2003 could be made without having to revise that tax return. There would still be the NIC registration, penalty to consider. There would also be some scope for a section 381 loss relief claim (ICTA 1988).

Date of first activity

3.17 When is first purchase/sale? What has happened? It is suggested that accounts are prepared from the date of first activity and the results reviewed.

Fact?

3.18 What is the right time to register the equine business? The textbooks will, of course, say this is 'fact'. An IT business has definitely started when it issues its first sales invoice but what triggers the start of the trade?

Likewise, a stud is trading when it sells its first item of stock or transfers it to racing, but what if that took a number of years to achieve? What of pre-trading expenditure? What business stock is entered into business? What premises are included in the business?

Equine stock would have to be introduced as cost. Cost of production could be complicated to calculate but necessary.

The inclusion of pre-trading expenditure (ICTA 1988 s 401) is set out in CHAPTER **11**: PLANNING FOR LOSSES.

These are all practical considerations to be reviewed by the tax adviser. It is hoped that this chapter helps highlight the pitfalls whilst being aware of the tax benefits of late registration.

Trading losses

Late claims

3.19 The question of when to register the equine business can be linked to the availability of losses and the ability to make a tax claim in respect thereof.

CHAPTER **11** sets out the rather 'tight' time limits for claims for losses under self-assessment. So can a late claim be made? If it is discovered that a business is registered late and a loss claim available, can a late claim be made?

The Inland Revenue's Inspector's Manual at IM3357 'Trading losses: late claims', states that:

> 'There is no express provision in the Taxes Acts for claims to loss relief to be made after the statutory time limit has passed. Other than in exceptional circumstances set out at IM3358 (which should in all cases be checked), late claims should not therefore be accepted and the reasons explained in full to the taxpayer or agent.'

Furthermore, IM3358 says with regard to the acceptance of late claims:

> 'Where a late claim is made for a year, which is the subject of an investigation settlement involving interest and penalties, the instructions at IH4111 should be followed. Relief should be allowed only against the amount of the additional assessment. As to other circumstances in which the normal time limits for claims are extended, see IM3356.'

The pragmatist will try to strike the correct balance between the desire to succeed with a late claim and causing unnecessary problems with the tax Inspector. Each case must be assessed on its merits – the size of the loss, the ability to offset losses in the future, the relationship with the Inspector, etc, will all be relevant.

Unacceptable reasons for late claims

3.20 IM3358 sets out the principles, which determine whether a late claim should be accepted:

> 'What constitute acceptable reasons for late claims will depend upon the facts of each individual case. However, there are a number of common explanations, which are not normally accepted. Tax Officials are told that they should not accept late claims where the reason given is one of the circumstances shown below. The reasons should be explained in full to the taxpayer or agent.
>
> (a) Where accounts disclosing the loss were not prepared until after the expiry of the time limit, except where IM3358 applies.
> (b) Where an agent was unaware a loss had been sustained although the taxpayer, or another agent where more than one acts (for example with partnerships), was aware.
> (c) Where accounts have not been agreed by the Revenue, except where IM3358 (e) applies. As IM3354 says, claims can be made in advance of the submission of accounts.
> (d) Where an agent, whether current or former, has been dilatory or given bad advice or is otherwise blamed for the lateness of the claim, except where IM3358 (c) applies.
> (e) Where the taxpayer and agent are in dispute, including cases where fees have not been paid.
> (f) Where the taxpayer was unaware that relief could be claimed in respect of the loss.
> (g) Where the taxpayer refuses to give a reason for the lateness of the claim.
>
> Any cases falling outside IM3358 in which the taxpayer insists that there are grounds for the Board to exercise its discretion have to be referred to the relevant Head Office Specialist for further advice before being refused finally.'

Use of private horses in the equine business

3.21 This was first looked at in 3.4 above.

In addition to the working animals, there may be one or more that are only used privately, perhaps for dressage, show jumping, eventing or other competition work such as show horses. Sometimes these special animals are not used at all in the business in case of injury.

The question of transfer of a horse for private use at market value as set out in *Sharkey (Inspector of Taxes) v Wernher (1955) 36 TC 275* has to be taken into consideration. If a horse is transferred from business to private use it must be made at market value.

Ascertainment that private usage of feed, tack, farrier, medicines, veterinary care etc, has been properly accounted for has to be made. Clearly, by extracting the private element of an equine business, a commercial and viable venture that satisfies the tax Inspector can go ahead (see 10.23 below).

The Inland Revenue's approach to the question of allowing expenses against income from equine activities is generally favourable for the business of buying and selling horses where there is a pure 'trade'. This is sometimes known as 'dealing' and sometimes as 'pin-hooking' However, where the costs of producing horses for sale includes competing, the Revenue can consider that it must give rise to considerable personal benefit. The tax adviser must try to protect this position.

Owning a Horse – Tax Planning 4

Achieving tax efficiency of racehorse ownership

4.1 As mentioned in CHAPTER 2 and throughout the book, horse-racing is generally regarded by the Inland Revenue as 'tax-free'. Owning a horse is essentially not a taxable activity. The arguments put forward by the Inspector's Manual for racing being non-taxable are strong and based on the desire to refuse loss relief for the high costs of involvement in this pastime.

The Government's decision to keep the Racehorse Owner's VAT Scheme is a significant opportunity for tax advisers, racehorse owners and racing authorities to work together and look at the maximisation of the commercial structure and tax efficiency of the industry of owning racehorses (see CHAPTER 17: PLANNING FOR VAT).

In order to establish that an activity is actually a properly taxable trade, it must be shown to be managed on a commercial basis with a view to the realisation of profit. As has been said, there is a case for racing to be regarded as taxable because a racehorse needs to be tested on the racecourse in order to determine whether it should be retained for a career in breeding. These tests are for speed, stamina and courage. If there is to be any prospect of agreement on this matter from the Inland Revenue it is perhaps more likely with fillies (the female of the species) since, statistically, a higher percentage return to the breeding function.

Racecourses are ideal locations for the entertainment of business contacts and although entertainment expenditures themselves are disallowable for tax purposes, (ICTA 1988 s 577), other costs of racing ought to tax deductible if a commercial venture is structured correctly.

Business motive of racehorse ownership

4.2 Most directors whose companies own racehorses would claim that they do so for advertising, marketing or public relations (PR) purposes. Tax Inspectors will obviously look very closely at such claims, as they have to satisfy themselves that they are granting tax relief for legitimate business expenses and not merely subsidising a hobby of one of the directors. The key issue here is MOTIVE. The following points will be taken into consideration.

- Is there an entertaining motive behind the acquisition of the racehorse? If so, the claim is likely to fail or at least fail in part.
- Is this a form of advertising in keeping with the company's size, structure and image? A company which has not previously had a substantial advertising budget is unlikely to succeed in a claim. The same applies to a company which would not otherwise advertise to the public.
- Is there any evidence that the horse is being used for advertising purposes? If a horse is named after the company which owns it, there is a stronger argument in favour of treating it as a business expense.
- It might be wise to try and carry out an analysis of sales and to prove that there is a direct benefit. Alternatively, an independent marketing or PR bureau could carry out a report. This might keep fellow directors and the tax Inspector happy at the same time.
- Is this form of advertising likely to generate more business? Has the decision to advertise in this way been based on sound commercial principles? If not, the claim is likely to fail.

Minimum sponsorship – the Racehorse Owners VAT Scheme

4.3 Guidance to the sponsorship angle can be found in the Racehorse Owners VAT Scheme ('the VAT scheme') – see CHAPTER 17.

The VAT scheme agreed between HM Customs & Excise and the racing industries means that owning racehorses can become significantly less expensive.

There were doubts about the scheme continuing but it was agreed in December 2002 that the scheme could continue with a review in 2005. Further extension depends on the owners complying with the code of conduct rules for proven sponsorship agreements.

Information can be obtained on Weatherbys' website at www.weatherbys-group.com/services/vatservices.html.

At the time of writing, the Weatherbys VAT services guide says that as a 'rule of thumb', keeping a horse in training costs around £16,000 a year. Weatherbys estimate that the scheme could mean a saving of around £2,800 a year per horse, quite apart from recovering VAT in the purchase price. Sponsorship agreements must be registered and must have minimum values to be attained. The minimum value is £300 per horse per year. For those horses intended to compete in Class A races, the minimum value is £750 per horse per year. Where the agreement extends to sponsorship of a group of ten or more horses the minimum is £100 per horse.

Can a company pursue a hobby?

4.4 In principle, it makes no difference whether an individual or a company owns a racehorse since corporation tax is largely based on income tax rules with some specific extensions and revisions. Inevitably there are minor differences due to the legal distinction between a company and an individual. The subject of incorporation is dealt with in detail in CHAPTER 9: THE EQUINE BUSINESS STRUCTURE.

For example, whereas the Inland Revenue regard racing as a hobby when carried on by an individual, it cannot be said that a company owning a racehorse is carrying on a hobby. It is either carrying on a taxable or a non-taxable activity – but what of benefits in kind for directors?

It is an interesting tax fact that it is the individuals behind a company – the members and/or directors – who pursue hobbies, not the company itself.

The company is merely carrying on a non-taxable activity at the directors' instigation. From the company's point of view, the distinction is academic since the effect is still to deny tax relief in most cases on losses. The position of director's benefits in kind and the requirements of form P11D must be considered by the company's management and the tax advisers.

Sponsorship, entertaining, marketing, advertising and PR

4.5 Horseracing is one of the most televised leisure activities and is thus an extremely high profile sport which can in turn be used to promote products through advertising and sponsorship. The relevant tax rule for allowability is ICTA 1988 s 74. Strictly, expenditure will need to be incurred demonstrably *wholly and exclusively* for the benefit of the trade of the company.

In general, an individual or a company cannot obtain tax relief for racing expenses and, conversely, will not have to pay tax on race winnings. The exception to this rule is where the Inland Revenue accept that a racehorse is maintained for the purpose of advertising or marketing, in which case the owner can claim the cost of keeping and racing the horse as a business expense. The disadvantage is that prize money becomes taxable, but relatively few racehorses generate enough money to cover the cost of keeping them. The vast majority of owners who keep racehorses for marketing purposes will be companies, although the rules also apply for individuals.

The advertising world of the 1960s and 1970s has moved into the whole new industry of marketing and PR. The travelling salesman is almost a rare beast replaced by a marketing and PR team. How does the ownership of a racehorse fit into the twenty-first century business life?

1994 saw a turning point for sponsorship. Owner-sponsorship was introduced in racing which allowed sponsorship through the medium of horse rugs, jockeys' breeches and silks. The key is to ensure that the sponsorship agreement is tax efficient. It is essential that maximum tax relief is obtained.

In today's world, one of the ultimate aims of the taxpayer and tax adviser alike is to try to obtain tax relief for expenses that the taxpayer 'enjoys'. This does not mean trying hopelessly to claim relief for a hobby, but to ensure that the business relationship between racehorse ownership and the taxpayer's business is commercially sound, well structured and tax efficient.

Questions that must be asked are whether the advertising expenditure is genuine advertising or a corporate entertaining package? Can the amount spent be justified in relation to the benefits achieved from the advertising? Are there commercial principles? Will the advertising generate more business? Is the advertising linked to the image, size and structure of the business? Where the horse is, say, named after the company the claimant's position vis-à-vis the Inland Revenue will generally be stronger.

The case of *Executive Network (Consultants) Ltd v O'Connor (HM Inspector of Taxes) [1996] STC (SCD) 29* can be a useful reference for the purpose of considering expenditure incurred by a company in sponsoring a horse riding business.

Tax efficiency of the sponsorship is a key issue. As set out at **4.2** above, the main benefit of the sponsorship expenditure must be to promote the trade of the company. The business should be able to show that the sole purpose of the sponsorship agreement is to help promote and market the company's products and services and that any personal benefits accruing from horseracing are merely incidental. The reason for the sponsorship should be documented. The BHB have guidance publications such as 'The Racehorse Owners' Guide to Sponsorship' and the 'Guide to Valuation of Ownership Sponsorship Sites'. The sponsorship should have a clear and defined benefit for the trade.

Another consideration is a structured corporate entertaining package for both staff and clients. Staff entertaining is allowable. There is a thin line between clients and staff. When employees help entertain clients then this is client entertaining. However, where the business is entertaining employees only, eg paying for a day at the races, it can be tax allowable, but there is a risk that the staff will be taxable on the benefit received. It may be possible to incur such expenditures within the 'tax-free' limit for the annual Christmas party, increased to £150 per head in the 2003 Budget statement, as the limit is not just available for the festive season but can also cover other staff entertainment events.

Owning a racehorse in the corporate entity

4.6 Ultimately, a company's ability to succeed in obtaining tax relief on a racehorse may well depend largely on the facts of the specific case and on the relative powers of negotiation possessed by the company's directors and advisers and by the company's local tax inspector. In practice, it should be relatively easy for a large company to claim relief if it has a substantial advertising budget and if the racehorse is named after the company's product. Conversely, a small company, which is unlikely to generate much business from this form of advertising, is unlikely to succeed in its claim for tax relief for the expenses, especially if its advertising budget would otherwise be a modest one.

The Inland Revenue will look at all cases closely. For a business to be able to obtain tax relief it will be necessary to satisfy the Inland Revenue that the expenditure will be deductible if it is wholly and exclusively incurred for the benefit of the trade of the business. If a business can obtain tax relief for racing expenses, it will, of course, be taxed on any race winnings. The Inland Revenue will have to see that the expenditure is incurred to promote the trade. Examples of this are increasing awareness of its products and brands. Successfully claiming a deduction for racing expenditure will generally be more troublesome when the owners or directors of the business have a known personal interest in racing.

The practical point for the tax adviser and the owner is to compile a plan in advance, a detailed folio of evidence about the reasons for the purchase of the racehorse looking at budgets, opportunities and possibly identifying by reference to marketing reports the expected benefits flowing from the purchase. Full consideration must be given to the previous section on sponsorship, entertaining, marketing, advertising and PR.

For all directors who pay UK income tax, and whose companies own racehorses, there is a danger that the Inland Revenue will regard the company's financing of the horse as the provision of a benefit in kind for the director, especially in cases where the director has a keen interest in horseracing and has enough influence to bring a racehorse into the company. The benefit in kind will have to be declared on the form P11D if appropriate.

Although many bloodstock breeders and owners of racehorses may be optimistic about the likely future profitability from these activities, more often than not, racing and bloodstock breeding will produce losses. It may be necessary to borrow to fund these activities and any interest payable on loans relating to the trading activities should be allowable for tax purposes. If an individual wishes to embark on bloodstock activities but is not able to fund these personally or by bank borrowings without providing generous personal guarantees, then he may wish to fund the activities by withdrawing funds from one of his trading companies. If that company owes him money, possibly by way of loans, which he has previously made to the company or credit balances on his director's current account, then these funds can be withdrawn without any adverse tax consequences.

The tax legislation ensures that the withdrawal of funds from any company (whether to purchase a racehorse or not) ensures that tax in some form is payable, whether it be by dividend, director's remuneration or director's loan (ICTA 1988 s 419). Taking profits/funds from a company is a complex subject, which warrants its own book. However, the author attempts to embrace the subject of incorporation in CHAPTER 9: THE EQUINE BUSINESS STRUCTURE.

Unincorporated businesses owning racehorses

4.7 The same basic taxation principles apply whether a bloodstock activity is operated personally or through a company. In general, an individual is likely to be carrying on a taxable bloodstock activity but the Inland Revenue may regard his racing activities as a hobby and non-taxable. Here we must again turn to the fundamental principles set out previously. However, these principles may be modified somewhat when dealing with a company owning a horse rather than an individual. The ability to obtain tax relief for the unincorporated business may again depend on sponsorship, entertaining, marketing and PR.

The entertaining element of ownership will be disallowed in the tax computation and likewise the element of the expenses that is not wholly necessarily and exclusively for the business will be disallowed.

Again, great emphasis should be placed on sponsorship agreements which should ideally contain clear, well-structured and documented evidence that the expenditure is expected to produce distinct and identifiable benefits to the business.

Detailed work by marketing/PR consultants would demonstrate how the ownership could help the business and evidence of success will be imperative.

VAT registration for the unincorporated business can be conducted under the owner's scheme.

Ownership of the stallion – the income stream

4.8 Stallions are looked at in more depth in **CHAPTER 6**, however, it is worth looking at the summary position. It has been said that owning a racehorse is a dream, owning a stallion is an income stream and this is a taxable income stream.

As mentioned earlier, bloodstock breeding is a high-risk, long-term business. Mares do not generate income until they produce progeny and it will be a number of years before a judgment can be made as to the quality of the foals. The owner must pay for their upkeep, together with the nomination fees to enable the mare to visit a stallion, so losses are likely to be made for several years. Stallions, on the other hand, are income producers once they return to the stud farm. The likely value of the stallion will depend upon its success during its racing career, but a stallion can be an extremely profitable asset from the outset.

The owner of a successful colt has a number of choices at the end of its racing career. He could sell it and, as the racing activity is generally not taxable, the proceeds will be received tax-free. However, the tax-free element will depend on what the horse costs – either purchased or bred. If he brings the stallion back into a stud farm it will enter the accounts at its then market value so that if it is sold by the stud farm at a later date, the increase in the value of the stallion during its racing career will be tax-free. The stallion could be used to cover the mares of the stud farm or other owners could send their mares to the stallion for the payment of a nomination fee.

A successful stallion valued at, say, £1m could be expected to generate nomination fees of approximately £6,000 per nomination, so that the owner or shareholders could sell 40 nominations and so produce income of £240,000 for that year. However, this income would be taxable and so the individual taxpayer would be liable to pay income tax at the highest rate of 40% under current legislation. Whether such income will be taxable under Schedule D Case I as part of a stud or under Schedule D Case VI is dealt with in **CHAPTERS 6 AND 7**.

Leasing racehorses

General

4.9 Due to the difficulties which may arise in funding the cost and expenses of keeping and running a racehorse, some owners of a breeding business acquire their racehorses personally and then lease them on to their business so that all the expenses are met by that business. It may be possible to show that the expenditure thus incurred is advertising expenditure so that the company receives tax relief, although, obviously, the commercial viability would have to be justified to the Inland Revenue. In addition, the company may pay the owner a rent for the use of the horse, although this would be taxable on the owner.

If the business leases and then races the horse, any winnings should accrue to the business. However, if the racehorse becomes extremely valuable, the terms of the lease could include a clause to terminate the agreement with the business and enable the breeder to sell it with the resultant profit being tax-free on the assumption that the breeder's trading activity is not taxable.

There are various forms of leases, which can be arranged between the owner of the horse and the company. All leases need to be registered with the Jockey Club under the Rules for Racing. A form of lease can either be obtained from the Jockey Club or a legal document can be drawn up which will clearly define the relationship between the parties so that there can be no confusion at a later date. Again, the leasing arrangement, which may be required, will depend upon the tax position of the parties and the likely profitability of the activity.

Leasing arrangements may also be entered into where the breeder does not wish to sell a yearling filly, but to retain her for breeding purposes, and cannot afford training expenses. In these cases, similar leasing arrangements to those outlined above may be entered into. Imagine the situation where a breeder or stud farm wants to retain ownership but cannot afford training fees. The owner could lease the horse (at a relatively low cost subject to the quality of the horse) to the business who could then name it in their business name and organise marketing and PR around the activity. If successful, the breeder/stud has increased the value of its stock (and possibly associated stock) and the business has undertaken valuable PR/Marketing.

Obviously, if the business was a company and the company and owner were connected, there would be disclosure requirements under the related party transactions provisions. If the business was unincorporated, disclosure to the Inland Revenue would also be required.

Share of winnings

4.10 In *Norman (Inspector of Taxes) v Evans [1965] All ER 372, 42 TC 188,* the taxpayer, a breeder of racehorses, appealed against assessments made on him under Schedule D Case VI in respect of sums received by him under agreements whereby he received one half of the winnings of horses which he had leased to other persons for the purposes of racing. It was contended on behalf of the Crown that the sums received were taxable profits under a contract of 'bailment. On behalf of the taxpayer, it was contended that he received one half of the winnings in his own right and not under the terms of a contract, and that racing horses was a non-taxable recreational activity. It was held that he was properly taxable under Schedule D Case VI since the sums received by him arose not from a recreational activity, but from a business transaction between him and the lessees.

Capital gains tax and horse ownership

4.11 Horses which form part of the bloodstock of the stud farm and racehorses in training should not be subject to capital gains tax (CGT). The bloodstock which forms part of the commercial activity of the stud farm will normally be treated as stock-in-trade and will not be a capital asset for the purposes of this tax.

The valuation of stock of a stud is dealt with in CHAPTER 7.

Racehorses were within the scope of capital gains tax from the introduction of the tax in 1965, until 1968. The Chancellor of the Exchequer at that time realised that as racehorses were more likely to produce capital losses than capital gains, a number of racehorse owners were accumulating substantial capital losses and these capital losses could be carried forward indefinitely and set against future capital gains. In the circumstances, it was decided to take racehorses outside the capital gains tax net.

What a pity this ruling was made. How useful the capital gains tax relief would be. But if losses are achieved through a trade such as a stud then income tax relief can be obtained under the correct legislation and this income tax relief is more advantageous.

CHAPTER **6** looks in detail at the principle of the sale of the stallion and the wasting asset.

Interaction with the stud farm

4.12 When the racehorse owner also owns a stud farm, when is the tax-efficient time to transfer to the racing activities? How can tax planning and stud ownership be reconciled?

As set out in CHAPTER **3**, if, in general, breeding horses is a taxable activity and owning racehorses is a separate and non-taxable activity, then the transfer of horses from the stud to and from racing back to the stud will be awarded special tax treatment.

This matter was considered in the 1955 case *Sharkey v Wernher (1955) 36 TC 275*, which held that the animal must be valued at 'market value' when it leaves the stud to go into racing. Reference to this case is used to determine that assets taken from a proprietor's business for private use must be at market value. The market value of the horse at that time will be reflected in the bloodstock accounts. Therefore, even though a horse has not been sold, any profit or loss from breeding is taxable or allowable when it leaves the stud and commences its racing career.

Such profit or loss will have been realised in this way even though the breeder will not yet have received any proceeds from the sale of the horse to meet the tax liability. However, if the cost of breeding the horse by the stud farm amounted to much more than its market value when the transfer to racing is effected, this would result in an immediate tax relief on the amount spent. The loss will be achieved in the stud accounts, and then in the tax computation.

When the horse returns to the stud, it is brought into the bloodstock accounts at its then market value. If a horse left the stud, and became an extremely successful racehorse and returned to the stud at a much higher value during its racing career, the gain will have accrued tax-free to the owner, but with no money received. Conversely, if the horse is worth less when it returns to the stud then a non-allowable loss will have accrued.

Thus, timing is an essential element in the tax planning here. Deciding precisely when horses go into training and when they should return to stud will generally be based on opinions as to their future development and potential. However, the stage at which this occurs can determine just how much tax they incur over their lifetime. The task of seeking to reconcile the opportunity to obtain all the tax-free gains of racing with the desire to obtain loss relief on commercial losses of the stud farm would seem impossible for the tax planner. The tax position of stud farms is dealt with in CHAPTER 7.

Buying and selling or loaning a horse

4.13 Horses are subject to the ordinary laws of contract and the sale of goods so far as the transfer of their ownership is concerned. The transfer of the ownership of a horse is dealt with in CHAPTER 5: OWNING A HORSE – LEGAL ASPECTS. The aim of this section is to emphasise the benefits of information provided by the BHS and other organisations on this subject and to provide examples of model agreements.

There is no implied condition as to the fitness of an animal for any particular purpose *except* where the seller carries on a business of selling such animals. Otherwise, there are no warranties whatever upon the sale of an animal, as to its quality or fitness for any particular purpose, in the absence of express agreement. The rule of *caveat emptor* (or 'buyer beware') applies, and there will be no comeback over unidentified defects or other problems. Therefore, when the purchase is from a private individual, it is vital that there is a written agreement, which expressly provides that the horse is of the particular quality or possessed of the particular virtue that the buyer desires. It is also prudent to have the horse examined by a veterinary surgeon prior to purchase.

The buyer will also want to ensure that he has an appropriate remedy in the event of breach of any express term of the contract as to the condition of the horse. If there is no express provision, the buyer cannot return the horse for a breach of warranty as to the condition of the horse, unless the term of the contract, which has been breached, is regarded as going to 'the root of the contract'. So the buyer will be restricted to a pecuniary claim in damages. Therefore, it is best to provide expressly when and how the buyer will be allowed to return the horse for breach of warranty. Notice of any defect should be given to the seller as soon as possible. Where the contract specifies a time limit within which a complaint must be made or the animal returned, no action could be brought if this time limit has passed.

If the seller *is* in the business of selling horses, the Sale of Goods Act 1979 imposes a statutory expectation that the horse should be 'fit for the purpose for which it is sold, and is of satisfactory quality' (see also **5.2** below). There is a right to return the horse upon discovery of a breach of either of these terms, following a reasonable time for examination. This can lead to uncertainty, and there can be dispute as to whether the seller was aware of the purpose for which the horse was to be purchased. Therefore, it is still highly advisable to have a written contract.

Two model agreements can be obtained from the BHS. Precedent VI is an agreement for a straight sale and purchase of a horse and Precedent VII is an agreement for a loan coupled with an option to purchase.

A solicitor should draft all legal agreements. The aim of these agreements is to give guidance (and guidance only) so that when the meeting with the solicitor is arranged, various complex matters have been given due consideration.

Planning the sale of the 'tax-free' racehorse

4.14 Consider the following.

1 *The successful racehorse is good enough to stand as a stud. When is the most efficient time to sell?*

Racing is tax-free. What happens when a racehorse becomes a stallion? Is this still tax-free?

The sale of a successful racehorse is tax-free. The sale of the syndicate is taxable. A racehorse owner might not want to own the whole of the stallion. As per the Inland Revenue's Inspector's Manual at IM2350, this is set out as follows:

> 'Since the cost of buying a successful stallion outright is prohibitive for some bloodstock breeders, ownership may be shared in a syndicate. The usual form of syndication is into 40 equal shares, representing the number of mares which, traditionally, was regarded as the standard for a stallion to cover in one season. Each syndicate member contributes towards the costs of keeping the stallion and is entitled to one "nomination" each season per share owned. The member may use the nomination to cover one of his own mares, or it may be sold on the open market. The shareholders appoint a committee which deals with the day to day management of the stallion.'

The sale of part of the racehorse is, as stated, tax-free, however, once the stallion is an established syndicate animal, the sale of the shares in the syndicate are taxable under Schedule D Case VI (or Case I if part of stud activities). Clients must be advised prior to establishment of the syndicate of the ability to take advantage of the tax planning opportunity.

The situation will be confused if the stallion is part of a stud operation.

Stud fees and sale of nominations will be taxed under Schedule D Case VI unless:

- the owner of the stallion share is not carrying on a trade of stud farming or horse breeding;
- the owner is carrying on such a trade but does not use the stallion share for the purpose of obtaining service for his own mare.

As mentioned above, these will be taxed as Schedule D Case I. Each case *must* be looked at on its merits. Every alternative *must* be planned in advance. Clients with racehorses must be encouraged to discuss and disclose their activities in full as there could be tax savings to achieve or tax pitfalls to avoid.

2 *The sale of a racehorse is tax-free but is the sale of a foal from the racehorse (broodmare) tax-free?*

The activity of breeding can be taxable and each case must be looked at individually. If the disposal is deemed to be taxable then obviously the expenses surrounding it will be taken into account. Breeding is an activity based on luck. A foal of very high value could be bred and sold.

Owning a Horse – Legal Aspects 5

by Mark Charter
White and Bowker

Livery agreements

5.1 A livery agreement is a contract made between a livery operator and a horse owner. In return for payment, the livery operator provides facilities and/or services (depending on the terms of the agreement) to the horse owner.

There are many different types of livery agreement. The British Horse Society (BHS) provides a useful classification of the main types as follows:

- 'grass livery' – the provision of grazing, and usually a simple shelter;
- 'do-it-yourself livery' – the livery operator provides stabling and grazing and the horse owner is fully responsible for care of the horse;
- 'working livery' – the livery operator provides full care for the horse, but is allowed to work the horse in his/her own establishment;
- 'part livery' – stabling is provided by the livery operator, but duties relating to the care of the horse are divided between the livery operator and the horse owner;
- 'full livery' – the livery operator provides stabling and all the care for the horse.

Livery agreements do not have to be in writing but, for the protection of both parties, it is advisable that they are. A livery agreement should fully record the details of the agreed arrangements between the livery operator and the horse owner and, as a minimum, should include the following:

1 the livery period;
2 the livery fee and when it is payable;
3 the provision of a deposit by the horse owner;
4 a clear definition of the services to be provided by the livery operator and the obligations on the part of the horse owner. In particular, the division of responsibility for the care of the horse as between the parties should be made abundantly clear – the parties typically having to consider:
   - feeding;
   - watering;
   - bedding/mucking out;
   - exercising;
   - grooming;
   - worming;
   - teeth examination;
   - inoculations; and
   - tack;
5 a warranty by the horse owner that the horse is in good health, free of infectious diseases and vices;
6 the right for the livery operator to call out a vet or farrier in an emergency at the horse owner's expense;
7 an obligation by the horse owner to maintain public liability insurance at least in respect of the horse (the horse owner may also wish to be satisfied the livery operator carries public liability cover and buildings insurance cover for the livery yard);
8 the livery operator may also wish the agreement to oblige the horse owner to wear a riding hat whilst on the premises conforming to current BSI standards.

Operators of working liveries should also note that their establishments will require licensing by the local authority (see **4.13** above).

Buying and selling horses

5.2 The buying and selling of horses can be as fraught as buying and selling cars and houses. In law, horses are treated as goods, and therefore subject to the provisions of the Sale of Goods Act 1979 and the Sale and Supply of Goods Act 1994. The legislation has been mainly drafted with the sale and purchase of manufactured or inanimate articles in mind, and consequently does not always lend itself to easy interpretation in the context of the sale of a living animal.

The Sale of Goods Act 1979 imputes certain terms into the sale contract for a sale of a horse. Not all of these conditions will relate to a sale between two private individuals. The main conditions are:

- the seller has the right to sell the horse (s 12(1));
- the horse is not subject to an interest of which the buyer has not been notified (s 12(2));
- the horse corresponds to any description included in the sale contract (s 13(1));
- the horse is of satisfactory quality (s 14(2)) – (of course what constitutes *satisfactory quality* will depend upon the particular circumstances including the description of the horse and its price). If a defect is disclosed to the buyer before the contract is signed, or an examination ought to have revealed the defect, there will be no implied term in respect of such defect;
- the horse is reasonably fit for any purpose of which the seller has been informed (s 14(3)) and the buyer in the circumstances is relying on the seller's skill and judgment. This term would not be implied if it would have been unreasonable for the buyer to rely on the seller's skill and judgment, or if the buyer does not, in fact, rely upon the seller's skill and judgment.

In private sales *caveat emptor* is very much in point. Consequently, in such sales there is generally no implied term or warranty as to the fitness of the horse for its intended purpose or as to the merchantable quality of the horse.

Further and more recent conditions (effective from 31 March 2003) have been introduced by the Supply of Goods to Consumers Regulations 2002 (SI 2002/3045). Many of the provisions are difficult to interpret clearly in relation to sales of horses. Once again, the drafting applies more readily to manufactured goods (eg tack and equipment). As case law develops in this area, more guidance will be available. Of particular relevance is likely to be reg 4 which provides that the passing of risk in 'consumer' sales is deferred until actual delivery to the consumer. Thus, delivery to a carrier cannot trigger acceptance of contractual obligations or terms. 'Consumer' is defined as a natural person acting outside the purposes of his trade, business or profession. Furthermore, goods returned within six months of contract are presumed to have been out of conformity at the time of delivery – this reverses the previous position as to the burden of proof, and now places the onus firmly on the seller to show that 'goods' were not defective at the time of delivery.

In practice, returning a horse to a seller who does not wish to take it back, notwithstanding that technically the buyer will henceforward be within his rights to do so, will often not be practicable. The seller may have made it physically impossible to do so and/or if there is any element of abandonment of the horse, the buyer may expose himself to both civil and criminal proceedings arising out of that abandonment, particularly on welfare grounds. It seems likely that the safest option for a buyer when faced with such a dilemma will be to initiate court proceedings immediately in order to determine the matter.

If there has been non-conformity with an express or implied term of a contract (as described above), the buyer can require repair or replacement (Sale of Goods Act 1979 s 48B). This may be straightforward in relation to tack, but less likely to be an achievable remedy in the case of a horse. Alternatively, he can seek a price reduction or a complete voiding of the contract.

If the seller gives a guarantee, for example, guaranteeing to take a horse back if within a certain period it is identified as not being suitable for the buyer, this is now a contractual obligation.

In a consumer sale, a seller cannot exclude or restrict liability for breach of contract in relation to the implied terms mentioned above (Unfair Contract Terms Act 1977 s 7(1), (2)). In a private contract of sale, a provision excluding or limiting liability in relation to such implied terms may be acceptable, provided such provision was reasonable in the circumstances (Unfair Contract Terms Act 1977 s 11 (1)).

Although an oral contract for the sale of a horse is effective in law, prudent sellers and buyers should insist on a written contract clearly setting out all the terms of the deal between the parties. The law makes a distinction between those terms of the contract which in essence are fundamental to the contract (conditions), and those that may be considered collateral to the main purpose of the contract (warranties).

The distinction determines the nature of the remedy open to an aggrieved buyer. A condition of the contract may be, for example, that the horse has a given pedigree or an established record in competitive performance. By contrast, a warranty is a statement that eg, the horse is 'good to clip or shoe'. The dividing line between *condition* and *warranty* can at times be a thin one, and will vary with the particular circumstances of each case. If the breach of contract comprises a breach of warranty, the buyer's remedy is to seek compensation (damages); if the breach is one of condition, the buyer can rescind the contract, and return the horse.

Loan agreements for horses

5.3 The British Horse Society also provides a helpful categorisation of the different types of horse-loan agreements as listed below.

- A Standard loan – essentially one relating to a fit horse in good health which can be worked.

- Breeding loan – for example, the borrower borrowing a broodmare to put in foal, with a view to the borrower then keeping the foal.
- Sharing – an agreement under which the horse owner shares the use of the horse with another party and that party typically helping with the expenses of keeping the horse and/or providing assistance in the form of carrying out certain duties, eg mucking out, grooming etc.
- Working livery – the horse owner allows the livery yard/riding stables to use the horse and in return the horse owner pays reduced livery fees.
- Companion or permanent loan – typically used for an aged or unsound horse or pony which the owner does not wish to keep himself (but does not actually wish to sell or destroy). The loan being made with the intention the horse's use will either be for light work only or frequently as a companion to another horse.

Whilst an oral loan agreement is again effective in law, because the circumstances under which a horse may be loaned out are many and varied; it is therefore good practice to reduce such agreements to writing and, in particular, to cover in the agreement essential issues such as:

- how long the loan is to last;
- a description of the horse;
- whether any fee is payable by the borrower;
- who is responsible for insurance cover;
- whether tack is included;
- the nature and extent of the uses to which the borrower can put the horse;
- if the horse is to be ridden who is permitted to do so;
- welfare responsibilities, including shoeing, worming, inoculations;
- which vet is to be used, who is responsible for vet's bills, the extent to which each party is to be consulted before veterinary treatment;
- rights of the owner to visit;
- where the horse is to be kept;
- requirements as to feeding, stabling and grazing;
- the documenting of any vices or unsoundness of the horse.

Loan agreements may also contain an option for the borrower to buy the horse or a right of pre-emption (ie a right of first refusal) in the event the owner wishes to sell. Therefore, the loan agreement in such cases will also need to make provision for the terms of the sale contract that will operate should the option or right of pre-emption be exercised. Here the considerations mentioned at **5.2** above will need to be borne in mind.

Where an option to purchase is to be at a predetermined price this should also be expressly included in the agreement. Alternatively, if the price is to be determined later, the agreement must contain clauses setting out the mechanics for establishing such price. It would also be prudent for the agreement to contain provisions for arbitration or expert determination in the event of a dispute between the parties.

Horse passports

5.4 To implement the European Commission Decision 2000/68/EC requiring horses to have passports, the Horse Passports (England) Order 2003 will come into force on 30 November 2003 (similar provision is made for Wales).

On or before 31 December 2003, all owners of horses (and, indeed, all forms of equidae) must (if not already then holding passports) apply to a recognised organisation for a horse passport. The website for the Department for Environment Food and Rural Affairs (DEFRA) contains details of the recognised organisations for this purpose (www.defra.gov.uk).

The recognised organisations include the British Horse Society and many of the major breed and specialist interest equine societies. Existing passports may need updating to record whether the horse is ultimately intended for human consumption and to record veterinary medicines administered. The rationale for the passport system is to prevent equines treated with certain veterinary medicines entering the human food chain. The identification of the horse in the passport will require completion of a silhouette, to be signed by a vet or person authorised by the issuing organisation. Other forms of identification (eg microchip) can be used but there is no legal requirement to do so.

If a horse enters England without a passport from an EU Member State, the horse owner must apply to a recognised organisation for a passport within thirty days of the horse entering the country. If a horse or pony is already listed in the registers kept by the New Forest Commoners Defence Association, Dartmoor Commoners Council or Exmoor Pony Council, a passport is only required when the animal is moved from the area on which it had grazing rights granted by one of these bodies. Paragraph 8 of the 2003 Order also includes special provisions as to the completion of passports for semi-feral breeds.

A horse under six months old will not require a passport until it leaves the premises on which it was born.

A horse owner must ensure that a passport is given to the keeper of the horse if that person is someone other than the owner. The owner or keeper of a horse must also ensure that a passport accompanies the horse when it is being moved within, or out of, Great Britain, to other premises for competition purposes, veterinary treatment, to a new keeper or for slaughter, in the case of semi-feral breeds when moved from the designated area and on 'any other occasion specified by the recognised organisation'.

Vets, when treating a horse, will have to ensure that they are given the horse's passport and must:

- satisfy themselves that the horse they are treating is the one described in the passport;
- record the treatment administered in the passport; and
- if the passport contains the owner's declaration that ultimately the horse is intended for human consumption, refrain from administering certain medicines.

On the sale of a horse, the seller must give the horse's passport to the buyer and within 28 days, the buyer must send the passport to the issuing recognised organisation for the new owner's details to be inserted.

Non-compliance with the Horse Passports (England) Order 2003 will be a criminal offence.

Escape or straying by horses

5.5 The facts and recent decision in *Mirvahedy v Henley [2003] UKHL 16, [2003] 2 All ER 401* on 20 March 2003 will no doubt have made many horse owners shudder and reach for their insurance policies. On 29 August 1996, a horse (which had apparently been 'spooked' by an unknown disturbance) broke out of a fenced field onto the A380 in Devon. The horse collided with a car driven by Mr Hossein Mirvahedy who sustained serious injuries. The horse died following the accident. Mr Mirvahedy sued the horse's owners, Dr and Mrs Andrew Henley.

The House of Lords agreed with the earlier Court of Appeal decision in the case that, although Dr and Mrs Henley had not been negligent in failing to fence in the horse, the limited form of no fault liability under the Animals Act 1971 applied. Central to the issue considered by the House of Lords were the relevant terms of s 2(2)(b) of the 1971 Act which impose strict liability where:

> 'the likelihood of the damage or of its being severe was due to the characteristics of the animal which are not normally found in animals of the same species or are not so found except at particular times or in particular circumstances …'

Dr and Mrs Henley were liable because whilst the horse's behaviour was normal for that horse and animals of that species, it was only normal in particular circumstances, namely having been panicked by some external stimulus.

The Animals Act 1971 s 4(1) stipulates:

> '… where livestock belonging to another person strays onto land in the ownership or occupation of another, and

(a) damage is done by the livestock to the land or to any property on it which is in the ownership or possession of another person; or

(b) any expenses are reasonably incurred by that person in keeping the livestock while it cannot be restored to the person to whom it belongs or while it is detained in pursuance to section 7 of this Act or in ascertaining to whom it belongs,

the person to whom the livestock belongs is liable for the damage or expenses except as otherwise provided for by this Act.'

Liability under section 4 is only avoided if:

- the claimant was at fault; or
- the livestock had strayed from the highway (having lawfully been on the highway) (Animals Act 1971 s 5).

The definition of livestock in the Animals Act 1971 s 11 includes horses.

At common law, the general principle applied by the courts in relation to damage caused by animals is that of the ordinary duty of care expounded in *Fardon v Harcourt-Rivington (1932) 146 LT 391 (HL)*:

> 'quite apart from the liability imposed upon the owners of animals or the person having control of them by reason of knowledge of their propensities, there is the ordinary duty of a person to take care ... that his animal or chattel is not put to such use as is likely to injure his neighbour.'

Under the Highways Act 1980, it is an offence for a horse to stray on, or lie on, the side of a highway (except where the highway runs over common, waste or unenclosed ground). The owner or keeper of a horse straying on a highway can be prosecuted and fined, and can also be required to pay the expense of the removal and keeping of the horse (Highways Act 1980 s 155).

Tax Planning for the Breeder and the Stallion Owner 6

What Type of Breeder?

6.1 There are normally two types of bloodstock breeder. First, the one who owns horses but not the stud farm itself, and so keeps his horse at a public stud. Secondly, the one who owns horses and owns or leases a stud farm (see CHAPTER 7: TAX PLANNING FOR STUD FARMS).

The breeder who occupies a stud farm will be taxed in the same way as a farmer, as if he were breeding cattle or sheep.

The profits of a business of horse breeding, with a view to the sale of the progeny, will be taxable as this is classed as a form of farming.

In principle, there should be no distinction between the tax treatment of income and expenses of keeping mares and stallions to be used for breeding purposes. This point was well illustrated by the case of *Lord Glanely v Wightman (Inspector of Taxes) (1933) 17 TC 63*. Lord Glanely received stallion nomination fees from the owners of visiting mares. He contended that relief should be given for the cost of maintaining both his stallions and his broodmares at the stud. Lord Wright, in judgment, said:

> 'The fee which is received for the covering of the visiting mares corresponds to the gain which the appellant has, or at least hopes to have, in respect of the foals of his own mares. But I think the similarity is deeper than that. The profit or income is, in truth, from the reproductive capacity of the animal and it is that which has the money value however realised, whether in cash or in kind. There is a natural tendency to think only of the procreative activity of the female animal, the mare, and ignore that of the male, the stallion.'

Clearly the activities of stallions and mares are an integral part of the stud farm's breeding activities and should be taxed accordingly.

However, in some circumstances the receipts from a stallion are taxed separately under Schedule D Case VI (see **6.4** below).

Once it is established that a breeder is carrying on a trade, it is necessary to calculate the profits on which he should be taxed. Accounts will be prepared as for any trader, taking credit for horses sold or transferred to racing. Deductions are then made for costs of sales and other overhead expenses.

Leasing mares

6.2 The situation may arise where the breeder either cannot afford the purchase price of an expensive mare or would prefer to use a particular mare for a limited period of time without the need for a large initial outlay. The problem can be overcome by the breeder 'leasing in' rather than actually buying the mare. Normally, the leasing payments will be at an agreed figure which is to be included in the lease agreement. The breeder will bear all costs of the mare during the lease period and such costs, including the leasing payments, should be allowable for tax purposes in the normal way. The leasing income will accordingly be taxable on the recipient, normally under Schedule D Case VI, unless they are themselves a breeder, in which case the receipts are likely to be taxable as normal trading income.

Foal sharing

6.3 Due to the fluctuating nature of the demand for the services of certain stallions, in some years it is difficult to provide a stallion standing at stud with a full complement of mares. The price of the nominations is obviously a determining factor and can be reduced in order to increase the supply. However, in recent years the practice of 'foal sharing' has evolved. This is where the owner of a share in a stallion will agree with the owner of a broodmare to split, in varying proportions, the resulting proceeds from the sale of the foal or yearling which is the outcome from the mare visiting the stallion concerned. This can have the advantage to the mare owner that no nomination fee is paid up front in cash, but is set at a figure dependent upon eventual foal sales. Again, this can introduce some complications with regard to stock valuations. The stallion owner is taxed on the stallion fees as well as the percentage of the foal proceeds for that year. If the stallion fees are part of the trade, the potential value of the foal should arguably be included as an asset in the balance sheet.

Stallion fees not as a trade

The Inspector's Manual

6.4 The Inland Revenue's Inspector's Manual at IM2350 states that where the occupier of a stud farm owns a share in a stallion for the purpose of obtaining service for his own mares, the tax treatment will depend on whether he has made an election for the herd basis. The proceeds of any sales of nominations are treated as trading receipts. Any contribution by the stud farmer towards syndicate expenses will be an allowable trading expense.

However, in the following situations the sales of nominations are assessable under Schedule D Case VI:

- the owner of the stallion share is not carrying on a trade of stud farming or horse breeding himself;
- the owner is carrying on such a trade but does not use the stallion share for the purpose of obtaining service for his own mares.

There are some disadvantages to having income assessed as Schedule D Case VI rather than a trade, not least the inability generally to claim for trading expenses. Stallion owners will need specific and tailor-made advice on just how a particular stallion should be dealt with for tax purposes.

Tax cases

6.5 *Malcolm v Lockhart (Surveyor of Taxes) (1919) 7 TC 99* provides an example of stallion fees not treated as trade receipts.

A farmer, who was assessed to income tax under the now obsolete Schedule B provisions, owned a stallion that was used for breeding purposes. In addition to serving the farmer's own stock, the stallion served mares belonging to other farmers for which 'service fees' were received. The farmer claimed that the fees, which he received in respect of the stallion's services, should be deemed to be part of the profits of his farm, the income tax liability in respect of which was covered by the then relatively nominal Schedule B assessment.

The court held that the farmer was chargeable to income tax under what would now be Schedule D Case VI in respect of the service fees.

There is clearly some debate on whether or not the keeping of a stallion to serve mares for the public in return for service fees has any direct relationship to the occupation of a farm? It is clearly not the occupation of land. A stallion kept for this purpose would seem to have no direct or 'necessary' relationship to the farming activities of a farmer. Such an animal may be kept in a separate stable, and may even be kept by a person who is not a farmer. There may well be obvious advantages of keeping the stallion at farm premises but these are arguably indirect considerations. He may be kept at a farm, and yet not be the property of the farmer on whose premises he is kept. He may not bring the farmer any profits or gains other than those derived from his keep. As this simply involves the consumption of farm produce it is arguably just one way of marketing or realising the fruits of the occupation of the farm.

In this context it is worth quoting direct from *Malcolm v Lockhart*:

> 'It is quite possible that an entire horse may be used by a farmer in connection with his farm in such a manner that its use outside will, in relation to its use for his own purposes, be so trivial and unimportant that there would be no tax eligible in respect of profits received for its services; or on the other hand it may be that the real use and purpose of the animal and its real advantage to its possessor lie in the moneys which can be obtained by the use of its services outside.
>
> My lord, this question is essentially a question of fact; the commissioners in this case have decided that the use by the Appellant of this stallion is a use that provides a profit, which does not arise in respect of the occupation of his lands. This seems to me no reason whatever why that finding of fact should be investigated more closely. Had it been found in terms it would have been outside the competence of a court to discuss it further. It is not found in exact language, but it is found inferentially, and the facts to which I have referred – namely, the number of mares on the Appellant's farm, the number of entire horses that he possesses, and the extent of the profits which this horse has earned – are, in my opinion, abundant to justify the conclusion which has been reached.
>
> For these reasons in my opinion this Appeal fails and should be dismissed with costs. The fees were not therefore an integral part of the stud.'

This case produced an adverse view to the case of *Lord Glanely v Wightman (HM Inspector of Taxes) (1933) 17 TC 634* and therefore considers the degree of integration with the activities of a stud farm to be more important, but each case must be assessed on fact (see **6.8** below).

There have been a number of cases where taxpayers have been assessed under Schedule D Case VI in respect of payments for the provision of facilities or the hiring of property. In some of these cases, it was held that the payments could be alternatively assessed under Case I as trading receipts.

It has also been held that a subsidy or contribution received by a statutory body not carrying on a trade can be assessed under Case VI. In *Severn Fishery Board v O'May (Surveyor of Taxes) [1919] 2 KB 484, 7 TC 103* licence fees, which the Fishery Board was empowered to charge, were assessed under Schedule D Case VI. It was held in that case, however, that the Fishery Board did not carry on a trade, and that there was no liability to tax in respect of the receipts. The basis of the decision was that the source from which the fees flowed was not analogous to a trade as defined for the purposes of ICTA 1988.

This decision was questioned later by the House of Lords in *Forth Conservancy Board v IRC [1931] AC 540, 16 TC 103* where the Conservancy Board was empowered to levy dues on vessels, goods, and passengers coming within its jurisdiction. It was held that the Conservancy Board's surplus revenues from these dues were profits or gains within Schedule D Case VI.

Local authorities and local authority associations are wholly exempt from income tax, whether under Schedule D Case VI or otherwise, by virtue of ICTA 1988 s 519. Where a statutory body which is not so exempt carries on a trading activity, it is assessable under Schedule D Case I (and not under Schedule D Case VI) on the amount by which any subsidy or contribution received by it exceeds its relevant expenses.

In *Carlisle and Silloth Golf Club v Smith (Surveyor of Taxes) [1913] 3 KB 75, 6 TC 198,* the court decided that profits derived by the club from visitors' fees were assessable under either Schedule D Case I or Case II.

The cost of replacing stallions has been allowed as a deduction from the service fees they produce, but not an allowance for depreciation in their value.

Gifts of free shares or nominations

6.6 The demand for excellence in the training and racing of potential stallions is such that top trainers and jockeys command very high fees. In certain cases, inducements are offered and are eventually paid on successful results. In this connection, trainers and jockeys may receive free shares or nominations on the syndication of a stallion when it retires to stud. The income which arises from this source is clearly taxable in the recipient's hands. Indeed, the value of a share in a stallion given to a trainer or a jockey would itself be taxable on the recipient as income arising from the particular profession of trainer or jockey. The precise tax position will depend upon whether the recipient is an employee of the provider or a freelance self-employed individual.

Where the recipient is self-employed, the Inland Revenue is likely to insist that the current value of the nomination is the measure of the taxable amount to be included as a receipt of the individual's trade. Where the recipient is an employee earning above £8,500 per annum, the measure of the taxable benefit should be the 'cost to the provider'. This will mean marginal costs in these circumstances and, in the case of an untried stallion, it could be argued that this will be negligible.

The 'cost' figure to be used is not the 'opportunity cost', it is the lost selling potential to the owner and the actual cost entailed in giving the nomination to the recipient. For employees earning below the £8,500 level, the value of the gift will be its market value at the date of the gift. However, the gift will be split between the value of the nomination and the future income from that nomination. Where the employee later sells the nomination or earns income from it, the Inland Revenue is likely to see this as assessable employment income (ie receipts from using the nomination certificate) or as Schedule D Case VI income (ie receipts from selling the nomination on).

In order to reduce the costs of the syndicate committee in respect of a stallion's keep it is sometimes agreed that a stud farm will receive free nominations in lieu of these expenses. Any income which arises to the stud farm from the sale of the nominations will be taxed in the normal way as part of its trading income. If a stud uses the nominations for its own mares this will, of course, be reflected in the valuation of the stock for the stud farm (see **CHAPTER 7**).

Strictly, the owner should show the offset of free nomination as income and the cost of boarding which has been set off as an expense. The accounts and tax treatment of this will be important, especially as regards timing issues.

Stallions are not plant

6.7 In *Earl of Derby v Aylmer [1915] 3 KB 374, 6 TC 665* it was held that stallions are *not* plant, ie not fixed assets.

The appellant owned two stallions at stud and was assessed in respect of the profits derived from stallion fees. He contended that in the computation of these profits for income tax purposes he was entitled under the legislation of the time to a deduction for depreciation 'by reason of the diminished value of the stallions year by year'.

It was held, that the claim did not fall within the scope of the legislation and could not be allowed. The judge said:

> 'I am clearly of opinion that the diminished value of the breeding animal, merely due to the fact that having lived a year it is a year nearer its end and therefore is from that point of view less valuable, is not within this section.'

The judge took the view that any diminution in value was not 'by reason of wear and tear'; it was simply a loss arising from reduction in value of an asset which was a source of production which was a wasting source of production.

If the stallion is part of the trade or stud then it would be included in stock and if the value falls (valued at the lower of cost or net realisable value) tax relief would be achieved in that way.

Stallion fees part of the stud farm – the tax case

6.8 The favourable case of *Lord Glanely v Wightman (1933) 17 TC 634* ruled that breeding, where the serving has been limited to animals on the farm, can be viewed as farming, ie part of a farming trade. The likely practical tax advantage will be that more expenses can then be claimed in respect of the keeping of the stallion.

In *Glanely*, the appellant was the owner of both a racing establishment and of a stud farm, comprising arable land, stud paddocks and pasture land, at which he maintained a stock of selected horses and carried on a breeding operation. Horses bred from the appellant's stock were sent to his training stables and raced, and those which were considered satisfactory were subsequently sent to the stud. Additions to the stock of horses at the stud farm were made, by purchase, from time to time and unsatisfactory horses were sold.

Mares belonging to other owners were served by the appellant's stallions at his stud farm in return for fees, and, on occasions, the services of the appellant's stallions to others mares were exchanged for the service of other stallions to the appellant's mares.

The appellant was assessed to income tax under Schedule D in respect of profits from stallion fees. He appealed to the Special Commissioners contending:

- that any profit derived from stallion fees was covered by the tax assessment on the stud farm; alternatively
- that the stallion fees should not be the subject of a separate tax assessment, but were receipts of the trading undertaking of breeding and racing horses, in which, as a whole, no profit had been made;
- that if the stallion fees were assessable as a separate item, a deduction should be allowed of the cost to the appellant of the service of his mares by the stallions of other owners, and therefore should not be exchanged for the service of outside stallions.

The Special Commissioners rejected the appellant's contentions and upheld the assessments in principle.

It was held that the occupation of the land being for the purpose of a stud farm, the use of the stallions upon the farm was not separable from the purpose of the occupation and the fees for their services were not taxable under schedule D.

It is interesting to look at other points raised in the case. Success in breeding thoroughbred horses could only be attained by submitting them to the test of the racecourse in order to find out whether they possessed the necessary speed and stamina. The test was essential to ascertain the value of both stallions and mares for producing high class progeny. It was only by the successful racing of the progeny of a stallion that the fee for his service could be assessed accurately. The potential and actual capabilities of the horses bred from him were only capable of being tested on the racecourse by the purchasers. The method followed by the appellant is the one usually adopted.

It is not generally believed to be conducive to successful breeding to send a mare every year to the same stallion. Better results will arguably be obtained by sending a mare to different stallions in different years. Furthermore, over time fillies bred at a breeding stud will finish their racing career and then return to the breeding stud. However, it is not uncommon to find that as a result of their close blood relationship to the stud stallions, they cannot be mated with any of them for fear of the ill-effects of inbreeding. Consequently, in *Glanely*, it was sometimes necessary to procure for the appellant's mares the service of a stallion or stallions belonging to other owners, for which fees were paid, or for which the services of stallions to the appellant were given in exchange. In these instances, the appellant, in addition to the stallion's fees, paid for the keep of his mares at the stud visited and the necessary travelling expenses.

Thoroughbred stallions must stand at a properly equipped stud farm and it is not practicable to send them around the country to serve other owners' mares. The owner of stallions must therefore either occupy sufficient land to accommodate the stallions and the visiting mares, or else the stallions must stand at some other similarly equipped breeding establishment.

In the case of a stud with 40 visiting mares such as in *Glanely*, a large number of paddocks is required for the accommodation of the visiting mares and the owner's own mares, in addition, a number of spare paddocks and loose boxes is also needed.

After foaling, mares must not be crowded and only two or three mares at a time can be put into a six or eight-acre paddock.

It is usual to find a high class stud farm with the paddocks divided by fences, lined by trees, with water laid on, and equipped with loose boxes lit with electric lights.

A mature stallion should serve 30 to 40 mares each season, and the appellant in *Glanely* did not have sufficient mares to keep his stallions fully employed. He was therefore obliged to let their services to the owners of other broodmares. Apart from keeping the stallion in health, the obtaining of nominations from first class mares is the best way of proving the value of the stallion as the sire of good progeny.

The appellant in *Glanely* did not expect to make a profit out of racing alone, but hoped he might make a profit out of the breeding and racing establishment as a whole. This might be possible if he obtained at least one more really first class stallion commanding a fee of 400 guineas. He contended that he had always run the whole establishment on what he considered to be commercial lines.

This case ruled that stallion stud fees could be regarded as an integral part of the profits of the farm.

Syndicate share in a stallion not a trade

6.9 The case of *Benson v Counsel (Inspector of Taxes) [1942] 1 All ER 435, 24 TC 178* gives a clear example of the tax position of the syndicate and the sale of stallion rights to nominations (stallion fees) as Schedule D Case VI income.

The appellants were two members of a syndicate formed in 1932 to purchase a thoroughbred stallion. By an agreement entered into after the sale, defining the rights and interests of the members of the syndicate, members became entitled each season to one free nomination to the stallion in respect of each share they held in the syndicate. There were no restrictions on a member selling his right to a nomination, provided the mare of the purchaser was approved by the syndicate.

During the seasons 1934 to 1940 inclusive, the appellants sold some of their nominations. On appeal, it was held by the Special Commissioners that the payments so received, while not receipts of a trade within Case 1 of Schedule D, were receipts of annual income chargeable under Case VI.

It was held, that the Commissioner's decision was correct.

If the tax planner's objective is to have stallion fees treated as Schedule D income, it is essential to look at reasons behind the appellants' failure in this case. The key issue is the identification of the existence of an 'integrated stud farm'. This is of paramount importance. If a syndicate share is used on a farmer's own mares then the income from the share should be taxed as farm income, eg Schedule D Case 1.

Irish tax position of stallion fees

6.10 The Irish stud industry has tax advantages that are the envy of breeders in Britain and France. The position was well explained in the Racing Post on Wednesday, 4 December 2002 (the day of the Irish Budget). A summary of the article is as follows.

Tax D-day for Irish breeders

Industry fears end to stallion fee tax exemption

The Irish bloodstock industry is bracing itself for a possible end to its much valued stallion tax exemption in today's Budget – a concession worth up to €42 million a year to breeders at present tax rates.

The Irish Thoroughbred Breeders' Association (ITBA) warned yesterday that any change would have a devastating effect and would lead to an exodus of the top sires.

Stallion fees have been tax-free in Ireland since 1969 and Irish breeders have taken full advantage, with Coolmore boss, John Magnier, leading the way, and as a result Ireland has long stood many of the top stallions in the world.

The tax concession is the envy of breeders in Britain and France, and the Thoroughbred Breeders' Association has tried many times, always without success, to get the British exchequer to follow suit.

However, Irish Minister for Finance, Charlie McCreevy, is under strong pressure, political as well as financial to bring the concession to an end.

ITBA manager, Niamh O'Sullivan said: "There is little doubt that the climate created, if this concession were removed, would lead to stallions being moved abroad, while the ability of most Irish studs to acquire new stallions would be seriously impaired. It would also decimate both employment and a world-class business that has been built up over the past 33 years.

The stallion tax exemption has been singled out for special criticism by Labour Leader Pat Rabbitte as benefiting the rich and many believe McCreevy, despite being a firm believer in its advantages, will find it politically impossible to retain the exemption.

For the past month the ITBA has been fighting a rearguard action to keep the exemption. It has sent every member of the Irish Parliament a three-page document setting out the benefits and warning of the consequences if it is removed.

Many commentators expect a compromise and believe that this will take the form of tax at the corporation tax rate of 12.5%.

However, such a move could well persuade Coolmore to stand some of its most expensive stallions at its Ashford division in Kentucky rather than in Ireland. Nobody from Coolmore was prepared to comment yesterday, with spokesman Richard Henry saying: 'It is up to the ITBA'.

The Irish tax position remained unchanged.

Whilst the advantages of standing stallions at stud in Ireland remain unaltered for the moment the UK regime does still offer some tax planning opportunities and advantages, they are perhaps just slightly more difficult to identify!

ICTA 1988 s 68 – 'Special Rules Where Property etc Situated in Republic of Ireland' – can have a further impact on taxpayers of Irish domicile living in the UK. It states:

> 'Rents and profits from the Republic of Ireland are assessed in the UK on the income arising on a current year basis, whether remitted or not, under Schedule D Cases IV or V. Deductions are allowed as if the income had been received or arisen in the UK and annual payments (other than interest) paid to non-UK residents may be deducted.'

As to relief for interest, see ICTA 1988 ss 353–368.

Subject to special provisions relating to income from trades, professions, vocations and pensions, tax charged on Irish income under Schedule D Case IV or V is computed 'on the full amount of the income arising in the year of assessment'. Whether Irish income is received in the UK is irrelevant; the 'remittance basis' never applies. This simple rule applies to Irish property and profits or gains generally.

Tax on such income, like other income arising in the Republic, is computed on the income arising in the year of assessment, ie current year basis. However, as an alternative, the inspector may direct as the basis for computing the tax a period which will yield an amount of income chargeable to tax equivalent to the amount which would have been assessed if the income had arisen in the UK. The Appeal Commissioners may review the Inspector's decision. The same allowances, reliefs and deductions as would have been available in respect of income arising in the UK are to be granted.

Thus, if someone of Irish domicile has a stallion standing in Ireland the income will arguably still be caught under ICTA 1988 s 68. The usual range of loss reliefs are available in respect of a trade, profession or vocation carried on in the Republic of Ireland as are available for other trades taxable on the arising basis under Schedule D Case V.

Stallions as a wasting asset

6.11 For the purposes of UK capital gains tax, no chargeable gain or allowable loss accrues on the disposal of (or of an interest in) an asset which is tangible movable property and which is a wasting asset. On the assumption that a stallion qualifies as a wasting asset then it is worth looking at the detailed CGT position associated with a wasting asset.

The exemption does not apply to a disposal of, or of an interest in, an asset if:

1 throughout the period of ownership of the asset by the person making the disposal, the asset has been used solely for the purposes of a trade, profession or vocation and that person has claimed or could have claimed any capital allowance for expenditure on the acquisition or enhancement of the asset; or
2 if the person making the disposal has incurred any expenditure on the asset or interest which has otherwise qualified in full for any capital allowance.

Expenditure on an asset is not deemed to have qualified for capital allowances for the purposes of (2) above unless the expenditure continued to be eligible for capital allowances at the time of the disposal of the asset. If capital allowances were originally given but were subsequently withdrawn because the expenditure ceased to satisfy the requisite conditions, the taxpayer is treated as if the allowances had never been made, in accordance with the decision in *Burman (Inspector of Taxes) v Westminster Press Ltd [1987] STC 669, 60 TC 418*. In that case, first year allowances made to the company in respect of expenditure on a printing press were withdrawn retrospectively because the press was never brought into use in the trade. It was held that the expenditure on the press had not satisfied the conditions of eligibility for capital allowances, and therefore the gain accruing to the company on the disposal of the press was exempt.

The most common example of assets to which exemption does not apply is plant and machinery used for the purposes of a trade.

Where an asset or interest has been used partly for the purposes of a trade, profession or vocation and partly for other purposes, or has been used for the purposes of a trade, profession or vocation for only a part of the period of ownership, or has otherwise qualified in part only for capital allowances:

- the consideration for the disposal, and any expenditure on acquisition or enhancement, are apportioned by reference to the extent to which that expenditure qualified for capital allowances; and
- the computation of gains or losses is made separately in relation to the apportioned parts of the expenditure and consideration.

Consequently, the exemption does not apply to any gain accruing in respect of the part of the consideration apportioned to use for the purposes of the trade, profession or vocation, or to the expenditure qualifying for capital allowances. The restricted exemption would apply, for example, where plant and machinery was used for non-business purposes.

Where a chattel is not exempt as a wasting asset, because expenditure in respect of it has qualified for capital allowances, the £6,000 exemption limit and associated marginal relief may apply instead.

Where a wasting asset is only partly exempt because of partial eligibility for capital allowances, it would appear that the limit applies to the part of the disposal consideration apportioned to the expenditure qualifying for capital allowances.

As it is extremely unlikely that a stallion will have been eligible for capital allowances, it is therefore clear that no chargeable gain or allowable loss accrues on the disposal of a racehorse or stallion, because a racehorse or stallion is tangible movable property which is a wasting asset. This is so even if the racehorse is immature. There should therefore be no capital gains tax concerns on the disposal of the racehorse.

Valuation of stock and transfers to racing

6.12 It might be that an individual carries on breeding activities which are regarded as merely a hobby and which do not have a commercial motivation. If so, this section should be regarded as reference material in the event that the motivations behind the activity changes and become commercial at some stage.

On the assumption that the breeder is trading the complex area of the valuation of stock, this subject is covered in detail in CHAPTER 7. Assuming that the breeder is paying fees at a public stud the calculation of costs should be relatively easy to calculate as opposed to operating a stud himself where the costs are internal.

As decided in *Sharkey v Wernher (1955) 30 TC 275*, the transfer of breeding stock from a commercial concern to a racing stable has to take place for tax purposes at full market value. This would apply to a small breeder and a stud farm.

However, as can be seen in CHAPTER 7, for the valuation of stallions in (see **7.8** below), a 'rule of thumb' method of valuation can be used to write off the stallion by equal instalments. This method is, however, only acceptable when a more accurate figure cannot be obtained. Similarly, with stallion syndicates the cost of the share in a stallion syndicate could be depreciated by equal instalments.

'Tax-free' sale of stallion to a syndicate

6.13 As the future value of a stallion and the likely length of its income producing life is uncertain, the owner may prefer to realise capital and still receive future income through nomination fees whilst also retaining the right to send his mares to the stallion. This could be achieved by the owner selling the stallion to a syndicate of which he would be a member. If he retained, say, eight syndicate shares so that he had a 20% interest in the horse, on the above assumptions, he could receive £800,000 tax-free. The definition of 'tax-free' is debatable here as it could be that the owner originally paid £2m for the horse and so has effectively made a loss with no tax relief. If he used, say, two of his nominations for his own mares, he would receive income of £36,000 from a sale of the other six nomination fees and this income could meet the expenses of the stud farm.

The difference between the sale of nominations to the stallion (the right to have a mare served), the sale of shares in a syndicate and the sale of shares in a potential stallion must be looked at. They are three different and separate activities.

Establishment of syndicates

6.14 Because stallions can generate high income as soon as they have been retired to stud, they generally have a higher value than broodmares.

The breeding season generally runs for five months from mid-February to mid-July. On average, each mare will be covered two or three times by the stallion. It is generally accepted that the optimum number of mares to be sent to a stallion during the breeding season (without subjecting the stallion to undue strain) is 40. Therefore, syndicates are normally formed with each owner of a syndicate share acquiring a fortieth interest in the horse. The syndicate share entitles the owner to a nomination, ie the right to send one of his mares to the stallion each season.

From the outset, UK bloodstock breeders were very interested in the principle of the syndicate as it was a way of owning an interest in a successful stallion at a relatively small initial outlay when compared with the entire cost of the stallion, and also the owners would only be responsible for their share of its upkeep. If the stallion became more valuable by producing successful progeny, then the value of their asset, ie the syndicate share, would accordingly increase. If the member did not want to send one of his own mares to the stallion, he could sell the nomination to another breeder. The proceeds from the sale of the nomination would be subject to tax under Schedule D Case VI, depending on the investment of the stud (this was looked at in **6.8** and **6.9** above).

Taxation of nomination fees from shares in syndicated stallions

6.15 As we have seen, the ownership of a share in a syndicated stallion by a bloodstock breeder can be used to enable his broodmares to be covered or can enable him to produce income by selling the nomination. As the syndicate share could be used as an income producing asset, there is a danger that the Inland Revenue could treat the share as an investment and tax any net income from the sale of nominations under Schedule D Case VI – and not Schedule D Case I as in the case of an investor who does not own broodmares. Any excess of the share of the upkeep of the horse over the nomination fees would be a Case VI loss, which could only be set against other Case VI income, but not against any trading or other income. It follows that if the syndicate share is held to be an investment, its cost would not give rise to a trading deduction for tax purposes, nor will it be valued as stock at the balance sheet date.

This line of argument by the Inland Revenue could be supported if the number and value of syndicate shares exceeded the number of broodmares. For example, if eight syndicate shares were owned and the stud farm only had five broodmares, then, at that time, three of the shares could not be used in the trading activities of the stud farm. Clearly, each case will be judged on its own merits, but if the number of shares were restricted to the number of broodmares then it would be easier to contend the shares were acquired with the express intention of being used for the stud farm's activities. Even if the nominations are then sold, the proceeds may have been used to finance the costs of an alternative stallion nomination fee for a broodmare.

The Inland Revenue can apply a similar argument where stallion shares are to be included in a herd basis election, ie if the number of syndicate shares exceeds the number of mares owned by a breeder, the surplus nominations cannot be required for the breeder's mares and are not therefore part of the herd. For further information about the herd basis, SEE CHAPTER 7.

Taxation of syndicate committees

6.16 A syndicate committee is normally formed to protect the interest of the stallion concerned and to be responsible for expenditures such as advertising, keep costs and insurance of the animal. To cover this expenditure, the committee is normally allocated a number of free nominations to the stallion to be used to raise revenue. Initially, the number is determined by the estimate of the quantum of the costs mentioned above. However, in certain cases where the stallion has become successful, profit can be generated for the syndicate committee. It is in these circumstances that the Inland Revenue may seek to tax the resulting profit.

Where stallions are less successful and it is difficult to sell nominations, a call may be made on syndicate shareholders to cover the syndicate committee's excess expenditure and, in these circumstances, the claimed apportionment from the shareholder may be a tax deductible item.

The taxation of the resultant profit can be looked at from two alternative approaches:

- Is the syndicate an unincorporated association?
- Is the syndicate a 'fiscally transparent entity' where the income is being taxed on the syndicate members in the appropriate proportions?

Unincorporated association

6.17 Where a syndicate is taxed as an unincorporated association it is taxed as if it were a company. The syndicate is under the control of a syndicate manager and committee. They have the power to distribute or accumulate any surplus income. In addition to the sale of nominations there will be the member's share of the income from the sale of surplus nominations.

Any breeding income will be treated as trade income where the member carries on an established breeding trade on a commercial basis with a view to profit. The income from the sale of surplus nominations will be taxed on the unincorporated association under corporation tax rules. Any surplus income generated by the syndicate will be regarded as distributions when it is paid out to members. The syndicate has to produce annual accounts for each stallion and profits shown in the accounts will be subject to corporation tax. The syndicate members will be taxed on the distributed income as if they are dividends received.

Fiscally transparent syndicates

6.18 A fiscally transparent syndicate (FTS) is one which is set up for the mutual benefit of the members directly and where the syndicate committee acts only as agent for the members. The difference between the unincorporated association and the FTS is that the income and expenses will be treated as accruing directly to the members in proportion to their shareholding, rather than to the syndicate. In effect, an FTS is somewhat akin to an investment club and treated in much the same way for tax purposes.

The applicable tax treatment turns on the wording of the syndicate agreement. If it is made clear that all rewards and risks of ownership are underwritten by the members, this will be an FTS. In this case, the income and expenses will be treated as accruing directly to the members of the syndicate and the division will be based on the proportion of their shareholdings. The syndicate manager will have no discretion as to distribution and the taxation of income will depend on whether the syndicate shareholder is a taxable breeder or a non-taxable breeder.

Tax pitfalls of breeding income

6.19 The aim of this chapter is to try and highlight areas of activities of the small breeder or stallion owner which could be charged to tax or which may need to be disclosed on the individual's tax return. Owners should make their adviser aware of all their breeding activities.

The fact that income arising from owning racehorses can be regarded as 'tax-free' does not prevent income receipts from the breeding elements of these activities being properly regarded as taxable. It is incorrect to assume that the racing losses and costs 'cancel' the taxable element of the breeding income.

The key points to be reviewed are as follows.

- Will a profitable small breeder incur tax liabilities on a 'one-off' high profit on sales?
- Will the profitable small breeder achieve full tax relief where a high profit is followed by large losses?
- Will income produced by an 'investment' stallion be taxable under Schedule D Case VI?
- What are the income tax implications of the allocation of future stallion nomination fees to jockeys and trainers (whether they are employed or self-employed)?
- What will be the tax status of shares of winnings paid to third parties as nomination fees – will these be taxed under Schedule D Case VI?
- Could stallion leasing produce more income – normally taxable as Schedule D Case VI income but possibly trade receipts in some cases?
- Will there be tax liability on foal shares under Schedule D Case VI?
- Will free 'board and lodgings' for the stallion in return for stallion nominations be taxable?
- What is the true status of Irish 'tax-free' stallion nominations taxable in the UK unless a 'bridge' is in place?

Tax Planning for Stud Farms 7

Stud farming is farming

7.1 As mentioned in CHAPTER 2: TAXATION AND THE EQUINE INDUSTRY, stud farming is regarded as farming for UK tax purposes (see the Inland Revenue's Inspector's Manual IM2350b) and with that come agricultural tax reliefs. Ensuring full compliance with the definition will therefore mean access to these valuable tax reliefs. Failure can mean extra costs both short and long term.

Whether or not an equine business qualifies as a farm depends on a number of factors. The Inspector's Manual at IM2260a provides guidance on the definition of 'husbandry' for these purposes:

> '"Husbandry" is not statutorily defined and one of its ordinary meanings is "farming". The statutory definition of farming (see IM2253) has a degree of circularity and should be given a common-sense interpretation to include activities normally recognizable as farming such as the growing of crops and the raising of farm livestock (see *Lowe v JW Ashmore Ltd (1970) 46 TC 597*).
>
> The definition does, however, presuppose a connection between the activity and the occupation of the land, which goes beyond the mere use of the land as a site for the activity (see *CIR v The Cavan Central Co-operative Society (1917) 12 TC 1*). Thus, certain intensive enterprises may fall outside the definition (see IM2260b).'

Thus the Inland Revenue accepts that stud farming can be regarded as husbandry and therefore as a form of farming.

If a stud farm is run on commercial lines then the trading results will almost certainly be taxable under Schedule D Case I whereas racing activities are not normally regarded as a taxable trade as has already been established. These principles apply whether the activities are run by an individual as a sole trader, through a partnership or a limited company. Before deciding on the operating or trading vehicle for the bloodstock and horseracing activities, it is necessary to consider the funding of the operation and the likely future trading results. The choice of business structure is dealt with in **CHAPTER 9: THE EQUINE BUSINESS STRUCTURE**. Agricultural building allowances are looked at in **CHAPTER 10: OVERVIEW OF EQUINE BUSINESS TAXATION.**

If the stud farm can be established with the Inland Revenue as a taxable trading business entity, it ought to obtain some of the benefits of the available reliefs for capital gains tax and inheritance tax, which may, in some cases, cover the stud house. These reliefs should not be put at risk.

Stud farms all treated as one trade

7.2 Stud farms are farming and hence the 'all farming one trade' rule in ICTA 1988 s 53 is applicable.

However, section 53(2) does not allow the amalgamation of profits earned from farming by different entities, eg an individual who carries on stud farming, both as a sole trader and as a member of a partnership, will be regarded as having two different taxable sources.

Some consequences of the 'all farming one trade rule' are as follows:

- if an individual carries on two quite separate stud farming businesses at two quite distinct locations, the trading results are nevertheless merged in order to arrive at adjusted profits or losses and capital allowances. The special tax rules for assessments of profits on commencements and cessations are not applied if a second stud farm business is acquired, or if one of two businesses is sold;
- if one stud farm business is sold and a new one started by the same entity within a reasonable space of time, the continuing basis will apply. A reasonable time can probably be as long as a year.

It is therefore important to ensure that stud and non-stud farming income is identified separately so that the two can be disclosed separately on tax returns.

It is also important to recognise that location within the UK is irrelevant to these tax rules. That one stud farm may be situated in Newmarket and the other in Cornwall is immaterial. Nor is it relevant that the two stud farms are managed as separate economic units, or that separate sets of financial accounts are prepared. The principle was argued in *Bispham v Eardiston Farming Co (1919) Ltd (1962) 40 TC*

322, where it was held that the company carried on only one trade, so that losses on the Worcester farm could be aggregated with profits of the farm in Scotland. Note, however, that the rule does not apply to amalgamate stud farming overseas with UK activities.

Stud liveries in addition to husbandry

7.3 The activities of a stud farm may include a number of activities other than just the act of husbandry, ie the raising of livestock and the production of horses. The stud may also introduce mares as livery 'boarders'. This will be very common with the public stud that has stallions standing for use by the public. Visiting mares will require board and lodging. Also, many small breeders will not want the responsibility of foaling the mare (being present at the birth) and will rely on the technology of a larger stud farm offering modern facilities such as CCTV, 24-hour staff etc. These are livery services which are not generally regarded as farming activities and which will not be eligible for the agricultural reliefs which follow. However, they should still be regarded as eligible for various business tax reliefs possibly, for example, qualifying for Enterprise Investment Scheme (EIS) status.

As the income from livery activities is not regarded as farming income, the profits will have to be removed from the farming Schedule D Case 1 computations before any 'farmers' averaging' adjustments to taxable profits are undertaken. Similar adjustments will need to be carried out if claims under section 397 for the eleven-year loss relief are to be made. The latter is of some concern as some studs approaching their eleventh year of loss have taken in 'boarders' to boost profits. This is, of course, another source of income not strictly regarded as farming income. The stud tax computation must be adjusted for non-stud farming income which must be disclosed separately on tax returns.

For IHT purposes, although these elements will not qualify for Agricultural Property Relief (APR) they will qualify for Business Property Relief (BPR) – see CHAPTER **10**: OVERVIEW OF EQUINE BUSINESS TAXATION.

Trading as a limited company

7.4 The choice of which trading structure is to be preferred is looked at in more detail in CHAPTER **9**.

Many stud businesses might look to the protection of limited liability in view of the high risk nature of the stud industry. Particular tax problems which may arise here, however, are that trading losses might become 'trapped' in the company (see CHAPTER **11**) and the stud land and buildings will not qualify for Business Asset Taper Relief (BATR) from capital gains tax (see CHAPTER **13**). Obviously, the latter will only apply to stud businesses, which own their own land and buildings. However, all equine businesses which own land inside a limited company will suffer the same problem. Of course, companies continue to accrue indexation allowances instead of taper relief, but at current low inflation rates this is unlikely to represent real compensation for the inability to claim taper relief inside a company.

If the stud activities are carried out at a stud farm it may be advisable to own the stud farm personally and to operate just the trading activities through a company. The shareholder would then be the landlord and grant a lease over the stud farm to the stud company. The owner could receive a market rent from the stud company for the use of the farm and this may offset any interest charge payable on the mortgage used to originally acquire the land. BATR would also then be retained as rented property of this sort qualifies in full.

The subject of letting equine property is covered in **CHAPTER 15: THE EQUESTRIAN LANDLORD – TAX PLANNING.** However, a specific problem area here will be reconciling the structure chosen with the need to try to retain entitlement to valuable capital taxation reliefs currently available in respect of agricultural and 'business' property for both capital gains tax (CGT) and inheritance tax (IHT) purposes. Fundamental to this situation will be ensuring that there is in place a properly drafted lease agreement which retains the right to vacant possession within 12 (or in some cases, 24) months for the landlord.

Similarly, the fact that generally the activity of the stud farm is taxable whilst horse-racing activities are not can also pose some difficult questions for a limited company carrying on a stud activity.

It may even be more convenient to separate taxable and non-taxable activities into separate limited companies. If this is not practical it will be important to ensure that the respective income and expenses from each source are clearly distinguishable from the company's records.

Alternatively, the non-taxable income could be retained outside the company in the taxpayer's own name. Consideration should also be given to looking at areas such as sponsorship, entertaining, marketing, advertising and PR. For example, does the stud owner have a separate business that could incorporate a sponsorship agreement? This is considered in **CHAPTER 4** (see **4.5** above).

For inheritance tax purposes, it is only controlling interests in shares in a limited company that may qualify for APR (IHTA 1984 s 122), however, a minority interest may attract BPR. If the company does not qualify as a trading company but as an investment company, then BPR will not apply. Furthermore, APR will only be relevant where one is dealing with a limited company trading as a stud farm. Other forms of equestrian businesses are not counted as agricultural but many still attract some BPR.

To attract the full APR on shares in a stud company the company must have occupied the relevant agricultural property for the purposes of agriculture (ie the stud farm) throughout the period of two years before the transfer of the shares. 100% APR is also available against the value of shares in such a company, if the company has owned the agricultural land and it, or another, has used it for agriculture, throughout a period of seven years before transfer, for example, where a company leases its land out to be farmed under a tenancy.

Where the shares have been acquired as consideration for agricultural land (normally on the incorporation of a pre-existing partnership or sole-trader's business), the shares issued as consideration are deemed to *stand in the shoes* of the original property in calculating the period of ownership, and in ascertaining whether the original property is still held on death (important for 'replacement property').

The inheritance tax relief of APR is restricted to the agricultural value. Agricultural value is set out in IHTA 1984 s 115(3) and is defined as:

> 'The value which would be the value of the property if it were subjected to a perpetual covenant prohibiting its use otherwise than as agricultural property.'

Agricultural value applies to that part of the value of shares in (or debentures of) a company, which is attributable to the agricultural value of qualifying agricultural property, provided that the particular conditions set out in IHTA 1984, s 122 are satisfied. This will be determined by the Shares Valuation Division (SVD). Also SVD will notify the District Valuer (DV) of any agricultural property owned by the company, which qualifies for relief (form VAL 63 or 63A) when referring the case to the DV (VOA manual, Ch 1B, para 16.21) (see **7.20** and **7.29** below).

A stud house owned by a limited company will potentially cause income tax accommodation benefits to be assessable on the occupants where they are the directors or are otherwise employees of the company. There will also be potential capital gains tax issues as there will be no principal private residence relief available on the stud house if it is not owned by the individual in occupation. These difficulties can sometimes be surmounted via the use of trust arrangements under which a qualifying beneficiary occupies the property which is let to the company in which the trust is also a shareholder.

VAT registration

7.5 VAT registration is only available for taxable businesses. This issue of all areas of VAT registration is dealt with in more detail in CHAPTER **17**: PLANNING FOR VAT.

The question of VAT registration is dealt with at **2.11** above.

It is clear that Customs and Excise accept that although a stud may be 'small and slow' in operational terms it may still be accepted as a genuine business in the eyes of Customs and Excise.

In order to recover input VAT against supplies, any goods or services purchased will need to have been purchased 'in the course or furtherance of the business of stud farming'.

VAT registration thresholds remain a subject of debate as, in relative terms, it is arguable that they are quite low in comparison with the costs and sales prices equine studs can produce. Therefore, stud transactions might result in an obligation for compulsory registration where turnover exceeds the thresholds and the taxpayers thus become unwittingly liable for registration.

Averaging of profits

7.6 When a stud is carried on as a commercial farming business the profits can be averaged if they fluctuate at the thresholds set out in the tax legislation.

According to the Inland Revenue's Inspector's Manual M2325: 'Farmers' averaging', averaging can be available in the following circumstances:

> 'Where the difference between the profits of two consecutive years of assessment is 30% or more of the higher of the two figures of profit (and regardless of whether the difference is a rise or a fall), the profit of the two years may be averaged. The sum of the two profit figures is simply divided by two and the resulting figure becomes the chargeable profits for each of the two years of assessment. The tax computation might need careful review to identify farming and non-farming activities but essentially the potential advantage is available.'

There is also some scope for tax planning here where there are activities which might be included as farming income which might otherwise not attract this averaging treatment if kept separate.

A trading loss is treated as a nil profit for averaging purposes. This enables loss relief to be claimed under the normal rules without the measure of the loss available for relief being affected by averaging.

Thus, where a stud has a one-off very profitable year, eg sells a yearling for an unusually high price which boosts the profits in one year, there may be losses in the years either side. In such cases the tax losses can still be claimed in full and the year of high profit will average with £nil figure for the year of the loss. This spreads the profit over two years and hopefully spreads the higher rate tax which is the aim of the tax relief. The mechanics of the averaging rules are set out in more detail in *Stanley: Taxation of Farmers and Landowners* (LexisNexis UK) Chapter 2 section F.

11-year loss rule followed by 5-year loss rule

7.7 The 11-year loss rule is dealt with in more detail **CHAPTER 11: PLANNING FOR LOSSES** and only applies to stud farming. It must be remembered that the 11-year loss rule is an 'initial set-up' loss period. Once a profit is achieved, the farming loss rule of a profit by the 6th year (ie, in the year following the fifth year) and every 6th year after that comes into force. Likewise, if a profit is gained in, say, year 2 or year 3, the benefit of the 11-year rule is cancelled and the 5-year loss rule for farming comes into place.

Valuation of trading stock used in the stud farm

7.8 All stock must be valued at the lower of cost and net realisable value and, therefore, the open market value of a thoroughbred will be important. This will also be important for assets transferred to and from racing which are at market value (*Sharkey v Wernher (1955) 36 TC 275)*.

The Inland Revenue's Inspector's Manual provides clear guidance here (see IM2350c: 'Farming: stud farms: open market valuations of thoroughbred horses'):

> 'Specialist advice on open market valuations of thoroughbred horses is available from the Inland Revenue's Bloodstock Section, Shares Valuation Division, Nottingham. Requests for advice should include:
>
> - The name(s) of the horse(s) to be valued
> - The valuation dates
> - Any opinion of open market value together with reasoning, if supplied.
>
> A written valuation will be supplied.
>
> Stud stock is valued individually at the lower of cost and net realisable value.
>
> The above principle was established in the case *CIR v Cock Russell & Co Ltd (29 TC 387)*.
>
> See also IM2350d – Farming: stud farms: stock valuation.'

Except where the herd basis has been adopted, both stallions and mares should be dealt with as stock in trade and valued individually at the beginning and end of each year on the basis of cost or net realisable value (see IM2350c), whichever is the lower. Stock valuations should also include any foals and, where appropriate, stud fees paid.

Inland Revenue Business Economic Note 19, which gives guidance on stock valuations for farms uses 'deemed' cost to arrive at cost. For example:

Cattle	60% of open market value
Sheep and pigs	75% of open market value

The deemed cost method should not be used for the valuation of thoroughbred horses. This would, however, be used if the stud farm is integrated with farming and the farm animals need to be valued and costs of breeding and rearing to maturity home-bred animals are not available or readily extracted for the farmer's own records.

When the foal is born the stud fee becomes part of the cost of the live foal.

Foals are also included in stock at the lower of cost or market value. However, as the foals may have been bred and not bought, the cost of foals and yearlings is the aggregate of

- the stallion nomination fee;
- the cost of keeping the mare for the whole year of gestation; and
- the cost of keeping the foal from weaning until it is sold or transferred to training.

In cases where no nomination fee has been paid because the nomination has been acquired via a syndicate share, generally the annual depreciation allowance on the share is substituted for the nomination fee. If a foal is purchased then it is included in stock at cost.

Valuation of stallions for stock

7.9 Whether or not a stallion is held as trading stock of a stud farm or a separate investment asset is a complicated and important issue which must be considered in detail.

On the assumption the stallion is used in the stud (note this rule is not applicable for mares), a rule-of-thumb method of valuation is generally accepted by the Inland Revenue under which the cost of the stallion is written off in equal annual instalments until it reaches the age of ten (age 15 for valuations as at dates up to and including 31 December 2000). This rule-of-thumb method is an attempt to arrive at an acceptable figure for net realisable value where this is less than cost. It is not, however, appropriate where:

- a better figure is available because the animal is valued at the balance sheet date; or
- it would give an unreasonable result. For example, in those exceptional cases where the value of an animal increases, or drops at a rate significantly slower than that used in the rule of thumb, because, for example, of very successful progeny, the figure computed using the rule of thumb should be increased to an amount not exceeding cost.

If a stud receives free nominations in return for keeping a stallion, the cost of the keep will have to be included in the value of the stock as if they were stud fees paid. This is, in principle, no different from the normal accountancy 'matching' concept. The cost of the keep of the stallion has been paid and should therefore be treated as a prepayment for accounting purposes. The basis of lower cost and net realisable value still applies.

What is the potential cost of the future foal? If there is clear evidence that net realisable value will be less, perhaps because there is a clear risk that the foal will be lost at birth or subsequently, then this potential loss should be accounted for.

The cost of the potential share of the foal should be included in costing accounts unless the net realisable value is considered to be less.

Where a mare is bought in foal, separate costs can be attributed to the mare and the foal.

Valuation of stud fees paid

7.10 The stud fee or 'nomination' fee paid by the owner of a mare for the services of a particular stallion can be a substantial sum. The fee paid should be reflected in the balance sheet valuation of the animal unless:

- the mare has already given birth, or is known not to have conceived, or has aborted, before the accounting date; or
- an 'adjusting event' (see IM563) occurs – for example, the discovery between the balance sheet date and the date the accounts were finalised of a congenital defect rendering the foal valueless.

The fee paid should be reflected in the balance sheet by one of the following methods:

- including the fee in a stock valuation of the embryo or foetus of the foal;

- increasing the value of the mare while she is carrying the foal by the amount of the fee;
- carrying forward the fee as a prepayment.

The valuation of stallion held by a syndicate share is very similar to the valuation of the stallion held separately.

As far as stallion syndicate shares are concerned, and because there will frequently be considerable difficulty in obtaining agreement among 40 shareholders on a market value of a share at any particular moment, a concessionary treatment is available. The cost of a share can be depreciated by equal annual instalments. If, however, at any date the market value of such share is clearly above the written-down value, the share can be revalued upwards subject to a maximum value equal to original cost. If the value increases in any year above its written-down value, a breeder may need to temporarily refrain from any further depreciation of the share until such time as actual value falls back below the depreciated value.

Part of the stock of a stud business may well consist of shares in stallion syndicates. Strictly, the value of such shares should be determined by reference to the lower of cost or realisable value. However, since as many as 40 shares might be held in one stallion, and each share owner might adopt a different approach to market value, the Inland Revenue accept a straight-line depreciation method which produces a £nil valuation for an animal by the time it reaches 15 years (this was reduced to 10 years from 2000), to reflect the likely or expected breeding life of a stallion.

If the owner of a syndicate share cannot convince his Inspector of Taxes that he is holding the share as trading stock, surplus income from it will be taxed under Schedule D Case VI. However, although the share will be a 'wasting asset' and will eventually become totally worthless, no trading deduction will be granted for the cost of the share by way of depreciation allowances.

Thus, the use of a stallion in the stud is a matter which merits close attention as this will impinge closely on tax planning issues as discussed above.

Practical tax planning around stock values

7.11 The equine industry is unique. It could be said that stud stock values are more volatile than teenage fashion. Outside factors such as the racing achievements of animals from associated bloodlines can have dramatic effects. Keeping stock fit and healthy and injury free is a real problem. Equine stock valuations may be viewed by some as an unimportant paper exercise but they can, in fact, produce tax refunds resulting from the tax losses that arise. If potentially valuable equine stock is held at cost, the timing of the profit can be planned around the date of the sale. However, if a disaster awaits in the form of a valuation fall, it can be realised as soon as possible by means of being reflected appropriately in the stock valuation, therefore accelerating the tax loss (or reducing the taxable profit).

The stud farmer must, therefore, take full cognisance of the importance of year-end valuation of stock for his bottom line. The timing of the sale of good and bad stock is critical as is the timing of any transfer to racing and owners and tax advisers alike need to give appropriate weight to this subject. It will frequently determine exactly when a profit is achieved. As with all tax planning issues, however, commercial commonsense should take priority such that when a good sales price can be achieved the adviser may need to accept that the owner will very likely ignore the tax planning advice given previously.

Mares and stallions will have been either purchased or transferred from training, ie racing. Those purchased in the market will have been brought in at cost, while those transferred from training will be brought in at market value. The accounts will reflect these amounts unless the current market value of the animal is lower, in which case this will be substituted. A number of factors can influence the market value of a horse, including its past performance, racing career, market conditions and breeding prospects, etc.

As stock values considerably affect the taxation position, the Inland Revenue tend to examine them closely and so it may be worth seeking a written independent valuation in certain cases.

Herd basis election for stock valuation – the detail

7.12 Horses kept on a stud farm are normally treated as trading stock, so that relief is given for the cost of the animal and in the event of sale, the proceeds are taxable. Where horses are kept for breeding, the owner may elect for the herd to be treated as a capital asset; ie put on the 'herd basis' under the provisions of ICTA 1988 Sch 5. The election is not available in respect of horses currently kept for racing.

The effect of the election is as follows:

- the initial cost of the herd and additions to the herd are not deducted as a business expense;
- the value of the herd is not brought into the trading stock valuation;
- the transfer of a horse from trading stock to the herd gives rise to a trading receipt.

Where a horse dies or leaves the herd and is replaced, any proceeds from sale are treated as a trading receipt. The replacement is effectively treated as a purchase but only to the extent that it is of an equivalent value to the outgoing horse. If the replacement is more expensive then the excess cost may not be allowable.

For this purpose, the value of the horse will be determined by such factors as its age and it's racing and breeding records.

If the entire herd is sold and not replaced, any profit arising is sheltered for income tax.

The Inland Revenue's Inspector's Manual 2316b sets out the time limits for making the election as follows:

- in the case of a sole trader, 12 months after the fixed filing date for the first year of assessment, other than the year of commencement, for which the farming profits or losses are computed by reference to a period during which the taxpayer kept a production herd of the specified class;
- in the case of a partnership, 12 months after the fixed filing date for the year of assessment in which the first period of account during which the partnership kept a production herd of the specified class ended;
- in the case of a company, two years from the end of the first accounting period during which the company kept a production herd of the specified class.

Once the election is made, it is irrevocable and it should be noted that each election covers one species of animal, therefore, a farmer keeping, for example, cattle and horses, may elect for the cattle to be treated under the herd basis while opting to treat the horses as trading stock.

Herd basis – should the election be made?

7.13 Although applicable to horses, the herd basis is more commonly associated with cattle and sheep. The idea, from a tax planning point of view, is that the herd will appreciate in value as a collective asset, without the owner having to suffer adverse tax consequences. Unlike cattle and sheep, horses have individual characteristics and are less likely to be sold as a herd. Because of this, the movement of horses in and out of the herd is less predictable than with cattle or sheep. The herd basis election, being irrevocable once made, is generally not flexible enough to be advantageous. Consequently, the herd basis is not normally recommended in respect of horses but each case must be assessed on its own merits.

If the breeder does decide to adopt the herd basis, he may include stallion shares in the herd, provided the nominations are used mainly for the breeder's own mares.

Reference should be made here to the Inland Revenue's Inspector's Manual IM2350f: 'Farming: stud farms: stud farms on the herd basis':

'The herd basis applies to horses as it does to other production animals but, because of the economics of the industry, elections are unusual. Any election for the herd basis in a case in which the progeny are not wholly or mainly for sale (transfers from stud to training not being regarded for this purpose as sales) should be submitted to BPD Farming.

Where an election for the herd basis is accepted, the guidance at IM2300 onwards applies. The following points should be noted.

- All immature stock should continue to be dealt with as stock in trade. Transfers of immature stock from or to training should be dealt with in accordance with IM2350e.
- Where exceptionally a mature animal is put into training, adjustments should be made as though at the time of transfer it had been sold from the herd at its then market value (see IM2305 and IM2308).
- If a mature animal is returned to stud after racing, its cost price for the purposes of the herd basis should be taken to be its market value at the time of return (see IM2304 and IM2305).'

The equine industry requires flexibility and arguably it does not receive it from the herd basis. The aim of the herd basis for farmers was that as they built up their herd they could increase the value and receive this 'tax-free'. However, if the stud stock is to fall in value then relief for this will not be obtained under a herd basis election. In practice, the election is probably not generally advisable for a stud farm. In general, horses are not a herd. However, the availability and advisability of the election should still be reviewed in every case.

Integrated studs and racing activities

7.14 There are strong arguments to say that racing activities cannot be split from a stud farm. In this context it is worth looking at one of the specific points raised in *Lord Glanely v Wightman (1933) 17 TC 634*. It was argued in that case that 'success in breeding thoroughbred horses could only be attained by submitting them to the test of the racecourse'.

Can this argument be put forward as justification for the contention that racing activities ought to be accepted as an integral part of the trade of stud farming? The result would be that prize money and increases in stock values would become taxable but the expenses relating to racing would then be allowable.

It is felt that this is not a view that would meet much favour with the Inland Revenue but there may well be cases which could justify the attempt. This would particularly be the case where a stud farm and integral racing activity both exhibited all the 'badges of trade' together as one integrated business entity.

Non-thoroughbred studs

7.15 This subject was considered at **1.14** and **2.29** above.

Evidence would seem to indicate that for tax purposes the Inland Revenue does not differentiate between non-thoroughbred and thoroughbred horses.

EIS – Can it apply to a stud farm?

7.16 The Enterprise Investment Scheme (EIS) was first looked at in CHAPTER 2. Stud farming currently does not qualify for EIS as, by definition, it is within the exclusion currently contained in the legislation aimed at 'farming'. The author has written to the Country Land and Business Association (CLA) chief tax adviser (and also co-author of *Stanley: Taxation of Farmers and Landowners* (LexisNexis UK) on this subject and has received the following response.

Reply from Adrian Baird (Chief Tax Adviser (CLA)):
Obviously, whether a particular activity is farming depends upon the facts of the case so any advice can only be in general terms. Taking the term 'stud farm' to mean breeding and rearing horses, this activity is within the definition of husbandry and therefore farming.

It is clear that the farming exclusion from EIS applied by ICTA 1988 s 297(2) is governed by the definition of 'farmland' in ICTA 1988 s 832(1). It is common that farming requires the occupation of certain land and that the purpose of this occupation must be husbandry. Thus an initial distinction can and should be made between the bloodstock breeder who owns horses or leases a stud farm and the person who owns horses but not a stud farm itself (but keeps them at a public stud). Only the former can be regarded as being in occupation of land within s 832(1).

It is in that context that IM2350b should be read. It is clear that where the breeder also owns the stud farm he is treated 'as farming'. This is surely correct as it stands but it extends the principle established in *Lord Glanely v Wightman 17 TC 634* that the breeding of horses where serving is limited to an animal on the farm is classified as farming (see *Stanley: Taxation of Farmers and Landowners*, para 2.41). I would therefore argue that the activity of occupying a stud farm for

> the purpose of breeding horses is farming and excluded from EIS. This, however, does not represent the full position. The horseracing element is not treated as a taxable activity (ibid IM2350b) and in any event would be excluded from EIS as not being a commercial activity; fees for outside serving of stallions should be regarded as Case VI receipts (ibid *Stanley*) and hence are not trading for the purpose of EIS. This then leads to the murky grey area of other activities, which may not be classified as farming. EIS could be available because these would surely fall within ICTA 53(3) if commercial and hence be commercial trading activities by definition.
>
> I agree, however, with the conclusion of your article (you will not be surprised by this) that the stud farming, as a diversified rural activity should, following our Reform to Perform, be subject to unified taxation as a business, and whereas EIS is not mentioned in that document, I would fully support arguments for EIS being available.

The author would like to thank Adrian Baird for these positive words and direction.

Agricultural Property Relief

7.17 Agricultural Property Relief (APR) was initially looked at in CHAPTER **2** at **2.5** above.

Where certain conditions are satisfied, relief from inheritance tax is available on the transfer of agricultural property in the UK, the Channel Islands and the Isle of Man. The relief known as APR is a percentage reduction in the value transferred by a transfer of value and is given automatically without claim.

Relief is also available on occasions on which tax is chargeable under the provisions relating to settlements without interests in possession. (IHTA 1984 ss 115(1)(5) and 116(1)), broadly discretionary trusts. This tax relief is of prime importance to the stud owner. The commercial stud farm (and commercial equine business) can be an enjoyable and efficient way to shelter wealth from inheritance tax.

It is imperative to look at the definition of 'agricultural property' or 'farmland'. Some guidance is given in IHTA s 115(2) for the purposes of this relief. 'Agricultural property' means agricultural land or pasture and includes woodlands and any building used in connection with the intensive rearing of livestock or fish if the woodlands or building is occupied with agricultural land or pasture and the occupation is ancillary to that of the agricultural land or pasture.

It also includes such cottages, farm buildings and farmhouses, together with the land occupied with them, as are a character appropriate to the property. The breeding and rearing of horses on a stud farm and the grazing of horses in connection with those activities is to be taken to be agriculture and any buildings used in connection with those activities to be farm buildings.

Livestock, deadstock and farm plant and machinery are not included but these may qualify for Business Property Relief (BPR). According to the CTO Advanced Instruction Manual, paras L246.2.2–2.4, land used for agricultural purposes may occasionally be used for other purposes (eg annual Point to Point horse races) without the relief being jeopardised. However, careful consideration is required where land is used for other purposes such as reeds for thatching (cultivation of a crop) and pheasants for sport, which are not agricultural. The equine equivalent is given in the case of *Wheatley v IRC [1998] STC (SCD) 60*. This case is considered at **7.23** below.

Agricultural land or pasture (IHTA s 115(2)) means the bare land (and does not have any wider meaning derived from the Interpretation Act 1978), as including buildings on the land (*Starke v IRC [1995] STC 689*). It will, however, include any interest, servitude or right over land. In the past it was argued that farmhouses were by definition 'agricultural land' and immediately qualified as such. The bare land or pasture must be used for the purpose of agriculture to qualify as 'agricultural' land or pasture. 'Agricultural' is not defined in the legislation though it is likely to include that within the Agricultural Tenancies Act 1995 s 38(1) wherein 'agricultural' includes horticulture, fruit growing, seed growing, dairy farming and livestock breeding and keeping, the use of land as grazing land, meadow land, osier land, market gardens and nursery grounds cottages, farm buildings and farmhouses (together with the land occupied with them) as are of a character appropriate to the property (IHTA 1984 s 115(2)).

Death of the stud farm owner

7.18 The liability to inheritance tax (IHT) primarily arises on death or on chargeable lifetime transfers. The deceased's estate is valued at that time and if the chargeable assets exceed the nil rate band (£255,000 from 6 April 2003) tax will be payable on the excess at the appropriate rate, currently 40%. If assets are left to a surviving spouse, IHT will normally be deferred until the death of the surviving spouse.

For stud farms there are various tax planning issues raised by the availability of APR, BPR, the nil rate band and the 'surviving spouse' exemption and these must be given due consideration. It is for this reason that will planning is of such importance.

It is hoped that the stud will escape inheritance tax liability under the provisions of APR. Careful attention to will planning should attempt to ensure that the business assets are covered by APR/BPR and that non-business assets are covered by £nil rate band and make optimum use of the surviving spouse exemption.

Lifetime gifts of the stud farm

7.19 Whilst a stud owner can currently enjoy 100% tax relief (APR – subject to conditions being in place), it is very tempting to make a gift of the stud now rather than delay it until later when reliefs may have been subject to reform. See **10.15** below on potentially exempt transfers (PETS) and failed PETS.

Lifetime gifts to an individual, to interest in possession trusts or to an accumulation and maintenance trust are potentially exempt from IHT so long as the donor survives seven years. However, lifetime gifts to, for example, discretionary trusts, are normally chargeable unless the property transferred qualifies for APR or BPR.

An accumulation and maintenance trust is most commonly set up for minor children by grandparents. The legislation requires that for the tax benefits to be available, a beneficiary must become entitled to an interest in the income of the trust by at least the age of 25, although they can be denied any entitlement to the capital until a later time, say, age 40.

APR takes precedence over BPR

7.20 Stud property will probably qualify for a mixture of APR and BPR. APR takes precedence over a claim for BPR if both forms of relief are available on the same item.

To ensure that the stud qualifies for APR it is essential to conform to the basic conditions for APR. The relief is available where an individual or partnership transfers land and buildings used for agricultural purposes (ie at death or by lifetime gift). It is also available against shares or securities in agricultural companies to the extent that their value is attributable to agricultural property. This is provided that the transferor has control of the company immediately before the transfer. Land and buildings at a stud farm used for the breeding, rearing and grazing of horses should generally qualify for APR.

Relief will only be available if one of the following conditions is satisfied:

- the property has been occupied by the transferor and used for agricultural purposes for a period of two years prior to the date of the transfer; or
- the property has been owned by the transferor for a period of seven years prior to the date of transfer and has been used for agricultural purposes throughout that period either by himself or another;

- if a transfer of agricultural property falls to be included in the gross estate of an individual on death (ie before reliefs are deducted), normally because it was made within seven years of the death of the donor, it must be held by the donee throughout the period up to the donor's death and still remain agricultural property and be occupied for the purpose of agriculture during that period for relief to be retained.

APR is restricted to Agricultural value. The expression 'agricultural value' of agricultural property is defined to mean the value which the property would have if it were subject to a perpetual covenant prohibiting of its use otherwise than as agricultural property (IHTA 1984 s 115 (3)) (see **7.4** above).

The effect of the definition is that APR only applies to the agricultural value of the property, not any enhanced value attributed to development or 'hope value'. Provided that the conditions are met, BPR should apply to any balance not attributable to agricultural value.

When a stud farm fails in its claim for APR it may well be possible that BPR can still be claimed. This is dealt with at **10.12** below.

Tax planning re stud loans or mortgage

7.21 Where a property is subject to a mortgage or charge, the amount secured is deducted from the open market value for IHT valuation purposes (IHTA 1984 s 162(4)) and only the balance is capable of being relieved from APR.

Thus, sensibly, such loans should always be secured as far as possible against non-business assets to maximize the BPR/APR.

Acquiring stud land on death of another person

7.22 The owner of a stud farm will also want to ensure that the person who acquires the stud will themselves satisfy the relevant inheritance tax conditions for the future.

Where the deceased acquired the land on the death of another person, he is treated for the purposes of the conditions as having commenced to occupy the land on the death of that other person (IHTA 1984 s 120(1)(a)).

If the land was acquired on the death of the deceased's spouse, then if the spouse satisfied the conditions at the date of death, the deceased is treated as having also satisfied the conditions at that date (IHTA 1984 s 120(1)(b)).

When grazing of horses is not agriculture

7.23 Stud farms engaged in the breeding and rearing of horses, and for grazing associated with that activity (IHTA 1984 s 115(4)), qualify as occupying agricultural land for the purposes of APR.

However, in *Wheatley v IRC [1998] STC (SCD) 60*, the Special Commissioners held that APR was not due in respect of a meadow which was the subject of a grazing agreement between the deceased and a grazier. It was accepted that the meadow constituted pasture within the meaning of IHTA 1984 s 115 but the claim failed because the horses were used for leisure pursuits and were not connected with use for agricultural purposes or with a stud farming business. This decision has been criticised on the grounds that the act of growing grass, which can properly be regarded as a 'crop', should be treated as an act of husbandry, irrespective of the way in which the crop is exploited or utilised, ie grazed by horses.

The stud house – APR

7.24 There have been a number of court cases over the years involving farmhouses and whether APR is available against the agricultural value of the farmhouse. On the basis that the stud farm is farming the tax planner should look to a claim for APR on the farmhouse.

The main tests are as follows.

- Is the property a farmhouse?
- Is the surrounding land farmland?
- Is the farmhouse of character appropriate to the surrounding agricultural property?

The first two points are fairly straightforward. The latter is more difficult to satisfy. The Inland Revenue looks at all three tests and then reviews the whole picture. The current trend seems to be for the Inland Revenue to consider each of the above aspects in turn and then to apply the 'elephant test' – 'a farmhouse is difficult to describe but you will know one when you see one!'. So how would the stud farmhouse be viewed by the Inland Revenue?

For the property to qualify it must be at the centre of stud farming operations and must be of a 'character appropriate' to the surrounding land over which the owner and occupier of the stud house must have beneficial interest.

For instance, if the owner and occupier of the stud house no longer own the surrounding stud land, even though it is being actively used by the stud itself, the stud house would not attract any relief. This is because the owner of the stud house does not have a beneficial interest over any stud land to give the stud house the necessary 'character appropriate'.

Conversely, if the owner of a stud house had given away the farm land, perhaps to his son, subject to the retention of a tenancy for him and his son as a partnership, he will retain a beneficial interest in the land, and the stud house will still attract relief.

Historical association

7.25 Has relief been given on the property previously under the current inheritance tax rules? Provided the transferor still has a beneficial interest in the acreage which satisfied a previous transfer, the 'character appropriate' test can probably be satisfied.

Geographical comparisons

7.26 Comparisons are made with similar holdings of land in the surrounding area. Although the size of the stud house does not form part of the character test, it is often a feature referred to in disputes over the availability of the relief. Other studs in the area would be compared.

Financial viability

7.27 This is a test being used more and more by the Inland Revenue. They attempt to question whether stud activities undertaken are sufficient to maintain the stud house. Many experts in this field believe this is an unfair test as it concentrates on activities conducted, not those that could be conducted. For instance, an elderly stud owner may reduce his farming operations concentrating more on letting land for grazing, which in turn may reduce his return from the land. This could then affect the availability of APR on the stud house.

The stud house – 'Antrobus'

7.28 The inheritance tax advantages of stud farming have been that the farmhouse and farm cottages are potentially business assets and eligible for inheritance tax relief as well as the stud land and buildings. There have been several recent cases, including *Lloyds TSB (Personal Representatives of Antrobus deceased v IRC [2002] STC (SCD) 468,* which challenged the availability of IHT relief on farmhouses and introduced some new aspects to the debate.

The APR on a farmhouse is restricted to the agricultural value, although again it is generally to be hoped that BPR could be claimed on the balance of any value not relieved by APR.

This can be a complex issue for the tax adviser. Throughout the period of ownership of a stud house, care must be taken to ensure that for capital gains tax purposes, best use is made of the CGT Principal Private Residence relief whilst trying to ensure that the farmhouse does not 'fail' but wins as in *Antrobus* for inheritance tax purposes.

It is worth noting that in the past it was argued that farmhouses were by definition agricultural land (IHTA 1984 s 115) and immediately qualified as such.

Although these cases relate to farming and not stud farming, they are still relevant to the potential tax relief on the farmhouse. Perhaps a test case will give the equestrian world more guidance at some stage on the future.

The main points on IHT and farmhouses raised by *Lloyds TSB (Personal Representative of Antrobus Deceased) v IRC* were as follows.

- Is the house appropriate by reference to size, content and layout to the stud buildings and land being used in the stud?
- Is the house proportionate in size and nature to the requirements of the farming activities conducted on the land in question?
- Does the house meet the so-called 'elephant test'?
- Would the 'educated rural layman' describe the property as a 'house with land' or as a stud farm?
- The historical dimension – how long has the house been associated with the land in question and has there been a history of agricultural production or stud activity?

The limitation of relief to farmhouses described as 'of character appropriate to the property' has caused difficulties. The Inland Revenue's view has been that in interpreting this section, 'agricultural property' means agricultural land or pasture. Farm buildings and farmhouses qualify if (and only if) they satisfy the stated condition. If they are not 'of a character appropriate to the property' they do not qualify for relief. A large and expensive 'farmhouse' standing in a relatively small acreage would thus be disqualified as 'inappropriate'.

The farmhouse must be of a character appropriate to the land that surrounds it. One of the tests of 'character appropriate' is that the occupiers of the farmhouse must be treated as farming the land.

Under a tenancy agreement, the occupier of the farmhouse is a landlord of the surrounding property and is not treated as farming the land. Under licence he is a trading farmer and the relief on the farmhouse should be available, subject to further complex conditions. Each stud farm owner who is anxious to preserve IHT relief in the stud house should ask their tax adviser to review their particular facts. Likewise, the tax adviser should make the stud farm owner aware of the potential pitfalls.

Agricultural value and the stud house

7.29 Agricultural value is considered at **7.4** above.

Agricultural value can have significant relevance to the farmhouse in view of current high property values.

Assuming the relief is available it is now important to ascertain the agricultural value of the stud house. This is the value of the property subject to a hypothetical restrictive covenant prohibiting the non-agricultural use of the property.

There are many who consider that the agricultural value is around two-thirds of the open market value of the property but this is subject to debate. Tax practitioners have argued that this should not be the case, particularly where the farmhouse is transferred together with the rest of the farm property. In this instance, the agricultural value of the whole unit should not be much less than the open market value of the farm as a whole.

There is also an argument put forward that the agricultural restriction is a restriction on use not occupancy. A non-farmer may wish to purchase such a property because the agricultural restriction on surrounding land protects the amenities sought. In this case, the agricultural value should be equivalent to the open market value. The relevance of this argument will depend upon the area in which the farmhouse is situated and whether it is attractive to non-stud farmers.

At the time of writing, land prices appear high as there currently seems to be a shortage and as a result the 'hope' value for possible development and alternative uses is increasing again.

The rented stud house

7.30 Reference should be made here to Inspector's Manual IM3377b: 'Farming and Farmhouse Rent'. This will be of particular use to the rented stud farm and how the farmhouse should be dealt with.

The stud owner or farmer can let grazing rights and still be a Schedule D trader with all the associated business reliefs. This can be essential if a large gain is in prospect (grazing agreements are considered in detail in CHAPTER **15**: THE EQUESTRIAN LANDLORD – TAX PLANNING).

The criteria for a well-drafted grazing agreement have already been set out. There are also important inheritance tax advantages under IHTA 1984 s 117(a). It is considered that the case for the claim for APR in the future is stronger when there is an established Schedule D trade as opposed to a letting arrangement.

The Farmer case – the stud cottage

7.31 Most stud farms employ staff who require accommodation on the premises so that they can deal with problems on site. The case of *Farmer (Farmer's Executors) v IRC [1999] STC (SCD) 321* is likely to be of great importance with regard to the availability of IHT reliefs available for stud farm cottages and may even extend the availability of the relief to cases in stud cottages, which were previously part of the stud operation but have since been let out. However, the capital gains tax eligibility of each property has to be looked at on a property-by-property basis.

In the *Farmer* case, Mr Farmer gave evidence that the farm was run for a profit but that it is very difficult to make a farming profit without the subsidies from the European Union. The evidence of the Inspector of Taxes was that the farm could have been run at a profit if there had been no lettings: there would not be a large profit but the farm could be self-supporting and there would be a healthy profit in some years. Over a ten-year period the farm would be viable.

The judge said that it was necessary to consider the business in the round. Of the five relevant factors, the overall context of the business, capital employed, the time spent by the employees and consultants in the business, and the levels of turnover, all supported the conclusion that the business consisted mainly of farming. The profit figures, and more particularly the net profit figures, on the other hand, supported the opposite view. Taking the whole business in the round, and without giving predominance to any one factor, the conclusion was that the business consisted mainly of farming.

The resultant theme of *Farmer* and the significance to the tax planner is that of 'unified management' with all aspects of the business being examined. Where this can be demonstrated, the case for the availability of the relief will be that much stronger. The letting of some *surplus* properties was indeed relevant but not fatal to the case. Until further cases emerge it will be essential for the tax planner advising studs to work very closely with land agents and the farmers alike. Key factors appear to be:

- ensuring that the letting of surplus stud buildings is incorporated into the stud as one unit;
- ensuring integrated accounts, ie treating all the financial activities as one integrated business unit;
- recording time spent on properties;
- using organisations such as the CLA and TBA to monitor APR/BPR claims and to report back on success and failures.

The Inland Revenue's statement that the business 'could have been run at a profit if there had been no lettings' is of interest. Could this statement still be made in 2003? Also, the business 'consisted mainly of farming'. Is this still likely to be the case in such businesses today? Hopefully, direction from case law or the Government will give future clarity, but in the meantime, the taxpayer should take note of the main points stressed above as far as possible in order to achieve maximum IHT reliefs.

The question of cottages as 'surplus to requirement' has been looked at in detail in the case of *Farmer* mentioned above. However, it is also important to look at the main cottages used by a stud.

There has previously been some confusion over the rate of agricultural property relief to be applied to farm cottages, CLA Chief Tax Adviser, Adrian Baird has now confirmed the position via the publication of a briefing note approved by Inland Revenue Capital Taxes Senior Officer, Peter Twiddy, obtained in September 1997:

> 'In order for agricultural property relief to be applied, two conditions must be satisfied first, that the cottage is occupied "for the purpose of agriculture"; secondly, that the cottages is "of a character appropriate" to any agricultural land or pasture in which the transferor has an interest. If either of these fundamental conditions is not satisfied, then the cottage does not qualify for agricultural property relief at all (eg a cottage occupied by a housekeeper).'

Thus to ensure retention of favourable tax status, all stud cottages should be checked for the status of their tenancies, the amount of legal protection the tenants currently have and the tax efficiency of such arrangements then reviewed. The advice for all equestrian activities is to review the tax status of the assets held and that includes cottages. Stud farms traditionally require a lot of staff and this will probably result in property being provided for their accommodation with all the potential tax consequence highlighted above that this may entail.

The equine limited company and APR

7.32 The IHT position and the availability of APR on the value of land used for stud farming but owned inside a limited company deserves specific attention.

Under IHTA 1984, in order to obtain APR, agricultural property, which is the subject of the transfer, must form part of the company's assets, and part of the value of the shares or securities of the company must be attributable to it. The transferor must also have control of the company immediately before the relevant transfer.

'Control' is defined as control of powers of voting on all questions affecting the company as a whole, which if exercised, would yield a majority of the votes capable of being exercised (IHTA 1984 s 269(1)). The fact that a company has one or more classes of shares with voting rights limited to the question of winding up the company, or any questions primarily affecting shares of that class, does not prevent an individual from having control (IHTA 1984 s 269(4)). No account is to be taken of the capacity of the shareholder or that of any other shareholders to exercise their votes.

In *Walding's Executors v IRC [1996] STC 13* the deceased held 45% of the voting shares of the company, and her four-year-old grandson held 24%. Her executors contended that as her grandson lacked legal capacity to exercise his votes, she therefore had control, but this argument was rejected, ie APR was denied. She did not have control.

In Walkers' Executors v IRC [2001] STC (STD) 86, the position there was that the deceased held 50% of the shares and was chairperson of the board of directors of the company, in which capacity she had a casting vote. The Inland Revenue contended that when exercising her casting vote she owed a fiduciary duty as an officer of the company, and if there had been conflict between her personal interest as a shareholder and that of the company, her use of the casting vote would have been constrained by her position as a director. The Special Commissioner held that, having particular regard to IHTA 1984 s 269(3), this fiduciary constraint did not mean she did not have control of the powers of voting, and he allowed the executors' appeal, ie in this case APR was given. It will, therefore, be necessary to consider carefully who has 'control' of a stud farm company to ensure that APR is obtained where required.

It is necessary to establish what proportion of the value of the shares held by a controlling shareholder can be attributed to the value of the land which forms part of the company's assets. The process of attribution can involve complex arithmetic. Where control exists before the gift, then gifts of minority holdings may qualify for relief. (As to the meaning of 'control', see IHTA 1984 s 269.)

A transfer of qualifying shares will attract APR at 100% of vacant possession value, provided the shareholder has owned the shares and the company has occupied the land for at least two years. This rule is modified where the shares owned on the date of the transfer have not been owned for the two-year period, but replaced other qualifying property, eg shares or other property attributable to the underlying property owned by the company. This would apply where there had been a company reconstruction or the incorporation of a business in exchange for shares. Where other eligible property can be established, the period of ownership of the shares transferred must amount to two out of five years ending on the date of transfer. Business property relief for IHT would produce the same result. Shareholders will normally be able to secure 100% business property relief, unless the company is a quoted company, which they do not control.

The stud company owning land – APR Issues

7.33 What is the position where a stud farming company owns 'agricultural' land and lets it out.

The result is generally that the relief is limited to the rate of 50%. However, 100% relief may be available where the agricultural property would carry 100% relief if it were owned by an individual and vacant possession could be recovered within 12 months (or by concession, 24 months) or where the tenancy commenced on or after 1 September 1995.

The controlling shares and the land must have both been respectively owned for seven years and occupied for agricultural purposes by the tenant of the company throughout the seven years immediately before the transfer of the shares.

Where eligible property is involved, the combined ownership period must amount to seven out of ten years ending on the date of transfer. Minority shareholders get no relief. This configuration has the additional disadvantage that a disposal of shares will not qualify for capital gains tax holdover relief, because the shares will not be shares in a trading company.

What happens if the shareholder of the Company owns the land and carries out stud farm activities on it?

Asset	*Controlling shareholder*	*Minority shareholder*
Land	Deemed to be occupied by the shareholder (IHTA 1984 s 119(1)) and hence relief available after two years occupation by the company. Relief will be at 100% even where the land is let to the company because of the second part of Extra-Statutory Concession F17.	There is no deemed occupation by the share holder and hence relief is only available after seven years of ownership by the shareholder and seven years occupation of the land for agricultural purposes (IHTA 1984 s 117(b)). Relief will be at 100% if the shareholder qualifies under the normal rules or otherwise at 50%.
Shares (agricultural value)	Any agricultural value attributable to the shares will qualify for 100% relief after two years of ownership of the shares.	No agricultural property relief, but business property relief available as for the non-agricultural value.
Shares (non-agricultural)	Will normally qualify for 100% property relief if the company is unquoted.	Will normally qualify for 100% property relief if the company is unquoted.

Advantages of integration with other farming

7.34 Pure livestock farming has a lot of tax and other advantages. In addition to the benefits of agricultural business rates and agricultural tax reliefs, integrated farm livestock can have clear advantages in the areas of grass maintenance and land management. Studs can often benefit from some of the grants available due to location, for example, the benefits of the Countryside Stewardship Scheme should not be overlooked.

The Irish stud farm and the UK taxpayer

7.35 The detail of overseas tax issues is beyond the scope of this book. However, it is worth looking at the evolution of the Irish stud farm and the relationship with the UK taxpayer. The 'tax-free' element of Irish stallion fees has been highlighted at **6.10** above. Although these stallion fees are tax-free in Ireland, they have tax consequences for the UK taxpayer. The 'bridge' that the UK taxpayer puts between themselves and this income is commonly a legal entity, eg an Irish company or trust that uses the stallion fees to fund, say, an Irish stud farm. The losses of the stud farm can probably be offset against the stallion income. The loss-making Irish stud farm can be very beneficial for those of Irish domicile caught under ICTA 1988 s 68 who could integrate the Irish stud fees with the Irish stud farm.

Tax Planning for the Professional Horseman 8

The trainer

8.1 Most trainers operate as a sole trader, a self-employed professional horseman. Some trainers are salaried employees. Training horses is not always profitable. CHAPTER **3** on the subject of business or hobby also applies to trainers. Many small trainers and permit holders have traditionally made losses.

Although most trainers pursue their business activities on a professional and commercial basis, the ability to make a profit can be difficult. The Inland Revenue divides trainers between commercial and non-commercial. The latter cannot claim tax relief for their expenses but then nor is their income regarded as arising from a taxable source.

One of the key issues will be the trainer's own horses if these are trained 'in-house'. Details of all horses owned by the trainer should be submitted to the Inland Revenue. Some trainers will try to avoid this ownership question by having other family members registered as owners. Part ownership will result in an apportionment of expenses. Trainers must ensure that they account for the costs associated with their own horses correctly. This is of particular concern if the training operation is run in conjunction with another business.

Trainers almost always need employees (the tax implications of which are set out in CHAPTER **12**). This may bring up issues such as the taxability of benefits in kind, (particularly in respect of living accommodation where staff live on the premises). Sometimes the tax issues they cause may be perceived as outweighing the advantages of having employees who are free to concentrate on the training work and who are not burdened with financial pressures, as will be the proprietor.

Another key tax issue is that of the trainer's house. The provision of hospitality to owners is generally perceived as an important area in the success of a training yard, both with regard to attracting new owners and keeping existing owners happy. The costs of entertaining owners are not allowable for tax purposes in the UK. A tax planning device can be the separate hospitality business which charges a fee to companies or individuals who take up the packages. This is tax deductible.

In order to attract owners the trainer might use the Racing Club as a device to introduce new people to racing. The division of the training fees and hospitality fees should be considered. The trainer could divide the charge to the members of the club between hospitality and racing.

The trainer's house

8.2 The taxable benefit for the accommodation of an employed trainer was considered above. However, a lot of equestrian businesses take place in rented premises. Racehorse training is no exception. The allocation of the rent to the trainer's house is a difficult subject.

Some guidance on the tax the treatment of farmhouse rents is given in the Inland Revenue's Inspector's Manual at IM2277b: Farming: Farmhouse rent:

> 'Farmhouse rents pose particular problems in arriving at a private use adjustment because the rent charged is often charged for the whole farm without a separate amount being attributable to the farmhouse itself.
>
> Farmers are assessed on the profits or gains of their farming trade under Case I of Schedule D because ICTA 1988 s 53(12) specifically directs that farming profit shall be so assessed. The definition of 'farming' for this purpose appears in section 832(1) which takes as its starting point the definition of "farm land" as meaning 'land in the United Kingdom wholly or mainly occupied for the purpose of husbandry, but excluding any dwelling or domestic offices', and goes on to say that farming shall be construed accordingly.'

This definition was introduced following the adverse decision in *Korner v CIR, (1969) 45 TC 287* and it is worth quoting from the speech of the Minister, Mr Taverne, who said in the committee stage of the debate on 16 June 1969 that:

> '... everyone in the committee wants to achieve the same purpose, which is to put the practice back where it was before the *Korner* case – that is, to apportion expenditure both on the farmhouse which is used as a dwelling house and on farm properties in such a way that what is a proper business expense for the run-

> ning of the farm is allowed, and what is an expenditure on domestic purposes is not allowed ... the clause, I am advised, will restore the previous practice ...'

Farmers are assessed to tax as occupiers of farm land excluding residential premises and it is only the rent of the farmland which can properly be deducted as an expense 'wholly and exclusively' incurred for the purposes of the farming trade. The fact that both the farmhouse and the farmland form the subject of a single lease cannot make the farmhouse part of the farmland in view of the clear direction to the contrary in ICTA 1988 s 832(1). As the rent paid covers both the farmhouse and farmland, it is necessary to apportion the total to arrive at the rent appropriate to each.

The portion of the rent, which relates to the farmhouse, will depend on the facts of the case concerned. The taxpayer may argue that the part of the rent relating to the farmhouse is represented by the difference between value of land without a house and the value of land with a house. However, that difference is not of direct relevance since you are dealing with land with a house. On the other hand, pointing to rents commanded in the open market by similar properties which are not farmhouses may well give a figure which is too high since the fact is the farmhouse is a farmhouse with the associated inconvenience of being used for the farming business. But these two views will, at least, serve to show the range within which a reasonable figure would be expected to lie.

In the past, adjustments were often based on the gross annual value and they can still be seen in some cases. Adjustments based on gross annual value may well have produced realistic figures in days gone by but are unlikely to do so nowadays since gross annual values have not been adjusted for many years. The aim should therefore be to produce an adjustment, which is realistic in amount and fair to both sides.

In cases of difficulty, the District Valuer will be able to assist in determining where the correct answer lies. The principles to apply when using his services are set out in IM1940a–IM1940j.

The next step is to establish the proportion of the rent relating to the farmhouse, which is to be allowed because it represents business use. This is, of course, a question of fact to be decided by agreement or by the Commissioners in the event of a disagreement.

The above will also be a useful tax guide for the stud farmhouse. As training horses is not classed as farming it might be questioned as to what relevance the farming guide IM2277b is to the trainer. The point is that the lease of the training establishment will probably be one lease to cover the house and stables. What proportion of rent will be allocated to the trainer's house? The tax adviser should try to achieve minimum rent allocated to the house and maximum to the training premises.

When the trainer lives in a rented house, the special CGT rules which permit an individual to have a main residence exemption for another property whilst living in the 'job-related accommodation' should be brought to the attention of the trainer.

Inheritance tax planning for the trainer

IHT reliefs available to the trainer

8.3 The inheritance tax reliefs available to a trainer who owns his own property can be very favourable. In broad terms, the yard, the gallops, the facilities and the lads' accommodation should be eligible for 100% relief from inheritance tax via the Business Property Relief (BPR) rules. The trainer is different from the stud farm as training is *not* agricultural for tax, however, there could be some elements of agricultural ownership combined with the training, such as breeding of horses and reference should therefore be made to **CHAPTERS 7 AND 1**, especially with reference to 'excepted assets', ie assets that might fail in their claim for the valuable BPR for IHT.

Examples of assets which might fail to qualify for BPR might be where parts of a yard are used for private use or used for training the proprietor's own racehorses. Strictly, racing is 'tax-free' and the ownership element should be removed from the trainer's accounts and the associated income and expenses should be treated as private. Also, the ownership element could cause some disallowance of IHT. Another example is where part of the yard is rented out – although arguments could proceed along the lines of *Farmer (Farmers Executors) v IRC [1999] STC (SCD) 321*, the tax relief is at risk. If the yard is proven to be non-commercial, relief might be denied on the basis that the business is not a commercial business (see **CHAPTER 3**).

The value of the tax reliefs here for IHT could be far greater than the minor disallowance of relief for annual income tax losses and must be given due weight.

Will planning for a trainer can be particularly complex with regard to the future allocation of assets. If all the assets are left to be divided among the children this can have problems for the future of the training yard. It might be that the children would not be the best choice for carrying on the training business and it would be better to pass the yard to a capable assistant or to sell the business as a going concern.

If there were, for example, two children and one wanted to carry on training and one did not, perhaps the property could be split between yard and gallops with the 'trainer' being left the core property and the gallops, etc left to the other who could then rent them back to the trainer in return for an income.

The trainer – CGT planning

8.4 The approach of this book is to attempt to emphasise the benefits of the UK tax system, especially where the trainer owns his own yard, whilst highlighting the pitfalls.

Business assets used by the trainer, eg yard, gallops etc, should be eligible for capital gains tax (CGT) taper relief and other relevant business reliefs, such as hold-over relief. **CHAPTER 13** deals with buying and selling the equestrian property of a stud. Although a trainer's yard is not commonly also a stud, many of the same criteria will be relevant.

Historically, training yards are situated either in the middle of small villages or on the outskirts of small rural towns. Sometimes in the interests of health and safety and general convenience it would be better to relocate to a more rural location. Sometimes the beautiful older yards are not the most labour efficient and a modern complex could serve better. The sale of such an older property with the benefit of planning permission having been obtained for development (usually only after a vast amount of work) can lead to large capital gains but these may be eligible for sheltering tax either through rollover relief or BATR.

The training activity is not agricultural and therefore it may be necessary to rely on the potential to claim BPR for relief from IHT (**CHAPTER 7** looks at the stud house). However, IHT is not the only consideration. The full implication of principal private residence (PPR) for CGT, expense claims for income tax relief and input VAT claims must be given consideration. If the trainer has another PPR for CGT purposes, maximising the business use of the trainer's house could have distinct advantages.

Maximising expense claims for all professional horsemen

8.5 The general view on equine expense claims is dealt with at **10.10** below.

The key ingredient to maximising tax reliefs is ensuring that the professional horseman remembers to record his expenses properly and to retain all relevant documentation.

A key issue relating to the professional horseman is whether there is deemed to be any element of hobby. The case of *Prince v Mapp (1969) 46 TC 169* dealt with the cost of a minor finger operation to enable a professional guitarist to continue playing as, on the evidence, he also played guitar as a hobby. Whilst a large number of expenses incurred in respect of maintenance of a professional horseman's general health are generally not allowable, recent serious operations undergone by Tony McCoy and Mick Fitzgerald enabled them to ride again are therefore almost certainly allowable for tax purposes. This is a difficult area where duality of purpose will often come into play. No doubt David Beckham kicks a football with his son for pleasure but he is still regarded as an employee and a professional sportsman for tax purposes. The cynic might advise the professional horseman to never admit to any hobby activities akin to their profession.

A lot of the equipment of the professional horseman will be of a replacement nature and therefore allowable as an expense under ICTA 1988 s 74(1)(d) as the renewal of 'utensils and loose tools'. Additional utensils and loose tools will probably be capital in nature but if not ranking for capital allowances may in suitable cases be regarded as a profit and loss expense, especially if it can be shown that they are not of a durable character (See *Hinton v Malden and Ireland Ltd [1959] All ER 356, 38 TC 391).*

Mallalieu v Drummond [1983] 2 All ER 1095, 57 TC 330 identified that whilst normal day wear will not be claimable as a tax expense, work clothes that cannot be worn socially are allowable, eg boots, jodhpurs, breeches, chaps, safety protection gear, etc.

Recent challenges by the Inland Revenue on the availability of tax relief for dietary needs and vitamins have been well documented. The Inland Revenue's view is that expenditure on maintaining the general health and fitness of a jockey is not allowable. Whilst it is also likely that the 'dual purpose rule' will taint a self-employed professional's travelling expenses with a private purpose it is likely that the Inland Revenue will accept an apportionment with some disallowance for the 'private' element in most cases. Care must be taken to document overseas riding assignments and travel thereto. Travel to races and competitions will generally be extensive. Travelling expenses such as air fares and rail fares are allowable if solely for business purposes. Hotel expenses incurred by a professional horseman or his own subsistence and accommodation whilst travelling on equine business are also allowable.

The ability to claim 100% first year capital allowances on computers and communication technology has been extended until 31 March 2004.

The timing of purchases of new IT equipment is of great importance to the professional horseman. The timing in relation to the year end and purchase should be reviewed carefully. The professional horseman is currently totally dependent on e-mail for instructions from owners and trainers and the IT relief can be a useful extra tax relief.

Likewise, 40% first year allowance claims on capital equipment, eg gyms, mechanical horses etc, can influence the timing of the purchase.

Interest on borrowing for business purposes usually qualifies for 100% tax relief. Personal borrowing qualifies for none. Consider borrowing first for business purposes, and when times are better repaying personal borrowings.

Incorporation and ICTA 1988 s 660A

8.6 The professional horseman might consider incorporation to take advantage of the fact that the current tax system favours companies. Business structure is looked at in more detail in CHAPTER **9**: THE EQUINE BUSINESS STRUCTURE.

Any professional horseman considering the pros and cons of incorporation will need to review carefully whether the savings will be real or minor.

Historically, a company has been a used by many 'husband and wife' teams as a vehicle for running their business. Current tax rates and bands for small companies also encourage this further. Such a structure also helpfully reflects the reality that in many traditional family businesses one spouse works at the traditional skills side of the business whilst the other provides backup and support. However, of significant concern to many tax professionals and business people alike, is the current Inland Revenue attack on these structures via the use of the 'settlement provisions'; in particular, where the Revenue identifies cases in which a 'non-working' spouse has been made a shareholder in order to transfer profits taxable on the working shareholder at higher rates of tax to the lower earning spouse in the form of dividends. See **8.7** below for a detailed commentary on this and see also the Inland Revenue's *Tax Bulletin* Issue No 64.

As most top flight professional horsemen will be spending less than they earn, leaving profits in a company to be taxed at 19% can be very tax efficient. Likewise, the dividend route for profits extraction is very attractive in that they currently attract no NIC charges.

If dealing with the tax affairs of a professional jockey who is considering the use of a personal service company, it is important to be aware of the provisions of ICTA 1988 s 775. This is anti-avoidance legislation and unlikely to be used in cases involving small amounts, but where the amounts involved are large then the possibility that the Inland Revenue might invoke it to prevent cases of abuse cannot be ruled out, although it is understood that cases of the application of these rules are rare indeed.

Inland Revenue *Tax Bulletin* April 2003

8.7 In April 2003 the Inland Revenue published *Tax Bulletin* Issue No 64 setting out their view of the settlement legislation of ICTA 1988 s 660A and how it affects husband and wife businesses. A recent article by Francesca Lagerberg, Tax Director of Smith & Williamson, which was featured in 'TAXline', the newsletter of the Tax Faculty, has summarised the main points of the *Tax Bulletin* and this is set out below.

'The Inland Revenue's April 2003 *Tax Bulletin* contains guidance on how the Revenue thinks the settlements legislation (ICTA 1988 s 660A) works in relation to individuals and businesses. In particular, it considers the situation where there is a family business involving a husband and wife. One spouse does the majority, if not all, of the work. The other spouse has shares in the business and receives dividends etc in relation to his holding. This spouse inevitably is a lower taxpaying individual.

The Revenue's view is that in certain circumstances this is an arrangement being used to divert income to someone else with the intention of saving tax. Thus it can be caught by the settlements legislation if the arrangements are bounteous, not commercial, not at arm's length or, in the case of a gift between spouses, 'wholly or substantially a right to income'. In such cases, the Revenue may seek to invoke the settlements legislation and claim tax, interest and penalties in relation to a reallocation of the income to the higher taxpaying spouse.

The Revenue gives its view in a series of examples ...

As the Revenue does point out, the settlements legislation has been in existence since the 1930s. Many of the points being raised by the Revenue now are not new and have indeed been its view for many years, not least the points which have appeared previously in the Trusts Estates and Settlement Manual. However, the series of examples go far further than many expected.

There are a wide range of arrangements that can potentially be caught by the settlement legislation which do not involve a trust. Each case will depend on the facts but some of the most common situations we see are:

- shares subscribed at par that carry only restricted rights;
- shares given away that carry only restricted rights;
- shares subscribed at par in a company by someone else where the income of the company derives mainly from a single employee;
- a share in a partnership gifted or transferred below value;
- dividend waivers;
- situations where dividends are paid only on certain classes of share;
- dividends paid to the settler's minor children.

These lists are by no means definitive of situations to which the settlements of legislation can be applied.

This appears to be a clear warning shot that certain arrangements may be subject to particular close scrutiny by the Inland Revenue in the future.

Some key points to note are as follows:

1 In spouse situations, the *Bulletin* may attach too much importance to the current state of affairs. Where one spouse gives to the other, shares which can only ever attract a dividend (eg non-voting preference shares) then clearly this can only be a transfer of a right to income. But if the gifted shares rank *pari passu* with the other shares for all purposes, how can the Revenue conclude that there is a settlement merely because currently the company has little or no capital value (eg where there are few assets and almost all profits are being paid out in expenses plus salaries plus (mainly) dividends)? Who can say what may happen next year or the year after, or ten years after? The dividend policy may change, a windfall profit or capital gain may arise, goodwill may increase substantially etc. Then the gifted shares will clearly become much more valuable. Will the Revenue's view change and, if so, when?

2 The breadth of the examples shows a very wide interpretation being taken. Example 2, where "beneficiary" is not the spouse nor the minor children, if correct, would appear to apply to every case in which there was a single controlling shareholder. Also Example 9 – where children are given shares by a grandparent – again has been criticised as overly wide. Is every dividend paid to a minority shareholder bounteous?

3 One solution to the above is the suggestion that shares could be transferred by the active spouse in the company into the joint names of the husband and wife, so that the shares were held beneficially and thus dividends would be assessed on the spouses equally. This would require the use of a trust deed. One possible difficulty with this approach is the operation of ICTA 1988 s 282A(5) which appears to let the settlement take priority.

There is at least one test case at the moment, which may challenge this Revenue interpretation. In the meantime, however, it would be sensible to give thought to structures which minimise the possibility of attack.'

Business use of home

Claim for expenses

8.8 Where business use is made of a property, the professional horseman should ensure that a proportion of the related expenses are claimed for tax purposes.

Many individuals use their properties to a greater or lesser extent for the purpose of a trade or employment carried on by them. This could mean that there is an entitlement to claim related household expenses for tax purposes.

A person carrying on a trade, profession or vocation can deduct any expenses, which are wholly and exclusively incurred for the purpose of the trade etc (ICTA 1988 s 74). This could include heating, lighting and power costs resulting directly from his use of the property for business purposes. Often this can be estimated based on the amount of time spent on business activities in the home and the space occupied.

In addition, where an individual exclusively uses part of the premises for business purposes (eg where it is used as a gym, sauna or as a self-contained office), it may also be possible to claim an appropriate portion of other expenses, such as rent repairs, insurance, interest charges and council tax. Strictly, such expenses are only deductible if they are exclusive to the business area being used. In practice, Inspectors of Taxes do allow pro rata expense claims provided an area is genuinely used for business purposes. However, the possible restriction in the capital gains tax exemption should be noted. In practice, the Inland Revenue is prepared to accept apportioned sums in respect of heating, lighting and council tax (rates in Northern Ireland) where business use of a room or rooms is not exclusive, as will usually be the case (see Inspector's Manual, para 601e).

Risk to capital gains tax and business rates

8.9 The claimant for the business use of home should be aware of the potential adverse affect on capital gains tax and the house.

Any claim that part of a residence is used exclusively for business will result in a restriction of the principal private residence exemption, ie the relief that an individual can claim the gain on their principal house tax-free.

If part of the house is used exclusively for business purposes, then it is not covered by the main residence exemption (TCGA 1992 s 224(12)). Examples are equine physiotherapists (who heal the professional jockey) who may have used two or three rooms within their house for the purpose of a surgery and waiting room. However, many individuals do set aside part of their house as a study or office informally or as a formal business address. In other cases, garages or sheds within a garden area are converted into stores for all the riding equipment.

If a claim is made that a particular room is being set aside wholly for business purposes, then it will be necessary to estimate the portion of the gain attributable to that room. This will be excluded from the main residence exemption. If one room in a ten-room house is being so used, then it may be reasonable to assume the figure is 10%, although it could be higher or lower depending on the size of the room in question relative to the rest of the house. In addition, it may be possible to claim a portion of the interest paid on the loan to purchase the property.

A higher-rate taxpayer may be better off with the income tax relief than the capital gains exemption.

More recently, of course, the availability of business asset taper relief (BATR) will bring down the chargeable gain significantly. After two years of ownership, 75% of the chargeable gain drops out of charge as a result of BATR if the individual is engaged in a trading activity (see **CHAPTER 13**).

As mentioned above, even if part of a house is exclusively used for business, the allowance of certain expenses on a pro-rata basis may be more a matter of Inland Revenue practice specific to the circumstances of the case.

The professional sportsman must also be aware of the impact of business rates.

Where part of a house is used as an office, this will turn the premises into a composite hereditament, and the extent of the property liable to rates will turn on the degree of business use in each part: (see *Fotherington v Wood [1995] RA 315*). Where there is a permanent adaptation and use of an area of the house to work use, such as the use of an integral garage as an office, then part will not be domestic for council tax purposes.

Where a person working from home just uses the dining room table and a filing cabinet, a non-domestic use cannot be established and this is likely to come within the council tax treatment of the whole dwelling. Where a room is used as an office, ie it is equipped with a desk, filing cabinet, computer and dedicated telephone/fax line, but in the evening it is used to catch up with the payment of domestic bills and for children playing computer games, this is borderline. However, the Valuation Office holds the view that where there is clearly dual use and the non-domestic use is not predominant, the room should not be assessed for rates. Therefore, perhaps in such a case the room will not be counted as non-domestic. The key considerations seem to be:

- the effect of the extent and frequency of the non-domestic use; and
- any modifications made to the property to accommodate that use.

All taxpayers must be made aware of the risk of the imposition of business rates on a property if space is given over to business use exclusively.

Prizes/gifts received by horse owners and professional advice

8.10 The market value of a trophy received for winning is normally assessable. If there is any doubt as to whether the trophy is assessable, details should be submitted to the Inspector of Taxes.

The case of *Wing v O'Connell Supreme Court (IFS) 1926 [1927] IR 84* ruled that a present to a successful jockey by the owner of a racehorse was taxable. This would apply in the situation of the employed and the self-employed professional horseman.

Strictly, all gifts received from third parties for the performance of employment duties or from the provision of services as a self-employed professional are taxable. Hunt staff are also professional horsemen and the case of *Wright v Boyce [1958] 2 All ER 703, 38 TC 160* ruled that gifts to hunt servants were taxable.

Monies receivable for advice about horses are taxable. Appearance monies payable by sponsors, owners and others are taxable.

Apprentice and conditional jockeys

8.11 Apprentices and conditional jockeys are employed by the trainer for whom they ride. Their income is taxed under employment income (ie PAYE). The riding fees and prize money received by the trainee jockey under the Rules of Racing are subject to PAYE. 'Home' rides, ie rides for the trainer who is the current employer are assessed under employment income (PAYE). 'Away' rides are, however, currently taxed under employment income, ie treated as self-employed income.

Apprentice and conditional jockeys can receive income from appearances, sponsorship, professional advice on horses and injury benefits. With regard to the latter, temporary disablement benefits received from the Professional Riders Insurance Scheme (PRIS) are taxable. Likewise, capital sums received under PRIS regulations are not taxable.

The professional jockey – ICTA 1988 s 775

Exploiting the earning capacity

8.12 This section focuses on ICTA 1988 s 775 itself and the supplementary provisions in sections 777 and 778. In short, the provisions attack schemes where personal earnings otherwise subject to income tax are converted to capital. Because capital gains tax treatment is generally more favourable than income tax treatment for such large sums as tend to be involved in such cases, strategies are sometimes devised to convert income into capital gain. The Inspector's Manual refers specifically to jockeys as one of the professions which might attempt this.

The struggling jockey might consider himself unlikely in the extreme to ever be in a position to be able to have enough income to consider the advantages of diverting it in this manner but the legislation can still potentially apply to even small cases, although in practice, this is unlikely. Similarly, there may appear a certain irony in being bracketed along with the high-earning sporting personalities such as premiership football players, pro-tennis players and other television and film personalities etc. This legislation, in practice is, only likely to be applied to the very top flight jockeys. The majority of professional jockeys (probably like a large number of professional footballers) only earn a standard living and many struggle to survive, and as such are unlikely to be deemed worthy of the attentions of the Specialist Technical Revenue sections which deal with this legislation.

Attempts by the tax planner to convert income to capital by such means may well be caught under the anti-avoidance rules of ICTA 1988 s 775. It is worth quoting the Inspector's Manual IM4682 in this context:

> 'Section 775 refers to any occupation of an individual and the individual's activities in that occupation. "Occupation" is defined in section 775(3)(a) and embraces all activities, which are of a kind pursued in any profession or vocation, irrespective of whether the individual is in fact carrying on a profession or vocation. Thus, although the individual may be an employee of, for example, his service company, if the activities, which he performs in the course of his employment, are a kind, which is performed as a part of a profession or vocation, those activities are within the terms of section 775.'

The use of the word 'vocation' in the subsection brings in activities, which do not fall within the normal meaning of the word 'profession'. For example, a jockey may well be carrying on a vocation without carrying on a profession. The words 'profession or vocation' embrace not only actors, actresses, pop stars and the usual TV and film personalities, but also such people as golfers, tennis players, footballers, boxers and so on.

With regard to jockeys, there are three conditions that need to be met before the provisions can apply:

- there must be transactions or arrangements that enable a person to enjoy the earning capacity of another individual;

- a capital amount must arise; and
- tax avoidance must be a main object (ICTA 1998 s 775(1)).

These three components are now considered in more detail below.

Diverting the income stream

Another person enjoying the earning capacity of the jockey

8.13 The anti-avoidance provisions require there to be 'transactions or arrangements'. It is suggested that the definition is wide enough (especially when considered with the other conditions) to cover any deliberate scheme that may be implemented.

These transactions or arrangements must have been put in place 'to exploit the earning capacity of an individual'. In other words, the transactions or arrangements must divert the jockey's earnings to another person, ie someone else 'enjoys' the jockey's earnings.

This other person may, but need not be, an individual or a company. Indeed, the typical case contemplated by the legislation involves the establishment of a company to employ the individual, with the company receiving the income stream generated by the jockey's personal activities. It will be seen, therefore, that in some ways the provisions were a limited precursor of the more recent IR35 legislation.

Provided all the relevant conditions are met, the legislation is so broadly drafted it catches cases where the other person is put in a position to enjoy:

> 'all or any part of the profits or gains or other income, or of the receipts, derived from the individual's activities in that occupation, or anything derived directly or indirectly from any such income or receipts.'

Although this would seem to be broad enough, ICTA 1988 s 775(3)(b) specifically includes within this 'payments for any description of copyright or licence or franchise or other right derived its value from the activities, including past activities, of the individual'. This would be less likely to apply to jockeys but could be used to capture other income from authorship for example.

Further, ICTA 1988 s 777(5) allows the Inland Revenue and the courts to look through any number of trusts, partnerships and companies to determine whether value derives from the jockey's occupation.

Section 775(3)(a) restricts the number of individuals caught by the legislation by limiting the occupations that are subject to it. In particular, it provides that the legislation only applies to 'activities of any of the kinds pursued in any profession or vocation'. This means that genuine jockeys who wish to incorporate their business are not unwittingly exposing themselves to future problems on this point. However, the wording of the legislation ensures that an occupation is caught if it is of a kind that is (by some individuals) pursued in a profession or vocation, even if the individual concerned is able to argue that he was not actually so engaged.

As long as the occupation is carried on at least partly in the United Kingdom, then the legislation bites. Furthermore, it bites whether or not the individual is UK resident (ICTA 1988 s 775(9)). A key point for overseas jockeys riding in the UK.

Capital amounts

8.14 The second requirement (ICTA 1988 s 775) highlighted at **8.12** above was that the jockey obtains a capital amount.

A capital amount is defined as any amount in money or money's worth that would (but for these provisions) not be subject to income tax (s 777(13)).

This capital amount must arise 'as part of, or in connection with, or in consequence of, the transactions or arrangements' referred to above. Further, the legislation bites even if the jockey obtains the capital amount on behalf of another person (again, not necessarily another individual).

It might appear that any capital amount obtained by another individual (for example the individual's spouse) is outside the scope of the legislation. However, ICTA 1988 s 775(8) extends this rule to cover cases where the individual has put some other person in a position to receive the capital amount by providing the other person with something of value derived (directly or indirectly).

This extension would catch the situation where a jockey channels his or her income through a company and shortly before winding up the company gives the shares of the company to the jockey's spouse. However, with a little foresight, it might still be possible to circumvent the provisions. Suppose the spouse were to form a company, which employed the jockey. It is then arguable that although the shares obtain their value from the individual's activities, it is not the individual who has provided the other person (ie the spouse) with something of value since the spouse owned the shares *ab initio.*

The alternative view is that section 777(2) requires section 775 to be interpreted broadly such that 'however indirect ... the occasion when the value of any property is enhanced may be an occasion when under section 775, tax becomes chargeable'. This would suggest that, in the above example, the increasing value of the spouse's shares is within the scope of section 775.

On the other hand, section 775 does not purport to impose a tax charge on any occasion other then the realising of a capital sum. As a result, the courts may take the view that section 777(2) does not bite in such a case. Such a view is reasonably likely when section 777(3) is considered. That subsection provides a number of examples of where section 777(2) is intended to apply and these do not seem to go anywhere near the example illustrated above.

As a result, there are certain occasions when a capital amount will not trigger the anti-avoidance provisions. These exceptions apply if both the following conditions are met:

1 the capital amount is obtained from the disposal of either:
   - assets of profession or vacation (including goodwill); or
   - a share in a partnership that is carrying on a profession or vocation; or
   - shares in a company; and
2 the profession, vocation or company's business is valued as a going concern (ICTA 1988 s 775(4)).

The second limb is itself subject to two qualifications. First, the reference to a company's business includes any business owned by a company whose shares are owned (directly or indirectly) by the company (ICTA 1988 s 775(6)).

Secondly, there is a qualification if the value of the jockey's business (or profession or vocation) is based largely on future income or receipts.

In such cases, the exemption provided by section 775(4) does not apply to any part of the capital amount that relates to the consideration due to the individual in their Schedule D profession or vocation or employment income employment (ICTA 1988 s 775(5)).

In addition, no tax arises on the receipt of a capital amount if the capital amount is a right or property, which derives its value (or substantially the whole of its value) from the activities of the jockey. This ensures that the jockey is not subject to the anti-avoidance rules when such shares are received. Instead, the occasion, subject to the anti-avoidance rules, is when the shares themselves are realised (ICTA 1988 s 775(7)). Similarly, if the jockey receives an option which otherwise represents a capital amount.

The tax avoidance motive

8.15 Finally, the last requirement for the anti-avoidance provisions (ICTA 1988 s 775) to apply is that the main object or one of the main objects of the transactions was the avoidance or reduction of liability to income tax. The test is always difficult to apply, as it is often hard to distinguish between a main object and an enjoyable secondary reason.

It is not sufficient, however, to show documentary evidence (eg board minutes and other memoranda) that purports to show that tax avoidance was not a main object. Section 777(4) provides that such evidence 'shall not be conclusive'. However, that does not mean that such records should not be made or pieced together later since there is nothing preventing them from being persuasive evidence.

If the anti-avoidance provisions apply, then the capital amount is treated as income of the jockey. This income is assessable under Schedule D Case VI (ICTA 1988 s 775(2)). The purpose of this provision is to remove any of the CGT reliefs available to the jockey (now principally the availability of taper relief, but historically the lower marginal rate and the use of the annual exemption).

Whilst this is meant to deter jockeys from going down this route, there can be an advantage. In particular, by treating what would otherwise be Case II or employment income as assessable under Case VI, the jockey appears to escape liability to National Insurance contributions. However, it should be noted that the deemed income would not qualify as relevant earnings for pension purposes.

It should also be noted that this deemed income does not arise until the capital amount is realised, thus section 775 still provides a method of deferring income recognition.

To ensure that there is no double taxation, TCGA 1992 ss 37 and 39 provide that amounts subject to income tax are excluded from calculations for capital gains tax. ICTA 1988 s 777(12) extends this to cases when the person receiving the capital amount is different from the person assessed to income tax.

As will be seen, it is possible for one person to be assessable to tax on a capital amount received by another. In such circumstances, the person liable for the tax can recover from the other person (ICTA 1988 s 777(8)(a)). The Inland Revenue can, if requested, issue a certificate stating the amount paid and such a certificate is to be conclusive (ICTA 1988 s 777(8)).

Conversely, if the person liable for the tax had not paid it to the Inland Revenue within six months of it falling due, the Inland Revenue may seek to recover it from the person who received the capital amount (ICTA 1988 s 777(8)(b)). In such circumstances, the person may seek to recover it from the person actually assessed (although the latter person too is apparently able to recover it in turn from the first).

Finally, if the person receiving the capital amount is resident overseas (eg overseas jockey), the Inland Revenue can require basic rate tax to be deducted from the capital amount. Such a direction does not prevent tax from being collected from that person under the provisions outlined at **8.14** above (ICTA 1988 s 777(9)).

The Inland Revenue has the statutory right under ICTA 1988 s 778 to obtain from any person information that may be necessary to enforce section 775. It should make its request by written notice giving the recipient at least 30 days to respond (ICTA 1988 ss 778(1) and 832(1)). (Failure to provide the information in time can render the recipient liable to penalties under the Taxes Management Act 1970 s 98.)

However, solicitors are not subject to the full powers of these provisions. In particular, a solicitor is not required to provide information of any transaction or arrangements with which he or she took part if his or her only involvement was as a professional adviser. Furthermore, without the consent of the solicitor's client, the solicitor is not required to say more than that he or she was acting on behalf of a particular client and provides the client's name and address (ICTA 1988 s 778(3)).

Specific tax planning for sportsman

8.16 'Property' is taxable for inheritance tax. The definition of property is changing. For example, do endorsements of products by a sportsman have a capital value, to be included in his or her estate at death? If so is it 100% relief under IHTA 1984 s 105(1)(a) or plant and machinery with possible 50% BPR under IHTA 1984 s 105(1)(d).

Costs incurred in engaging the services of an agent or secretary for booking rides and dealing with associated paperwork are an allowable expense for income tax and corporation tax purposes. Travelling to and from race meetings (which with the growth of the evening meeting can perhaps be two a day), can be expensive but will generally qualify as wholly, exclusively and necessarily for the purpose of the business. This can include a driver and helicopter flights.

A jockey can provide his services through the medium of service companies. The jockey will have to enter into a contract of employment with his company. The company will then have to enter into various contracts to supply the jockey's services. The structure of the company is dealt with in CHAPTER **9** and the diversion problems of ICTA 1988 s 775 have been dealt with at **8.12–8.15** above. Care will also need to be taken here to ensure that the jockey's company does not fall foul of the rules (IR35) by virtue of FA 2000 Sch 12.

Where Jockey Club rules specify prizes payable direct through Weatherbys or by the owner, these are taxable. The winning percentages pool allocated to the Jockeys Association Pension Scheme are taxable. The value attributable is the amount shown on the certificate of premium payments provided by the nominated insurance company and should be shown as part of the prize money receipts. Temporary disablement benefits received from the Professional Riders Insurance Scheme (PRIS) are taxable. Capital sums received under PRIS regulations are not taxable.

If a jockey is given shares in a stallion syndicate he is assessable on their market value when receivable. Likewise, annual nominations in stallions will be assessed on the value received, (although this will sometimes be difficult to quantify). Any commissions received on sales or syndication of horses will be assessable to tax.

The earning capacity of a professional jockey can be restricted by early retirement and it is normal for jockeys to expand their equine interests. For example, the profit of a business of horse breeding with a view to the sale of the progeny will be taxable.

Overseas income can have tax deducted from the payments. The overseas tax deducted will normally be eligible for set-off against the UK tax liability of the jockey. See also the taxation of overseas sportsmen at **8.17** et seq below.

Non-resident sportsmen

Background

8.17 With the large number of overseas (non-resident) sportsmen riding in the UK it would be impossible to ignore this subject.

The UK tax position of non-UK resident entertainers and sportsmen altered radically from 1 May 1987. Before that date there was little necessity for tax planning as although such people were taxable on their UK earnings – and indeed the UK specifically reserved the right to tax them in virtually all of its double taxation agreements – in practice, the Inland Revenue rarely raised assessments. Since 1 May 1987 there has been a need for tax planning, but unfortunately little scope for doing so.

Under the current system a non-resident entertainer is, in most cases, chargeable to UK tax on his UK earnings as a performer as if they form the income of a notional trade carried on wholly in the UK – and unlike other trades, taxable on a fiscal year basis instead of the normal accounts year basis.

Furthermore, collectibility of the tax has been reinforced by an extremely widely drawn withholding tax. Withholding taxes are, by their nature, difficult to avoid as the person responsible for the tax is the withholding agent, and this is the person who makes the payment and is legally subject to the withholding tax. Such a person is likely to resolve any doubt as to whether or not an obligation to deduct exists in favour of the Inland Revenue. As a safe fall-back position, if he did not take such an approach he would be at risk that the Inland Revenue would look to him, and not the entertainer, for any tax he improperly failed to deduct Worse, by the time that they came to the withholding agent, he could well no longer have any relationship with the entertainer and might find it very difficult to recover the tax from him.

Under the specific rules dealing with non-resident entertainers, a payer must deduct tax at the 22% basic rate (unless the Inland

Revenue otherwise direct) from any payment to any person – not just the entertainer or sportsman – who has a connection of a prescribed kind with a relevant activity, or one which in any way derives directly or indirectly from a relevant activity.

The withholding tax

8.18 Where tax is deducted from a payment that is not covered by the withholding requirements, the Inland Revenue will repay it to the intended recipient. Nevertheless, in practice, it is generally easier to convince the Revenue that a payment is not taxable if the Revenue are trying to collect money from a non-resident (which generally is not the easiest of tasks for them) than it is if one is trying to persuade the Revenue to make a repayment to the individual concerned.

The first obvious area to consider is whether the services need to be performed in the UK. If a sportsman is to be paid for making a TV advertisement to be shown to coincide with a sporting event in the UK, can the commercial be shot or videotaped outside the UK? If the individuals services are performed outside the UK, a payment for those services is outside the scope of the withholding rules, and also outside the scope of the special rules for assessing an artiste, as the scope of his deemed trade is, broadly speaking, the same as for the withholding rules.

In relation to the jockey, clearly the riding of a race takes place in a specific country but any videos and publicity that surround the ride might take place outside the UK.

The next possibility is to analyse exactly what work the sportsman or entertainer will do in the UK and to remunerate him separately for any service not carried out in his capacity as a sportsman or entertainer. For example, an actor who also directs the show in which he stars is not classed as carrying on a relevant activity. Similarly, if a pop star devises the lighting or sound rigging for the show and supervises its erection such work is not a relevant activity.

A word of warning, however. Whilst such work is not a relevant activity, the need for it, and thus the payment in respect of it, could well be said to derive directly or indirectly from the relevant activity, ie the actor's activity as an actor or the pop star's activity as a singer, and thus will be within the scope of the tax for that reason. The Inland Revenue does not seem to be taking this point if the individual involved is, in reality, performing a distinct function. If activities were to be hived off to create a wholly artificial job that in practice would never be performed by an independent person, there is a significant risk that they would seek to attack the division.

There are four exceptions to the need to deduct tax. The first is if a payment of withholding tax already falls to be deducted under some other provision of the tax legislation. At first sight this is not very helpful. Nevertheless, if a double taxation agreement provides, for example, for royalties to suffer a nil or a 5% withholding tax, it can be worthwhile trying to structure things so that an individual receives royalties instead of fees.

The second exception is that certain payments are made to a person who is both resident and ordinarily resident in the UK and is neither connected with, nor an associate of, the entertainer concerned. The payments are those made for the provision of services ancillary to the performance of the relevant activity, provided that the price does not exceed an arm's length price. This does not leave much scope for planning except in a negative way. It demonstrates that the incorporation of a UK company owned by the entertainer will not automatically take payments out of the scope of the withholding tax. It should be noted that this exception does not cover goods, only services. Accordingly, the entertainer should preferably not ask the UK promoter to provide goods, such as costumes, even if they will be purchased in the UK, but should endeavour to convert the items to services (eg hiring charges rather than purchase cost) and a promoter should endeavour to ensure that services are provided by UK rather than foreign residents (eg British Airways rather than United Airlines). However, it will be important not to lose sight of the fact that the entertainer can generally claim a deduction for expenses so the withholding tax is likely to be a prepayment rather than an additional charge. Accordingly, if a service can be acquired more cheaply from a foreign supplier the tax considerations should take a back seat.

The third exception is payments to the entertainer in respect of the proceeds of sales of records provided that these are calculated by reference to such sale proceeds. Again care is needed here. The exception does not extend to payments to third parties such as the entertainer's personal services company.

The final exception is payments which (together with any connected payments) do no exceed in aggregate £1,000 in the course of a year of assessment.

In summary, the payments or transfers from which tax need not be withheld under these provisions are as follows:

- a payment subject to deduction of tax under some other provisions of the Taxes Acts than ICTA 1988 s 555(2) and The Income Tax (Entertainers and Sportsmen) Regulations 1987 (SI 1987/530);
- an arm's length payment made to a person resident and ordinarily resident in the UK, who is not connected or associated with the payee, for services ancillary to the performance of a relevant activity;
- payments representing royalties from the sale of sound recordings;

- any total amount paid in a tax year by a payer, together with persons connecting or associated with him, to a non-UK resident entertainer or sportsman, together with persons connected or associated with him, which does not exceed £1,000.

Arrangement with the Inland Revenue

8.19 There is a procedure under which either the non-resident sportsman or entertainer (or other recipient of a relevant payment) or the person who is due to make the payment can approach the Inland Revenue in advance and agree with them that either tax need not be deducted or that it should be deducted at a reduced rate.

The objective is for the Inland Revenue to require deductions equal in aggregate to the entertainer's likely liability for some or all of the payments due to him and to authorise any further payments to be made gross. As an alternative, the Inland Revenue could agree that no withholding tax at all need be deducted if the entertainer can instead provide acceptable security for payment of the tax, eg by a bank guarantee or by paying the estimated tax direct to the Inland Revenue. An application for such an arrangement needs to be made at least 30 days before the payment falls due. The Inland Revenue does not have the power to waive this 30-day requirement, but, in practice, does not take this point if the payer and the entertainer agree to defer making the payment until the arrangement has been entered into.

Where a sportsman or entertainer will incur heavy expenses in relation to his UK performance he should normally seek such an arrangement, as 22% of the gross income could well exceed the anticipated net profit. Even if expenses are relatively small there could be merit in entering into an arrangement.

Where an arrangement is entered into, the Inland Revenue generally seem to regard the amount withheld under it as satisfying the sportsman or entertainer's tax liability, so there is probably merit in seeking to agree the taxable profit (or budgeted taxable profit) with them as early as possible, rather than waiting to claim excess withholding tax, which cannot be done until the following fiscal year – by which time their attitude to allowable expenses may have hardened.

On the other hand, the Inland Revenue's normal procedure is to review an entertainer's past UK performances – including appearances before 1 May 1987 – and to seek to collect any outstanding past tax as a condition of granting an exemption or reduced withholding certificate for a current tour.

If such an arrangement is to be entered into, the Inland Revenue requires details of projected income and expenses, a list of tour dates, and a copy of all contracts relating to the UK appearance or appearances. Obviously, these documents need to be assembled, and the budget prepared, before the approach to the Inland Revenue is made. Equally obviously, the budget should include all expenses relating to the entertainer's UK appearance, including those incurred outside the UK, as the making of the arrangement is likely to be regarded by the Inland Revenue as the occasion of agreeing the entertainer's UK tax liability.

In practice, the opportunity should also be taken to review whether the entertainer is liable to UK tax in respect of UK appearances in the last few years. The Inland Revenue explanatory booklet FEU 50, which is obtainable from the Foreign Entertainers Unit, 2nd Floor, Royal House, Prince's Gate, 2–6 Homer Road, Solihull, West Midlands B91 3WG, states that allowable expenses will normally include general subsistence expenses, commissions, manager's and agent's fees, UK travel, and international air fares to the UK.

The Inland Revenue consider that the return fare to the taxpayer's own country is not an expense of his UK performance, although the logic for this is difficult to discern. They also seek to impose arbitrary limits on accommodation costs if these are unduly extravagant, or there are more than a few days in the UK between performances. In addition to items specifically relating to the UK work, it is worth claiming a reasonable proportion of general expenses, such as promotion, if these have contributed to generating the UK income. Telephone calls, telexes, faxes, etc from the overseas country in connection with arranging the UK performance should not be overlooked.

The regulations provide for arrangements to be made in writing between the payer, the entertainer or sportsman, or other recipient of the payment, and the Board of Inland Revenue for a reduced tax payment representing, as nearly as may be, the actual liability of the entertainer or sportsman, to apply. Such application must be made not later than 30 days before the payment (or transfer) falls to be made and the full basic rate deduction must be made from any payment or transfer made before the Board gives approval. There are provisions to prevent any payment suffering withholding tax more than once where it passes through an intermediary and for reductions to apply where there is a double taxation agreement in force. Similarly, there are anti-avoidance provisions to prevent payments or transfers being routed through third parties such as controlled companies and similar entities.

The sum accounted for to the Inland Revenue is treated as paid on account of the income or corporation tax liability of a person other than the person so accounting for it, whether a liability under the regulations, under ICTA 1988, s 555 et seq or under any other provision of the Taxes Acts. The charge under ICTA 1988, s 555(2) applies in place of any charge under emloyment income (any amount charged under which shall be treated as an expense of the 'Schedule 11 trade'). Under ICTA 1988, ss 660–685 (settlements) or under Schedule D (where the connected payment is a receipt falling to be included in the computation of profits of a company which provides the services of the entertainer or sportsman). A recipient is entitled to claim in writing that a tax payment deducted is excessive and TMA 1970, s 42 applies to such claims.

It must be understood that the Government has sought to block attempts to circumvent the withholding tax – and has, in some cases, imposed what in effect were penalties for trying. If payments have been made in kind, ie via the transfer of goods, eg a car, or services instead of cash, the Government takes the view that withholding tax still needs to be accounted for even though it cannot be deducted! The value of the goods must be regarded as a net sum for the purpose of calculating tax, ie the tax is deemed to be due on a grossed up figure in the Inland Revenue's view. For example, the payment of a fee of £5,000 attracts withholding tax of £1,100; the transfer to the entertainer of a car worth £5,000, on the other hand, will attract withholding tax of £1,410. Nor can the tax be avoided by making the individual a loan whilst he is in the UK, with the intention that he will be paid his fee in a later year when he does not come to the UK and repay the loan at that stage. The loan is a payment from which tax has to be withheld, and there is no provision enabling the tax to be refunded when the loan is repaid. The parties must wait for the Inland Revenue to refund it to the entertainer following a repayment claim – which cannot be made until the next fiscal year. Clearly, temporary loans to the individual should be avoided.

In some cases it may be possible to avoid the withholding tax by arranging for the payer to be an overseas company. Such a company is probably outside the scope of the withholding tax, as the UK cannot legislate to tax overseas activities of foreign companies. This is not practical in the case of some activities where the income is generated in the UK, as even if the immediate payer is a non-UK resident, there will be a UK payer further down the chain and the withholding of tax will bite at this stage. It may well be possible in the case of endorsement fees for sponsorship payments, particularly if the advertiser is an international rather than a UK company. Unlike in the USA, it is not possible to avoid tax by the formation of a UK company owned by the artiste. Tax must still be deducted from payments to that company. Furthermore, the income must be treated as the income of the artiste, not of the company, so this would not even obtain the benefit of the lower corporation tax rates for higher earning artistes.

The personal service company rules in FA 2000, Sch 12 also need to be borne in mind in appropriate cases. There is a specific exemption from these where a withholding obligation arises under the foreign entertainers' scheme. Avoiding that scheme brings the personal holding company legislation back into play. The Schedule 11 trades, 'Computation of liability of entertainer or sportsman' (known as the 'Schedule 11 trade' because these provisions were originally enacted in FA 1986, Sch 11). Where a payment or other transfer is made within these provisions, the relevant activity is treated as performed in the course of trade, profession or vocation exercised in the UK and thus chargeable to tax under Schedule D Case I or II (to the extent that it would not otherwise be so treated) unless it is performed in the course of an office or employment.

Payment of tax is due, whether or not it has been withheld from the connected payment or transfer, before, or at the time when, a quarterly return is made, whether or not an assessment has been made.

An assessment to tax may be made, in relation to a tax year or other period, on a current year (not preceding year) basis and any apportionment, division or aggregation by reference to tax years or other periods may be made as is just and reasonable. The 'Schedule 11 trade' is thus treated separately from the 'worldwide trade' of an entertainer or sportsman, but for the purposes of loss relief under ICTA 1988, ss 381 and 385, they are treated as the same trade, although losses in early years will be relieved only by reference to the date of commencement of the worldwide trade. Terminal loss relief under ICTA 1988, s 388 will only be given in respect of the Schedule 11 trades if the worldwide trade ceases in the same period.

All other provisions of the Taxes Acts as to the time within which an assessment may be made apply to such an assessment, as do the provisions for out of time assessments. Tax charged by an assessment is payable within 14 days of the issue of the notice, or by the due date of the payment of the tax if this is earlier. The collection and recovery procedures and the provisions relating to interest on overdue tax in the Taxes Management Act (TMA) 1970 apply to such assessments. The penalty provisions of TMA 1970 s 98 also apply. Returns (including returns of payments of which a nil deduction rate applied) must be made quarterly in respect of the periods to 30 June, 30 September, 31 December and 5 April, within 14 days of the end of each period. The Board may require, in writing, within a specified time, certain information regarding payments, payees and relevant activities. The penalty provisions of TMA 1970 apply to failure to submit returns.

Double taxation agreements

8.20 An area that might give greater scope for planning is the study of double taxation agreements for non-resident sportsmen. The legislation on the taxation of overseas entertainers is, as always, subject to the provisions of such agreements. The Inland Revenue's booklet FEU 50 makes clear that they accept this – although it states that a withholding agent should ignore the existence of double tax agreements and leave it to the Inland Revenue to refund to the artiste any tax that the UK was not entitled to impose on him. This seems of doubtful propriety as, if the UK is prohibited by an international agreement from taxing a person, it is doubtful if it meets its obligation under the treaty by imposing a tax and later refunding it. Unfortunately, the legal cost of opposing the deduction could not be justified.

All of the UK's double tax agreements (other than that with Gambia, which has not spawned many international entertainers) reserve to the UK the right to impose tax on UK performances of foreign entertainers. However, the scope of what the UK can tax varies. In most cases, the UK is only entitled to tax the income of entertainers 'from their personal activities as such'. It is doubtful whether this is wide enough to tax income from sponsorships or endorsements or from opening shops or similar events where the entertainer is acting as a 'personality' rather than as an entertainer. It is certainly not wide enough to allow the UK to tax the singer's remuneration from acting as a record producer or the film star's fee for acting as producer or director.

Although the 'artistes and athletes' Article in a double tax agreement generally overrides the business profits and personal services Articles, it does not override the royalties Article. There may accordingly be scope for turning the artiste's remuneration into a royalty if the relevant double taxation agreement provides an exemption from UK tax on royalties. It should be borne in mind that an actor's participation in a film's income is not normally a royalty.

Most double taxation agreements entered into by the UK before 1974 – and some entered into after that date – allow the UK to tax only income of the artiste. In such circumstances the use of a personal services company (or loan-out company) should be effective. Although the UK domestic law deems the income to be the income of the artiste, it is in truth income of the company and the protection of the double taxation agreement would therefore apply. Even where the double taxation agreement allows the UK to tax income in respect of personal activities of the entertainer where it accrues to some other person, the charge will normally extend only to his activities as an entertainer and would not include ancillary income. In many cases there may be scope for the company to provide services supporting the performance. Its fee for such services would not be caught by the artistes' and athletes' clause as it is exempted from UK tax under the business profits provision. However, as mentioned earlier, if a company is used this could trigger the application of the Finance Act 2000 rules on the provision of services through intermediaries.

The freelance instructor

8.21 The infrastructure of the equestrian world is supported by the freelance instructor and equestrian trainers.

As mentioned earlier the changing nature of the equestrian world has brought a move away from riding schools to livery yards and pony paddocks and this has meant that instruction and tuition is now often provided on a freelance basis. There are a number of types of freelance instructor: those who teach the very basics of riding, those who carry out work for a number of riding schools, the pony clubs and those who work for individual clients with their own ponies and their own paddocks. Some instructors are effectively equestrian trainers rather than a freelance instructor. The equestrian trainer has an expertise in a discipline such as polo or show jumping, dressage etc, and they will have a client base that they teach or train.

Sometimes the individual will combine this with competing themselves, there is no set pattern. Sometimes they will subsidise their income by carrying out regular duties at, say, a trainer's yard, riding out a couple of lots early in the morning so they have time to instruct their clients later.

In view of the English winter it is very difficult to carry out instruction work during those months unless there is the facility of an indoor school. Some such instructors might seek positions abroad in winter or carry out work for freelance livery yards or riding stables, particularly those with the jump racing or all-weather disciplines which need help.

The first question to be addressed is whether or not such individuals are genuinely and effectively self-employed? (See further **CHAPTER 12** which deals with the issue of employment.) In some cases it will be clear that part of an individual's working life falls into the self-employed category and part falls into the employed category.

It will be necessary to consider whether or not turnover is sufficient to warrant VAT registration. (See **CHAPTER 17: PLANNING FOR VAT**.) Similarly, there may come a time when it is advisable to consider whether or not the income has risen to a level at which the individual ought to consider incorporation so as to save on tax and National Insurance. (See also **CHAPTER 9: THE EQUINE BUSINESS STRUCTURE**.)

Other issues to be considered would be the maximisation of expense claims, such as claims for the business use of the home. These individuals will also face other problems that a lot of members of the equestrian community have to consider such as keeping accurate books and records and ensuring that, above all, any cash transactions are recorded. Where the individual keeps their own horse which is also used for riding lessons, what will be the relative business and private proportions?

Often a freelance instructor will combine this work with running a livery yard, thus producing a combination of different income streams. Again, the income level and the liability for VAT registration must be kept in mind along with whether the freelance work should be run as a separate business from the livery yard.

It is unlikely that there will be any higher rates of income tax to shelter in these cases. Such freelance work tends in many cases not to be highly rewarded and might almost be categorised to be a labour of love. The work is often carried out to subsidise the costs of the individual competing on their own horse. Clarity between business and personal use of items such as the horse, the motor vehicle used in the trade, the equipment used for the business etc must be achieved.

The position of freelance instructor may evolve from a leisure activity or hobby over a period of time. The key issues for the tax adviser here are ensuring that the business is registered within three months of starting to trade so as to avoid the £100 fine and to try and capture the correct recording of pre-trading expenditure. It might be that the income is of a sundry nature before the business starts and decisions will have to be made by the tax planner as to whether this should be recorded as sundry income on the tax return or a formal Schedule D source of income and dealt with accordingly.

Some equestrian employers who have a 'transient workforce' try to redefine as many as possible as self-employed or freelance. Here it will be essential for tax adviser to help these newly freelance staff understand all the concepts and rigours of self-employment such as Class 2 and Class 4 National Insurance contributions, proper books and records, the requirements of the self-assessment tax return, the accounting period and what expenses count as business and which do not etc, not to mention all the other commercial and legal liability aspects of running and risking a business activity on one's own account.

The tax planner might be faced with a difficulty over whether the relationship really qualifies as employed or self-employed and the standard rules will apply here. See also in this context **CHAPTER 12: EMPLOYMENT ISSUES**.

Other activities of the professional horseman

8.22 The basic disciplines of polo, eventing, dressage, show jumping, showing etc, were explained in **CHAPTER 1**. Each of these disciplines has within their structure professionals who earn their living from their specific area of sport, perhaps through being paid to ride an owner's horse, instructing (as mentioned at **8.21** above) or owning a string of horses on which to compete. The source of income comes from a combination of riding fees, winnings, profit on sales of horses and sponsorship.

Often the professional horseman will also run a competition yard or a livery yard to support their earnings and, as a result, what starts out as a simple professional sports activity can expand into a complex business, rather than the trade of a freelance individual (see CHAPTER **18**). Like all areas of the equestrian world there is no standard format and there is often a thin line between the professional and the non-professional and an equally thin line between the amateur and the fully-developed professional business.

The harsh reality is that to survive as a professional in the equestrian world, sponsorship money is needed and invariably the activities have to be underpinned by selling good horses or bringing on young horses or trying to combine a multitude of income streams to survive. The income streams can range from appearance monies, gifts from owners for successes, television appearance money, instruction and conferences. This can create a minefield of tax compliance work for the tax adviser before moving on to tax planning work.

Some of the points that should be considered are, as always, the differentiation between business and hobby, the clarification of ownership of the horse – is it a business asset or not? Does owning a horse come under the category of racing? If so, will it be tax-free? The tax adviser will have to be aware of some equine professionals who would argue that if they made a large profit on a horse it was for their personal use and if they made a loss it was a horse they used in their business.

Employed professional sportsmen – diverting income

8.23 Highly paid sportsmen have traditionally tried to 'divert income'. Although this would only apply to a handful of professional sportsmen, it is worth considering further.

An interesting case on whether income is received by virtue of the employment is *O'Leary v McKinlay [1991] STC 42*. David O'Leary was resident in England and domiciled in Ireland. His employer, Arsenal FC Ltd, entered into an arrangement designed to pay him an additional £28,985 per annum. To achieve this, a third party set up a Jersey trust with a nominal £10. Arsenal lent the trustees £266,000 interest free and repayable on demand. The trustees invested this to produce £28,985. This money was paid to O'Leary but not remitted by him to the UK. He contended that this income was income from a foreign possession taxable under Case V of Schedule D on a remittance basis. It was held, however, that it was an emolument of his employment and thus assessable under employment income on a rising basis.

The test in this case posed by Vinelott J was 'how would an ordinary member of the public have perceived the money?' He would have said without hesitation that it was an emolument of the taxpayer's employment by Arsenal. The judge was very much influenced by the fact that there was an overall scheme. If an employer lent money to an employee interest free and the employee was free to exploit the money in any manner he chose, his employment could not be said to be the source of the income it generated. However, in O'Leary's case he never had the free use of the £266,000. The purpose of the arrangement was to provide him with the income of £28,985. The trustees could not have invested it in any other manner without O'Leary's consent (and undoubtedly Arsenal's too).

The reason for setting out this case is to show that there are many interesting ways of trying to minimise the tax due by professional sportsmen. The higher profit element of the taxpayers in question almost certainly means that they can expect greater scrutiny from the Inland Revenue of their affairs. The warning is clear!

Full-time education and providing for the future

8.24 The professional sportsman has the risks of injury, the need to capture income in a short earning space, to provide for a further career and to provide for early retirement.

CHAPTER **20** deals with the financial planning elements of this subject.

The past is littered with those professionals who have not maximised the opportunities of providing for the future.

With the problems of obtaining staff in the equine industry the tax relief position on full-time education courses should not be overlooked. Likewise for the young (and in some cases not so young) professional starting out as this can be very tax efficient. Payments made by employers to employees for periods of attendance on a full-time educational course, including a 'sandwich' course, are regarded as covered by the general exemption for scholarship income in the following circumstances:

- the employee is enrolled at a university, technical college or similar external establishment for at least one academic year;
- the employee actually attends that establishment for an aggregate period of at least 20 weeks a year; and
- the rate of payment (including lodging, subsistence and travel expenses, but excluding any course fees paid by the employee) does not exceed £7,000 per annum (£5,500 prior to 6 April 1992) (SP 4/86 as amended by IR Press Release 1 November 1992).

If the payments exceed £7,000 per annum, the whole amount, not merely the excess, is taxable. If it can be shown that a public grant-awarding body, such as a research council, would have paid a higher grant to an individual in similar personal circumstances, the exemption is increased to that higher amount. The relief does not apply to payments to the employee for periods actually spent working for the employer – whether during vacations or term time. Nor does it apply to education at an employer's own training centre or one run by an employer's association.

The Equine Business Structure 9

Benefits of sole trader/partnership

9.1 The unincorporated business plays an important, if not vital, role in the equine world. Many, if not most, businesses start their life as a sole trade or partnership.

The key initial tax planning point for the equine business is that an unincorporated structure is also preferable if the early years are likely to produce trading losses. A sole trader/partner would normally be able to claim prompt repayment of income tax by making a loss relief claims against their other current or prior income (of the three previous years) under sections 380 and 381 of ICTA 1988 respectively. If such losses fall within a company they could not be relieved until it generated profits (see **CHAPTER 11: PLANNING FOR LOSSES**).

There are no legal formalities in establishing a partnership (other than one under the Limited Partnerships Act 1907 or the Limited Liability Partnerships Act 2000) and a written agreement is not necessary, although it is advisable. The mutual rights and duties of partners, whether ascertained by agreement or defined by the Partnership Act 1890, may be varied by the consent of all the partners, such consent being either express or inferred from their actions (Partnership Act 1890 s 19).

Whether or not a partnership exists is a mixed question of fact and law, and it is obviously more difficult to prove the existence of a partnership if there is no written agreement. But the mere existence of a written agreement is not proof, and it must be supported by the facts (see, for example, *Dickenson v Gross KB (1927) 11 TC 614).* The Inland Revenue may require proof that there is a partnership by requesting sight of contracts, agreements, VAT registration details and bank accounts. On the other hand, a partnership may be regarded as existing even though the individuals considered they were not partners

(*Fenston v Johnstone (1940) 23 TC 29*). There are many cases in which the existence of a partnership has been considered by the courts.

Decision to incorporate (or not?)

9.2 The decision to incorporate must not be undertaken lightly. Once a company is formed, for the decision to be reversed it has to be sold, wound-up or 'struck-off'.

Accounts have to be filed at Companies House and there are administrative concerns that should be given consideration as well as the tax advantages and disadvantages. In some cases for equine businesses the tax disadvantages can be punishing.

In the current climate, many professional practices such as vets are looking to incorporate their partnerships subject to their professional body's approval. Likewise, with farriers and other successful equestrian establishments.

Once a certain level of profit has been achieved, a company may now offer many clear advantages over sole trade or partnership but the equestrian world must not be unduly influenced by this incorporation fever (see **9.18** below).

Undoubtedly the current fiscal infrastructure is balanced heavily in favour of companies, particularly in relation to the taxation of retained profits on capital distributions. While remuneration drawn from a company is taxed and suffers National Insurance contribution (NIC) liabilities less favourably than the profits/drawings of an unincorporated business, this difficulty is usually minimised by extracting the required amount of profits as dividend which do not attract PAYE or NICs (subject, of course, to IR35 considerations).

Limited liability partnership

9.3 Professional practices such as vets can involve a large number of partners, which may itself present distinct problems. A half-way stage is to go down the limited liability partnership (LLP) route. The increasing number of practices displaying LLP next to their trading name indicates that this is becoming an increasingly popular route.

Whilst looking at the advantages of the limited liability partnership, all practices may consider going one stage further and fully incorporating the practice. There are a number of advantages in incorporation for the professional practice, these include: the fundamental principle of limited liability, an easier method of allocating profits, a clear structure illustrating the share holdings of the owners and directors and a shareholders' agreement which can be a more flexible document than a partnership agreement. There are also potential tax savings as set out below.

Potential tax savings of limited company

9.4 This was first considered at **2.9** above.

Incorporation brings with it some distinct tax advantages and specific reliefs. These include the first £10,000 of profits being taxed at nil%, the ability to take money out of the company through dividends without any National Insurance problems and the ability to retain profits in the company at a much lower rate of tax.

Due to recent changes in tax legislation, it is probably true to say that almost all profitable sole traders and partnerships would save at least some tax and NICs by forming a limited company. However, many equestrian businesses may not conform to this rule (see **7.4** above).

The structure that gives the most potential tax savings is generally based upon the assumption that only a small salary will be drawn from the company and that the rest of the profit will be paid as dividends. The reasons behind these assumptions are explained in more detail below. However, where the proprietor can afford to leave funds in the company, then the tax saved (or at least deferred) could be even greater. This would particularly be the case where the proprietor would otherwise have paid income tax at the higher rate of 40% by drawing the funds retained in the company. References apply to sole traders, but, suitably adapted, the comments would also apply to partners. The impact on high earning professionals in the business is obvious.

The tax benefits of incorporation are dealt with at **10.5** and **10.17** to **10.21**.

Salary versus dividends in the company

9.5 Until a couple of years ago, most accountants and tax advisers would not recommend forming a company until a sole trader's profits had reached at least around £45,000. However, that was only the approximate break-even point. There was little tax saving at that level unless the client could either afford to leave excess profits in the company (though they would be taxed later if withdrawn) or it he/she were able to take drawings in the form of dividends rather then salary.

The distinction between dividends and salary is important. As far as the company proprietor (a shareholder-director) is concerned, a dividend is taxed more favourably than salary. He/she pays no income tax on dividends if his/her taxable income does not exceed the basic rate of income tax, £30,500 (£35,115 – if you take into account basic personal allowances) for 2003/04. If the 'proprietors' income takes him/her into the higher rate, he/she only pays tax on dividends (which are treated as the top slice of income) at a rate of 32.5%. This produces an effective rate of only 25% on the net dividend received by the shareholder. This compares with the normal 40% he/she would pay on salary or which they would have paid on profits earned as a sole trader. Secondly, National Insurance is not due on dividends, while it is on both salary and a sole trader's profit.

Choice of equine company name

9.6 In broad terms, those forming a company are free to choose any name for it provided that

- it is not too similar to an existing company name;
- it does not infringe another's trade or service mark;
- it is not offensive; and
- its use would not be a criminal offence.

Some words and expressions may be used in company names only with official consent. Examples of such 'sensitive' words include 'British', 'international', 'holding', 'group', 'royal' and 'United Kingdom'. This could be of relevance to many equine businesses.

A UK company may also use a business or trading name under which to conduct its business. The only restrictions on a business name are that it:

- is not too similar to another business name; and
- does not require prior official approval because it contains 'sensitive' words.

As a safeguard for customers, suppliers and others, a company must show its company name on all business letters and contracts, including invoices.

Equine directors' duties and responsibilities

9.7 The directors of a UK company are appointed by the shareholders and are typically entrusted with the day-to-day management and conduct of the business and to represent the company in its dealings with the outside world. There are various legal safeguards to prevent any abuse of power by company directors. Directors have both statutory and common law duties and are subject to a large number of restrictions and controls.

Directors must exercise due skill and care in carrying out their duties but no specific qualifications are required. They must disclose certain personal information to the company and to Companies House to be kept with the public records of the company, eg date of birth, residential address and other directorships.

Like the shareholders, directors of a limited company are generally protected from personal liability. In extreme cases, however, directors may be personally liable for any wrongdoing on their part. A director's duty is first and foremost to act honestly and in the best interests of the company itself rather than individual shareholders. A director also owes a duty to the company's creditors and must have a regard to the interests of the company's employees. Directors must not make a secret profit from their position as directors (ie without the company's consent) nor show bad faith towards the company.

The Companies Act 1985 also imposes various restrictions on directors to ensure fair play by them in relation to the company's business and assets. For example, a company is generally prohibited from lending money to its directors and directors must declare any interest which they have personally in any contract or arrangement which the company proposes to enter into.

Directors are not appointed for any fixed period and may be removed by the shareholders at any time. In small private companies, the directors are typically all executive directors. They are, therefore, employees of the company and may enjoy the benefit of service agreements (employment contracts) which will govern the company's ability to remove them whether with or without compensation. In larger companies or in subsidiaries, it is typical for some, if not all, of the directors to be non-executive.

Meetings – directors and shareholders

9.8 Given their authority to bind the company, the directors should hold regular board meetings to make important decisions concerning the company. The Companies Act 1985 does not expressly require meetings of directors to be held. Nonetheless, it is difficult for directors to establish that they have acted properly unless they meet regularly. This is often overlooked by the equine business.

Whilst the management of a company is, in effect, delegated by the shareholders to its directors, a company must generally hold an annual general meeting of its shareholders to deal with the regular shareholder business (such as presentation of the annual accounts). Other specific types of transaction or business require the directors to obtain shareholder approval and to call extraordinary general meetings as required. The Companies Act 1985 specifies the period of notice required for all types of shareholder meetings although a private company may elect to dispense with various notice requirements and certain other specific requirements of the Companies Act 1985. In addition, shareholders may pass resolutions in writing without needing to meet formally. A similar option is open to the directors if the articles of association of the company permit (as they usually do).

Records of all directors' and shareholders' meetings should be kept in the form of formal minutes.

Administration and records of the company

9.9 All UK companies must (unless they are dormant), keep accounting records and prepare annual accounts, which require them to prepare a profit and loss account and balance sheet for each financial year. The accounts are subject to strict requirements as to form and content in the Companies Act 1985. A UK company must not only appoint accountants to prepare its accounts but it must also file its accounts at Companies House within ten months of the end of its accounting reference period. Only dormant and small companies escape the additional legal requirement that accounts should be audited. The auditors and the directors must report to the shareholders on the accounts.

In addition to accounting records, a company must keep statutory registers recording details of directors and company secretaries, directors' interests in shares or debentures of the company, shareholders, charges and mortgages affecting the company's assets and debenture holders.

Statutory restrictions on company activities

9.10 The Companies Act 1985 is designed to ensure that in return for the limited liability of shareholders, companies are regulated so as to protect their creditors. This leads to various general restrictions on day-to-day corporate activities. For example, a UK company is either not permitted or is permitted, but only subject to certain conditions, to:

- pay dividends other than out of distributable profits;
- purchase its own shares;
- give financial assistance to a person to enable that person to buy shares in the company;
- reduce its share capital.

Overseas companies

Setting up in the UK – the choices

9.11 This book does not have the scope to deal with the overseas tax planning but aims to present some very basic information surrounding the overseas company trading in the UK. It can also be of importance for those in the equine world trading with overseas companies in the UK to be aware of some of the basic principles. Equine company transactions can be of high value and in need of protection.

If an overseas company decides to set up business there are three options. It can:

- establish a representative office;
- establish a branch;
- set up a separate UK subsidiary company.

In deciding whether to set up a representative office, branch or subsidiary, a company and its shareholders/directors must consider the commercial objectives, the nature and scale of the proposed activities in the UK and the potential tax treatment of the preferred structure.

There are no statutory definitions of the terms 'representative office' and 'branch'. However, the distinction is important because of the different tax treatment applied by the UK tax authorities to a branch and a representative office.

Representative office

9.12 The term 'representative office' is used to describe an office that advertises and promotes the business of its head office. It typically collects and distributes information and introduces and refers potential customers to its head office abroad. To maintain its status as a representative office (which is relevant for tax purposes), it should not negotiate to conclude contracts directly with local customers and third parties.

If the overseas company does not operate through a UK resident subsidiary, it will be subject to UK tax on its trading income only if it is carrying on a trade *in* the UK. Whether the UK business activities make the company liable to UK tax will depend upon whether the company is trading *in* or trading *with* the UK. In general, the following factors are relevant in determining whether a business is trading in the UK:

- where the contracts are concluded;
- where the goods or services are supplied;
- where any goods are manufactured;
- where the purchase price is paid.

Overseas branch

9.13 A 'branch' is part of an overseas limited company organised to conduct business through local employees in the UK rather than referring that business abroad. The term 'branch' therefore implies a permanent place of business, which has its own management and is authorised to negotiate contracts with third parties without reference to head office.

UK subsidiary company

9.14 The most common form of company in the UK is the private company limited by shares. It is also the most popular choice for overseas businesses setting up a UK subsidiary company.

'Stuck with a limited company from a former life'

9.15 The problems of asset ownership in the limited company have been well documented. The significant lack of BATR for assets owned by the company under the current CGT regime in the UK should be carefully considered by tax planners. The limited company is, however, eligible for rollover relief on assets that it owns.

Some tax planning problems can arise when an equestrian business is purchased. Purchasers sometimes want to buy assets, not a limited company. In these days of risk avoidance and the pressures of due diligence, the desire for the purchaser to avoid the risks inherent in a share purchase is obvious. The vendor of the business (the investor in the new equine business) is therefore stuck with the limited company which holds all the proceeds from the sale of the company's business.

Suggestions are first for a sale of shares but sometimes commercial considerations overcome tax planning and there is no alternative but an asset sale.

The problem with this is that the gain on the asset has to be rolled over into the assets of a new business, which may be another equestrian business, although this is not a requirement of the tax provisions for rollover relief. With careful planning this can be achieved with £nil tax *but* the end result will be that the new equestrian business is again owned in the limited company with all the attendant compliance and tax issues, such as benefits in kind and potentially trapped trading losses which this brings. In addition, there will be the need to try to ensure that, for the future, the business owner's shares qualify for BATR and BPR or APR for inheritance tax. In particular, where a company contains investment type assets valued at more than 20% of the balance sheet, this may invalidate the business asset taper relief qualifying status of the shares.

It is therefore important to consider whether the assets of equine business should stay in the limited company or be taken out. Also to push for a share sale as opposed to an asset sale has obvious advantages in future transactions to minimise capital gains tax.

Incorporate only part of the business

Full incorporation not possible

9.16 Full incorporation is not the only possibility. It may be that other structures rather than a straightforward incorporation of the whole business might be appropriate. For example, incorporation of the higher risk activities leaving unincorporated the non- or lower-risk areas.

The main initial benefit for smaller business from the corporate structure is the current availability of the first £10,000 at a £nil corporation tax. It may, therefore, be possible to isolate one suitable part of a business and to incorporate it – thus provide this level of profit tax free.

However, quite apart from the tax problems associated with incorporating part of a business, the FA 2000 Sch 12 rules (IR35) may also throw up some difficulties which could invalidate the strategy.

There could be VAT advantages of a split business, but the potential for a challenge from HM Customs & Excise over business 'disaggregation' must be kept in mind.

Partnership with a limited company

9.17 Whilst at first sight, this seems to add complications by requiring two sets of financial statements, it has some interesting possibilities. In England and Wales (the position is different in Scotland) the partners do not own a particular share of partnership assets; they own a share of the partnership as a whole. This means that the financial statements of the company will be straightforward, showing the interest in the partnership as an asset at cost, and the partnership share of income as a one-line entry for revenue. The only expenses will be those specific to the company (Companies House fees etc) and anything that is deliberately put through the company because it is more tax efficient (eg a mobile phone in the company's name).

The partnership sharing ratio would be skewed towards the company, but should not be as extreme as to permit an argument that profits are not really being 'shared'. The following might be appropriate:

- first £4,000 to the individual;
- next £35,000 to the company.

Any profits above this to be split 5% to the individual and 95% to the company.

The company could then pay a small salary to the individual for acting as a company director, which would justify pension contributions being made direct from the company if desired.

Assets would generally be partnership assets, and the problem of the company car would therefore not arise. There is, however, a rather complex relationship between the rule for taxing corporate partnerships and the general principle that capital allowances are now given as a deduction in computing the profits of the trade.

ICTA 1988 s 114(1) requires the profits of the partnership to be calculated as if it was a company initially, but without any deduction for capital allowances. The partnership split is then carried out, and section 114(2) then charges the company to tax on its part of the profits as if it was from a trade carried on by the company alone. At this point, the capital allowances do not come into the calculation. However, since the company does not actually own the assets it is not always entirely clear how to attribute them. This book does not have the scope to go into this in greater depth. The aim is to flag up the potential and highlight the need for review.

Incorporation 'fever' – the practical problem

9.18 At the time of writing, incorporation fever has dominated the UK tax world because undoubtedly, as set out at **9.4** above, the UK tax regime favours companies.

Whether a limited company is a suitable vehicle for many small businesses is one of concern. A company is a legal entity in its own right and one perennial problem for accountants and tax advisers is making clients understand that they cannot treat the company's assets as their personal property.

A limited company is regulated by the Companies Act 1985 and by its own written constitution. It must file accounts annually with Companies House and is subject to more onerous record keeping and other requirements than unincorporated businesses. Moreover, a company's accounts, albeit in an abbreviated format, are public information and may be accessed by creditors, competitors, etc. The equine industry is known for its desire for privacy.

Although a company does not require an audit where its turnover for any year is below £1m, the preparation of company accounts is likely to cost more in professional fees than would those of a sole trader. This is because the company's records will generally be more extensive, and accounts must be prepared in accordance with accepted accounting practice as laid down by a joint committee of the various professional accountancy bodies.

Another practical problem is that the proprietor becomes an employee of the company and is therefore subject to quite harsh rules over the claiming of expenses against any salary or other employment income. This is looked at in CHAPTER **15**: THE EQUESTRIAN LANDLORD – TAX PLANNING and should not be overlooked when reviewing the decision to incorporate.

The benefits in kind tax charges in respect of motor vehicles should also be borne in mind.

It is not easy for financially unsophisticated sole traders to get to grips with the complexities of operating as a limited company. If, for example, drawings are made without regard to whether they consist of salary, dividends or withdrawals from a director's loan account, this will cause accounting problems and may give rise to claims from the Inland Revenue for PAYE income tax and National Insurance. Any tax savings may easily be eaten up in additional professional costs in sorting out such problems. Therefore, before recommending that a sole trader should form a company, the professional adviser needs to explain what is involved and the client needs to be sure that he can cope with the requirements.

Once brought into existence, a company cannot simply be abandoned if no longer required. Formal procedures must be completed to dissolve the company, and until then annual accounts must be prepared and filed with Companies House (even if the company is no longer active). Substantial penalties may be imposed for failing to meet Companies Act 1985 requirements.

If a business disposal takes place by way of a sale, often the purchaser will want to acquire the individual assets and not the shares as has been said already. The purchaser's legal advisers will be worried about hidden liabilities and risks associated with shares. The onerous task of due diligence, will often push the buyer towards asset purchase, which can have onerous tax consequences. There is no BATR (see **9.6** above) within a company. It could be that the main asset purchased will be goodwill. The shares of a trading company do generally attract BATR but assets it holds do not. This could have serious tax disadvantages.

An important non-tax advantage, which is fundamental to the attractions of a limited company, is that its liabilities are limited to its available funds. The personal assets of its shareholders are thus not exposed to claims of creditors of the company. This is perhaps not quite as attractive as it sounds, since banks will generally require personal guarantees from the directors/shareholders where the company needs to raise finance. However, a company is able to give a 'floating charge' over all its assets as security, which is unique to limited companies.

A major shake-up of private pensions happened in April 2001 when the new stakeholder pension's rules were introduced. Under the old rules, an individual had to have relevant earnings in order to make pension payments, and these were limited to a proportion of those earnings depending upon age. Under the new rules, up to £3,600 a year can be paid into a stakeholder policy without any evidence of earnings, and above that level it is only necessary to provide evidence of earnings once every six years. For pension planning, see CHAPTER **20**.

As far as the proprietor of a company is concerned, it will normally be better to take dividends rather than salary. Under the new rules, as long as once every six years he/she pays himself/herself enough salary to support the level of pension contributions, in the intervening five years he/she can draw dividends instead. In fact, the detailed rules provide that a payment can be made only once every eleven years in cases where no remuneration at all is paid for the last five of those years.

Operating the six-year salary/dividend strategy has become standard tax planning. However, care is needed because drawing funds from the company as a dividend requires appropriate paperwork to be completed, and the more frequently dividends are drawn, the more paperwork there is.

A company must also have sufficient 'reserves', ie accumulated profits after tax, out of which to pay the dividend or otherwise it is unlawful.

It is a requirement that companies show a note of related party transactions in their accounts. It was noted that a set of company accounts are for the public record. Again, this can be a cause of much 'angst' among the equine business world who also want ultimate discretion in all matters equine. They are often very 'private'.

The onerous disclosure requirements of the Companies Act 1985 and the directives from the joint accounting bodies should be made fully aware to the equine client.

There are circumstances of potential risk which will leave the equine businessman to seek the protection of limited liability. The tax adviser must obviously warn of all the tax advantages and disadvantages of such a decision.

Overview of Equine Business Taxation 10

Benefits of the UK equine tax position

10.1 The author would like to defend the advantages of the UK equine tax system. Racing is tax-free in the UK. If there are large amounts of tax losses achieved in the UK, with good UK tax planning these can be captured very tax-efficiently.

The current UK tax reliefs are very favourable towards business assets for both capital gains tax and inheritance tax and very valuable tax reliefs can be achieved, especially with regard to studs and farming.

All overseas aspects should also be carefully reviewed when carrying out tax planning for a client overseas as these can often produce additional tax-saving potential.

Income tax rates and allowances

Income tax and personal savings

10.2 At this point it is worth looking at the full rates of income tax, which are applicable to 2003/04 (and 2002/03).

Income tax rates	*2003/04*	*2002/03*
Starting rate tax band to	£1,960	£1,920
Tax rate	10%	10%
Basic rate band – next	£28,540	£27,980
Non-savings rate	22%	22%
Savings rate	20%	20%
UK dividend rate	10%	10%
Higher rate – income over	£30,000	£29,900
Tax rate excluding UK dividends	40%	40%
UK dividend rate	32.5%	32.5%

Personal allowances

10.3 Rates announced for 2003/04 are as follows (ages at the end of the tax year).

	Age	*2003/04*	*2002/03*
Allowances that reduce taxable income:			
Personal allowance	Under 65	£4,615.00	£4,615.00
	65 to 74*	£6,610.00	£6,100.00
	75 and over*	£6,720.00	£6,370.00
Allowances that reduce tax:			
Married couple's allowance	Under 75*	£556.50	£546.50
Age of elder spouse	75 and over*	£563.50	£553.50
	minimum	£215.00	£211.00

* Higher allowances for those aged 65 or more are scaled back when income exceeds £18,300.

Tax credits

10.4 Two new tax credits – Child Tax Credit and Working Tax Credit – replace the Children's Tax Credit, Working Families' Tax Credit and Disabled Person's Tax Credit from April 2003.

Rates vary, but people on middle incomes may qualify, especially where they are paying for childcare. For more information visit the Inland Revenue's website at www.taxcredits.inlandrevenue.gov.uk/Kome.aspx.

Tax benefits of incorporation

10.5 One of the changes as a result of the Finance Act 2002 was to the rate of tax payable by companies making only small profits. From 1 April 2002, a company will pay no corporation tax if its profit for any year does not exceed £10,000. Thus, a sole trader making profits of up to about £15,000 a year could pay no tax or National Insurance at all, or only negligible amounts, by incorporating his business, compared with total tax and National Insurance payable as a sole trade of about £2,900 a year. To achieve this, he would take a salary from the company of no more than the National Insurance primary threshold. This is the level of earnings above which National Insurance becomes payable, and is the same as the income tax personal allowance, ie. £4,615 for 2003/04.

The salary paid is deducted from the company's taxable profit, which would reduce it from £15,000 to just over £10,000. Money drawn as dividends does not reduce the company's profit for corporation tax, but the company pays no corporation tax if its profits do not exceed £10,000 (here there would be a small corporation tax liability of about £90 as the profit would exceed £10,000 by £385). As far as the proprietor is concerned, the salary would be 'covered' by his personal allowance and the dividends drawn are clearly within the lower rate and basic rate band of up to £30,500.

The result is no income tax to pay. No National Insurance is due either, since the salary drawn is equal to the primary threshold, although for State pension purposes, credit is given as if contributions had been paid on a salary of £10,000.

Clearly, the company has distinct advantages to the sole trade service providers in the equine world, such as the freelance jockey or groom who works for a number of yards in the Lambourne/Newmarket area. Similarly, farriers could also benefit.

The position of losses in the limited company are dealt with at **11.18** below.

The disadvantages are that the earnings might be caught under the IR35 regime. It has been possible for people such as nannies and gardeners working for private individuals to set up service companies and thus avoid PAYE and NI by paying themselves via a dividend. This created an anomaly in that individuals supplying such services to a business would have been caught under IR35. The Finance Act 2003 incorporated measures which, broadly speaking will bring such individuals within the IR35 regime. The new rules apply to services provided after 9 April 2003.

There are problems of incorporating an equine business. The two key factors associated with equestrian businesses are that they often involve tax losses and they own land that is needed for the activity. This presents two problems.

First, losses can be trapped in the company without the right of offset against total income and, secondly, a limited company that owns assets such as land and stables does not receive Business Asset Taper Relief (BATR) for CGT, on those assets. The shares in the company (provided that it is a trading company) would attract BATR.

The answer to this can be to have ownership of the land and stables in individual names and the 'trade' carried on by the limited company if no real losses are anticipated. The legal/tax relationship between the owner of the land and the trading company must be carefully reviewed.

Corporation tax rates

10.6 The corporation tax rates and bands are as follows.

Financial year to:	**31 March 2004**		**31 March 2003**	
Taxable profits	*Amount*	*Percentage*	*Amount*	*Percentage*
First	£10,000	0%	£10,000	0%
Next	£40,000	23.75%	£40,000	23.75%
Next	£250,000	19%	£250,000	19%
Next	£1,200,000	32.75%	£1,200,000	32.75%
Over	£1,500,000	30%	£1,500,000	30%

Small company's marginal relief fraction		
£10,000–£50,000	19/400	19/400
£300,000–£1,500,000	11/400	11/400

Equine plant and machinery

10.7 Plant and machinery is very important to loss planning so it is relevant to consider the definition of plant and machinery and how it can be used to help maximise tax relievable losses or reduce taxable profits.

Plant and machinery are not defined in statute so must be given their ordinary commonsense meaning. Whilst machinery is rarely the subject of debate, the nature of plant has been considered in many decided cases.

Permanent employment demands some degree of durability, see *Hinton (Inspector of Taxes) v Maden and Ireland Ltd [1959] 3 All ER 356, 38 TC 391* (in which a shoe manufacturer's knives and lasts, with an average life of three years, were held to be plant). In practice, a useful life of two years or more is sufficient, and this applies equally as regards animals functioning as apparatus with which a trade is carried on (see Revenue Capital Allowances Manual CA 1540, 1571). To this end, it is worth quoting from the Inland Revenue's Inspector's Manual 21220: 'CAA 2001 s 38':

> 'Accept a claim for PMAs on an animal if the animal functions as apparatus with which the trade is carried on and it has an expected life of two years or more. For example, it is likely that a horse used in a riding school or show jumping business, a guard dog or a circus animal is plant.

> Do **not** accept a claim that a farm animal such as a horse, cow or sheep is plant, unless it is a working animal such as a sheep dog. Farm animals are normally trading stock and their cost is revenue expenditure which bars a capital allowance claim. Alternatively, the farmer may have made an election for the herd basis under ICTA 1988, Sch 5, para 2. This also means no capital allowances may be made claimed on these animals.
>
> You should treat a share in an animal in the same way.'

Clear examples of equine plant and machinery are show jumps, horse walkers, and schooling fences. Further examples of plant and machinery where there could be some debate with the Inland Revenue are:

- fire alarm systems;
- sprinklers and other equipment for extinguishing or containing fires;
- burglar alarm systems;
- swimming pools;
- movable buildings (eg temporary stabling and staff accommodation);
- towers to support floodlights (eg use in outdoor school);
- solariums;
- box heaters.

40% first year allowances are available on plant and machinery subject to the threshold for small and medium-sized businesses. 100% first year capital allowances on investments in IT up until 31 March 2004 for qualifying 'small' businesses (see **10.9** and **10.20** below).

In practice, few horses are capitalised as plant. *Stanley: Taxation for Farmers and Landowners* (LexisNexis UK) says that farm animals can be treated as plant or stock but the treatment must be *consistent.* Most working horses are, in practice, always for sale and therefore more likely to be shown as stock. If capitalised working horses would attract 40% first year allowance so it is always relevant to consider whether capitalisation or stock treatment will achieve faster tax relief. If the net realisable value is likely to fall below cost, then 'stock' treatment is likely to be preferable.

Plant and machinery includes apparatus kept for permanent employment in the trade etc, but a line is drawn between that which performs a function in the business operations (which may be plant) and that which provides the place or setting in which these operations are performed (which is not). See *Cole Bros Ltd v Phillips [1982] 2 All ER 247, 55 TC 188* (electric wiring and fittings in department store held not to be plant) and *St John's School v Ward [1974] STC 69, 49 TC 524* (prefabricated school buildings held not to be plant).

The case of *Yarmouth v France (1887) 19 QBD 647* concerned the 'function test' for plant. In this instance a vicious horse was considered plant because it was used for haulage.

If an item used for carrying on a business does not form part of the premises and is not stock-in-trade, then it may be plant (*Wimpy International Ltd V Warland [1989] STC 273, 61 TC 51*) (lighting and décor of licensed premises held to be plant).

Equine establishments should ensure that when property improvements are carried out or new buildings are erected, the correct apportionments are made to plant and machinery expenditures in order to maximise eligibility for capital allowances. All plans for new stables, stud offices and indoor schools etc, should be examined carefully with a close eye on what allowances could be available on included plant and machinery expenditures: here *Wimpey International Ltd v Warland* will probably be highly relevant.

Unfortunately, the Inland Revenue currently strongly resists claims for capital allowances in respect of all-weather riding surfaces and since 1995 has taken the line that these surfaces do not qualify for capital allowances.

Some guidance on the types of items which can qualify as plant can be found in *Jarrold (Inspector of Taxes) v John Good & Sons Ltd [1962] 1 All ER 141, 40 TC 681* which considered the status of movable office partitions and *(Schofield v R & H Hall Ltd [1975] STC 353, 49 TC 538)* which dealt with grain silos.

Each addition to plant and machinery or improvement to a building (eg lighting for an indoor school) or any new building work must be reviewed on its own merits. The choice between what to include in, or exclude from, a capital allowances claim can be an important tax planning tool.

The availability of capital allowances and the Inland Revenue's response to claims throws up a number of grey areas in the equestrian world, eg sand schools, new fencing as opposed to replacement fencing, sports surfaces and specialised lighting for indoor arenas etc.

One of the most important criteria is the distinction between something which is performing a business function and something which is merely providing the workplace or business setting or premises. Again, each has to be looked at on its own merits. Other areas sometimes questioned are claims in respect of expenditures on saddlery and riding/horse equipment which can be a direct cost (and carried forward at the year end in stock) or dealt with as 'apparatus'.

Capital allowances on equine staff accommodation

10.8 Caravans can be used for equine staff accommodation. They do qualify as plant on which capital allowances may be given, provided the caravan does not occupy a fixed site and is regularly moved as part of normal trade usage, even if it is only moved from its summer site to winter quarters.

Caravans occupying residential sites do not qualify as plant for capital allowances purposes, the exception being a caravan provided by a farmer to house a farm employee, which may qualify as 'plant' even if the caravan occupies a fixed site and is used solely for residential purposes.

Most equestrian businesses use caravans from time to time as temporary accommodation etc and maximum tax relief should be claimed where appropriate.

The availability of agricultural building allowances (ABA) on stud farm staff accommodation should also be considered by the tax planner (see **10.11** below).

IT Capital allowances – tax advantages

10.9 As mentioned at **10.7** above, 100% first year capital allowances are available to small enterprises for expenditure on computers and information and communications technology until 31 March 2004. This measure was welcomed by many equine businesses, especially those which will be redesigned as 'small' enterprises when the definition is realigned later in 2003. The definition of 'small and medium-sized enterprises' is also set to change, extending the availability of the 40% first year allowance on most plant and machinery.

The timing of the purchase of equine plant and machinery and especially IT equipment is often an essential element of tax effective loss planning. As mentioned, capital allowances can increase a loss as well as reduce a profit and the 100% relief on IT expenditure prior to 31 March 2004 represents a clear example of this. Over the last few years, the equine industry has become very dependent on e-mail and website communications and investments here needs to be clearly identified to ensure that maximum tax relief is obtained.

Equine expense claims

10.10 This was first considered, in relation to the professional horseman, at **8.5**.

The provisions of ICTA 1988 s 74(1) deny tax relief against business profits for any expense which is not been incurred 'wholly and exclusively ... for the purposes of the trade'.

It is therefore a key consideration to be able to identify cases where an expense is for a material private purpose. In such cases, the whole cost is strictly disallowable as not wholly and exclusively for business purposes. In practice the Inspector of Taxes will generally agree a fair apportionment where an expense had objectives additional to those of a purely business nature, especially where it can be shown that these were merely incidental to what was primarily a business purpose.

In *Mallalieu v Drummond [1983] 2 All ER 1095, 57 TC 330* it was held that the sober clothing worn by a lady barrister to comply with Bar Counsel guidelines was for the dual purpose of her profession and her requirements as a human being.

The courts decided that it is important to look into a taxpayer's mind at the time of making the expenditure. The same considerations will be relevant when attempting to maximise expense claims for a professional jockey. There will be many instances in which a fair apportionment of business expenditure between business and personal motives occur within equine business. Examples are where:

- the stud and racing functions are combined;
- the business has an element restricted as hobby under ICTA 1988 s 384 and s 397;
- the business combines non-taxable and taxable, eg professional training which is taxable and race-horse ownership which might be non-taxable.

Agricultural building allowances

10.11 Any stud farm that qualifies, as a farm for agricultural purposes must make sure that it achieves the 4% writing down allowance for agricultural building allowances (ABA) on relevant agricultural buildings. ABA is a straight line claim so that the allowable cost is extinguished for tax relief after 25 years.

However, capital allowances are superior to ABAs. On the assumption that the maximum claims for plant and machinery have been made, it is worth considering qualifying expenditure for ABAs after first year allowances (FYAs) and written down values (WDAs).

The following conditions must be satisfied in order for a claim for ABAs to be valid.

- The expenditure must be capital expenditure (Capital Allowances Act (CAA) 2001 s 361(1)). Capital expenditure excludes items of maintenance or repairs, and any amount which the claimant is able to claim as a deduction in computing profits, or from which any person paying it is entitled to deduct tax at source.
- The money must be spent on the construction, reconstruction, alteration or improvement of farmhouses, farm or forestry buildings, cottages, fences or other works. 'Works' includes drainage and sewerage works, water and electricity installations, walls,

shelter belts of trees, glass-houses on market garden land, and the reclamation of former agricultural land.

- It is important to note that where items are included amongst repairs and renewals, and are disallowed by the Inspector as representing 'improvements', the amount disallowed may then be made the subject of an agricultural buildings allowances claim. A similar situation arises where, shortly after the acquisition of the farm, expenditure is disallowed under the rule in *Law Shipping Co Ltd v IRC (1923) 12 TC 621* that is, on the grounds that the farm was bought at a low price because it was in a dilapidated condition.
- The expenditure must be incurred for the purposes of husbandry on agricultural land or forestry land, of which the person incurring the expenditure is owner or tenant (CAA 2001 s 361(1)(b)). (Stud farming does count as husbandry for this purpose.)
- If the expenditure is paid partly from a subsidy, grant or contribution from government, public or local authority, the allowance is limited to the net amount after deduction of that subsidy (eg under the Farm Capital Grant Scheme or the Farm and Horticulture Development Scheme) (CAA 2001 s 532).

The ABA claim is normally made by the owner or tenant who has incurred the qualifying expenditure. Landlords may claim, where they have provided the building for use in the trade carried on by a tenant, or have made a contribution to the total cost. A tenant who has erected the building or provided part of the cost, is treated as having incurred expenditure of the net amount after deducting the landlord's contribution.

Where a tenancy comes to an end, there is a special test to determine who shall enjoy the remainder of the allowance given to the for mer tenant. If the incoming tenant buys the buildings etc on which relief has been claimed, he becomes entitled to these allowances. If not, the buildings are treated as reverting to the immediate landlord, and the allowances are accordingly allotted to him (CAA 2001 ss 368 and 367).

Where only part of the land in question is transferred, only the allowances attributable to that part are accordingly transferred.

Special problems arise on ABA claims where land has been settled on trust. In *Sargaison (Inspector of Taxes) v Roberts [1969] 3 All ER 1072, 45 TC 612*, a farmer settled his land on trust, and the trustees leased it back to him. He claimed that he had not parted with the whole of his interest in the land, and was therefore entitled to the remainder of the allowances for expenditure incurred before the settlement and lease back. It was held that he was so entitled. This precedent may be relevant where farming partnerships are created during the currency of existing allowances.

ABA entitlements should not be overlooked when a stud is bought. It will be important to correctly research and establish the tax allowances and WDVs (written down values) in the vendor's tax computations and thus the residues which will be available to the purchaser of the buildings after the transaction is completed. It is unlikely that the claim will greatly influence the overall decision to purchase but it may do in some cases.

It must also be noted that far more can be achieved through re-defining buildings as plant, ie the capital allowances on plant and machinery are much more beneficial than the 4% ABA on agricultural buildings expenditures.

A brief checklist of the main tax planning issue on ABAs (CAA 1990 s 123) is as follows:

- change of use has no effect on the claim for ABAs;
- seller and buyer get ABAs in year of sale/purchase;
- it may be beneficial to consider such an election where building is demolished.

An anti-avoidance measure has also been introduced to prevent businesses claiming excessive balancing allowances on the disposal of assets on which capital allowances had been claimed, by entering into artificial transactions at below-market value. The provision applies to industrial buildings, mineral extraction, flat conversions, agricultural buildings and assured tenancies. It applies to events occurring on or after 27 November 2002.

BPR – equestrian business not a stud

10.12 In *Wheatley v IRC [1998] STC (SCD) 60* (see at **7.23** above in relation to studs) APR was denied on a meadow which was accepted as within the meaning of IHTA 1984 s 115(4) because the horses being grazed in the meadow were used for leisure pursuits and not connected either with agricultural or stud activities. A claim for BPR was allowed. This ruling is arguably one of the most significant tax case judgments in the equestrian business world in recent years.

Provided that an equestrian business is run with genuine commercial inspiration, its assets etc should qualify for business property relief (BPR) from IHT. This is of extreme importance in the equine industry where, despite frequently low annual incomes and profitability, there are often very high asset values with high levels of stocks, equipment and property on balance sheets.

BPR is available for transfers of certain categories of business and of business assets if they qualify as 'relevant business property' and the transferor has owned them for a minimum period. The relief is available for transfers in life and on death. It is also available when relevant business property is chargeable as settled property. The relief reduces the value transferred by a transfer of relevant business property.

Relevant business property and rate of relief

10.13 So how will an equestrian business qualify for BPR? Transfers of property may qualify for relief. 100% relief is available for equestrian activities in respect of:

- a business or an interest in a business (such as, a partner's interest);
- securities owned by the transferor, which are not listed on a recognised Stock Exchange, which themselves or with other unquoted shares or securities give the 'transferor' control of an unquoted trading company.

Relief is also available at 100% where the transfer combines the transferor's business and qualifying settled property used in that business.

Availability of BPR

10.14 Relief is not available if the:

- business or company is engaged wholly or mainly in dealing in securities, stocks or shares, land or buildings, or in making or holding investments (see CHAPTER **11**);
- business is not carried on for gain (IHTA 1984 s103(3)) (see CHAPTER **3**);
- business is subject to binding contract for sale, unless that sale is to a company which will carry on the business, and the sale is made wholly or mainly in consideration of shares in the company buying the business;
- shares in a company are subject to a binding contract for sale or the company is being wound up, unless the sale or winding up is part of a reconstruction or amalgamation to enable the business of the company to be carried on (IHTA 1984 ss 105(5) and 113).

If the property is an unincorporated business or an interest in such a business, its value for the purpose of the relief is its net value. That is, the value of the business assets, including goodwill, less any liabilities secured on the asset which were incurred for the purposes of the business (IHTA 1984 s110).

Any money that has been loaned to a business is not part of its net value, so will not qualify for business relief.

Property that is regarded as an 'excepted asset' does not qualify for relief (IHTA 1984 s112).

An asset is excepted if it is:

- not used wholly or mainly for the purposes of a business throughout the two years immediately before the transfer (or since its acquisition by the business if more recent);
- not required at the time of the transfer for identified future use for the purpose of the business; or
- used wholly or mainly for the personal benefit of the transferor, or a person connected with the transferor (eg the spouse, a child or other relative of the transferor).

If any land or building is an excepted asset but part of it is used exclusively for the purposes of the business, that part is regarded as a separate asset. Provided the above conditions are satisfied, that part is taken into account in determining the value of relevant business property (IHTA 1984 s112(4)).

Special rules apply if the relevant business property is a controlling shareholding in a holding company. If the group includes any company whose own business falls outside the scope of the relief, business relief is only given on the value that would be appropriate if that company were not part of the group. In applying the rules for excepted assets, the group is considered to be one concern (IHTA 1984 ss 111 and 112(2)).

The general rule is that property is not relevant business property (and so does not qualify for relief) unless it was owned as such by the transferor throughout the two years immediately before the transfer.

The following are points to note.

1. If the transferor became entitled to property on the death of a spouse, any period during which the spouse owned that property is counted for determining eligibility for the relief.
2. If the transferred property was acquired on an earlier transfer within the two-year period, relief is available if:
   - the earlier transfer was eligible for business relief;
   - the earlier transfer was made to the current transferor or spouse;
   - one of the transfers was made on death; and
   - the property, apart from the two-year rule, would qualify for relief.
3. Relief is available when the transferred property replaces other relievable property, eg one equine business is sold and replaced with another within one year of death.
4. If the transferor inherits the property on a death, the Inland Revenue considers the ownership to run from the date of that death.

PETS and failed PETS

10.15 PETS were first considered at **2.27** above.

A potentially exempt transfer (PET) made seven years or more before the death of the transferor falls out of the charge to IHT. Any other potentially exempt transfer is included in the computation of the total estate on death and then becomes a chargeable transfer (IHTA 1984 s 3A(4); FA 1986 Sch 19 para 1). A potentially exempt transfer is assumed to be an exempt transfer during the seven years following the transfer or, if earlier, until immediately before the transferor's death (IHTA 1984 s 3A(5); FA 1986 Sch 19 para 1).

As potentially exempt transfers are assumed to be exempt at the time of the transfer, no IHT is payable at the time. If the transferor makes a subsequent chargeable lifetime transfer (eg a gift to a discretionary trust) the earlier potentially exempt transfer does not enter into the transferor's cumulative total at the time.

Thus the transfer by gift of a stud which is deemed to be *non-commercial* could be dealt with under the PET provisions provided the donor survives seven years. The gift of a *commercial* stud should normally be eligible for APR/BPR at the point of transfer.

It is, however, important to be alert for 'failed PETs' should a gift change from being a commercial stud.

A 'failed PET' is not necessarily an animal who does not behave but a tax complication with potentially serious tax consequences. Gifts to the next generation should not be considered without giving proper consideration to CGT and careful thought to the possibility that they might fail to qualify for IHT relief should they no longer be in use as business or agricultural property by a donee at the date of a donor's death.

In order for BPR to be retained on the death of a donor within seven years, two conditions must be satisfied.

1 The property must qualify as a 'relevant business property' for BPR at the time of death (IHTA 1984 s 113A(3)b).
2 The recipient of the lifetime gift must have retained the gifted property until the death of the transferor or if earlier his own death (IHTA 1984 s113A(3). The conditions apply strictly.

Chapter 13 of the author's book *Tolley's Tax Planning for Farm and Land Diversification* (2002) (LexisNexis UK) goes into some detail on how to avoid a failed PET.

Where a transferor dies within seven years of transfer and the gift does not meet the above conditions, it becomes a chargeable transfer treated as having occurred at the valuation relevant at the original date of the gift. Tax is calculated at the full death rates applying at the time of death, subject to IHT taper relief. Tax on subsequent chargeable lifetime transfers may, therefore, not only need to be revised under the rule for transfers within seven years before death but will also be affected by the revision of the transferor's cumulative total.

Examples of a failed PET would be:

- a non-commercial stud which did not qualify for APR/BPR gifted as a lifetime transfer where the transferor dies within seven years; and
- the a death of a transferor within seven years of a transfer of a stud which qualified for APR/BPR at the point of transfer but which does not qualify at the date of death.

Practical APR/BPR planning

10.16 Tax planning and APR/BPR was first considered at **7.17** and **7.20** above, in relation to studs.

Clearly, it is important to review all equine assets and establish which are likely to qualify for these valuable APR, BPR and CGT reliefs. All assets should be identified to the client and their tax eligibility for both IHT and CGT established and, wherever possible, preserved.

Any tax planning exercise on behalf of the equine client must include a close and detailed scrutiny of what assets are held and whether or not they currently qualify for these capital tax reliefs. Detailed advice should then be given as to how property which does not qualify might be used or its ownership restructured in order to maximise available reliefs and eligibility for them.

Inheritance tax savings can perhaps be achieved by 'chattel leasing' in an attempt to avoid gifts with reservation of benefit (GROB) problems. In the case of property, which is an interest in land or a chattel (or corporeal movable in Scotland), retention or assumption by the donor of actual occupation of, or actual enjoyment of an incorporeal right over, the land or actual possession of the chattel (corporeal movable in Scotland) is disregarded for the purposes of the gifts with reservation rules if it is for full consideration in money or money's worth (FA 1986, Sch 20 para 6(1)(a)(3)). The Inland Revenue consider that for this provision to apply full consideration should be provided throughout the relevant period, so that any rent passing should be reviewed at appropriate intervals to reflect market changes. Any consideration passing will be treated as full if it lies within a range of values reflecting normal valuation tolerances (Inland Revenue *Tax Bulletin* November 1993).

Equine enthusiasts inevitably own equine 'chattels' with very high value and often wish to minimise any inheritance tax. This can be achieved by leasing the chattel. Examples could be equine art, equine trophies and lots of other areas of equine treasures.

So when is a claim for BPR at risk? For the purpose of BPR, 'business' includes a profession but does not include ownership of tenanted land which is regarded as the holding of investments (IHTA 1984 s 105(3)). Nor does it include a business carried on otherwise than for profit, ie where loss relief has been denied under the 'hobby-farming' rules (IHTA 1984 s 103). Opinions on this differ and each case needs careful consideration to ensure that tax reliefs are preserved.

Another risk can arise with assets which initially appear to qualify as part of a business in their own right but, in fact, on closer examination, turn out to be capable of being regarded as merely part of a larger, non-qualifying business (IHTA 1984 s 105(3)). For example, woodlands on an agricultural estate may be held to be part of a larger non-qualifying business of letting land. Steps should be taken to establish that the woodlands amount to a separate business in their own right, for example, by establishing and maintaining Forestry Commission dedication schemes where appropriate and by preparing separate financial accounts. Similarly, if a genuine commercial equine trade or activity is part of a larger non-qualifying activity it may be appropriate to seek to segregate it so that it does qualify.

The equine limited company and BATR

10.17 Shares in a limited company carrying on an equine trade should qualify for BATR. The tax planner's aim must, therefore, be to ensure that nothing is done to put this status at risk.

Most equine activities have high asset values. The proprietor will want to achieve BATR on any sale of the shares in cases where there is likely to be significant capital gain on rising property values.

Full BATR continues to be available as long as a company or group is substantially engaged in trading activities. To avoid losing the favourable status for shareholders, it will be important to ensure that any investment activity does not broadly exceed 20% of the overall activity (see Inland Revenue *Tax Bulletin* Issue No 53, June 2001) – or perhaps to conduct the activity through a different business entity. Furthermore, for some companies, periods of inactivity should also be avoided as these can stop the taper relief clock running.

Having introduced a favourable capital gains tax relief for primarily trading situations, the Inland Revenue has had to distinguish situations, which are trading and not trading. The Government has not specifically set down this distinction in legislation so the Inland Revenue has made its own pronouncements on when it considers investment activities to be sufficiently significant as to affect trading status for taper relief purposes. It considers investment activities more than incidental when they broadly exceed 20% of the overall activity of the company/group in question (see Inland Revenue *Tax Bulletin* Issue No 53,

June 2001). That percentage could be applied in a number of ways, for example:

- turnover;
- net or gross profit;
- asset/balance sheet value;
- management time.

The Inland Revenue recognise that the circumstances of any particular case will need to be individually examined in order to ascertain which of these criteria is most appropriate and that there can be leeway for unusual circumstances. Specifically, the Inland Revenue have indicated that where the 20% test is breached, for instance because the company has surplus cash earmarked for future investment in the business, those funds will not necessarily be included for the purposes of the 20% test.

The risk of a company falling foul of these tests of 'investment activity' cannot be understated and are relevant for both capital gains tax and inheritance tax. An 'investment company' does not qualify for any CGT or IHT tax reliefs.

The areas of equine activity potentially at risk here are the letting of equine property, holding large cash balances or reserves, and possibly holding non-trading assets in a company such as expensive horses kept for personal use. Consider also the position of a valuable stallion – is it being retained as an investment or a trading asset?

The equine limited company – is it a trading company?

10.18 An equine limited company risks being regarded as a non-trading company for a variety of reasons. It might, for example, choose to invest surplus funds in a property for letting. Alternatively, former trading premises such as stables or stud land may be retained long-term for investment purposes. A company or group could lose its trading status by virtue of a property's investment performance improving relative to the trading activities during a particular period and rising above the 20% threshold mentioned above. The message is that carrying on investment activities within a trading company or group can jeopardise the taper relief status of shareholdings in that company/group. As a result, the effective capital gains tax rate on a sale could be much higher than the 10% (see **13.6**) achievable under the more generous business asset regime with relief at the maximum of 75%. If any investment activity is to be carried on it will be vitally important to monitor its significance. Alternatively, the activity should be carried on outside the company, possibly by the owners personally or in a separate company.

It is possible for the equine company to apply to its Inspector of Taxes for confirmation of his/her opinion on this issue. Inspectors have been instructed to respond 'positively' to such requests. This does not mean that they have to answer 'yes' but at least they must give some clarification of their views based on the known facts as they stand. Such an application can be made after the end of a particular accounting period and would be considered in relation to the accounts of that period.

For inheritance tax purposes, some guidance on whether a company is an investment company, ie 'making or holding investments' can be found in IHTA 1984 s 105(3).

Incorporation of an equine business

Section 162 relief

10.19 Capital gains tax affects equine companies twice, first on incorporating an existing business and secondly when transferring or selling the company shares or when the company sells its business assets etc.

The transfer of a business into a company will almost always involve the disposal of at least one chargeable asset, eg the goodwill of the business if there is any.

Minimising a charge to CGT on incorporation can be achieved under one of two sections; TCGA 1992 s 162 or the less obvious but often more flexible section 165.

The provisions of TCGA 1992 s 162 are intended to assist in incorporation of the equine business by rolling over gains on chargeable assets against the cost of the company shares.

TCGA 1992 s 162 requires three main conditions to be met:

- the business must be transferred by the sole trader or partnership to the company as a 'going concern';
- all the assets (or all assets except cash balances if preferred), must be transferred to the company);
- the consideration given by the company for the business must be wholly shares in the company if full relief is to be given.

As the rollover is against the value of the shares, rather than the value of the assets transferred, it follows that if a property is transferred into the company, it is acquired by the company at its then market value and it is the value of the shares that is reduced for CGT purposes. This means that a subsequent sale of the property by the company will trigger a reduced capital gain and the ultimate chargeable gain will only arise when the shares are sold (which may then attract full BATR).

However, note the asset within the company does not have the benefit of any BATR.

Historically, the problems with TCGA 1992 s 162 relief have been:

- its all-inclusive nature, ie the whole of the assets of the business and the business itself must go across;
- it is automatic, ie mandatory application meaning that valuable BATR could be lost if the shares were sold within two years of incorporation.

The latter issue has now been solved by TCGA 1992 s 162A (introduced by FA 2002) which enables an individual to disclaim the relief if preferred. (See **10.21** below for more detail.)

Section 165 relief

10.20 The other alternative is to claim relief under TCGA 1992 s 165, which is aimed at gifts of business assets.

The mechanics of the relief are that the company is formed and shares are issued to the proposed shareholders. Assets that are wanted in the company are gifted in and others can then be retained personally, perhaps for letting or other uses. The holdover is against the acquisition cost by the company. Typically, this means that both the company's base costs for chargeable assets *and* the base cost of the shares are very low.

TCGA 1992 s 165 does, however, allow non-chargeable assets to be transferred into the company at full value, with the balance left on the loan account. This can then be drawn down in future years, typically being used to 'top up' dividend payments that are designed to use up basic rate bands.

It is this 'draw down' facility, which is considered so important to the incorporated business where the proprietor is a higher rate taxpayer. This can be used to secure basic rate tax liability only for a number of years with careful planning.

A further refinement may be to leave some chargeable assets outside the scope of the holdover claim and actually have some assessable capital gains on the transfer of the business. This might, of course, generate a tax liability, but this will probably only be chargeable at 10% (see **13.6** below).

Also, of course, if full 75% BATR is available the chargeable gain may not actually be assessable. This may be a price worth paying for the ability to draw down significant amounts from the loan account in future years, where it will effectively only suffer a further 19% tax liability (see **10.6** above). This is the basic rate of corporation tax to 31 March 2004. For example, if goodwill were to be valued at £100,000 for a transfer during 2003/04, the company could pay consideration of £31,600 (by credit to the director's loan account), with the balance of the gain (£68,400) being held over. The cash consideration is ostensibly chargeable as it exceeds the cost of the goodwill (assumed here to be nil), but BATR at 75% (£23,700) would reduce the assessable gain to the level of the annual CGT exemption (£7,900) so no tax would be payable.

Clearly for a husband and wife partnership, the consideration left on the loan account could be £63,200. Thus, the normal reluctance of the tax professional to accept Inland Revenue arguments that there was goodwill on the occasion of such a transfer may actually have gone into reverse with the advent of the generous BATR regime.

A lot of businesses will have goodwill value, eg vets with a large client base or farriers with high profits etc. The problem of having to pay some capital gains tax now compared with large amounts of income tax in the future is a barrier that some equine taxpayers find hard to overcome. Goodwill is one of those assets on which capital gains tax will be payable. The ability to draw down a director's current account 'tax-free' should not be overlooked.

Unless the equine trader is currently operating on a 31 March/ 5 April year end, the potential impact of overlap or transitional relief brought forward from earlier years must be considered. When the trade ceases, the full profit from the end of the last accounting period to the date of incorporation will become chargeable, less the overlap relief available. For a business on a rising trend of profits this may prove expensive. The extra tax due will be weighed against potential savings. In some equine businesses it could be that profits are in decline, which would mean that the overlap relief is a benefit as it reduces a profit or creates a loss.

If the incorporation goes ahead, it may well be appropriate to complete a CAA 2001 s 226 election, which will carry over the written down value (WDV) of the qualifying assets into the company's corporation tax computations. This does not, however, change the fact that capital allowances will not be due in the final period of the trade. This may be particularly important given the current availability of 100% FYA on ICT equipment (see **10.7** and **10.9** below). It may well be a good idea to set the incorporation for a date a few weeks into a new accounting period for the sole trade, thus securing the FYAs against the profits of the penultimate unincorporated assessable period.

The position of TCGA 1992 s 165 is considered again at **13.13** below.

Incorporation relief

10.21 One of the changes introduced by the Finance Act 2002 concerned the transfer of a business to a company wholly in exchange for shares in the company. In those circumstances, any assets liable to capital gains tax, eg property or goodwill, are deemed to have been disposed of for their market value. This could give rise to a capital gains tax liability were it not for the long-established relief under section TCGA 1992 s 162 mentioned at **10.19** above.

However, taper relief now also offsets gains on business assets. As little as 25% of a chargeable gain is taxable if the asset has been held for more than two years. Thus, in some circumstance, it might conceivably be better to be taxed on only 25% of the gain at the date of a transfer to a company rather than being taxed later on a higher amount when the newly acquired shares in the company were sold with the benefit of less taper relief. This could occur where the shares in the company are sold soon after incorporation.

For businesses incorporated on or after 6 April 2002, an election may be made under TCGA 1992 s 162A so that incorporation relief is not automatically given and any gains are not deferred. Admittedly, this change will affect only a few people.

Horserace Betting Levy Board

10.22 Under the Betting, Gaming and Lotteries Act 1963, a Horserace Betting Levy Board (HBLB) collects contributions from bookmakers which is then used to fund improvements in breeding and horseracing, and for the advancement or encouragement of veterinary science or education. For more detail on this, see extract from the Inland Revenue's Inspector's Manual IMI880.

Competing on horses owned by the business

10.23 If a commercial sponsorship deal does not exist then there should be a private adjustment to expenses claims against business profits for the calculation of the costs of their own competition horses, ie adjustment for private usage. However, if the horses promote the *business* then there is scope to include a business proportion (see **3.21** above).

Planning for Losses 11

Relief for losses

11.1 Equine businesses involve highly individualistic people so tax planning will often need to be 'tailor-made'. Dealing with losses in particular can be problematical and it will generally be advisable to keep a full record on file to control the timing of claims, maximise cash flow and ensure that they are fully utilised.

Care should be taken in deciding how to claim loss relief and whether to claim or disclaim capital allowances.

Careful consideration should always be given to the optimum use of personal allowances and to ensure wherever possible that income is not taxed at higher rates. Similarly, accelerating loss relief claims can have useful cash flow consequences especially in the early years of a business.

The ability to claim equine tax losses can affect commercial decisions such as who is formally involved in an equine trading partnership and arrangements for the share of profits/losses.

The importance of commerciality

11.2 It is fundamental to loss relief claims that the equestrian business can demonstrate that it is being run on a 'commercial basis and with a view to profit'. If this cannot be established, the Inland Revenue may seek to restrict any claim for losses.

Perversely, an early claim for losses may actually be of benefit in establishing commerciality. The dispute process may actually help to show that there is a reasonable expectation of profit being earned by the business in future years. Once this is established, it should enable a business to claim other reliefs including capital gains tax (CGT) and inheritance tax (IHT) business reliefs.

If there is a precise date at which an equine activity turns from a hobby to a commercial trade then care must be take to claim losses within the time limit.

Choices available to the equine business owner

11.3 The equine taxpayer has a variety of alternatives to select when planning how to claim the trading loss. Reliefs available for companies are set out at **11.18** below. For individuals and partners, income tax loss relief is available as follows:

- set off against other income in current or preceding year (ICTA 1988 s 380);
- set off against other income in first four years of trade (ICTA 1988 s 381);
- set off against capital gains on business assets (FA 1991 s 72);
- carry forward against future profits of *same* trade (ICTA 1988 s 385);
- expenditure in seven years before start of trade set off in first year of trade (pre-trading expenditure) (ICTA 1988, s 401);
- terminal year loss set off against profits of three preceding years (ICTA 1988 s 388).

In general terms, all the usual rules which apply to income tax trading losses apply equally to equestrian businesses.

In order to see how losses are treated in the context of averaging claims for stud farms, see CHAPTER 7: TAX PLANNING FOR STUD FARMS.

Setting tax losses against general income (s 380)

11.4 Once an equine business is proven to be commercial then the losses will be allowable for tax purposes.

Section 380 provides that a loss from the equestrian business can be set against other income of a tax year or, if this is insufficient, or if the claimant prefers, against other income of the previous tax year.

A loss in the current year must be used to relieve profits before a loss carried back from the subsequent year. For example, if a loss in 2001/02 is set off against other income of that year and a claim is also made for a loss in 2002/03 to be set off against other income in 2001/02, priority is given to the loss claim for 2001/02 before the claim for 2002/03.

Relief cannot be given for the same loss twice. For example, a loss in the year ended 30 April 2003 falls in the tax year 2003/04. This can be set against other income in 2003/04 and in 2002/03. Since there is an overlap between the two basis periods, it is possible that the loss could be included in both tax years. To prevent this from happening, the loss is excluded from the second year by ICTA 1988 s 382.

The claim must be made within one year from 31 January following the year in which the loss arises. For example, a trading loss in the year to 5 April 2003 must be claimed by 31 January 2005.

This relief can be very beneficial where the business owner has other income from another business, employment income or income from investments. It is not possible to claim only a part of the loss except to that extent that it exceeds available income. Therefore, some careful planning is needed when making a claim so as not to waste personal allowances, but this might not always be possible.

Time limits for claiming the loss

11.5 From 1996/97 onwards, the time limits for claims are one year (ICTA 1988 ss 380 and 381) and five years (ICTA 1988 s 385) after 31 January following the tax year of the loss.

These time limits are tight and the taxpayer and adviser must ensure prompt adherence to the deadline. This can also be of importance with regard to the late registration of a business (see **CHAPTER 3**).

Opening year losses (s 381)

11.6 ICTA 1988 s 381 allows losses sustained by an individual in the year of assessment in which he commences a trade and in the three following tax years to be set against his other income in the three tax years before that in which the loss is made, offsetting losses against income for earlier years before that of later years.

As with claims under s 380, relief cannot be given for the same loss twice (s 382) and the claim must be made within one year from 31 January following the year in which the loss arises.

Where an individual starts an equestrian business after retiring from some other activity or employment, a high-income source may cease and the facility to offset losses against total income under s 380 may be very beneficial if there is sufficient total income to absorb the losses, especially if large tax refunds can result. The facility to carry back losses of the first four years of a new business can be extremely useful to maximise loss relief against these high income years.

It is of paramount importance for such loss claims to be able to show that the trade is carried on in such a manner that profit can be expected to be realised within a reasonable time. This is of particular importance to the taxpayer who retires from a high-earning business or employment and moves into equine activities. A tough approach is taken by the Inland Revenue in this regard and careful consideration must be given to this when thinking of making claims for losses under ICTA 1988 s 381.

Losses offset against capital gains

11.7 Finance Act 1991 s 72 enables trading losses of an individual to be set against capital gains. This provides scope for planning when considering the timing to realise potential disposals likely to give rise to capital gains.

The relief under FA 1991 s 72 can only be given after trading losses have first been set against a claimant's other income under ICTA 1988 s 380. It is not possible to claim trading loss relief against capital gains only, and so it is inevitable that personal allowances for the year could be wasted.

As with claims under ICTA 1988 s 380, trading losses can only be offset against gains for the same or preceding tax year. Any trading loss which is not offset in this way may be carried forward and set against future trading profits under ICTA 1988 s 385.

Non-commercial losses do not qualify for relief against capital gains tax under FA 1991 s 72.

The maximum amount of any trading loss claim under FA 1991 s 72 is the amount chargeable to CGT in any year before deducting the annual exemption for CGT. Therefore, the claimant may lose the benefit of the annual exemption from capital gains tax. However, the trading losses are set against the gains of the year before unused capital losses brought forward from earlier years, so this may facilitate these capital losses being used in future years while helping to preserve the annual exemption.

For equine trading losses realised after 5 April 2004, the maximum trading loss that can be set against capital gains is equal to the total gains before taper relief and annual exemption. For farming losses realised before 6 April 2004, the maximum trading losses that could be offset against capital gains was the gain *after* taper relief but before the annual exemption (although the maximum trading losses that can be offset in 2002/03 and 2003/04 can be calculated before the application of taper relief if the taxpayer makes a specific election before the respective deadlines on 31 January 2005 and 31 January 2006).

The claim must be made at the same time as the claim against general income under ICTA 1988 s 380 even if there is no income to absorb the loss (one year from 31 January following the year of the loss), although the Inland Revenue may accept separate claims.

Only the trading losses of the year of assessment or the year preceding the year of assessment, are available to offset a capital gain. Any trading loss which is not set against income or gains of the current or preceding year is available to be carried forward and set against future trading profits under ICTA 1988 s 385 (see **11.8** below).

Losses carried forward (s 385)

11.8 Where no claim is made under the provisions outlined above, or where such a claim is made but excess losses remain unused, trading losses can be carried forward and set against future profits from the same trade (ICTA 1988 s 385). This is much more restrictive than other claims where the losses can be set against other income. For this reason and also for cash flow reasons, it is generally preferable, where possible, to avoid carrying forward losses.

On the other hand, there may be times where losses can be used more beneficially in future years where, for example, profits would otherwise be taxed at a higher rate.

A claim to carry forward a loss must be made within five years from 31 January following the year of loss. Since the time limits for ICTA 1988 ss 380, and 381 and FA 1991 s 72 claims are much tighter, this longer time limit is not as relevant because it will be apparent long before the expiry of the time limit whether losses are to be carried forward or not.

Terminal losses (s 388)

11.9 On the permanent discontinuance of any equine business any losses sustained in the twelve months before the date of cessation may be carried back and set against profit of the same trade (ICTA 1988 s 388). This is subject to the provision that they are relieved elsewhere.

The carry back of losses is restricted to the three tax years prior to the year in which a trade ceases. Relief is given first for the latest of those three years. This means that the eligible profits that are available for set off against terminal losses are those for the tax year in which the trade ceases and the three tax years preceding it.

Pre-trading expenditure (s 401)

11.10 A large proportion of equine businesses take a long time to get off the ground and can incur considerable expenditure before the actual commencement of trading.

Tax relief can be achieved on this expenditure under ICTA 1988 s 401 if it is incurred in the seven years before commencing to trade. Expenditure may be the subject of such a claim if it would be allowable under normal rules had it been incurred after commencement.

Pre-trading expenditure is treated as incurrent on the day an equine business starts to trade. The relief does not extend to expenditure that would be deductible as a trade expense. An example of this is pre-trading purchase of stock of horses which will be shown as opening stock.

Restriction of loss relief

11.11 Relief is only available for losses which arise from a trade carried out on a commercial basis. The Inspector of Taxes may decide to review claims if the losses continue made year after year. If he considers that an activity has not been carried on commercially, he may seek to deny tax relief for the losses of past years and raise assessments to recover the tax due.

Where an enterprise is clearly not being carried out on a commercial basis and with a view to the realisation of profits, an Inland Revenue challenge under ICTA 1988 s 384 should be anticipated.

ICTA 1988 s 384 restricts loss relief (see Inspector's Manual at IM2336b) where the trade was not run on a commercial basis with a view to the realisation of profits (see Inspector's Manual at IM2340a onwards).

Stud farms and averaging claims

11.12 In order to see how losses are treated in the context of averaging, see CHAPTER 7. This will apply to farming profits, eg stud farm but not to equestrian businesses that do not generally qualify as farming. The loss for averaging is treated as £nil for the purposes of an averaging claim so that the facility to claim relief for a loss is left intact.

Stud farms – the 11-year loss rule

11.13 It became apparent when the loss relief provisions were originally introduced that the test under ICTA 1988 s 384 was arguably too subjective for stud farms (ie it was necessary to review what was in the mind of a farmer starting a business). A further test was enacted under ICTA 1988 s 397 which is based on a more objective test of losses having been sustained for five successive years. When that occurs, there is a statutory inference that the farm is not being run on a commercial basis and so loss relief may be denied.

ICTA 1988 s 397 applies only to farming and market gardening (which includes stud farming) and provides that if losses have been sustained for five consecutive years then any subsequent loss cannot be set off under ICTA 1988 s 380. For this purpose, profits are calculated before capital allowances are deducted.

In 1982, the Inland Revenue agreed with the Thoroughbred Breeders Association, to extend this relief from the first five to the first 11 years from commencement of a stud farming business.

The scope the restriction is, however, qualified in subsection (3) of section 397, which provides that the relief shall not be restricted if it can be shown that a profit could not reasonably be expected in the first five years of the business but that there was a reasonable expectation of profits in the future. This recognises that some farms or market garden enterprises require a start-up period of more than five years and equally, in the case of stud farms, more than 11 years. Each case must be assessed on its own merits.

The Inland Revenue's Inspector's Manual IM2350g states:

> 'It has always been recognised that some ventures are by their nature unlikely to show a profit by the sixth year of trading and section 397(3) provides for loss relief to be continued after the fifth year where the claimant is engaged in a particular farming activity of an intrinsically long term profit making nature. We have long accepted that the breeding of thoroughbred horses is such a long term venture, and provided that a stud farming business is potentially profit making, we would not normally seek to invoke section 397(1) until after 11 years from the start of the business.'

The Thoroughbred Breeders Association has circulated this text to its members. It does not mean, however, that all stud farming losses can be claimed against other income up to 11 years from commencement. The requirement that the business should be potentially profitable, in other words, the question of whether ICTA 1988 s 397(3)(a) is satisfied, is very important and should not be overlooked. Nor should it be assumed that the five-year period is extended where a run of losses arise in periods following a profitable year, or where a business is taken over as a going concern.

Relevant tax cases on this topic tend to relate to thoroughbreds and racing and it can generally be accepted that the principles are the same for non-thoroughbreds. The emphasis has to be on evidence of commerciality and each case reviewed on this basis.

The 11-year loss rule does not apply when a profit occurs. Once a business has made a profit the five-year rule applies. This is not too much of a problem if the profit is in, say, year 9, 10 or 11, but if it crops up unexpectedly in year 2 it can cause a lot of problems. No matter how commercial their approach, nor how disciplined, knowledgeable and experienced a stud owner might be, their business is dependent on a large element of luck. Infertility, miscarriages and the loss of foals sometimes cannot be avoided. On the other hand, a surprise superstar foal may arrive without warning. This could cause a profit in, say, year

2 or 3, which would mean that the five-year loss rule comes into play with detrimental effects on the 11-year loss rule. A profit in year 2 will mean that a profit must be achieved again in year 8 just to secure the five years' loss reliefs. If an early profit is achieved the tax practitioner must warn their client of the problem.

Eliminating a loss

11.14 It will at times be desirable to plan to reduce or eliminate a loss in a particular year so as to protect other tax reliefs.

If a partnership has substantial interest payments, consider arranging for the partners to borrow individually and use their new loans to introduce capital into the firm. This will improve the stud farm trading result, and the interest on the personal loans is deductible from other income under ICTA 1988 s 362. Clients and adviser should, however, be aware that Inspectors are specifically instructed to examine such 'refinancing' tactics carefully to ascertain whether or not they were commercially inspired or undertaken with a view to manipulation of the loss relief rules. The Inspector's Manual specifically warns against obvious manipulations of profits, such as pulling in income into one year, reducing expenses in a particular year or the manipulation of stock valuations etc.

To avoid 11 consecutive years of stud farm losses, planning well in advance to ensure a profit in one particular year may be achievable without running such risks. Consider also what rates of depreciation are relevant for business and non-business equine fixed assets as this can have a marked effect on whether a profit or loss arises.

Opening year loss rules – s 381

11.15 ICTA 1988 s 381 allows losses sustained by an individual in the year of assessment in which he commences a trade and in the three following years to be set against his other income in the three preceding years, taking income for earlier years before that of later years.

Using capital allowances to augment/reduce a loss

11.16 Capital allowance and agricultural buildings allowances are dealt with in CHAPTER **10:** OVERVIEW OF EQUINE BUSINESS TAXATION. These allowances are treated in the same way as business expenses and so augment the losses (or reduce profits) in the same way as expenses. If loss relief is denied on the grounds that a business in not run on a commercial basis, it follows that any related capital allowances will not be allowed.

There is scope to reduce losses by restricting the amount of capital allowances claimed. This would be a useful tax planning technique where the taxpayer could not make good use of the allowances. Some reasons for not claiming capital allowances include:

- the reduction of losses to avoid wasting the benefit of the personal allowance;
- the desire to utilise losses brought forward instead of current year losses;
- the inability to relieve current year losses in a tax-efficient manner;
- wanting to avoid having to carry forward current year losses;
- wanting to carry forward a higher written down value for the capital assets, in particular if an asset is to be sold in the future – increasing the amount of unrelieved capital expenditure would increase a balancing allowance or reduce a balancing charge thus increasing future losses or reducing future profits which otherwise may be taxed at a higher rate.

The restriction for capital allowances does not mean that an exact amount of tax relief can be claimed in a future year but that there will be extra allowances to claim due to the increased amount of the written-down value of the assets carried forward.

Augmentation of losses by capital allowances – a summary

11.17 For certain classes of loss the amount of the loss claim can be increased by including certain qualifying capital allowances. The augmentation of different losses by capital allowances is set out in the table below.

Section	*Class of relief*	*Capital allowances to be included*
ICTA 1988 s 383	Set off against total income of tax year.	Capital allowances for the year of assessment for which the year of loss is the basis year.
	Carry forward against subsequent profits.	Capital allowances exceeding balancing charges and taxable profits for the relevant year, but allowances brought forward can be applied first against profits and charges.

Section	*Class of relief*	*Capital allowances to be included*
ICTA 1988 s 388	Terminal loss relief against earlier profits.	Capital allowances for year in which the trade is permanently discontinued plus the appropriate proportion for the preceding year.
ICTA 1988 s 381	Relief for losses in early years of trade.	Capital allowances for the year of loss so far as not carried back effective for that year.

Trading through a company

11.18 Losses made by a business run via a limited company are not available for offset against the income of the shareholders or directors.

Companies can claim relief for the loss from equestrian businesses as follows:

- against their total profits in the period or against the profits of the preceding period (if the trade was carried on during that period) under ICTA 1988 s 393A;
- if the company is part of a group or consortium then the loss can be set against the profits of the same period of another group or consortium company (ICTA 1988 s 402);
- against future profits of *same* trade under ICTA 1988 s 393; and
- in the case of terminal losses, against total profits of the preceding three years under ICTA 1988 s 393A.

The hobby farming/non-commercial restrictions apply equally to losses incurred by companies and individuals. The provisions of ICTA 1988 s 397 will mean that if losses are sustained and restricted under s 384, the trading status of the company will be at risk. Losses restricted as non-commercial in this way will not be allowable to be offset against other income of the company, for example, property that is let.

Other loss reliefs

11.19 There are two other potential loss relief claims not explained previously, ICTA 1988 s 386 (claims against income received from a company after incorporation of a business) and ICTA 1988 s 574 (income claims for capital losses on unquoted shares becoming of negligible value) as their application is rare within the equine industry. However, these are dealt with in detail in *Tolley's Income Tax* (2003–04) by Gina Antczak, Glyn Saunders and David Smailes (LexisNexis UK).

Other planning points

11.20 CHAPTER **10:** OVERVIEW OF EQUINE BUSINESS TAXATION sets out the provision of ICTA 1988 s 53 (all farms treated is one trade). There are clear tax planning implications there as this section can have a significant impact on the use of loss relief. It is not uncommon for a UK stud owner to have a number of stud farms throughout the UK and overseas. The impact that this rule has on loss claim, ownership structures and future plans should be considered for tax planning.

The matter is complicated by the fact that stud farms are rarely dedicated studs; they often have other equestrian activities running alongside the stud as well. It is possible that the stud farm could 'escape' under the non-farming rules.

For any equestrian establishment, which has problems of profit making and cash flow, a high earning partner who can introduce capital and utilise some initial tax losses may have considerable tax benefits for tax planning.

The tax planning implications of the use/allocation of profits/losses will have to be reviewed in the light of commerciality. Historically, partnership losses have been allocated to those with the highest income to offset. There is a risk that this may be attacked by the Inland Revenue (see the Inland Revenue's *Tax Bulletin* April 2003).

If a realistic view is that losses will be incurred in the early years of a business it is imperative to consider in advance how these will best be used.

Historically, a problem that faces the tax adviser is ensuring a sensible 'marriage' between land ownership and the trading vehicle. For example, who should own assets and who should be a partner in the business? Is the chosen structure tax-efficient? IHT and CGT reliefs which are linked to business assets could be lost if this 'marriage' of ownership and trading vehicle is not achieved in a tax-efficient manner.

Whether, when and how to claim the loss

11.21 In summary, care should always be taken in deciding whether to claim a loss and how to claim loss relief and whether any claim should be augmented by the relevant capital allowances.

As in any situation, interaction of personal income tax allowances, basic rate bands for income tax should be considered. Likewise, the cash flow considerations of the claim for losses to reduce tax as soon as possible should be reviewed including the carry back of losses.

The ability to claim equine tax losses might affect commercial decisions, such as who is formally involved in the equine trading partnership and what the profit/loss share provisions are.

Tax planning for capital gains tax losses

11.22 The majority of this chapter has been devoted to the position of tax planning surrounding income tax and corporation tax rules with the interaction of the hobby farming rules. It would be impossible to look at equine tax loss planning without giving due consideration to capital gains tax losses.

This was first reviewed with the interaction of BATR. It was also explained in relation to the use of income tax losses offset against capital gains (FA 1999 s 72 – see **11.7** above). On a practical point, a memorandum of losses for each client (capital and income) will be essential, as will clients advising of transactions prior to the event.

Conclusion

11.23 Consideration of practical equine tax loss planning ranges from whether or not the business is commercial to what loss can be claimed and where it can be claimed. It is hoped that this chapter directs the tax adviser on an area of tax planning of great importance to the equine business.

Employment Issues 12

Problems of employing staff

12.1 One of the biggest problems facing any equine business is finding and keeping stable staff. The problems can be alleviated somewhat by good tax planning to ensure that the remuneration package offered to the staff is as tax-efficient as possible. One method used to keep good staff is the promise of future rides in races/competitions. However, that is totally unrelated to tax planning and the tax-efficient remuneration package that can be made available to staff. Tax planning to help employees must be tailor-made to the equestrian business and the employees' circumstances.

This book does not have the scope to deal with the full issues surrounding the taxation of employment. The latter can be found in depth in *Tolley's Taxation of Employment* by Robert Maas (LexisNexis UK).

Freelance service provider

12.2 With all the problems of employing staff it is often tempting for the equestrian business to use self-employed service providers rather than employed staff. The tax position of the freelance instructor and the professional horseman are dealt with in CHAPTER **8**.

The flexibility and cost savings on employers' NICs can certainly be advantageous to the business.

The service provider must look at the compliance issues of self-employment, eg registration with the Inland Revenue (there is a £100 fine if registration is not within three months) and consideration as to VAT registration. Recording expenses, documentation of expenses and maximising expense claims are standard considerations. These points are raised in CHAPTER **8**. The key to self-employed status is the service provider being 'in business on their own account'.

Proactive encouragement of self-employed status can be a tax planning tool of the equine business but one that must be handled carefully. Any business travelling this path must consider the factors which define the difference between employment and self-employment.

The *Market Investigations Ltd v Minister of Social Security [1968] 3 All ER 732* case concerned part-time interviewers for a market research organisation. Cooke J considered a number of previous authorities including that of Denning LJ in the *Bank voor Handel* case (*[1954] 1 All ER 969*), Lord Wright in a Canadian case, *Montreal v Montreal Locomotive Works Ltd [1947] 1 DLR 161*, and various US cases from which he concluded:

> 'The observations of Lord Wright, of Denning LJ and of the judges of the Supreme Court in the USA suggest that the fundamental test to be applied is this: "Is the person who has engaged himself to perform these services performing them as a person in business on his own account?". If the answer to that question is "Yes", then the contract is a contract for services. If the answer is "No", then the contract is a contract of service. No exhaustive list has been compiled and perhaps no exhaustive list can be complied of considerations which are relevant in determining that question, nor can strict rules be laid down as to the relative weight which the various considerations should carry in particular cases. The most that can be said is that control will no doubt have to be considered, although it can no longer be regarded as the sole determining factor; and that factors, which may be of importance, are such matters as whether the man performing the services provides his own equipment (eg own tack, grooming equipment etc), whether he hires his own helpers, what degree of financial risk he takes, what degree of responsibility for investment and management he has, and whether and how far he has an opportunity of profiting from sound management in the performance of his task.'

Practical points to be taken as evidence will be:

- the number of customers;
- the regular nature of the work; and
- having equine equipment to perform tasks.

In some equine areas a group of freelancers will work together, standing in for each other and offering a genuine freelance 'bank' of workers.

The Inland Revenue, in their leaflet IR56, say that the distinction between employment and self-employment 'is something to be decided in a commonsense way'. Unfortunately, some commentators take the view that this is not always how they approach the question in practice.

Mixture of employment and self-employment

12.3 It is quite feasible (and, indeed, not at all uncommon in the equine world) for the freelance service provider to have a mix of employment and self-employment. An alternative approach would be to say that the insecurity of self-employment can be underpinned by the security of employment.

General expenses of employment

12.4 The employees' costs of upkeep, replacement or repair of protective clothing or of uniforms (recognisable as such) are allowable where their duties require them to be self-financed (Inland Revenue Schedule E Manual, SE 32465 et seq).

Use of a room at home for business purposes has been allowed (*Newlin v Woods [1966] 42 TC 649*).

For those with mixed employment and self-employment it should be noted that expenses of part-time employment not allowable as employment expenses under ITEPA 2003 may not be deducted in computing the profits of an associated business within Schedule D (*Mitchell and Edon (Inspector of Taxes) v Ross [1961] 3 All ER 49, 40 TC 11).*

Specific provisions allow an employee to deduct from his salary expenses that he incurs in the course of his employment. These are to be found in ITEPA 2003 ss 336–344 (previously ICTA 1988 ss 198–201). Unfortunately, ICTA 1988 s 198, the main provision (now repealed and replaced by ITEPA 2003 s 336), was very narrowly drawn and over the years the courts have interpreted it extremely restrictively. Because of this, a paraphrase of section 198(1) would be dangerous and it is accordingly set out in full below (although the split into sub-paragraphs and the use of italics is the author's). The provision was substantially recast by the Finance Act 1998 with effect from 1998/99 onwards, although most of the old wording which had previously been judicially interpreted was preserved.

ICTA 1988 s 198 (now repealed and replaced by ITEPA 2003 s 336):

> 'If the holder of an office or employment is *obliged* to incur and defray out of the emoluments of that office or employment:
>
> (a) qualifying travelling expenses; or
> (b) any amount (other than qualifying travelling expenses) expended wholly, exclusively and necessarily in the performance of the duties of the office or employment;

there may be deducted from the emoluments to be assessed the amount so incurred and defrayed. [s 198(1)].

"Qualifying travelling expenses" means:

(a) amounts necessarily expended on travelling in the performance of the duties of the office or employment; or
(b) other expenses of travelling which:
  (i) are attributable to the necessary attendance at any place of the holder of the office or employment in the performance of the duties of the office or employment; and
  (ii) are not expenses of ordinary commuting or private travel. [s 198(1A)].'

Up to 1997/98 the text of s 198 read:

'If the holder of an office or employment is *necessarily obliged*:

(a) to incur and defray out of the emoluments of that office or employment the expenses:
  (i) of travelling *in the performance* of the duties of the office or employment; or
  (ii) of keeping and maintaining a horse to enable him to perform those duties; or
(b) otherwise to expend money wholly, exclusively and necessarily in the performance of those duties;

there may be deducted from the emoluments to be assessed the expenses so necessarily incurred and defrayed.'

It will be seen that the changes relate wholly to travelling expenses apart from the consignment to history of the relief for keeping and maintaining a horse (perhaps a shame in the minds of those operating in the world of equine taxes?).

Travel expenses

12.5 'Qualifying travelling expenses' are amounts necessarily expended on travelling in the performance of the duties of the office or employment, or other travel expenses which

- are attributable to necessary attendance at any place of the holder of the office or employment in the performance of those duties; and
- are not expenses of either 'ordinary commuting' or 'private travel'.

Expenses of travel between two places at which duties are performed of different offices or employments under, or with, companies in the same group are treated as necessarily expended in the performance of the duties to be performed at the destination. Companies are members of the same group for this purpose if one is a 51% subsidiary (by reference to ordinary share capital) of the other or both 51% subsidiaries of a third company. The tax planning key to the equine world is an equine employee who has to travel to different yards, studs or locations and the ability to claim expenses.

'Ordinary commuting' means travel between home (or a place other than a 'workplace' in relation to the office or employment) and a place which is a 'permanent workplace' in relation to the office or employment. 'Private travel' means travel between home and a place that is not a 'workplace' in relation to the office or employment, or between two places neither of which is a 'workplace' in relation to the office or employment.

Travel which, for practical purposes, is substantially ordinary commuting or private travel is treated as such. 'Private travel' is travelling to the equine yard or stud every day. If travel to a 'temporary' yard takes place then the expenses of travel are allowable.

A 'workplace' is a place at which attendance is necessary in the performance of the duties of the office or employment. It is a 'permanent workplace' if it is not a 'temporary workplace' and attendance there in the performance of those duties is regular. Except it is a 'temporary workplace' if the purpose of attendance there is to perform a task of limited duration or some other temporary purpose.

A workplace is not a 'temporary workplace' if attendance there is in the course of a 'period of continuous work' at that place lasting more than 24 months or compromising all (or almost all) of the period for which the office or employment is likely to be held, or if it is reasonable to assume that it will be in the course of such a period.

A 'period of continuous work' at a place is a period over which, looking at the whole period and considering all the duties of the office or employment, those duties fall to be performed to a significant extent at that place (ie 40% or more of working time is spent there – see Inland Revenue booklet 490, para 3.12). Actual or contemplated modifications of the place at which the duties are performed which do not have any substantial effect on the journey or on the travelling expenses are disregarded. This explains when a temporary yard or stud becomes permanent.

A place regularly attended in the performance of the duties of the offices or employment which forms the base from which those duties are performed, or which is the place at which the tasks to be carried out in the performance of those duties are allocated, is treated as a permanent workplace.

Similarly, where the duties are defined by reference to an area (whether or not requiring attendance outside the area), and attendance is required at different places in the area (none of them a permanent workplace) in performance of the duties, then that area is treated as a permanent workplace if it would be so treated (as above) were it a place. An example here would be where an employee's permanent place of employment is a Newmarket Stud and the temporary employment is, say, a visit to help out at the stud in Norfolk which deals with 'overspill' horses. If visits to the Norfolk stud became regular, expenses would cease to be allowable subject to the exact facts.

Inland Revenue Booklet 490 'Employee Travel: A Tax and NIC's Guide For Employees' also provides comprehensive general guidance, and pamphlet IR161 is a short guide.

As competitions are generally nationwide, equine employees often have to travel extensive miles and a car, van or pool car is often provided.

Benefits in kind for staff

General

12.6 Equine staff should normally be able to take advantage of the tax-efficient 'job-related' accommodation, ie the exempt status for the purposes of the benefit in kind legislation in respect of employee housing. This is dealt with at **12.13** and **12.14** below. The 'pool car' for trainers is also a possible benefits exemption. Staff will have to travel extensively and incur considerable costs. The interaction of tax-efficient travel expense claims is covered at **12.5** above.

There are three main hurdles that need to be overcome to obtain a deduction for an expense against employment income.

- the employee must be 'obliged' to incur it;
- it must be incurred 'in the performance of' the duties of the employment (other than travelling expenses within ICTA 1988 s 198(1A)(b) (now repealed and replaced by ITEPA 2003 s 338(2)).
- except for travelling expenses, it must be 'wholly, exclusively and necessarily' incurred.

Obviously, it is very difficult to meet all three of these tests.

'Obliged' has been held to connote an expense that is not personal to the employee but that each and every holder of the office or employment would have to incur. The leading case is *Ricketts v Colquhoun [1926] AC 1, 10 TC 118*. A barrister who lived and worked in London was appointed to the office of Recorder of Portsmouth. He claimed to deduct his travelling expenses to Portsmouth. It was held that he could not do so as he would not have incurred the expense had he lived in Portsmouth. 'In the performance of the duties' is an equally hard test to satisfy.

For full-time box drivers, who can be classified as lorry drivers, there are special concessions. No tax charge will arise if an employer reimburses to the driver the extra cost of travelling and subsistence which the employee incurs because he is away on duty. Where a driver travels full time in the course of his duty, the additional cost of meals at restaurants and cafes over what he would have spent if he were able to get home for meals can similarly be reimbursed – unless the driver travels only in a limited area. The driver is expected to produce bills or vouchers (Statement of Practice 16/80).

Cars

The 'green' car

12.7 The 'green' car issue is one of great debate. There are those who consider the costs far outweigh the tax benefits, but as the cost-effective formula of the green car develops it is a matter that many equine employers find of interest.

Car benefits have been the focus of much attention of late. The recent increase in tax on car benefits has hit some taxpayers hard and everyone has been looking at ways of making sure that these costs are minimised.

One recent innovation for the green car is the advent of the availability of 100% first-year allowances in FA 2002 which could mean that the employee can negotiate with the employer to try and help compensate for the extra benefit in kind.

The100% first-year allowance is available for low-emission cars used in a business or by employees and refuelling equipment for vehicles using natural gas or hydrogen. Businesses can also claim 100% allowances on the cost of designated energy saving technologies for leasing, letting or hire. To qualify, the vehicles must be registered on or after 17 April 2002 and either be electrically propelled or emit less than 120 g/km of carbon dioxide.

One of the problems associated with benefits in kind in the equine business, and particularly motor vehicles, is that historically, the racing industry likes its cars like its horses – fast and expensive! Likewise, some of the other equestrian activities need strong but expensive four-wheel drive machines! These are afforded considerable tax protection in the unincorporated business, but on incorporation can become taxable benefits for the new director/shareholder.

The benefits in kind position must not be overlooked and trying to convince directors of the favourable tax benefits of vans (no matter how amazing the sign writing) or twin cabs (no matter how much tack you can carry in the back) can be difficult! It is also important to look at 'greener' alternatives.

Computing car benefits

12.8 The tax payable on a 'company car' is governed by four factors:

- the list price of the car, on the day before it was first registered, plus certain accessories;
- the rate at which the car emits carbon dioxide (CO_2);
- the fuel type (for most types of car, this is all the information you need to work out the taxable benefit);
- the individual's highest rate of income tax.

An individual can find their taxable percentage of the list price for 2003/04 using the following table.

CO_2 *g/km*	**Taxable** *Petrol*	*Diesel*	**CO_2** *g/km*	**Taxable** *Petrol*	*Diesel*	**CO_2** *g/km*	**Taxable** *Petrol*	*Diesel*
Less than 160	15%	18%	190 to 194	22%	25%	225 to 229	29%	32%
160 to 164	16%	19%	195 to 199	23%	26%	230 to 234	30%	33%
165 to 169	17%	20%	200 to 204	24%	27%	235 to 239	31%	34%
170 to 174	18%	21%	205 to 209	25%	28%	240 to 244	32%	35%
175 to 179	19%	22%	210 to 214	26%	29%	245 to 249	33%	36%
180 to 184	20%	23%	215 to 219	27%	30%	250 to 254	34%	37%
185 to 189	21%	24%	220 to 224	28%	31%	255 and over	35%	38%

For how to find out how much CO_2 a company car emits, see the following:

- the car's V5 registration document;
- the dealer;
- the data pages of car magazines for current models;
- the Vehicle Certificate Agency at www.vca.gov.uk;
- the Society of Motor Manufacturers and Trades at www.smmt.co.uk/co2/co2search.cfm.

Reliable emissions data is not widely available for cars registered before 1 January 1998. For those cars the following taxable percentages of the list price apply, regardless of fuel type.

Engine capacity	*Taxable percentage*
Up to 1,400 cc	15%
1,401 cc to 2,000 cc	22%
Over 2,000 cc	32%

It is important to remember that the rate of the taxable benefit will rise in 2004 – for the comparative rates, simply deduct 10 from all the CO_2 figures in the table. The rate may very well rise again in 2005.

The 'greener' alternatives

12.9 Starting from the emissions-based taxable benefit rate (15% or more – see the table above), the taxable benefit is then discounted by:

- cars running on electricity only, 6% (so, emissions being zero, the percentage of list price chargeable to tax is 9%);
- for petrol/battery hybrids, 2% plus a further 1% for each 20g/km by which the CO_2 emissions are less than 159;
- for diesels meeting Euro IV standards, 3% (that is, the 3% diesel supplement is waived for these cars);
- for cars running on gas, 1%, plus a further 1% for each 20g/km by which the CO_2 emissions are less than 159;
- for gas/petrol hybrids the discount varies – the discount is as for cars running on gas, alone, if the car was built after 31 December 1999 to run on both petrol and gas.

The van and the twin cab pick-up

12.10 The benefit in kind on a van is so beneficial that a review was announced in the 2003 Budget. At the time of writing the details are awaited.

In the desire to pay as little tax as possible on the benefit of a motor vehicle, taxpayers have recently looked more and more towards 'vans' or at least to vehicles which purport to be vans! The taxable benefit on a 'van' is £500. For a 40% taxpayer this means £200 tax payable. Now that the phrase 'white van man' has become part of the English language there are some who might squirm at the very prospect of such an idea but it is important to look at what qualifies as a van. The very popular twin cab (also known as crew cab or dual) pick-up may qualify as such. The Inland Revenue and HM Customs and Excise take the view that a vehicle will qualify if its load bearing capacity is at least 1,000 kilograms. If pick-up owners are VAT registered they can reclaim the input VAT. To claim the VAT refund, owners must have businesses which require the use such vehicles.

Note, however, that the addition of a 'hard-top' to a pick-up may reduce its load-bearing capacity below this level!

In the very difficult times that have been facing the motor industry recently, suppliers have not been slow in stressing the tax benefits of these vehicles with marketing even featuring Pamela Anderson. Such 'vans' often include air conditioning, leather seats and a good sound system. They are seen as seriously trendy because of the rugged looks.

So for those pondering over whether or not to have a company car and, if so, which one or how to deal with it, pick-ups should not be dismissed.

The Government's consultation on vans is likely to take into account the level of private use and whether or not free fuel is provided. It is also proposed that, consistent with the Government's environmental policy, the reduction for 'older, more polluting vans' should be abolished and a higher charge for them should be considered. No figures are known yet, but it seems likely that the new scale charge could be based on some crude measure of emissions (perhaps engine size and fuel type), with incentives for the use of cleaner fuels. Vans cannot be dealt with in the same way as cars because there is no EU or UK legal requirement for them to have a CO_2 rating on which the charge could be based. Nor, as yet, is there any obvious way of dealing with the distinction between those vans used as real tools of the trade and those more comfortable models bought mainly for tax-efficient private use.

Mileage rates

12.11 Mileage rates, for business travel, paid at the following rates do not attract a charge to tax or NICs for 2003/04.

Vehicle	*First 10,000 miles*	*Thereafter*
Cars	40p	25p
Motorcycles	24p	24p
Bicycles	20p	20p

Car – fuel only advisory rates

Engine capacity	*Petrol*	*Diesel*	*Gas*
Up to 1,400 cc	10p	9p	6p
1,400 to 2,000 cc	12p	9p	7p
Over 2,000 cc	14p	12p	9p

The Inland Revenue advisory rates can be applied as a tax-free maximum rate for employees claiming for petrol used on business journeys and for employees' reimbursing their employers with the cost of petrol used for private journeys. The Inland Revenue will consider claims for a higher maximum rate, if it can be demonstrated that it is *necessary* for an employee to use a car with higher than average fuel costs.

If the employee pays for the full cost of all fuel for private journeys (usually including home to work) there will be no car fuel benefit. In *all* other cases the full tax charge will be due.

The taxable car fuel benefit for 2003/04 is calculated by multiplying £14,400 by the same percentage as applies (or would apply) for the car benefit.

Example

A company car driver has a car which, on the day before it was first registered, had a list price of £18,000.

It runs on petrol, and emits 182 g/km of CO_2.

If we assume the driver pays tax at 40%, the annual tax bill on the car is:

£18,000 × 20% × 40% = £1,440.

If the employer provides any fuel used for private journeys and is not reimbursed for the cost, the 2003/04 tax bill for the fuel is:

£14,400 × 20% × 40% = £1,152.

VAT on scale charge for quarters commencing on or after 1 May 2003.

Engine Size	*Petrol*	*Diesel*
Up to 1,400 cc	£35.29	£33.51
1,401 cc to 2,000 cc	£44.68	£33.51
Over 2,000 cc	£65.82	£42.14

National Insurance

12.12 One of the biggest problems facing any equestrian employer is the headache of National Insurance.

National Insurance contributions (NICs) for 2003/04	**Employer**	**Employee**
Class 1 – not contracted out:		
Weekly earnings band:		
Up to £89.00	Nil	Nil
£89.01–£595.00	12.8%	11%
Over £595	12.8%	1%
Men aged 65 and over	As above	Nil
Women aged 60 and over	As above	Nil

National Insurance contributions (NICs) for 2003/04	Employer	Employee
Class 1A:		
On relevant benefits	12.8%	Nil
Class 2:		
Self-employed	£2 per week	—
Limit of net earnings for exception	£4,095 pa	—
Class 3:		
Voluntary	£6.95 per week	—
Class 4*:		
Self-employed on profits		
£4,615–£30,940	8%	—
Over £30,940	1%	—

* Exemption applied if state retirement age was reached by 6 April 2003.

Board and lodging

Racehorse training staff

12.13 The tax treatment is set out in the Inland Revenue's Inspector's Manual SE68502. The detail is found in ICTA 1988 s 19(1)(1) (now repealed and replaced by ITEPA 2003 ss 10(2), 15(1), 21(1) and 22(1)) and Extra-Statutory Concession A60:

> 'Because of the traditional practice of providing board and lodging for stable lads, the Revenue accepts that no tax charge arises to those who are outside the scope of the benefits legislation if certain conditions are satisfied. The conditions are those which apply to farm workers – see the Revenue's Schedule E Employment Manual SE50012.
>
> Where living accommodation is provided, instead of board and lodging, (SE11351) about possible exemption from charge.'

The stable staff of racehorse trainers who live on the premises and certain other key workers who live close to the stables can live in the accommodation provided without being regarded as in receipt of a taxable benefit.

Full details of the agreement covering the treatment of accommodation provided to stable staff in the horseracing industry can be obtained from Personal Tax (Technical), Solihull.

The national agreement made between PriceWaterhouseCoopers, the NTF and the SLA on the tax treatment of living accommodation provided to stable staff is discussed at **12.19** below.

Agricultural workers

12.14 See the Inland Revenue's Inspector's Manual SE50012 for the tax treatment of agricultural workers and the relevant board and lodgings exemption for 'lower paid' workers. This is available on the basis that certain conditions are met.

The full text of the Extra-Statutory Concession A60 is:

> 'Income tax will not be charged on the value of free board and lodging provided for agricultural workers by their employers despite their entitlement to take a higher cash wage in lieu provided by the Agricultural Wages Act, where all the following conditions are satisfied:
>
> (a) The worker is not a director or in employment to which Chapter II of Part V, ICTA 1988 applies.
> (b) The contract with the employer provides for a net cash wage with free board and lodging.
> (c) Where the board and lodging is not provided in the farmhouse, the employer has a contract with a third party for its provision and payments under the contract are made direct to the third party.
>
> Where, instead of being entitled to a net cash wage and free board and lodging, the worker is entitled to a gross cash wage, he is assessable on the gross amount even if the employer, with his agreement, deducts a sum to pay for his board and lodging in the farmhouse or elsewhere.'

For the purposes of condition (c) above, a contract between the employee acting as agent for the employer and the third party providing the accommodation, is acceptable. Provided such a contract exists, no objection should be raised if the landlady is the mother of the employee concerned. The payments under the contract should be made direct to the landlady by the farmer. An arrangement whereby the farmer gives the employee a sealed addressed envelope containing the payment for board and lodging to be handed to the landlady should be accepted as meeting this requirement.

Rent-a-room scheme

12.15 Extra-Statutory Concession C60 makes direct reference to accommodation being provided by third parties.

A practical point worth mentioning here is the 'rent-a-room relief' scheme.

In any equestrian activity, finding good staff is very difficult and, as most activities take place in a combination of isolated rural outposts or in the over-crowded equestrian centres of, say, Newmarket or Lambourne, then finding accommodation can be difficult. Persuading locals with a desire for a tax-efficient income stream to allow staff to rent a room from them can be extremely beneficial for both the equine employer and the recipient of the money.

This relief was introduced as from 6 April 1992 to encourage those with spare rooms in their houses to let them out (Finance (No 2) Act 1992 Sch 10). Residences in which the rooms are let must be the individual's only or main residence.

'Residence' means a building (or part of a building) occupied or intended to be occupied as a separate residence. It includes a caravan or a houseboat. A residence qualifies if it is an individual's only or main residence at any time in the basis period. The test is based on the income tax rules for mortgage interest relief, and not the capital gains tax principal private residence exemption.

It appears that the relief can be claimed by both owner occupiers and tenants. Relief is given in terms of the gross rent accruing for a particular period up to an amount of £4,250 from 6 April 1997, but it is possible that this figure will be varied by Treasury Order in future years. If the gross amount accruing (not allowing any deductions) exceeds £4,250, the recipient may elect to:

1 pay tax on the amount by which the rent exceeds £4,250 without any relief or deductible expenses; or
2 calculate the profit from the letting by deducting expenses incurred from the gross rent, and paying tax on the net profit in the ordinary way.

The choice of alternative (2) is effectively an election not to claim the relief, which will be more advantageous, of course, if for example, deductible expenses produce a net allowable loss. Alternative (1), on the other hand, is likely to be advantageous where the gross rents marginally exceed the threshold of £4,250.

There are no stipulations concerning the length of the tenancy, so that the exemption is arguably applicable to bed and breakfast accommodation offered to holidaymakers in a farmhouse, although there is some debate about this. Relevant sums for the purposes of the exemption include those receivable for goods or services, including meals, cleaning and laundry. However, relief will not be available on cottages let to holidaymakers, which will not qualify as a 'main residence', unless such a cottage had been separately occupied by a member of the farming family.

Rent-a-room relief is not available if a residence is let for use as an office or for other trade or business purposes, rather than for providing furnished living accommodation. The Inland Revenue's view is that for the relief to apply, the rent must be receivable for the use of 'furnished accommodation' meaning 'a place to live'. However, relief is not denied where a lodger living in the house is provided with the use of a room with a desk as a study, eg a student (Inland Revenue *Tax Bulletin* 12 August 1994).

If a farmhouse is in multiple occupations, and each occupier takes in paying guests, the exempt amount of £4,250 is divided amongst the occupiers. Participation in the rent-a-room scheme will not prejudice principal private residence exemption from capital gains tax.

Family members employed in the business

12.16 Many equine businesses employ family members, especially the children. Often children are paid a sum just below the NIC limit. For the purposes of employment legislation, they must be at least 14 years old. Tasks carried out by family members should be evidenced to prove that their remuneration is not simply 'disguised pocket money' or income diversion. Duties will normally include grooming, exercising horses, travelling to competitions in the role of groom etc.

Claim for future liabilities

12.17 The nature of the equine industry is such that staff do suffer accidents and compensation may have to be paid in some cases. Adequate insurance cover is obviously important. However, an expense claim cannot be made for future payments of damages in respect of accidents to employees unless liability has been admitted or established.

The ruling of the case of *James Spencer & Co v IRC (1950) 32 TC 111* emphasises this point. The case of *Albion Rovers Football Club v IRC (1952) 33 TC 331* states that wages are deductible where paid. Future liabilities of wages to equine staff cannot be provided in financial accounts (see also FRS12 in this context).

P11D dispensations and treatment of expenses

12.18 An employer can apply for a dispensation in respect of certain benefits and expenses payable to employees. To do this, he must send to the Inspector of Taxes a statement of the circumstances in which such benefits or expenses are provided for employees. If the Inspector is satisfied that no tax would be payable on the expenses, eg because they are bona fide business expenses or because the employee will reimburse the full cost of personal expenses, he can exempt them from these provisions. The Inspector may revoke such a dispensation at any time if, in his opinion, it is reasonable to do so. He can revoke it with retrospective effect to the day it was originally given if he thinks fit, or with effect from any later date that he feels appropriate (ITEPA 2003 s 96(5)–(8)).

Equine employers should always consider the benefit of dispensations.

National agreement on the tax treatment of living accommodation provided to stable staff

12.19 PriceWaterhouseCoopers, who are the tax advisers to the National Trainers Federation (NTF), agreed with the Inland Revenue the national treatment of living accommodation provided to stable staff.

Living accommodation (as opposed to 'board and lodging') provided to stable staff will be tax exempt for all stable staff living within the curtilage of the training establishment. It will also be exempt if the employees can reach the yard within ten minutes or the staff have access to motorised transport and live within a five-mile radius of the yard.

Stable staff cannot sublet, cannot be reimbursed and the staff do not have the right at any time to give up the accommodation in return for higher wages. Trainers should be aware that very few staff can meet the strict exemption from tax conditions on board and lodgings and the straight provision of accommodation is generally more efficient.

The agreement between the NTF and the Stable Lads Association (SLA) defined grade 'A' staff as 'head lad, travelling head lad, assistant trainer and other senior staff'. The member of staff must be able to comply with the conditions mentioned above. The key is how close they live to the yard.

The employee will be taxable on the costs of the accommodation paid by the employer, eg telephone bills, use of furniture, appliances and repairs, internal decoration, heating, lighting and cleaning.

When there is a tax charge on living accommodation the tax due will be:

- where the employer rents the accommodation, the employee will be taxed on the amount equal to rent paid;
- where the accommodation is owned by the employer (freehold or leasehold) the tax charge is based on the Gross Rateable Value (GRV). This is complex when the cost of the property is over £75,000 (this needs to be changed).

Buying and Selling Equestrian Property – Tax Planning 13

Practical equine tax planning and BATR

13.1 It is beyond the scope of this book to look at all the complications of capital gains tax (CGT) and, particularly, business asset taper relief (BATR). The aim is to highlight to the equine taxpayer and adviser how beneficial the various reliefs can be. The whole issue of tax planning for land disposals is dealt with in the author's book, *Tolley's Tax Planning for Farm and Land Diversification* (2002) LexisNexis UK, at Chapter 14. It is sufficient to repeat in broad terms that the rate of CGT at 10% for business gains is a tax advantage that should not be overlooked by the tax adviser and the equine business (the calculation is set out at **13.6** below, see also the table at **13.9**).

Principal private residence relief (PPR) was first introduced at **2.5** and **2.34**, and the importance of the Stud House and the complexities of APR planning was looked into at **7.28**. This is also looked at in more detail throughout chapter 4 of the author's book *Tax Planning for Farm and Land Diversification* (2002) LexisNexis UK. When considering any purchase or sale of equestrian property the fine tax balance between business usage and PPR of the house must be planned for. PPR includes not only the house but the garden and extensive curtilage if appropriate. Property development in the garden and curtilage can be achieved with £nil tax rate of PPR as opposed to 10% BATR. What a dilemma.

Avoiding 'tainted taper' relief – CGT

13.2 During the relevant period of ownership, it is possible that an asset may have been, at different times, both a business asset and a non-business asset, perhaps because an individual did not trade throughout the period or because of a change in the statutory definition of a business asset during the period. An example would be where a stud that was, say, let from 1998 to 2001 and then farmed by the owner.

In such cases, an apportionment is necessary. To do this the tax-payer must ascertain the proportion of the relevant period of ownership for which the asset disposed of was, or was not, a business asset.

'Tainted taper' has been the subject of volumes of lectures, articles and debate. It arises when a business asset goes through a period of 'non-business status' for the purposes of the relief. In relation to a stud or equine property, this would be if, from 6 April 1998, the property (or part of the property) had for some time been:

- let out;
- used for personal use;
- redundant; or
- the trading activities had lost business status.

If the potential capital gains tax is likely to be significant then 'new ownership' to avoid tainted taper could be looked at as a tax planning tool, ie to start a fresh taper relief time period.

Rollover of gains from/into an equine property

13.3 In broad terms, 'rollover relief' is the capital gains tax relief under which a chargeable gain arising on the disposal of an equestrian business can be rolled into another business asset. In tax terms, there are several forms of relief which may enable chargeable gains arising on the disposal, or deemed disposal, of assets to be rolled over and the gain subtracted from the cost of acquiring a replacement asset or which enables gains to be deferred until some later event. There are a number of reliefs by virtue of the Taxation of Chargeable Gains Act (TCGA) 1992 and the relevant provisions are set out as follows:

- section 23 – capital sums applied to replace or restore assets;
- section 152 – replacement of business assets;
- section 162 – transfer of business to a company;
- section 165 – gift of a business asset;
- section 229 – transfer of shares to a QUEST;
- section 247 – transfer of interests in land to certain authorities;
- Schedule 5B – enterprise investment schemes (EIS);
- Schedule 5C – venture capital trusts (VCT);
- Schedule 7C – transfer of shares to an ESOP.

In addition, the Finance Act 2000 Sch 15 provides relief for corporate venturing.

It is likely that the most frequently used provision will be TCGA 1992 s 152.

It will sometimes be necessary to compare two or more potential reliefs before making a final selection of the relief to be obtained by the stud. For consideration of why the EIS will probably not apply to a stud farm but could, perhaps, apply to other equestrian activities, see **13.4** below.

Provided the stud qualifies as a business, gains on its assets may qualify for rollover relief.

The key planning point is that a gain does not have to be from, or to, an equestrian business so long as there is a 'trade' being carried on, eg a gain from assets of an engineering business can be rolled over into an equestrian business and the gain from an equestrian business could be rolled over into assets of an engineering business.

For example, where a specific *part* of the equine business is sold at a gain, such as, perhaps, an old stable block near the village centre is sold off for residential development. The proceeds of this gain might be spent on another business asset within the equine operation, eg a new stable block, indoor school and all-weather gallop. Rollover relief ought to be available if the relevant conditions are met.

For full relief to be achieved the 'whole' of the proceeds of the gain have to be spent.

It is most likely that TCGA 1992 s 152 will be used against replacements of business assets. The new asset must be purchased 12 months before, or 36 months after, the disposal of the old asset.

Rollover of gains into an EIS company

13.4 The availability of the CGT deferral relief using the Enterprise Investment Scheme (EIS) can be of key importance to the equestrian business which is looking at the twin problems of how to shelter a gain and how to raise the capital of a business tax efficiently.

Essentially, stud farming is farming and although this does receive all the tax reliefs of farming it suffers restrictions under the EIS. One of the key factors to trading through a limited company can be the ability to raise capital through EIS. In principle, all equine activities other than a stud should qualify. The possibility of relief via the EIS is one of the few clear advantages of equine activities not being classified as farming.

Note that it is possible to indefinitely defer tax on the sale of a property investment company by reinvesting the gain into an unquoted trading company if it qualifies as an EIS company.

Property investors have never been able to benefit from the capital gains rollover relief available to traders who reinvest the proceeds of the sale of trading premises into new premises, goodwill and/or other trading assets. However, individuals and trustees can defer gains by reinvesting into shares in suitable companies that qualify for the EIS. If the equine business qualifies for EIS then it should be eligible.

Currently, an individual or trustee that realises a gain on the sale of an asset can defer any tax on the gain by subscribing for shares in companies which satisfy conditions for the EIS (TCGA 1992 Sch 5B).

The company must be unquoted and carry on a trade but some trades are excluded. The excluded activities are:

- dealing in land, commodities, futures, shares, securities or other financial instruments;
- dealing in goods other than in the course of an ordinary trade of wholesale or retail distribution;
- banking, insurance, money-lending, debt factoring, hire purchase financing or other financial activities;
- leasing or receiving royalties or licence fees;
- providing legal or accountancy services;
- property development;
- farming or market gardening;
- holding, managing or occupying woodlands or other forestry activities;
- operating or managing hotels or comparable establishments;
- operating or managing nursing homes or residential care homes;
- providing services to a commonly controlled company which itself carries on one of the above trades.

[TCGA 1992 Sch 5B para 1(2); ICTA 1988 s 297].

The key areas which the equine business should be wary of are farming, woodlands, leasing of equine assets and potential property links with dealing in land or property investment.

Another EIS condition is that the funds raised by the company must be used for a qualifying trade carried on wholly or mainly in the UK. The company need not be UK resident.

A further condition of EIS relates to the size of the company. To qualify for reinvestment relief, the company issuing the shares must not have gross assets in excess of £15m immediately before the shares are issued, nor £16m afterwards. Where the company has subsidiaries, that test is applied to the group as a whole (TCGA 1992 Sch 5B; ICTA 1988 s 293).

Although the company must be unquoted, companies whose shares are dealt solely on the Alternative Investment Market (AIM) can qualify.

Finally, the company in question cannot be a 51% subsidiary, or otherwise be under the control of another company. Nor can it control another company which is itself not a 'qualifying' subsidiary (ICTA 1988 s 293(8)).

To qualify for the EIS relief, the individual or trustee must subscribe in cash for shares in a qualifying company up to one year before, or within three years after, the disposal giving rise to the gain. The shares must be ordinary shares with no preferential rights or rights to be redeemed (TCGA 1992 Sch 5B para 1).

It should be noted that unlike the replacement of business asset relief dealt with in **CHAPTER 3**, it is sufficient to reinvest only the gain to obtain full tax deferral under reinvestment relief. For section 152 relief, the entire proceeds of sale have to be reinvested for full deferral (TCGA 1992 s 152). Thus the EIS deferral relief is arguably cheaper.

There are provisions for clawback of the EIS relief if certain things happen within three years of the issue of the shares (or five years, if the shares were issued before April 2000), for example:

- the acquired shares cease to be eligible shares;
- the company ceases to be a qualifying company;
- the person holding the shares becomes resident and/or ordinarily resident outside the United Kingdom (unless the reason for this is a short-term working assignment abroad).

The relief is also clawed back if the person holding the shares or any associate receives value from the company during the four-year period which starts one year before the issue of the shares. The whole of the gain would then be brought into charge, no matter how much or little value was received, subject to the EIS de minimis limits on value.

Of course, the deferred gain also comes into charge whenever EIS shares are disposed of, unless the disposal is a transfer to the disposer's spouse at no gain, no loss.

As presently drafted, there is no doubt that the conditions for the EIS reinvestment relief are somewhat restrictive. The EIS rules are complex and contain many pitfalls that can result in denial of the relief. The new shares acquired would potentially attract 100% business property relief for inheritance tax purposes should there be a future chargeable gift of them or legacy on death.

Temporary business use

13.5 The ability to rollover a gain into an asset with temporary business use can be a useful tax planning device. For example, if a gain is rolled over into a genuine working stud or a new stable block under TCGA 1992 s 152 and subsequently, due to problems of profitability, the property is let out, the rolled-in gain does not crystallise unless, and until, there is a disposal of the asset. Non-business use does not cause the gain to come into charge.

Business asset taper relief – use to the equine industry

13.6 The CGT benefit of taper relief which has introduced a potential minimum effective CGT rate of 10% has brought a dramatic advantage to equestrian and farming property. The rate of 10% is calculated using the current highest rate of UK income tax of 40% and the highest rate of BATR of 75% (see the table at **13.8** below). 75% of 40% is 10% for business assets. (It is also set out in the table at **13.9**.)

BATR now makes it less likely that a rollover relief claim will need to be considered.

By the mid 1990s, it was widely thought that CGT was too complicated to operate – particularly considering its relatively modest yield. Whilst some voices were suggesting abolition, no doubt the fear of income being converted into capital gains made that option unattractive to the Government. Instead, one of the complicating factors (indexation allowance) was abolished by the incoming Labour Government in its first full Budget in March 1998. In its place came taper relief.

BATR and capital losses

13.7 Taper relief is applicable if a taxpayer's total capital gains exceed the taxpayer's total capital losses available for the year (TCGA 1992 s 2A(1)). This means that the losses can be wasted to the extent that they reduce an individual's gains to the annual exempt amount if a similar reduction could have been achieved by using taper relief. There was always a risk of same year losses being wasted under the pre-taper relief rules. For the trading losses realised after 5 April 2004, relief is given against gains after the application of taper relief. Prior to this it was before taper relief subject to a specific election for 2002/03 and 2003/04.

The whole question of tax planning and the use of capital losses brought forward against business and non-business gains is a complex area and one that tax planners ignore at their peril. The key issue here has to be liaising with the client on potential capital disposals and keeping in full a memorandum of losses for both income and capital.

BATR table of relief – business and non-business

13.8 The table below lists the taper relief percentage rates from 1998 to 2002.

Rate of taper relief (TCGA 1992 s 2A (5))

Number of whole years in qualifying holding period	*Non-business assets*	*Business assets*		
	Disposals from 6 April 1998	Disposals from 6 April 1998 to 5 April 2000	Disposals from 6 April 2000 to 5 April 2002	Disposals from 6 April 2002
0	0%	0%	0%	0%
1	0%	7.5%	12.5%	50%
2	0%	15%	25%	75%
3	5%	22.5%	50%	
4	10%	30%	75%	
5	15%	37.5%		
6	20%	45%		
7	25%	52.5%		
8	30%	60%		
9	35%	67.5%		
10 or more	40%	75%		

The table shows the 'time' benefit of BATR as opposed to non-business asset taper relief and also the different benefit in the size of the relief. To equine businesses that might have problems proving the business status (see **CHAPTER 3**) this can be of great importance.

If an asset qualifies as a business asset throughout the relevant period of ownership, then the amount of business asset taper relief is simple.

Simple table for business assets

13.9 The table at **13.8** above focused on the comparison of business and non-business. The following table has the focal point of comparing 2002 rates at 2000 rates and emphasising the resultant benefits.

This table shows the benefits of the reliefs for disposals of business after 6 April 2002 in comparison to the previous period. This shows clearly the calculation of a 10% potential rate as set out at **13.1** and **13.6**.

	FA 2000 rates	
Whole years held from 6 April 1998	*Percentage of gain charged to tax*	*Effective rate of tax for higher-rate taxpayer*
<1	100%	40%
1	87.5%	35%
2	75%	30%
3	50%	20%
4 or more	25%	10%
	New rates (Disposals from 6 April 2002)	
Whole years held from 6 April 1998	*Percentage of gain charged to tax*	*Effective rate of tax for higher-rate taxpayer*
<1	100%	40%
1	50%	20%
2	25%	10%
3	25%	10%
4 or more	25%	10%

Shares in a limited company and assets in a limited company

13.10 For shares to be classed as business assets, a company generally has to be trading.

Assets held in a limited company do *not* attract BATR – see CHAPTER 9: THE EQUINE BUSINESS STRUCTURE.

Separate land and buildings – tax planning

13.11 For rollover relief purposes, 'buildings' and 'land' are the most widely used class of assets (TCGA 1992 s 155). They are defined as follows.

- Building – any building or a part of a building and any permanent or semi-permanent structure and the nature of a building occupied (as well as used) only for the purpose of the trade.
- Land – any land occupied (as well as used) only for the purpose of the trade. Schedule 1 of the Interpretation Act 1978 requires that unless the contrary intention appears the word 'land' includes 'buildings and other structures, lands covered with water and any estate interest, servitude or right in or over land'. This approach is somewhat modified by TCGA 1992 s 288(1) which defines land as including 'messuages, tenements and hereditaments, houses and buildings of any tenure'.

Note that that buildings and land are treated separately. It can be extremely useful when matching acquisitions or disposals in support of a claim for rollover relief to identify sales of land and buildings so that the sale proceeds may be apportioned between two different assets, ie the building and the land. A similar approach may be used when land and buildings are purchased. This may facilitate smaller self-contained rollover relief claims in some cases. An example would be where an equine business sells the land and stables for development. The owner does not want to roll over the whole of the proceeds into the new purchase as the proceeds are too high. The CGT computation can be divided between the land and the buildings (stables). Capital gains (after BATR) can be paid on one element and the other rolled over into the new purchase.

It may, therefore, be possible to rollover a gain arising on disposal of only one of two assets leaving the gain on the other asset to absorb the annual exemption or perhaps losses. This could also interact with taper relief.

Holdover relief

Gift to family members

13.12 A gift, although potentially free of inheritance tax (IHT) as a potentially exempt transfer (PET), may still trigger a CGT charge. The provisions of TCGA 1992 s 165 may be used to hold over gains arising on a gift made directly to a family member or other connected person. The detail of TCGA 1992 s 165 has already been considered with regard to incorporation of an equine business at **10.20** above. If the gift is made into a discretionary trust, TCGA 1992 s 260 will achieve the same result. It should be noted that these holdover provisions can apply equally to the gift of let land if it falls within the definition of agricultural property for IHT purposes (TCGA 1992 Sch 7).

Note, however, when making gifts to separate the ownership of buildings from land with which they have been historically associated, entitlement rights to agricultural property relief (APR) on the buildings may be lost.

Holdover relief is available if an asset has been used for the purposes of a trade carried on by the transferor. This means that it has to have been in trade use just before it is gifted. The fact that there may be a change in the nature of the trade should not affect the operation of the relief. However, if there is a period of non-business use (including any gap period between successive trades), or part of the asset is not used for business purposes, apportionments will have to be made so that only part of the gain will qualify.

The agricultural link

13.13 Agricultural property, eg stud property, qualifying for APR for IHT purposes qualifies for holdover relief where it is not used for the purposes of trade carried on by the transferor, or his personal company (TCGA 1992 Sch 7 Pt 1). This effectively means that relief is available on the gift of let land even where the transferee does not actually use the property. Switching to non-agricultural lets, eg industrial units, will mean relief is lost.

The converted barn in residential use, even though previously used for trade purposes by the transferor, will not qualify as it would neither be used for the purposes of trade nor be occupied for the purposes of agriculture at the time of a subsequent gift.

Under current rules, a claim for holdover relief can be made under TCGA 1992 s 165 for disposals of business assets. In order to make a claim for holdover relief, it is important to identify persons involved that are eligible and also the assets which are capable of supporting a claim for holdover relief. It is worth looking at the definition of transferor's personal company.

Assets which qualify are those assets (or an interest in an asset) used for the purpose of a trade, profession or vocation, by the transferor's personal company or a member of the trading group of which the holding company is the transferor's personal company. This also includes shares or securities of a trading company or the holding company of a trading group where:

- shares or securities are neither listed or recognised by the Stock Exchange nor dealt with on the unlisted securities market; or
- the trading company or holding company is the transferor's personal company.

Part disposals

13.14 There is a Statement of Practice issued by the Inland Revenue that stipulates that where part of an estate is disposed of, for example, the sale of a field, the Inland Revenue will accept that such part-disposal can be regarded as a separate asset and any fair and reasonable method of apportioning the total cost or March 1982 value will be accepted by them. This cost is then deducted from the original cost or March 1982 value, whichever applies for the purposes of future disposals.

The advantage of the part-disposal rule is that there can be short-term benefits in reducing the chargeable gain by being able to allocate a higher base cost against the gain, which can be very beneficial.

The availability of BATR has, in some circumstances, made the use of the part-disposal rule less attractive. It was traditionally used as a short-term measure so as to alleviate immediate CGT charges, pay the minimum amount of CGT and leave a lower base cost for future capital gains.

Other items relevant for CGT planning as follows:

- death is not a chargeable event, ie there is no CGT payable on death and so short-term CGT benefits should be weighed against long-term aims;
- BATR post-5 April 2002, ie very favourable rates.

The timing of disposals will be important when looking at the part-disposal rule because it gives the tax practitioner and the landowner some degree of choice over what the base cost will be.

Small part-disposal rule

13.15 Another element of the part-disposal rule is that known as the 'small part-disposal rule'. Under TCGA 1992 s 242, the transferor may claim that the sale of land does not constitute a disposal where the following conditions are met:

- the consideration does not exceed £20,000;
- the consideration does not exceed 20% of the market value of the entire holding at the time of the transfer; and
- the consideration for all transfers of land made by the taxpayer in the year in question does not exceed £20,000. In this instance the sale proceeds would be deducted from the base cost.

Once again, both tax planning and tax calculation in relation to disposals of land is not straightforward and there are some factors, which could influence the decision-making process surrounding a disposal. These would include the use of annual exemptions and the use of BATR.

Of particular use may be the treatment given to small part-disposals of land available under TCGA 1992 s 242. Under this provision, proceeds from a small part-disposal of land used to finance new ventures can be maximised by taking advantage of the relief. The transferor may claim that the sale of the land does not constitute a disposal where the conditions as set out above are met.

If a parcel of land were to be sold, for example, by a husband and wife trading in partnership, it will be sensible to see which is preferable: using the annual CGT exemption or claiming part-disposal treatment. Now, it will also be relevant to consider BATR. There could be strong advantages in not claiming the relief so as to secure a higher base cost for future use.

The permutations of taper relief, part-disposal treatment and using the annual exemption along with other possible reliefs and claims for CGT mean that, in future, CGT planning will rarely facilitate quick over-the-telephone answers on planning decisions. From a practice management point of view, this highlights the need for the tax practitioner to document the choices clearly for clients. Ultimately, the decision on which action to take rests with the taxpayer, and all options must have been thoroughly considered and documentary evidence of this retained.

Artificial transactions in land

13.16 Property developers can be caught by the provisions of ICTA 1988 s 776(2)(c) which encompasses cases where 'land is developed with the sole or main object of realising a gain from disposing of the land when developed'. The aim of this section is for the Inland Revenue to prevent property dealing profits being treated as capital gain rather than income.

It has been said that some farmers and landowners enjoy 'growing houses' more than growing crops and after one genuine disposal they start to 'trade' in land. The purpose is to prevent property dealing profits being disguised as capital. The circumstances are generally limited to two situations:

- the disposal of shares in a property company (*Yuill v Wilson [1980] 3 All ER 7, [1980] STC 460*); or
- where a UK resident passes the opportunity to make a trading profit on UK land to an overseas company.

The scope of ICTA 1988 s 776 is broad and may catch transactions which have little or no element of artificiality; therefore the avoidance can be accidental or unwitting by the landowner. With the current shortage of houses, farmers and landowners may find themselves unknowingly caught by these provisions.

The rules apply in the following circumstances:

1 land is developed with the sole or main object of realising a gain from disposal later;
2 land is held as trading stock; or
3 the land or any interest that has its value derived from it (eg shares in a landowning company, interests in partnerships, etc) is acquired with the sole or main object of realising a gain on disposal.

In order for ICTA 1988 s 776 to apply, a gain of a *capital nature* must result. This means that the gain must not be chargeable as income under any of the Taxes Acts if it is trade. If a trade exists, it will be caught in the trading in land provisions.

'Slice of the action' schemes

13.17 One of the most common applications of ICTA 1988 s 776 arises under point 1 at **13.16** above involving 'slice of the action' schemes. These schemes involve the landowner selling surplus land to a developer, receiving a fixed sum, followed by future contingent payments based upon the success of the development. The developer himself will be trading and will, in effect, be passing some of the trading profits on to the former landowner. The receipt will be of a capital nature in the landowner's hands and accordingly will be caught by s 776 as a Schedule D Case 1 profit has emerged in a capital form. The Inland Revenue's authority for treating additional payments in this way can be found in *Page v Lowther [1983] STC 61*. The fixed sum, however, will remain chargeable to CGT. It is the contingent payments that must be taxable as trading profit.

Section 776 cannot be invoked where the landowner could be charged under Schedule D Case 1 – refer to the 'badges of trade' to see if it is pure trading (see **3.3** above).

Section 776 cannot apply in respect of the disposal of a main residence which is exempt from CGT (TCGA 1992 s 222) or would be if it were not for TCGA 1992 s 224(3), regarding residences acquired wholly or partly for the purpose of realising a gain from the disposal.

Option agreements

13.18 In many of cases the farmer will sell his land to a professional developer, and this will be classed as a CGT disposal.

The possibility of progressive and deferred sales and the use of option agreements should be considered. In the nature of things, developers are often only too ready to defer completion of transactions, and this readiness needs to be taken advantage of in terms of tax planning.

If a series of options are entered into with the sole aim of maximising the use of successive years' CGT annual exemptions, then the basic principles of *WT Ramsay Ltd v IRC [1981] STC 174* with extension by *Furniss (Inspector of Taxes) v Dawson [1984] AC 474, [1984] STC 153* cannot be overlooked, ie the Inspector of Taxes will be very aware of general anti-avoidance rules.

So as to avoid the loss of rollover or business asset taper relief, ensure that land over which a client has granted an option to a developer does not stand unused, or become incapable of use because it is inaccessible as a result of work that the developer has started on adjacent land.

This can happen during the construction of motorways or other developments. The Inland Revenue's *Tax Bulletin* Issue No 2 February 1992, highlighted the point that the Inland Revenue accept that rollover relief on replacement of business assets is available in respect of grants on the option over land by reference to the underlying land.

It may be prudent to preserve photographic or other evidence of farming use of the land right up to the day when the option is exercised.

Deferred consideration may fail to qualify for rollover relief, and the timing of both a grant and the likely exercise of option agreements requires careful consideration in conjunction with time limits for reinvestment.

An option is not a part disposal of the underlying land over which the option is granted (TCGA 1992 s 144). The grant of the option is the disposal of a separate asset – the option itself. Because it is not a part disposal, it does not matter how long the underlying land has been held by the person granting the option.

In a straightforward situation where the option is never exercised the capital gain arises on the grant of the option and no BATR will be due.

Once the option is exercised the disposal created by the grant of the option is cancelled (TCGA 1992 s 144(2) and (3)) and the sums received for both the grant and the exercise of the option are aggregated in one disposal at the time of the exercise. Taper relief then applies to the aggregated consideration, and is determined by reference to the date of the exercise, and by reference to the period of ownership of the underlying asset disposed of (TCGA 1992 Sch A1 para 13).

If the asset changes from being a business asset to a non-business asset between the date of the grant and exercise of an option the apportionment rules will apply to the whole gain and part of the gain will lose favourable business asset status. Similar restrictions apply where there is partial non-business use of the asset between the grant of the option and its exercise.

Where either change is unavoidable a contract that crystallises accrued gains at the date the change of status in the asset occurs will ensure the whole gain to date qualifies for the higher business rate of taper relief.

Where it is known that it will take time for a particular development project to move into profit it will be prudent to preserve evidence of both commerciality and profit seeking motive (business plans, budgets and cash flow projections of the equestrian business). This will give the opportunity to claim Schedule D Case 1 losses now in anticipation of future trading profit.

Planning consent for residential development may be difficult to obtain, but in terms of the value involved, this may be the most profitable route for the equine business to follow.

Commercially, it may be beneficial to retain some right over land to keep some control over future development. Ransom strips or covenants can be used to protect the landowner. Ransom strips result in the application of the CGT part-disposal rules. Covenants are a capital asset and so again their disposal may result in a part disposal. Their value will be difficult to ascertain and they are likely to have negligible costs attributable to their acquisition.

Land sold and leased back

13.19 Consider also the tax planning applicable to arrangements within ICTA 1988 s 779 for land sold and leased back. Where a lease when sold has no more than 50 years still to run and the period for which the premises are leased back is 15 years or less, any increased rent payable, so far as it does not exceed a commercial rent, is allowable as a deduction from profits. However, of the consideration received by the lessee for giving up the original lease (or undertaking to pay an increased rent), a proportion equivalent to one-fifteenth of that consideration multiplied by the number of years by which the term of the lease-back falls short of 16 years will be treated as an income receipt instead of a capital receipt.

An appropriate adjustment must be made where the lease-back is of only part of the property previously leased. For the above purposes, the term of the new lease is deemed to end on any date where after the rent payable is reduced, or, if the lessor or lessee has power to determine the lease or the lessee has power to vary its terms, on the earliest date on which the lease can be so determined or varied (ICTA 1988 s 780).

Buying and Selling Equestrian Property – Legal Aspects 14

Guy Hurst
Withers[LLP]

Introduction

14.1 It is a fact universally acknowledged that the three most important aspects of any sale, whether it be of a two-up two-down terraced property in the middle of a city or a 12,000 acre country estate, are preparation, preparation and preparation. If this applies to any run of the mill property, then it is even more applicable to the sale of 'specialist' properties such as stud farms, racing stables and estates. The whole process, from agreeing a sale to completion, should resemble a textbook race win – a finely tuned thoroughbred trotting over the winning line, lengths ahead of its nearest rival, with seemingly little effort – but behind the scenes a tremendous amount of activity and months of preparation, all falling into place at the right time to achieve the desired effect.

The following discussion is not intended to be an in-depth legal treatise on conveyancing, but rather a brief canter through the process involved in ensuring that a satisfied seller can efficiently sell property to an equally satisfied buyer.

The purpose of this chapter is to point the reader in the right direction to ensure that any sale or purchase is undertaken as effortlessly, speedily and enjoyably as possible.

Estate agents

14.2 So let us suppose that you have decided to sell your 600-acre stud farm and retire to the South of France to live off the proceeds of the sale of that rather nice foal by last year's Derby winner which you managed to sell for a seven figure sum. Most sellers' first instinct is to contact the local estate agent for a valuation and pass everything over to them. You should get at least three agents to provide a valuation (which should be free of charge) and you can then decide which agent to appoint based not just on the highest valuation given but also on the professionalism and the quality of the agent. There are certain specialist agents who deal only with equestrian property, and bearing in mind the specialist nature of the property, you should always consider bringing in a London agent to quote. Often an agent falling outside the area will bring a different perspective to a sale with possibly a resulting higher sale price.

You may decide to appoint a firm of agents to act as sole agent or two agents to act as joint sole agents (ie this means they split the commission between themselves 50/50) or you may choose to appoint more than one agent to act independently, in which case whichever agent sells the property claims all the commission.

Any agent you appoint will present you with a legally binding contract setting out the terms of business of the firm and these should be scrutinised to make sure that you know exactly what you are letting yourself in for. Some agents will attempt to claim commission for any sale arranged during the period of their agency, even if a private sale to a party not introduced by them is arranged. Others will also attempt to claim the full commission from you should they arrange a sale but then you take the property off the market for a perfectly legitimate reason. The terms of business provided by the agent should be checked by your solicitor to avoid any onerous conditions.

It is possible to do some 'horse trading' with agents on commission, so do not assume that you have to accept the first proposal made. Most agents will charge a flat rate percentage of the sale price as their commission and on top of this you will be expected to pay for the costs of advertising and the production of brochures.

Other professional advisers

14.3 At the same time as instructing an estate agent, you should also inform your solicitor that you are placing the property on the market or if you don't have a solicitor who specialises in the sale of such property, then you should find one immediately.

The same is true of an accountant who, from the outset, should be giving specialist advice on tax issues, which are dealt with elsewhere in this book.

The solicitor's role

14.4 For any sale to proceed quickly and efficiently, the aim must be to present a buyer with a draft contract and all necessary supporting documentation literally within hours of a sale being agreed in principle. This keeps the pressure on the buyer to go ahead with the purchase and also prevents a sale from being bogged down because, for example, five weeks after the sale has been agreed, the buyer has still not carried out his local authority search and in the meantime has found another property which he prefers.

If the correct amount of preparation has been carried out by your solicitor, then there is no reason why exchange of contracts should not realistically take place within 21 days at the outside of contracts being received by a buyer's solicitor. Any buyer's solicitor who tells you otherwise is not doing their clients any favours. The author was recently involved in the sale of a 12,000-acre estate in Yorkshire which had numerous cottages, tenancies, rights of way, ancient monuments and so on. As the seller's solicitor the author had carried out all imaginable searches and had provided every conceivable piece of information relating to the property. After a well-organised marketing campaign, two 'would-be' buyers both offered exactly the same price, and the sole determinant of who should be the successful buyer was the speed at which they would be able to exchange contacts. Some 14 ring binders of information were provided to the solicitor acting for each would-be buyer. Having looked through the information, the successful buyer's solicitor said that he would be able to exchange contracts in less than 21 days. The other solicitor said that it would take at least six weeks before he would be in a position to even consider an exchange of contracts. Not surprisingly, his client did not buy the estate.

Once you have confided in your solicitor your intention to sell, he should then immediately begin the preparation of a seller's information pack to be presented to the buyer's solicitor at the moment a sale is agreed. If the property is charged to a bank or building society, it is doubly important to ensure that you involve your solicitor the moment you decide to sell as he/she will have to obtain the title deeds to the property from the lender. If the property is charged to one of the private banks, this is usually not a problem, but obtaining title deeds from one of the high street banks or building societies can often be an uphill struggle because in many cases their systems for dealing with these matters are woefully inadequate. It is not unheard of for it to take upwards of six weeks to obtain title deeds from such an institution, which defeats the whole object of a quick sale. The earlier your solicitor is involved, the better.

Seller's property information pack

14.5 The exact content of any pack will depend on the particular property in question but, in general terms, a well thought out informative pack will deal with the following matters.

Title

14.6 The title to the property will either be registered at HM Land Registry or it will be unregistered.

If the title is registered, then the pack will contain what is known as Official Copies of the Land Certificate, which will define the exact area of the property, give details of the owner or owners of the property and, in addition, detail any onerous covenants which affect the property. One phone call to HM Land Registry will produce the necessary Office Copy Entries.

If the property is unregistered, then it is necessary for the seller to prove that he has a good root of title to the property going back for at least 15 years and your solicitor will produce what is known as an 'Epitome of Title' detailing all matters affecting the title of the property in a universally accepted form. The sale of any unregistered property will trigger first registration at HM Land Registry.

Local authority search

14.7 This will be submitted by your solicitor to the District Council and is a set pro forma requesting such details as planning permissions, highways and many other factors which may affect the property and which are vital to give a buyer as much information as possible to enable him to make an informed decision whether to proceed with the purchase. The cost of such a search varies between authorities and can cost several hundred pounds, but this amount is negligible in the context of the average sale. The length of time it takes for an authority to respond also varies considerably from a few days to a few weeks and so it is vital that such a search is submitted as soon as possible. Such a search is considered valid for six months.

Public index map search

14.8 This is a search submitted to the Land Registry to confirm whether any, all or none of the property is already registered at HM Land Registry.

Commons registration search

14.9 Under the Commons Registration Act 1965, all common land had to be registered and records of such common land are held by the County Council for the property in question. The search will reveal whether any of the property is registered common land and who owns it. It will also reveal whether any commoners have rights over the property, for example, to collect firewood, take peat or stage such events as a parade on Oak Apple Day. This may sound quaint, but consider the problem of hoards of strangers going on to your property in the middle of the foaling season.

It is a criminal offence to drive a motor vehicle over common land without an express legal right, and so a Commons Registration Search should be carried out, not only against the property being sold, but also the access to the property. If access to the property is over common land owned by a third party, in the past he has effectively been able to charge whatever sum he likes to grant rights of access. This ability to charge has been modified by the Countryside and Rights of Way Act 2000, which limits the charge to a certain percentage of the freehold value of the property, depending on its age.

The same Act can have an adverse affect on rural properties in general and stud farms in particular. Members of the public will have a statutory right of access for recreational purposes to so-called 'access land' which is classed as mountain, heath or moorland, downland, registered common land and land over 600m above sea level. On the face of it, this might seem to have no impact for stud farms, which do not tend to be up mountains, but it is the common land aspect which could possibly give rise to problems. You may buy a 250-acre stud farm, no part of which is subject to the 'right to roam'. However, that hill which overlooks the yard may be, and every Tom, Dick, Harry and racing tout would be fully entitled to spy on you from there with his telephoto lens, just to see how your promising three-year-old is performing on the gallops. Now more so than ever, when buying you should not only investigate the property itself, but also the surrounding area.

Chancel repair search

14.10 For historical reasons, certain properties carry with them the liability for the repair of the chancel of the local church. The cost of the search is currently £100 plus VAT, which is insignificant in the scheme of things with current high property prices.

Utility searches

14.11 A well-informed seller's property information pack will contain searches carried out with the relevant utility body to show water, electricity, gas, telephone, etc services which affect the property.

Environmental search

14.12 With the increasing liability for pollution etc, it is advisable to carry out an environmental search of the property with a specialist search agent. This will reveal any possible sources of contamination within the property and the search will be certified as to whether or not the information revealed has a detrimental affect on the property.

Pre-contract enquiries

14.13 Normally, a buyer's solicitor will raise a whole raft of enquiries designed to obtain as much information about every aspect of the property as possible. It is far better to pre-empt this by providing in the seller's pack pre-contract enquiries together with replies. The enquiries should be tailor-made to fit the particular property in question and will cover every conceivable aspect from disputes with neighbours, the condition of the property, the terms of any tenancy agreements or licences at the property to EU subsidies, the incidents of any contagious diseases on the property and whether or not the current telephone number will remain.

As the seller, you will be asked to confirm that the answers prepared by your solicitor to the enquiries are correct. It is important that you do not just glibly agree to the replies but ensure that each reply is carefully checked and considered. If you give a reply which subsequently is found to be incorrect and the buyer relied on that reply in deciding whether or not to go ahead with the purchase, then you as the seller may be liable for damages for misrepresentation. For example, you may have indicated in a reply that the property was on mains drainage. If subsequently this was found not to be the case but the buyer had relied on this information in deciding to go ahead with the purchase, then the buyer may be able to sue you for the cost of putting the property on mains drainage.

A 600-acre property may have a main house, a set of buildings, three staff cottages, two grazing licences and a farm business tenancy. In order adequately to deal with pre-contract enquiries on this scale, it may be necessary to provide replies to upwards of 750 questions. When faced with page after page of enquiries, it may seem a chore to consider every one in great detail, but it is vital that you do so to avoid any nasty surprises after completion.

If a comprehensive set of pre-contract enquiries and replies is provided to a buyer's solicitor, then it is unlikely that additional enquiries will be raised at the eleventh hour with the potential to delay exchange of contracts. In the sale of the 12,000-acre estate referred to above, a comprehensive set of enquiries and replies was provided with the result that the buyer's solicitor raised only four additional enquiries.

Miscellaneous searches

14.14 Depending on the location of the property, the seller's solicitor should consider carrying out certain specialist searches, for example, a coalmining search or a brine search.

The contract

14.15 Under English law a sale is not binding until a written contact between the seller and the buyer has been exchanged. This means that even after three weeks of intensive negotiations, investigations and burning of midnight oil, either party is entitled to walk away from a sale or purchase at any time. It is therefore vital that contracts are exchanged as soon as possible after a sale has been agreed. Depending on the type of property involved and the complexity of any sale agreement, a sale contract may vary from a pre-printed single A4 sheet to a document running to 100 pages plus, together with assorted schedules and plans. Each contract will be tailor-made for the particular property in question.

On exchange of contracts, a completion date for the sale/purchase will be agreed and it is unusual for this date to be any longer than 28 days after exchange of contracts, although a delayed completion can easily be arranged to allow a seller to find a suitable alternative property etc.

The transfer/conveyance

14.16 Although the standard conditions of sale which apply to most property transactions in the UK put the onus on the buyer's solicitor to prepare the transfer (for registered land) or the conveyance (for unregistered land), it is much more satisfactory if the sale contract contains a draft transfer/conveyance prepared by the seller's solicitor. This enables the seller's solicitor to keep control of the whole transaction right through to completion and takes away any possible delay by the buyer's solicitor in preparing final documentation.

The buyer

14.17 If you are buying a property, then the above comments with respect to selling will apply to the transaction, albeit from a different perspective. As a buyer you will need to obtain exactly the same information as set out and if a seller's solicitor does not have such information readily to hand then alarm bells should start ringing and further enquiries may be necessary. Other considerations include the drafting of an exclusivity or 'lock out' agreement, which gives a prospective buyer sole rights, subject to certain conditions, to deal with the seller. In practice, this will not compel a seller to actually sell a property but may give a buyer the comfort that for a set period he will not be in competition with another potential buyer.

Further considerations

14.18 As a buyer, in addition to the purchase price you will be responsible for stamp duty assessed at a percentage of the purchase price which is currently (2003) as follows:

Purchase price	*Percentage*
£0 to £60,000	1%
£60,001 to £250,000	2%
£250,001 to £500,000	3%
£500,000 plus	4%

If the property is owned by a limited company, then you may be able to buy the company rather than the property and as such a transaction only attracts stamp duty at 0.5%, there is potential to save a substantial sum of money depending on the value of the property. However, detailed investigation of the limited company in question will be required to ensure that you are not taking on any onerous debts, liabilities and so on which have been incurred by the company.

Mortgage

14.19 If, as a buyer, you are taking out a mortgage to buy the property, it will normally be the case that the bank/building society will instruct your solicitor to act on their behalf in carrying out the necessary legal work and investigation of title required before a mortgage will be granted. Again, it is essential that you arrange your finances as speedily as possible as some lenders can take a considerable time to consider applications and any undue delay may result in you losing the property of your dreams.

Conclusion

14.20 To achieve a straightforward quick sale or purchase, it is necessary to:

- appoint and subsequently involve all your professional advisers the moment you decide to market your property or decide to buy;
- ensure that a comprehensive seller's property information pack is compiled by your solicitor;
- make sure that you are fully aware that the information being provided on your behalf is correct;
- ensure your solicitor keeps up the pressure on a buyer to proceed as quickly as possible.

The Equestrian Landlord – Tax Planning 15

Letting grazing for horses

15.1 Note that this chapter should be read in conjunction with CHAPTER **16**: THE EQUESTRIAN LANDLORD – THE LEGAL ASPECTS.

The first step in deciding what grazing agreement to use for horses is to decide whether the horse owner is to be given exclusive rights to the land, or whether the land may be grazed by horses belonging to more than one owner. For of the former, where just one horse owner is to be allowed to graze the land in question – this will be a tenancy. In the latter, where the landowner wishes to allow the horses of other owners to graze the land in question – this is most easily done through an agreement called a 'profit of pasturage'. This is similar to a grazing licence.

The grazier will have a tenancy where he is given exclusive possession of an area of land, even if the agreement is described as something else (such as a licence). Exclusive possession means that the grazier has sole use of the land, to the exclusion of the landowner (except for any specific rights reserved by the landowner in the tenancy agreement, such as a right of way or the sporting rights). So the landowner does not have the right to let other people's horses onto the land in question (see **15.2** below).

The letting of land for grazing by horses will create a tenancy of one of three types:

- common law tenancy;
- farm business tenancy (FBT) under the Agricultural Tenancies Act 1995, or
- business tenancy under the Landlord and Tenant Act 1954, depending on the *terms* of the tenancy and of the use of the land.

The difference between these three types of tenancy can be crucial if the landowner wishes to be able to recover possession of his land.

Income from the receipt of rents is charged to tax under Schedule A and is treated as non-trading income. The differences between non-trading and trading income means that the land will not qualify for other capital gains tax (CGT) and inheritance tax (IHT) reliefs if it is not trading. A farm business tenancy (FBT) is IHT efficient but not CGT efficient.

Profit of pasturage

15.2 Where the landowner desires that the horse(s) of more than one owner may share the grazing of the land in question, then there can be no tenancy of the land, since no one person has exclusive possession of the land. It may also be that the landowner wishes to use the land for his own purposes, so long as not inconsistent with the purpose of the agreement. For instance, the landowner may put his own horse(s) on the land, or use it for recreational purposes such as exercising himself and/or his dog.

In this case, the most appropriate form of agreement is a profit of pasturage (this is not dissimilar to a grazing licence). This is an agreement whereby one or more graziers are merely given a right of pasture (or herbage) for a fixed or periodic term. In legal terms, the landowner is still regarded as being in possession of the land and as growing the crop of grass. Indeed, the landowner will normally be treated as farming the land for tax purposes, if he actually performs (either himself or through his agents) such acts of husbandry commensurate with growing a crop of grass (eg weeding, seeding and fertilising the land), this should be taxable under Schedule D with all the IHT and CGT advantages. However, as an occupier, the landowner will also want to maintain third-party insurance in respect of the land.

Under a profit of pasturage, the grazier obtains an incorporeal rather than a corporeal hereditament, ie a profit rather than a lease of the land itself. An incorporeal hereditament cannot come within the Agricultural Tenancies Act 1995 or the Landlord and Tenant Act 1954 Part II, because it is not a tenancy of the land. Therefore, there is no question of any security of tenure arising, and common law principles will apply. Likewise, because there is no tenancy of the land, under a profit of pasturage the landowner will continue to enjoy all rights over the land not inconsistent with the grazier's rights. So the landowner will automatically continue to enjoy the sporting rights, may use the land for recreational purposes, and may grant rights to third parties. It is not necessary to expressly reserve any of these rights in the agreement.

Under a profit of pasturage agreement, the landowner has no responsibilities to care for a horse whilst it is on his land.

Although a profit of pasturage gives rise to an incorporeal hereditament, it is still a tenancy in contractual terms. Therefore, all applicable terms that might go into a tenancy, such as break clauses, can be included in an agreement for a profit of pasturage (hence the inclusion of a clause against assignment etc, in the absence of which assignment would be prohibited).

Stamp duty

15.3 It is considered that the pasturage agreement is exempt from stamp duty. Those using the profit of pasturage agreement who are particularly concerned about the stamp duty position and want confirmation, should submit the executed deed for adjudication by the Stamp Office (Stamp Office, Ridgeworth House, Liverpool Gardens, Worthing, West Sussex, BN11 1XP). This applies to any stamp duty question about any rent agreement in this chapter.

Contract of agistment

15.4 A contract of agistment is similar to a contract of bailment. A bailment takes place where a person's goods are delivered to another person, normally by virtue of a contract, on condition that they are redelivered to their owner after a certain period of time. A feature of contracts of bailment is the obligation on the person taking the goods to keep them safe.

To agist means to take in animals to graze for payment. A contract of agistment is therefore the term used to describe an arrangement whereby one person (known as the agister) takes in animals belonging to another person to graze his land for a fixed sum of money on the implied condition that the animals will be redelivered to their owner on demand. An important feature of contracts of agistment is that animals are taken in to feed but no particular part of a farm of land is allocated for this purpose. An agreement of this kind will not confer on the owner of the animals any interest in the land.

An agister of animals must take reasonable care of the animals which he takes onto his land, and supply them with food and water. A breach of the duty to take care resulting in injury to the animals in question may lead to a claim being made against him for damages. An agister has been held liable, for example where:

- he put a horse in a field where there was barbed wire concealed by long grass; and
- in another case where, owing to negligence of the agister's servant, a horse escaped through an open gate and was injured.

If the agister has taken all reasonable care, and can prove this, he will not be liable for any damage to the animals, eg if the animals are stolen, despite the gate being locked – here, whilst he must still use his best endeavours to recover them, he will not be liable to the owner if they are not recovered.

An agister of animals does not have a lien (a right to obtain possession until a debt is paid) upon the animals agisted unless there is a special agreement to this effect.

Before a tenant enters into a contract of agistment he should check the terms of his tenancy agreement because tenancies commonly prohibit the tenant from taking in any livestock of a third party.

A landlord's rights to distrain for rent (to seize the goods in order to satisfy unpaid rent) are limited by the Agricultural Holdings Act 1986 s 18. Certain animals are absolutely privileged from distress. These include livestock present on the land solely for breeding purposes belonging to a third party (s 18(1)(b)). Other livestock may only be distrained if there is no other sufficient distress available (s 18(2)).

Licences and profit à prendre

15.5 A tax efficient way to hold agricultural or equine business property is under licence.

Licences differ from tenancies as under a licence exclusive right of occupation is not given to the licencee. Other individuals, usually the landowner, are entitled to occupy the land. A license agreement, however, can give the licencee exclusive possession. In such a case, the agreement may be called a licence but for tax purposes may be deemed to be a tenancy. Licences are also usually granted for a short period of time, and the licencee has fewer rights then a tenant under a normal farm tenancy agreement.

The usual use of a licence is to allow a licencee to graze his or her animals on the land. This is known as a 'grazing agreement'.

Under a tenancy, the owner of the land is the landlord, and income received is taxable on him as Schedule A income (rental income).

Under a licence, any income received by the owner is treated as trading income under Schedule D and, accordingly, the owner is still treated as trading as a farmer. To maintain this title of trading, the owner must be responsible for the upkeep of the land including manuring, fertilising, seeding, hedging and ditching the land.

The differences between tenancies and licences become most apparent in relation to whether the farmhouse would qualify for APR.

An alternative to the licence is profit à prendre. The limitations to the use of profit à prendre are as follows:

- grazing only;

- private recreational horses; and
- for a short duration.

Clear advice on the legal relationship between landlord and tenant should be dealt with by a solicitor.

Common law letting

15.6 Where land is let to an individual or individuals for grazing for purely private or recreational purposes, the tenancy will be governed by common law. This means that the length of the agreement is exactly as the agreement states and can be terminated as stated in the agreement.

The agreement could be:

- for a fixed term, such as a year, where it would automatically terminate at the expiration of a year;
- on a monthly basis, where it would be terminable upon giving one month's notice to coincide with the same day of the month as the commencement of the agreement (the parties could provide for a shorter notice period in the agreement if they wished);
- a mixture of the above, for example, for six months and then on a monthly basis; or
- where the tenancy is for a fixed term, a break clause could be included in the agreement (ie there could be provision for the agreement to be terminated on, say, one month's notice).

This could be provided to operate at any time, or on the occurrence of a specified event, such as:

- the death of one of the parties;
- the obtaining of planning permission; or
- the placing of the land on the market.

The key requirements for a common law tenancy are that the letting is to an individual(s) (ie as opposed to a club), and that the land is used for private purposes only and not in connection with a business or trade. Therefore, it is important that the agreement prohibits the use of the land in connection with a business or trade. In such a case, it does not matter if the tenant is permitted to erect jumps or a shelter.

The conventional recreational pony agreement granted to a single individual will usually be a tenancy under common law. A common law fixed term tenancy will simply expire at the end of its contractual term without any special notice provisions. Periodic common law tenancies can be terminated by giving notice for the relevant period. The tenant has no right to compensation for improvements unless written into the tenancy agreement. This is of impact for the tenant who is proving commercial VAT status.

Business tenancies – Landlord and Tenant Act 1954

15.7 Where the land let for grazing is also used for a non-agricultural purpose, such as for the training or exercising of horses, then the tenancy will be governed by Part II of the Landlord and Tenant Act 1954. This confers a degree of security of tenure (unlike a farm business tenancy) on the tenant. Therefore, it will be essential to include appropriate covenants that restrict the use of the land to grazing only if this is to be avoided. Equally, if the land is not bare land, but includes any buildings, the agreement cannot be said to be just for grazing. Accordingly, the tenancy will not be within the definition of agriculture, and again will fall under the 1954 Act.

If it is unavoidable that the tenancy comes within the 1954 Act for either of the foregoing reasons, then an application can be made to the courts to take the tenancy outside Part II of the 1954 Act – this is neither a complicated nor expensive process, in most cases involving no more than form filling. Alternatively, the tenancy could be restricted to six months or less, thereby taking it outside the security of tenure provisions of the 1954 Act. It will be essential to see a solicitor.

If a protected business tenancy is established, the landowner has not necessarily lost the right to recover the land indefinitely. If the appropriate notice is served, then the landowner can recover possession as of right if he intends to occupy for his own purposes (and so long as he has owned the land for the five years previous to tenancy). However, in the event that the landowner recovers possession on this basis, he has to pay compensation of several times the annual rent to the tenant (in addition to any other compensation that is due).

If the land is to be used by an individual(s) for private purposes only, then there are no problems recovering possession. Nor does it matter whether a shelter or building is included, or the land is used for jumping etc. However, it is highly advisable that the (common law) tenancy agreement expressly restricts use to private purposes only, and prohibits use in connection with a business or trade.

If the land is to be used in connection with a business or trade, then it is greatly preferable that the use if the land is confirmed to grazing only (and not training or tuition). It is also important that no building or shelter is included within the agreement. If these two things are ensured, then the tenancy will be a farm business tenancy and there will be no security of tenure (although 12 to 24 months' notice will be required in respect of tenancies from year to year, and fixed term tenancies of more than two years).

Farm Business Tenancies – Agricultural Tenancies Act 1995

15.8 Where bare land is let to a horse owner who uses the land just for grazing, and this is done in connection with a trade or business, this tenancy will be a farm business tenancy (FBT), under the Agricultural Tenancies Act 1995. This will be the case even if the trade or business is non-agricultural, so long as the non-agricultural activities take place elsewhere and let land is used just for grazing; see *Rutherford v Maurer [1962] 1 QB 16*. In that case, a field was let for a year to the proprietor of a riding school for grazing her horses. This was held to be within the definition of 'agriculture', which definition includes 'the use of land as grazing land'. It does not matter whether the grazing is done by live-stock, or by other animals such as horses. So where, for instance, land is let for grazing by horses used in connection with a commercial riding school, then, so long as the land let is used just for grazing by the horses (and not for instance, for training or riding tuition), the tenancy will still be a FBT. Therefore, it is important to restrict the use of the land to grazing only. The FBT might contain a covenant by the tenant to occupy only for agricultural purposes. The taxation of the landlord's asset will be based on what actually happens on the ground, not what the landlord stipulates should happen.

If the agreement is for a fixed term of two years or less, or is a periodic tenancy other than an annual one (eg weekly or monthly), there is no restriction on the agreement. In other words, the normal common law applies in this respect and the parties can agree what terms they wish.

Even if the agreement is for a fixed term of more than two years, or is a yearly one, the landowner must serve a notice to terminate of between 12 and 24 months (this requirement also applies to any break clause in the agreement). Obviously, this reduces the flexibility of the tenancy, and therefore may not be desirable; but the important point is that, under a farm business tenancy, a landowner can always get possession back.

The key points for an FBT are:

- commenced after August 1995;
- character of the property must be wholly or primarily agricultural;
- fixed terms of two years or less.

The introduction of the FBT in 1995 was heralded as a breakthrough for IHT tax planning because henceforward the landowner had an opportunity to secure 100% agricultural property relief (APR) where previously this had not been available. However, the income tax and CGT position of these tenancies for the landlord should be reviewed by the tax adviser.

When land is let under an FBT the landowner is no longer regarded as trading for the purpose of capital gains tax reliefs. Rollover relief on any capital gain that may arise will usually be restricted on a time apportioned basis. Eligibility to business asset taper relief (BATR) for CGT would previously have be lost under an FBT. However, after 6 April 2004, let land where in use by a trade, ie a farmer, will qualify in full for BATR whether let to a company or individual tenant.

The creation of a new FBT is a relatively straightforward matter. Much greater complications arise when there is an existing tenancy under the Agricultural Holdings Act 1986 or there is no right to vacant possession within either 12 months or 24 months. In order for the landlord to achieve 100% APR the tenancy should come to an end.

In order to achieve this there must be a clear surrender of the old tenancy and a grant of the new. In his book *Business and Agricultural Property Relief* (3rd edn, LexisNexis UK), Toby Harris goes to some length into explaining the provisions of IHTA 1984 s 116 (2) and explores the position where the tenant of an old tenancy dies and the new tenancy commences.

In summary, the provisions of IHTA 1984 s 116 apply to all land subject to an FBT, thus they are IHT efficient but beware of the other complications of the loss of income tax and CGT reliefs together with possible loss in APR on the farmhouse.

Contract farming/stud arrangements

15.9 With current stud cottage rents as high as they are, the cost of a stud employee becomes greater and the employment law problems surrounding this become worse. A contract farming/stud arrangement is essentially a landowner using the services of a contractor or another stud owner to farm the land. The landowner supplies fixed cost items, ie the property of the stud, and the contracting farmer supplies labour, machinery and management.

A contract farming arrangement can be used effectively at the time of intending retirement of a stud manager; or when a tenanted stud has fallen vacant due to the departure of the tenant and the landlord does not wish to manage the stud himself. He may lack the capital or the inclination to do so but, nonetheless, wishes to retain vacant possession, perhaps having in mind that one of his family might wish to have a stud career in the future.

Generally, the contractor receives a set fee for the services provided and a bonus as a percentage of the calculated surplus from the venture. The contracting income received by the contractor must be reviewed carefully.

Contract farming agreements generally centre around a memorandum of 'joint venture', which will contain an arithmetical calculation to establish how much the contractor should be paid for the services. It is often advisable in a contract farming agreement to set up a separate bank account in the landowner's name with all transactions relating to the agreement going through the account. This would automatically apportion the interest calculation on working capital as the account becomes overdrawn to fund variable costs. It is essential that a correctly drawn up agreement should aim to enable the landowner to carry on the stud trade and provide reasonable return for both parties, even within the current falling income position in the UK. This should then ensure that the landowner will preserve his business reliefs, not just for IHT, but also for CGT. Additionally, the IHT reliefs on the stud house are also preserved as this is normally one of the assets specifically dealt with in the arrangement.

Although contract farming arrangements might not be as universal to the equine industry as they have been to the farming industry, they should not be dismissed by the equine world. They can prove a cost-effective and tax-efficient way of dealing with stud land management.

Business tenancies of stables

15.10 What is the best way of letting stables with or without some pasture, to a person who is proposing to run a riding establishment, or to keep horses at livery by way of business? Lettings of this kind may be a suitable way of making use of redundant farm buildings. However, where premises are let for business purposes, Part II of the Landlord and Tenant Act 1954 will apply, so as to give limited protection to the business tenant.

When letting premises for a riding establishment or livery stables, it is advisable to have a business tenancy agreement properly drawn. Under section 38(4) of the Landlord and Tenant Act 1954, it is possible for both parties to apply jointly to the courts for authority to contract out (Landlord and Tenant Act 1954 ss 24 28). This is a relatively uncomplicated and inexpensive process, in most cases involving no more than form filling. Usually, the courts will readily authorise contracting-out of the security of tenure provisions of the Act. Alternatively, the tenancy could be restricted to six months or less, thereby falling outside the security of tenure provisions of the 1954 Act, although in most cases this would be too short a time.

If, inadvertently, a protected business tenancy is established, the landowner has not necessarily lost the right to recover the land indefinitely. If the appropriate notice is served, then the landowner can recover possession as of right if he intends to occupy for his own purposes (and so long as he has owned the land for five years previous to the tenancy). However, in the event that the landowner recovers possession on this basis, he has to pay compensation of several times the annual rent to the tenant (in addition to any other compensation that is due).

A business tenancy should set out precisely the repairing liabilities of the parties, and it is advisable that a record of the condition of the premises should be made at the commencement of tenancy. Rights of access should be clearly described, by references to a plan large enough to identify the way or ways described. That is particularly important where the stables are situated near the owner's house. Disputes often arise where the agreement does not make clear what ways may be used, and for what purpose.

Where a tenant is granted a lease for a term of years, he may be expected, or may wish, to carry to improvements. If he does carry out improvements, he will be entitled to claim compensation at the end of the tenancy under the Landlord and Tenant Act 1927 ss 1–3. Compensation will be assessed on the following principles: the sum paid must exceed.

- the net addition to the value of the holding directly resulting from the improvement; or
- the reasonable cost of carrying out the improvements at the termination of the tenancy, less the cost of putting the work into a reasonable state of repair, except so far as that is covered by the tenant's repairing liabilities.

For tax purposes the landlord might try to establish that he is not a landlord and that livery income is a trading activity (Schedule D) opposed to the exploitation of the proprietorial rights over the land (Schedule A). IHT relief can be of prime importance here. To achieve trading status it is considered necessary for the livery provider to remain in occupation of the land to make absolutely sure that they continue to trade the land and achieve IHT reliefs.

The tax-efficient tenant

15.11 Historically, the definition of a good tenant is one who commits to the type of lease that the owner requires, always pays on time and looks after the property in a very satisfactory way. It has not always been the role of the landlord to have to consider which tenant is the most tax-efficient.

In this context, recent changes to the tax rules for BATR have made the choice of tenant more relevant to the equestrian landlord. Some tenants can help the equestrian landlord secure BATR on the property in relation to a potential CGT disposal.

The equine property will not be a business asset for taper relief purposes for any period from 5 April 1998 to 5 April 2000 unless:

- the tenant is a partnership in which the landowner is a partner (TCGA 1992 Sch A1 para 5(2)(a); or
- the land or property is used by a company which is a qualifying company in relation to the landowner or property ownership (TCGA 1992 Sch A1 para 5(2)(b)); or
- the asset is used within a group (51% subsidiary test) where the holding company of that group itself qualifies as a holding company of a trading group (TCGA 1992 Sch A1 para 22).

For the company to be a qualifying company in relation to the landowner or property owner, it must be a trading company or the holding company of a trading group, and the landowner or property owner must either hold shares with 25% of the voting rights, or 5% of the voting rights if he is a full-time working officer, or employee, of the company, or of a company that has a relevant connection with it.

For periods after 5 April 2000, it is sufficient for the land or property to be let to any unlisted trading company (or holding company of a trading group) to qualify for business asset taper relief.

For other unincorporated tenants, for periods between 6 April 2000 and 5 April 2002, the landlord will still have to be in partnership with them, or for a listed company he will need to be employed by the company, or hold 5% of the voting rights in the company.

However, the Finance Act 2003 has removed this inequality between letting to unlisted trading companies and other business entities and, as from 6 April 2004, BATR is also due on assets let to unincorporated trading tenants.

The BATR will not be reduced if the tenant pays a full market rent.

Contrast the position with rollover relief where there will be a restriction of relief for periods when the land is occupied by others (TCGA 1992 s 152(7)).

However, when considering the position of either landlord or tenant the capital gains tax treatment must not be looked at in isolation and full consideration must also be given to the inheritance tax implications of the situation, ie all taxes must be 'considered'.

In addition, the change of pre- and post-5 April 2000 and 2004 requirements can restrict the relief available for capital gains and must be considered carefully now rather than just prior to any disposal as there could be 'tainted taper relief'.

Surrender of the tenancy – replacing a tenant

15.12 Unfortunately there are tax consequences of replacing a tenant, including stamp duty implications, disposals for capital gains tax purposes, and possibly inheritance tax in family situations.

The surrender of a tenancy may constitute a transfer of value if not done on a commercial basis. No APR would be available on the surrender if the tenant dies within seven years under the claw-back rules, as the tenancy would have disappeared.

There is also the problem of how to value the tenancy surrendered. In a Lands Tribunal case *Walton (Executor of Walton deceased) v Inland Revenue Commissioners [1996] STC 68* it was held that the value was about 50% of the difference between the vacant possession value and its tenanted value. This is known as 'the vacant possession premium'.

A similar valuation may be used to calculate the value for the disposal for capital gains purposes. If the surrender is between connected parties, or full commercial value is not paid for surrender, the tenant could be treated as disposing of the tenancy at full market value.

Holdover and rollover relief should be available on the capital gains arising on the surrender. Be aware, however, that reinvesting the gain in the new farm business tenancy will be a rollover into a depreciating asset. This means that unless a subsequent rollover in made of this gain into a non-depreciating asset, the gain may be triggered as early as ten years after the initial rollover into the farm business tenancy.

If farmers are considering surrendering their tenancies early, both the tenant and the landlord should be separately advised.

National Insurance for the equestrian landlord

15.13 Is the letting of several equine properties a trade in which there will be a liability for NIC?

The subject of property letting also arose in the case of *Rashid v Garcia [2003] STC (SCD) 36* in which the question for consideration was whether income from the letting of four properties could be regarded as a business, allowing Mr Rashid to be an employed earner for NIC purposes.

The Special Commissioner looked particularly at the context in which the term 'business' was used in the Social Security Contributions and Benefits Act 1992 s 122(1). This provides that 'employment' includes any trade, business, profession, office or vocation. The Commissioner said that this is implied activity in contrast to mere investment. A property rental activity could be an investment business, but whether it was a business within the meaning of s 122 depended upon the degree of activity involved. He decided that there was insufficient activity for it to constitute a business and Mr Rashid was not therefore in employment for the purposes of the NIC legislation.

Once upon a time there was a clear distinction between an investment activity and a trade but the increased use of the word 'business'

– particularly the concept of 'Schedule A business' – has confused matters somewhat, and so has the concept of an investment business.

We now have the position that a clear investment activity (that is, the letting of investment properties) is a business (but maybe not a real business, just an investment business, the distinction being dependent upon activity) and possibly eligible for advantageous tax treatment that was otherwise confined to trade. The continuing uncertainty about whether a Schedule A business is eligible for relief under TCGA 1992 s 162 on the transfer to a company in exchange for shares is an important example.

Under the circumstances, Mr Rashid may regard himself as rather unlucky. He clearly had a property rental business and, even though it may have been an investment business, it was surely still a business and specifically within the terms of s 122. It might be argued that the term 'business' has to be constructed in the same way as surrounding words 'trade, profession, office or vocation,' but that does not necessarily lead to the conclusion that the property rental business should be excluded.

At the time of writing the letting of property is not a trade for NICs. Further cases might change this.

Furnished holiday letting

15.14 The equine business often has spare accommodation and this can be dealt with tax-efficiently though the furnished holiday lets scheme. Likewise, equine activities can revolve around the tourist industry and incorporate furnished holiday lettings.

In order to qualify for preferential treatment:

- a letting must be commercial, with a view to profit;
- it must be furnished accommodation;
- the accommodation must be available for commercial letting to the public generally, for periods totalling in aggregate not less then 140 days;
- it must actually have been let for periods totalling 70 days;
- for a period comprising seven months, not necessarily continuous, it must not have been in the same occupation for a continuous period exceeding 31 days.

For tax purposes, these tests need to be satisfied with reference to the tax year, for persons other than companies, and with reference to a 12-month accounting period for companies. If they are satisfied, then for all practicable purposes, the furnished letting is to be treated as if it were a trade with all the relevant deductions and loss reliefs for income tax purposes (ICTA 1988 ss 380 and 385) including capital allowances, and relief for annuities and personal pensions; and qualifying for important business asset taper relief, rollover relief, and hold-over relief for capital gains tax.

The question as to whether furnished holiday lettings qualify for loss relief under ICTA 1988 s 381 (set-off against total income) is, however, a complex one, and the Inland Revenue have issued an Interpretation (RI October 1997) describing the special tests to be applied, following the Special Commissioners' decision in *Brown v Richardson [1997] STC (SCD) 233.*

The facts in that case were that the purchase of a holiday home was financed by mortgage secured on the taxpayer's main residence, and loss relief arose primarily because of significant finance charges. The lettings were commercial. An agent had been engaged and the number of letting days was well in excess of the minimum of 70 days per annum. Disregarding the interest payments, the Case VI computation showed the lettings were profitable. However, it was decided that a letting must be with a view to the realisation of a commercial profit, not profit as calculated for tax purposes. In this case, it was found that the expectation of making a profit was unrealistic and that the property had been bought as a holiday home, with a view to generating revenue to offset costs, rather than with a view to the realisation of profit. Thus, the letting failed to qualify for relief.

In general, the Inland Revenue approach may be summarised as follows:

- 'profits' means commercial not tax-adjusted profits;
- the taxpayer's expressed intentions are not conclusive, where other facts suggest otherwise;
- there exists a principle that an activity may be carried on with a view to offsetting costs rather than realising profit, and that this may equally apply to farming and other trading activities;
- the size of a mortgage may jeopardise the commercial credibility of an activity;
- the Inland Revenue expects a written business plan to be prepared at the outset showing credible figures.

Where the general test in ICTA 1988 s 504 is satisfied, the letting may still fail the stricter test in s 381(4), which provides that there must be a reasonable expectation of profits in the relevant period, or within a 'reasonable time' thereafter. See, in this connection, *Walls v Livesey [1995] STC (SCD) 12.* In that case, the Special Commissioner observed that profits needed to be 'expected' not later than a reasonable time after the end of the four-year period for which claims under the section are permitted. The Inland Revenue do not accept this view, and insist that a 'reasonable time' depends on the facts and the nature of the loss making activity. They normally consider that there should be a reasonable expectation of profit within five years of the date of commencement of the activities.

The deemed trade treatment for furnished holiday lettings given for income tax and most capital gains tax purposes is specifically not applied for inheritance tax. The Inland Revenue Capital Taxes has traditionally allowed a claim to business property relief for furnished holiday lettings provided that at least three or more cottages were so managed. However, more recently, the Inland Revenue Capital Taxes has confirmed that it is now prepared to allow relief for a single cottage where the lettings are short term and even if the lettings are for part of the year only, provided the owner (whether himself or through an agent) is 'substantially involved' with the holidaymakers in terms of their activities on and from the premises, (See the Inland Revenue's Capital Taxes Advanced Instruction Manual at para L.99.3).

Rollover relief will be due on the disposal of property which has been let commercially as furnished holiday accommodation providing the conditions above are complied with.

In addition, the Inland Revenue have indicated that rollover relief will be due when properties are let out during the main holiday period on a short term basis, but during the quieter part of the year are let on a long term basis. Some of these longer lettings may be to the same person for more than 31 days. The Inland Revenue's view is that providing the letting during the main holiday period satisfies the above tests, the longer lettings in any other part of the same year of assessment will not preclude relief (ICTA 1988 ss 503, 504 and TCGA 1992 s 152).

Non-resident landlords scheme

15.15 The cost of purchasing an equine freehold can be an impossible achievement for many aspiring equine businesses. Renting premises is often a standard cost to the equestrian business.

Traditionally, a lot of training yards, studs and equestrian businesses have non-resident landlords, ie individuals, companies and trusts which are not resident in the UK.

The non-resident landlords (NRL) scheme is a scheme for taxing the UK rental income of non-resident landlords. The scheme requires UK letting agents to deduct basic rate tax from any rent they collect for non-resident landlords. If non-resident landlords do not have UK letting agents acting for them, and the rent is more than £100 a week, their tenants must deduct the tax. When working out the amount to tax, the letting agent/tenant can take off deductible expenses.

Letting agents and/or tenants do not have to deduct tax if the Inland Revenue authorises them not to under this scheme. The Inland Revenue will tell an agent/tenant not to deduct tax if non-resident landlords have successfully applied for approval to receive rents with no tax deducted. But even though the rent may be paid with no tax deducted, it remains liable to UK tax. So non-residential landlords must include it in any tax return the Inland Revenue sends them.

Non-resident landlords who are eligible can apply at any time for approval to receive their UK rental income with no tax deducted. This includes applying before they have left the UK or before the letting has started.

The Inland Revenue may refuse approval if they are not satisfied that:

- the information of the application is correct; *or*
- the non-resident landlord has or will comply with their UK tax obligations.

The Inland Revenue may withdraw approval if:

- they are no longer satisfied that the information in the application is correct; *or*
- they are no longer satisfied that the non-resident landlord has or will comply with their UK tax obligations; *or*
- the non-resident landlord fails to supply information requested by the Inland Revenue.

The Inland Revenue will authorise an agent/tenant not to deduct tax if the non-resident landlord has successfully applied for approval to receive rents with no tax deducted. But rent paid with no tax deducted remains liable to UK tax. All non-resident landlords who receive rents with no tax deducted will have a tax district. Individuals who are not resident in the UK for tax purposes are still sent an annual tax return automatically, even though they have sufficient UK personal allowances to cover any liability.

A letting agent is a person who:

- has a 'usual place of abode' in the UK; and
- acts for a non-resident landlord in the running of their rental business, and has the power to receive income of the non-resident landlord's rental business, or has control over the direction of that income; and
- is not an 'excluded person'.

An 'excluded person' is someone whose activity on behalf of the non-resident landlord is confined to providing legal advice/services. However, solicitors who draw up a lease and collect the rent for the first person are not excluded persons.

The Centre for Non-Residents have produced a booklet called 'Non-resident landlords – Guidance notes for letting agents and tenants', that tells people what their responsibilities are under the scheme. In addition, there is a brief letting agents' guide to the NRL scheme which outlines the main features of the scheme.

Tenants of the non-resident landlords have to operate the scheme if:

- the rent they pay is more than £100 a week; and either
- they pay the rent direct to a non-resident landlord; or
- they pay the rent to a person outside the UK; or
- they pay the rent to a person who is not a letting agent in the UK.

The Centre for Non-Residents may sometimes instruct tenants to operate the scheme even where the rent paid is less than £100 a week.

Non-resident landlords are persons (this term includes individuals, companies and trustees) who have:

- UK rental income;
- a 'usual place of abode' outside the UK.

Non-resident landlords can apply to receive their rent with no tax deducted on the basis that either:

- their UK tax affairs are up to date; or
- they have not had any UK tax obligations before they applied; or
- they do not expect to be liable to UK income tax for the year in which they apply; or
- they are not liable to pay UK income tax because they are Sovereign;
- they are immunes (these are generally foreign heads of state, government or government departments).

When approval has been given, the Inland Revenue sends:

- a notice of approval to receive rent with no tax deducted to the non-resident landlord; and
- a separate notice to the letting agency or tenants named on the application form authorising them to pay rent to the non-resident landlord without deducting tax.

Authority to pay rent to a non-resident landlord with no tax deducted is generally backdated to the beginning of the quarter in which the Inland Revenue approves the application. The non-resident landlord's year starts on 1 April, the quarters are the three-month periods that end on 30 June, 30 September, 31 December and 31 March. Therefore, if a non-resident landlord applies to the Inland Revenue on, say, 20 September, the authority that is sent to his letting agent/tenant will usually take effect from 1 July.

It is the landlord's 'usual place of abode' and not strictly their non-resident status that determines whether a landlord is within the scheme or not. In the case of individuals, the Inland Revenue normally regard an absence from the UK of six months or more as meaning that a person has a usual place of abode outside the UK. It is therefore possible for a person to be a resident in the UK yet, for the purposes of the scheme, to have a usual place of abode outside the UK.

Where the Inland Revenue refuses, or withdraws, approval to receive rent with no tax deducted, the non-resident landlord can appeal to them within 90 days. Where the Inland Revenue and the non-resident landlord cannot reach an agreement, the appeal will be referred to the General Commissioners or, if the non-resident landlord wishes, to the Special Commissioners. Both of these bodies are independent appeal tribunals.

Letting agents that have to operate the non-resident landlords scheme must:

- register with the Centre for Non-Residents;
- account quarterly for the tax due under the scheme;
- by 5 July following the year ended 31 March, complete an annual information return; and
- where they have deducted tax, give the non-resident landlord a tax deduction certificate NRL6.

Tenants who have to operate the non-resident landlords scheme have to:

- account quarterly for any tax due under the scheme;
- by 5 July following each year ended 31 March, give the non-resident landlord a tax deduction certificate NRL6; and
- complete an annual information return.

Letting agents or tenants must generally tax the rental income they pay to the non-resident landlords unless the Inland Revenue has authorised them not to do so. In calculating the amount of tax, they take into account any 'deductible expenses' they pay in a quarter. These are expenses that they can reasonably be satisfied will be allowable expenses for the non-resident landlords when the profits of their rental businesses are computed. The Inland Revenue has published a booklet IR150 'Taxation of rents – A guide to property income' that gives advice on allowable expenses.

When calculating the amount of tax, letting agents/tenants should:

- add together the rent they actually receive in the quarter plus;
- any rent that they had the power to receive; and
- any rent paid away at their direction to another person.

Less:

- any deductible expenses that they paid in the quarter; and

- any deductible expenses that were paid away in the quarter at their direction by another person.

Broadly, in calculating the profits of a rental business, expenses are allowable where:

- they are incurred wholly and exclusively for the purpose of the rental business; and
- they are not of a 'capital' nature.

Information about what constitutes an expense of a 'capital' nature is provided in Revenue booklet IR150 'Taxation of Rents – A Guide to property income'. For example, the cost of land and buildings and the cost of improvements and alterations is expenditure of a capital nature.

Expenses paid by letting agents and tenants which will normally be allowable expenses are as follows:

- accountancy expenses for the rental of the business;
- advertising costs of attracting new tenants;
- cleaning;
- costs of rent collection;
- council tax while the property is vacant but available for letting;
- gardening;
- ground rent;
- insurance on building and contents;
- interest paid on loans to but land or property;
- interest paid on loans to build or improve premises;
- legal and professional fees;
- maintenance charges made by freeholders, or superior leaseholders, of leasehold property;
- maintenance contracts (for example, gas servicing);
- provision of services (for example, gas electricity, hot water);
- rates;
- repairs which are not significant improvements to the property, including:
  - — mending broken windows, doors;
  - — furniture, cookers, lifts, etc;
  - — painting and decorating;
  - — replacing roof slates, flashing and gutters;
- water rates.

Letting agents and tenants can deduct only those expenses which they pay or which are paid on their direction. This means they cannot deduct:

- expenses which the landlord pays, even if they have details of the expenses;

- expenses which have accrued in a quarter but which have not been paid in the quarter;
- capital allowances; and
- any personal allowances due to the landlord.

If an equine tenant is aware that they have an overseas landlord then they must take note of these provisions.

Acquisition of an equine property through a non-UK resident company

15.16 A company resident outside the United Kingdom is a useful vehicle for the ownership of investment property such as an equine property in the United Kingdom, since capital gains on the sale can be realised free of UK tax. However, the tax benefit can only be fully exploited by individuals who are or become non-UK resident or domiciled.

The principle advantages enjoyed by a non-UK resident investment company are:

- exemption from tax on capital gains realised on the disposal of investment assets (TCGA 1992 s 2). The exemption does not extend to assets used in connection with a trade conducted in the UK (TCGA 1992 s 10);
- income arising in the UK will only be subject to a basic rate income tax. Non-resident companies are not subject to corporation tax unless they carry on a trade in the UK (ICTA 1988 s 11);
- income arising outside the UK cannot be subject to UK tax.

These benefits may not be fully available where the non-resident company's individual shareholders (or ultimate shareholder) are resident or ordinarily resident and domiciled in the UK when the capital gain is realised. It is important that the residency position of the shareholders is reviewed in detail.

The capital gains exemption provides an important tax planning opportunity. A company not resident in the UK can realise tax-free gains on the sale of an investment property, such as an equine property which has not been used for trading purposes in the UK. This should also include the letting of commercial furnished holiday accommodation, which, although regarded as a trade for some purposes of the Taxes Acts, will not be so regarded in this context (ICTA 1988 s 503 (1)).

The Equestrian Landlord – Legal Aspects 16

Mark Charter
White and Bowker

The occupation of land with horses

16.1 The author's experience in practising in this area, and anecdotal evidence, would suggest that a large section of horse owners and proprietors of equestrian businesses keep their horses on land they do not own. The arrangements under which horses are kept on land belonging to someone other than the horse owner are many and varied. Unfortunately these arrangements are frequently entered into without prior professional advice, and without the landowner or horse owner fully appreciating the full legal context and potential consequences of the arrangement. Problems with the 'horsey' occupation of land regrettably are not unusual. This may be partly attributable to the tradition in the countryside of transactions being conducted by verbal agreement – this is problematic because the law is complex, and the only record of the agreement will be individuals' recollection which may have become hazy over time.

There is also a danger that 'one thing leads to another'; for example, a farmer allows a teenage girl to graze her pony on a field. Over time, the girl puts up stables, keeps a number of horses on the land, and expands her equine activities onto adjoining fields. The farmer dies, leaving the farm to his son. The son has plans to increase revenue from the farm which entail recovering possession of the land used for horses. When he approaches the 'tenant' to discuss the handing back of the land she claims she has a business tenancy. The farmer's son then faces the daunting prospect of potentially lengthy and expensive litigation, in which he is at a disadvantage because he was not party to the original agreement (the first-hand knowledge and evidence as to the terms of the agreement from the landlord's perspective having died with his father). It is, therefore, important to make sure the arrangements for the occupation of land by horses are thought out and correct from the outset, failure to do so may result in:

- an inability for the landowner to recover possession of the land when he wants to;
- adverse or unexpected tax effects;
- the occupant claiming compensation from the landowner;
- devaluation of the landowner's property;
- considerable expense in recovering possession or resolving problems; and
- stress and worry.

However, before the reader despairs, provided the appropriate arrangement is identified in the first place, potential problems can be obviated. It should be said that any freehold landowner whose land is mortgaged, before entering into any of the arrangements mentioned below, should first obtain his mortgagee's consent to do so. The terms of modern mortgage deeds are invariably such that failure to obtain the mortgagee's consent would constitute a breach of the landowner's covenants or obligations as mortgagor under the mortgage. Similarly, if the person permitting someone else to use his land for horses is a tenant himself, he should first check the terms of his lease to see if the proposed arrangement would be permitted, and indeed whether his landlord's express prior consent is required. Failure to comply strictly with the terms of his lease may be disastrous for a tenant, not least because it may lead to the early termination of the lease. A tenant in this situation would also be prudent to take professional advice as to whether there are any other ramifications of the proposed arrangements with the horse owner or proprietor of an equestrian business to be established on the land (for example, could it result in an increase in the rent on a rent review)? In this chapter reference to the 'landowner' is shorthand for either the freehold owner of land, or an existing tenant of the land, looking to allow another to make use of the land under the landowner's control.

The landowner must also consider whether the proposed arrangement will be such that planning consent is first required from the local planning authority. A common misconception is that equine or equestrian activities for town and country planning purposes are synonymous with agricultural use, and consequently the necessity for a planning consent is often overlooked. Consideration of the town and country planning regime is outside the ambit of this chapter, suffice to say, however, that the circumstances in which an equine use will qualify as an agricultural one for planning purposes are extremely limited.

In essence, the possible arrangements can be categorised as follows:

- livery agreements;
- licences;
- profit à prendre;
- agistment;
- common law lettings;
- Farm Business Tenancy agreements;
- business tenancies (within the Landlord and Tenant Act 1954).

We shall look at each of these arrangements in turn.

Licences

16.2 A licence is a simple form of agreement between landowner and horse owner, and is used typically to permit the horse owner (non-exclusive) use of land for grazing. In the author's opinion, the use of simple licences (and profit à prendre) are, in most cases, better limited to situations where the proposed arrangement is of short duration and relates to grazing only for private recreational horses.

If the licence purports to grant the horse owner exclusive occupation of the land, that will be fatal to it being construed as a licence (it is of the essence to a licence that the licensee is not granted exclusive rights of occupation). Furthermore, to avoid the risk of a licence being construed as a tenancy by the courts, the licence should not:

- use the language of landlord and tenant (eg the use of the expression 'rent'); or
- impose tenant-type obligations (eg for hedging and ditching, maintenance and repair).

The danger to the landowner of a licence being construed as a tenancy is that the horse owner may have conferred on him rights which the landowner never intended the horse owner should have the benefit of; this is particularly so if what purports to be a licence, is subsequently determined by the courts to be a business tenancy.

Profit à prendre

16.3 A 'profit à prendre' is a right to take something from the land, which in the case of horses is grass by grazing (a 'profit of pasturage'). It is in the parties' (and particularly the landowner's) interest that the granting of a profit of pasturage should be documented by deed. A profit of pasturage comprises an incorporeal rather than a corporeal hereditament and, accordingly, no tenancy of land arises. The horse owner does not acquire exclusive possession of the land and, indeed, the landowner is treated as remaining in possession of the land, and remains free to exercise all rights over the land (including granting rights to third parties), which are not inconsistent with the right of pasturage granted to the horse owner.

This arrangement can be attractive to landowners who wish to be treated (commonly for tax reasons) as continuing to farm the land (ie by growing a crop of grass on the land). As with licences, the deed granting the profit à prendre (to be treated as such) must avoid language or terms which infers any exclusivity of occupation on the part of the horse owner, or seeks to impose tenant type obligations on the horse owner. Again, as with licences, all responsibility for care of the horse will lie with the horse owner (although the prudent landowner will maintain public liability insurance in respect of his land).

Agistment

16.4 A 'contract of agistment' is an agreement whereby the landowner (in this context referred to as 'the agister') agrees to take in someone else's animals to graze on the agister's land for a fee. The horse owner in such an arrangement obtains no tenancy or interest whatsoever in the agister's land, and no part of the agister's land is designated for the purpose of the arrangement. Under such arrangements, the horse(s) are returnable to the horse owner on demand; it is important the contract of agistment expressly provides that the agister will have a lien on the horse(s) until any monies owing under the contract are paid, otherwise the agister will not be entitled to retain a horse until the horse owner has paid his debt to the agister.

Common law lettings

16.5 The conventional grazing agreement to an individual or individuals in respect of ponies or horses kept for private recreational use, will usually be a tenancy under common law. It is essential (for the tenancy to be treated as a common law letting) that the proposed tenancy is not for a horse owner's use in connection with a trade or business. There is, however, a catch for the unwary in that a landowner granting a tenancy to a group of people, such as a riding club, may unwittingly create a business tenancy. The definition of business in the Landlord and Tenant Act 1954 s 23(2) includes 'any activity carried on by a body of persons, whether corporate or unincorporate'.

A common law letting for a fixed period will simply expire at the end of its contractual term without any special notice provisions.

Periodic common law tenancies, however, require termination by notice, the relevant period of notice being dependent on the type of periodic tenancy:

Type of periodic tenancy	*Notice required*
Weekly	One week
Monthly	One month
Quarterly	One quarter
Year to year	At least 6 months (the expiry of the notice period to coincide with the end of the tenancy year)

It is worth noting that a common law tenant has no right to compensation for improvements to the property let, unless provision for such is written into the tenancy agreement.

Farm business tenancies

16.6 The Agriculture Tenancies Act 1995 introduced a new regime for agricultural tenancies by the introduction of Farm Business Tenancies (FBTs). There was a recognition that increasingly there was a need in the agricultural industry for a more adaptable form of tenancy that could accommodate farmers wishes (or indeed economic need in many cases) to diversify farm activities into areas outside traditional farming ones.

The essential elements of an FBT are that it:

- must have commenced after August 1995, and the property the subject of the FBT used for business;
- the character of the property must be wholly or primarily agricultural – or notices must have been exchanged between landlord and tenant before the tenancy is entered into, stating it is intended to be an FBT;
- FBTs for fixed terms of two years or less expire at the end of their contractual term (without the need for service of notices);
- FBTs from year to year or fixed terms longer than two years run on until either the landlord or tenant serves notice to terminate (of at least 12 months). In practise, this may mean that a notice with a notice period of between 12 and 24 months has to be served, as the expiry of the notice must coincide with expiration of the relevant tenancy year.

Subject to complying with the requirements of Part III of the 1995 Act (which relates to landlords consent to improvements) tenants' improvements can qualify for compensation. Improvements in this context can be both tangible ones and intangible ones, for example, a planning permission. In essence, the compensation the landowner may have to pay for qualifying improvements equates to the increase in the letting value of the property at the end of the tenancy as a result of the improvements.

FBTs may be suitable where, for example, the land in question is to be used as grazing ancillary to an equestrian business (eg a riding school) or where the land use is diversifying out of an agricultural use. At the moment, there is no substantive body of case law to give guidance as to the extent to which land use can diversify out of an agricultural use, and the tenancy remain an FBT within the ambit of the 1995 Act. Accordingly, in the equine context the terms of an FBT need to be very carefully thought out, and in many cases the preferred route may be the creation of a business tenancy contracted out of the provisions of the Landlord and Tenant Act 1954 ss 24–28.

Business tenancies under the Landlord and Tenant Act 1954

16.7 Where an equestrian business is to be carried out on the land, a business tenancy, governed by the provisions of the Landlord and Tenant Act 1954, will often be the most suitable form of tenancy.

A wide range of activities can fall within the Act's definition of business (as mentioned at **16.5** above).The 1954 Act potentially:

- gives the tenant long-term security of tenure (as, subject to what is said below, the tenant at the expiry of his tenancy has a statutory right to apply for a new tenancy through the courts, which in turn the landlord can only resist on certain statutory grounds);
- provides for an outgoing tenant to be paid compensation in certain circumstances.

There are, therefore, real dangers for landowners who unwittingly create a 1954 Act business tenancy, particularly where the landowner had only intended the tenancy arrangement to be of relatively short duration before the landowner taking the property back in hand. However, professionally drawn business tenancy agreements will avoid traps for the landowner and provide a good structure for regulating the relationship between landlord and tenant.

Furthermore, the tenant's statutory right to apply for a new tenancy at the expiry of a current tenancy can be removed, if before the grant of such tenancy, a court order is obtained to sanction the landlord and tenant in the tenancy agreement 'contracting out' of the provisions of Landlord and Tenant Act 1954 ss 24–28.

Whilst a court application is necessary prior to the tenancy being granted, the application will not normally necessitate the parties attendance at court (particularly where it is evident that each party is represented by a solicitor), and the matter will be dealt with through the post. At the time of writing, it is proposed to change the procedural requirements for 'contracting out' (to obviate the need for a court order), to one involving notice so that it is quite apparent to a tenant that statutory rights are being waived on his part before the tenancy is entered into.

Planning For VAT 17

By Allison Broadey ATII
The VAT Consultancy

Planning for VAT

17.1 Value Added Tax (VAT) always seems to be the forgotten tax – one that is always ever present but is largely ignored as just a cost component of a transaction. This is highlighted by the wonderful use of the 'margin' or second-hand scheme which even ensures that the cost of VAT is hidden in the sale or purchase price of horses so that few are even aware that the tax has been paid.

Whilst the general public may not realise that the cost of their purchases might include this hidden tax, the businessman is probably all too familiar with it, and should be seeking steps to ensure that he maximises his VAT recoveries whilst minimising the output liability due to be paid. This chapter seeks to explain some of the VAT basics that individuals or businesses can use to minimise this VAT burden. The topics covered are summarised below:

- background to VAT – the basic principles;
- the business question – is a VAT registration possible?;
- the person liable for registration;
- registration scheme for racehorse owners – a brief guide;
- other VAT registration schemes;
- flat-rate farmers' scheme;
- flat-rate scheme for small businesses;
- margin scheme for horses and ponies;
- overseas trade – goods;
- EU purchases and sales;

- non-EU purchases and sales;
- bloodstock – services;
- equestrian activities;
- livery services;
- tuition;
- partial exemption – the basics;
- land and property – the basics.

Background to VAT

17.2 VAT was introduced 30 years ago on 1 April 1973. Since that time the principles of the tax have remained relatively constant but the complexities have ensured that the VAT adviser is kept busy and that the 'simple tax' has become unintentionally complicated with much scope for misinterpretation and unintended error.

The basis of VAT is governed by the EU Sixth VAT Directive under which the UK Government has interpreted and legislated through its domestic powers under the Value Added Tax Act 1994. Largely speaking, the UK has to work within the framework set by the EU and therefore the broad principles of VAT are enacted and adhered to by all the EU Member States. However, whilst the EU aims for harmonisation throughout the Member States, there is scope within the Sixth VAT Directive for Member States to have discretion in certain areas. Thus the harmonisation starts to drift in places and the treatment of supplies and the VAT rates chargeable can therefore vary from Member State to Member State.

In the UK, HM Customs & Excise ('Customs') polices the VAT regime as well as being the responsible body for monitoring the movement of goods into and out of the UK. Unlike many of the EU Member States, the UK has a separate body, the Inland Revenue, which polices the personal and corporate taxes. Whilst the two bodies remain distinct there is a growth in the exchange of information between the organisations and it is now common for trading information to be examined and passed between the departments on a regular basis. It is now very common for information provided to one department to end up assisting the other department in its own tax investigation affairs. It is, therefore, essential that the taxpayer adopts a consistent approach when dealing with both revenue departments.

The basics of VAT

17.3 In the UK we have three 'taxable' rates, being a 0% zero rate, a 5% reduced rate and a 17.5% standard rate. By supplying goods or services at a taxable rate, the right of VAT recovery is secured on the cost of related purchases. There are also exempt supplies which do not carry VAT but the making of them means that there is no recovery of the input VAT incurred on related purchases, unless such input VAT is beneath a de-minimis limit.

When a mixture of supplies is made at both the taxable and exempt rates, then the business will be able to recover a proportion of the input VAT incurred. This proportion is calculated under a 'partial exemption' method and it is essential to consider which method will allow the fairest recoverable percentage.

A VAT registration can only be sought if the business makes some taxable supplies. If only exempt supplies are made a VAT registration will be invalid. The current (2003) VAT registration limit is £56,000 per annum. This is the value of gross income in a rolling 12-month period. If the taxable turnover is above this limit then a compulsory VAT registration must be sought.

If the taxable turnover is below the VAT registration limit then a voluntary or intending registration can be applied for. This gives the benefit of input VAT recovery on costs whilst the business is still in its infancy or prior to the actual making of any taxable sales. These voluntary registrations mean that VAT must still be accounted for on the taxable sales made, but do offer significant cash flow advantages and formed the basis of the Registration Scheme for Racehorse Owners.

The business question

17.4 The ability to register for VAT, and to recover input VAT on expenses, is wholly conditional upon there being a taxable business purpose. For the equine industry in particular, this has often been the root of its VAT problems. When does a hobby become business or a business become a hobby? Only if Customs are satisfied that there is a genuine commercial business activity will they allow a VAT registration to be considered. If the activity is being carried out under the umbrella of an existing VAT registration, then Customs will need to be satisfied that the activity is still one of business – if not, then any associated input VAT cannot be recovered.

Whether an activity is one of business or hobby has been the subject of many VAT Tribunals and there are a considerable number covering the equine activities carried out by sole proprietors, partnerships and companies alike. Some of the more important cases include *Ian Flockton Developments Ltd v Custom & Excise Commissioners [1987] STC 394, Triangle Thoroughbreds Ltd (MAN/90/470) (1990 VTD 5404)* and *Brian Gubby Ltd [1985] VATTR 59 (1985 VTD 1961)* which concerned whether the racing of horses was carried out for private pleasure or for the furtherance of continued economic activity.

In particular, Customs used to view the ownership of racehorses as a non-business activity, but in 1993 it entered into agreement with the bloodstock industry to regularise the VAT treatment and to simplify some of the previously complex rules regarding the business question. This (now slightly amended) agreement is still in place and is reproduced below at **17.30**. Many of the decisions held by VAT Tribunals that were heard before 1993 are thus no longer relevant but it is still absolutely crucial to be able to identify a business purpose behind an activity in order to qualify for the benefits that a VAT registration might provide.

For the proposed activity to be 'business' for VAT purposes, there must be a clear and realistic intent to make taxable supplies on a regular and continuing basis.

Person liable for registration

17.5 VAT registration can be in the name of a sole proprietor, a partnership, a corporate entity or an unincorporated body, ie a Club or Association. It is important to remember that if a sole proprietor is VAT registered then all of his business activities will be covered by that VAT registration – he does not need to register for each activity and it is crucial that VAT is declared correctly on all business supplies made by him no matter how diverse his supplies are.

For businesses already VAT registered, they will only be able to recover input VAT on those costs put to a taxable business use. If there is no existing VAT registration, and the only intention is to enter into a sponsorship agreement for the racing of horses, then Customs will accept an application, not as a voluntary or intending registration, but under a special scheme – the Registration Scheme for Racehorse Owners.

The Registration Scheme for Racehorse Owners

Background

17.6 The agreement reached by Customs and the British Horseracing Board in 1993 came about following a long period of negotiation between the parties and all those involved in the bloodstock industry. Customs' refusal to accept that the business test was being met had the effect that VAT at the standard rate was being suffered as an additional cost to all those struggling to keep the British racing industry alive. The extremely generous tax and VAT treatments in place in other EU Member States (particularly France and Ireland) meant that the UK authorities were being forced to reconsider the impact that its decisions were having on the nation's equine industry.

On 16 March 1993, Customs introduced the Registration Scheme for Racehorse Owners ('the Scheme'). This acknowledged that those owners who were actively seeking sponsorship and appearance money for their horses would be treated as being in business and therefore could apply to be VAT registered. Once registered, owners must account for VAT on their business income including prize money and sales of horses, and can recover, subject to the normal rules, VAT incurred on the purchase and upkeep of racehorses and other general overhead expenses associated with the ownership.

In 1997 the scheme was reviewed and, with effect from 1 January 1998, all owners with racehorses wishing to register can only apply for VAT registration if:

- the racehorses are covered by a sponsorship agreement registered at Weatherbys; or
- the racehorses are covered by a trainer's sponsorship agreement registered at Weatherbys; or
- the owner can demonstrate that they have received, and will continue to receive, business income, ie from appearance money or sponsored number cloths.

Note that a sponsorship agreement must obtain a minimum level of fees to be seen as a business activity. The minimum level for 2003 is currently:

1–9 horses:	£300 per horse per annum; or £750 per horse per annum for a Class A race.
10 or more horses:	£100 per horse per annum.

Full details on the sponsorship requirements can be found in 'A Code of Conduct for Owners' Sponsorship' which is available free of charge from the British Horseracing Board (BHB).

Another review was recently carried out in 2001/02 and in December 2002, Customs confirmed that the Scheme will continue unchanged, in structure at least, until a further review in 2005. The further review in three years' time will take account of the wider impact of the tax system on racehorse owners, including recent reforms to betting taxation.

Whilst the Scheme's structure will not be changed, the Treasury invited the British Horseracing Board to participate in discussions with Customs about tightening up on compliance, including those rules concerning the securing and maintaining of sponsorship income.

Customs' recent review of the Scheme was an attempt to withdraw its use, as it considers that the majority of sponsorship deals are not commercial contracts but simply an opportunity to ensure that the business test is being met and that input VAT recovery on, sometimes significant, costs could be recovered. The devastating effect that its withdrawal would have on the British racing industry meant that Customs were persuaded not to make any changes to the Scheme, but there is likely to be a tightening of the rules regarding sponsorship in the future, especially if Customs consider that there is manipulation of the sponsorships received by current owners.

The Scheme

17.7 Full and comprehensive information on the Scheme can be found in Customs leaflet 700/67 (updated in January 2002) and can be found at their website at www.hmce.gov.uk/forms/index.htm or by calling their National Enquiry Line on 0845 010 9000. The BHB also provide 'A Guide to the VAT Scheme' which can be obtained free of charge from their website at www.bhb.co.uk or by calling 020 7396 0011.

The Scheme registration requires completion of a VAT 1 registration form, just like any other VAT application. However, it is also necessary to complete a D1 form (for sole ownership of horses) or a D2 form (for shares in horse ownership) and to send this completed form to Weatherbys. The 'D' forms are obtainable from Weatherbys and they have a useful VAT team on the helpdesk number, which is 01933 440077. The 'D' forms confirm that there is a sponsorship agreement or that business income has been received from the horses owned. Weatherbys will confirm the details that they have been given and then return the stamped 'D' forms to the owner. Once received, the 'D' forms and the completed VAT 1 should be sent to the VAT registration unit which covers the owner's business address postcode (Customs can confirm the local VAT registration office by contacting them on their National Enquiry Line).

Once the completed and stamped 'D' form (s) and the VAT 1 have been sent to the VAT registration unit the owner will be sent confirmation of the VAT registration number and normal VAT rules should then be applied to all sales and purchases (although see paragraph **17.8** below for variations to some of the basic VAT rules). It is important to notify Weatherbys of the VAT registration number as soon as it is allocated as this will ensure that any prize or appearance money is paid with the addition of VAT (rather than as VAT inclusive).

Registered person

17.8 The legal entity to be registered for VAT should be the owner of the racehorse who is registered at Weatherbys, ie sole proprietor, partnership or limited company. If only a part share in a racehorse is owned then registration as a sole proprietor will only be allowed if this share is at least 50% of the horse. If less than 50% is owned then registration will only be accepted in the name of a partnership with the other part share owners.

The Scheme only applies to those owners that are not already registered for VAT. Where a business is already registered for VAT and it purchases a racehorse for advertising and promotion purposes they should treat the activities under normal business rules. This means that if the racehorse is used partly for advertising purposes and partly for providing entertainment or for private purposes then the input VAT should be apportioned to reflect use.

Although Point to Point racing is regulated by the Jockey Club, owners are not eligible to register under the Scheme until their horses graduate for racing as hunter chasers. Permit holders, ie national hunt trainers with amateur status, may register under the Scheme provided they meet the normal requirements mentioned above, but they must remember that input VAT can only be recovered on business expenses. The costs relating to non-racing horses cannot be recovered under the Scheme, therefore an apportionment will need to be made.

Note that prize money is only standard-rated if the horse is covered by the Scheme and thus no output VAT will be due if the horse is unregistered – such prize money remains outside the scope of VAT.

The normal VAT rules for output VAT and input VAT vary slightly under the Scheme and, in particular, the following VAT liabilities apply:

- sponsorship income – standard-rated supply;
- prize money/appearance money – standard-rated supplies. Note that the value for VAT purposes of prize money is the amount calculated under the Rules of Racing as receivable by the owner less entry fees etc collected by the racecourse;
- sale of racehorses – standard-rated supply if the horse is in the UK but see 17.18 below for the place of supply rules for goods and bloodstock;
- racehorses given away or put to a non-business use – output tax is due;
- sale of a share or shares in a racehorse – this is standard-rated supply unless the sale of the share creates a new partnership, in which case the supply is disregarded for VAT purposes. Note that the sale of a share is a supply of services and thus will be standard-rated is the owner is established within the UK (see further **17.19** below).

With regards to the recovery of input VAT, Customs allow the following.

- The purchase, training and maintenance of a racehorse put to training is a business expense. VAT may be recovered on such costs, including any costs incurred when the racehorse is unable to run due to injury provided there is an expectation it will run in the future.

- Owner subsistence – where the horse is racing some distance from the principal place of business, and it is unreasonable to expect the owner to travel to and from the principal place of business, VAT may be recovered on hotel accommodation and breakfast/evening meals in line with the normal VAT rules. Note that Customs will not normally allow the VAT recovery on meals or drinks taken at the racecourse.
- Telephone usage has been agreed as a 10% VAT recovery unless there is evidence to support a higher percentage recovery.
- Lease of executive boxes – where an owner leases a box at the racecourse, the VAT recovery will depend upon the extent of business use. If used for meetings with potential customers and suppliers during racing as well as for their own personal use or for corporate entertaining then Customs will allow 50% of the VAT incurred on the lease of the box to be recovered as input VAT. If the owner feels a higher percentage recovery is warranted, evidence should be retained to justify the amount of VAT reclaimed.

Other VAT registration schemes

17.9 For those businesses that carry out other trading activities they will probably be VAT registered under the normal VAT rules. For these entities there is the opportunity to consider other VAT schemes which may make their VAT affairs simpler.

Two such schemes are the flat-rate farmers' scheme and the flat-rate scheme for small businesses.

Flat-rate farmer's scheme

17.10 The flat-rate scheme for farmers was introduced as an optional scheme for businesses. The scheme refers to supplies made by farmers, but the nature of activities included within the scheme means that any business supplying farming and agricultural goods and services could be eligible. By registering under the scheme the 'farmer' receives certification and is no longer VAT registered. The scheme can only be used for designated supplies but means that VAT no longer becomes due on sales made and that there is no VAT recovery on costs. Instead, the farmer is able to add a 'flat-rate' charge of 4% on sales of designated produce to VAT registered customers. The farmer can retain this 4% addition and the VAT registered customer can recover it on his normal VAT return. As the farmer is able to sell to the public without the addition of either VAT or the flat-rate 4%, he can increase his sales price in order to make a little more profit whilst these prices still remain below his VAT registered competitors.

The designated supplies covered by the scheme are varied but include stock farming, crop production, forestry, fisheries, certain processing of farm products and supplies of agricultural services. However, activities that involve animals which are not eaten by humans or produce food which is eaten by humans are largely excluded. In particular, the training of horses bred for racing, specialist training of horses and activities involving animals such as pony trekking, riding and hunting are also excluded. This means that these supplies must be treated outside of the scheme and, if the value of these taxable supplies exceed the VAT threshold, the farmer must leave the scheme and a VAT registration is required to cover all supplies.

The main benefit of the scheme is to those farmers that have a majority of sales included within the designated services but who also have some stabling or livery that produces a small amount of additional income each year.

The following is an example where VAT planning in the use of the scheme may bring benefits.

Example

A business currently lets 20 acres of land to a tenant farmer (an exempt supply) and has 150 acres of managed woodland. In addition to this, he also has a couple of stables where his horses are kept and where he charges ten other horse owners for the care, exercising and stabling of their horses. Currently, the farmer is VAT registered and has to account for VAT on the charges that he makes for his livery services. Note that these livery services do not qualify for exemption (see Equestrian Activities: Livery at **17.23** below) as they are primarily care related, not DIY livery services. In order to be competitive, the farmer has to meet some of the VAT cost himself as he does not want his customers to feel that they are being charged VAT. By using the flat-rate scheme, the farmer could de-register from VAT until such time as the livery income exceeded the current VAT threshold. He would need to charge VAT registered customers 4% flat rate on the woodland timber sales (which he retains), however he can avoid accounting for 17.5% VAT on the livery services and on any timber sales to the public. He needs to consider the loss of recoverable VAT on assets and overheads but, if these costs are low, then the benefits could be very welcome.

There are of course always conditions to the use of the scheme and the farmer is not entitled to use the scheme where his retention of the flat-rate 4% would exceed previously recoverable input VAT by more than £3,000.

Flat-rate scheme for small businesses

17.11 This is a relatively new VAT scheme having only been introduced in April 2002. The scheme is available for those businesses with a taxable turnover of less than £150,000, although the inclusion of exempt supplies increases the turnover to £187,500.

The scheme operates on a relatively simple level – the business remains VAT registered with the same VAT number and still has to complete the normal quarterly VAT returns. If supplies are made to VAT registered customers then a VAT invoice will be raised as normal and the VAT shown will be at the normal rate, ie 17.5%, 5% or 0%. However, when the VAT return is completed the calculation of VAT will depend upon the flat-rate that is applicable to the main business activity carried on.

Example

As an example, the flat-rate for animal husbandry is 11% and that for forestry and fishing is 10%. If we have a business that offers livery services and fishing rights then we need to determine which is the greater part of the business by reference to turnover. In our case this is the livery. At the VAT quarter end we take the gross sales receipts (including VAT if any was separately invoiced) and apply the 11% flat-rate to all turnover. The resulting figure is the output VAT that needs to be declared.

In theory, in the above example, this should result in a saving of VAT than if normal VAT rules had been used. However, the right to input VAT recovery on overheads and other costs is lost and so great care is needed to determine whether a saving will be made under this scheme as opposed to the normal VAT rules.

There are also a few surprises and the business should be aware of the following:

- input VAT can still be recovered if goods of a capital nature are purchased with a gross value in excess of £2,000 per item. Beware that output VAT of 17.5% must then be declared when the item is disposed of – the sale cannot be treated under the flat-rate;
- the flat-rate applies to sales of goods and services even when these would normally be liable to the zero, reduced or exempt rates;
- the flat-rate must be applied to the gross value of sales so that if VAT is charged to a VAT registered customer at 17.5%, then the

flat-rate applies to 117.5% of the value of the goods. This means that the flat-rate is effectively increased by one or two per cent.
- only one flat-rate can be used for the entire business – the rates cannot be apportioned unless there is a change to the most significant activity part way through a year.

The scheme will largely benefit those that supply standard-rated goods and services and where the level of input VAT is relatively low. As with all VAT schemes, there will be winners and losers and the business should be careful to consider its own customer base and nature of supplies before making a decision to adopt the scheme.

Margin scheme for horses and ponies

17.12 A margin scheme operates for second-hand horses and ponies and is available to a VAT-registered person, although not in conjunction with either the flat-rate farmers' scheme or the flat-rate scheme for small businesses. The margin scheme can, however, be used by persons registered under the Registration Scheme for Racehorse Owners.

The use of the margin scheme is optional and can be applied to all or just some of the horses or ponies owned. The basis of the scheme is that the VAT to be declared on the sale of an eligible animal is calculated on the margin made between the purchase and selling price. This margin is treated as being VAT inclusive and therefore 7/47ths of the margin must be declared to Customs as output VAT.

There are a number of conditions that must be met in order for the scheme to apply so care needs to be taken, as inappropriate use could result in hefty VAT liabilities.

The scheme cannot be used for:

- horses or ponies which have been bred within the business as these are not 'second-hand' animals;
- horses or ponies that have been purchased from outside the EC and have therefore been subject to import VAT;
- horses or ponies whose purchase price was subject to a VAT charge.

Providing the purchase has not been subject to VAT, the scheme can be used either for purchases of equine animals for resale or for retention within the business.

It is a legal requirement that a stock book, or similar record, is retained and that details of the purchase (stock number, name of vendor, purchase price and date of purchase) sale details (invoice number, buyer, sale price and date, margin made and VAT due) and description of the animal are clearly shown. The description of the horse must include the following:

- colour;
- sex;
- type, ie cob, chestnut, gelding etc;
- age;
- height;
- stable name; and
- any distinctive markings.

The purchase and sales invoice should normally have a declaration that 'input tax deduction has not and will not be claimed in respect of the goods sold on this invoice'. This is the evidence that shows that the animal is eligible for use within the margin scheme. If buying from a private individual it is important to ensure that an invoice or purchase document is still obtained.

As an alternative to the above accounting rules, Customs also allow the use of a special three-part invoice set which is available through the British Equestrian Trade Association. These forms comprise of:

- Part A for the stock records;
- Part B acts as the seller's sales invoice; and
- Part C as the buyer's purchase invoice.

The use of this three-part form obviates the need to retain the stock book and declarations mentioned previously.

The purchase or sale of animals through an auction will still be eligible for the margin scheme providing all the accounting conditions are met and that the auctioneer is aware that the margin scheme is to be used.

The margin scheme is operated throughout the EU which means that the sale of an animal under this scheme to a buyer in another EU Member State will be treated in exactly the same way as a sale to a UK buyer, ie UK VAT must be accounted for on the margin. A sale to a buyer resident outside the EU can be supplied VAT free providing the horse or pony is exported from the EU within three months of the date of the sale. It is important to retain evidence of the export to support the zero-rating.

There are also restrictions on the amount of VAT that can be recovered in relation to the costs of caring for a horse that has been purchased for sale under the scheme, and it is recommended that these rules are checked carefully before deciding the scheme's benefits. Full details of the margin scheme can be found in Customs Notice 718.

Overseas trade – goods

17.13 The purchase and sale of horses into, and out of, the UK are treated as supplies of goods and the VAT rules determining place of supply will be used to identify whether VAT is chargeable or payable on the supplies of these animals. There are different VAT rules for the movement of goods within the EU and those outside of the EU. The differences are highlighted below. The following paragraphs only cover the supply of goods and not the supply of services or the use of those goods to make supplies of services. Paragraph **17.18** covers the VAT issues affecting the supply of services.

EU dispatches and acquisitions

Dispatches (or sales)

17.14 If an animal is being temporarily moved to an EU Member State for a period of less than two years, then there is no need to register for VAT in that EU Member State or to account for any VAT on the movement. The temporary movement is 'ignored' for VAT purposes. However, if the horse is sold whilst away or does not return within the deadline, then a supply will 'crystallise' and VAT issues will arise.

The sale of a horse to a private individual or to a non-VAT registered business within the EU should be liable to UK VAT. If the margin scheme is being used, the profit margin will need to be treated as VAT inclusive.

Should the horse, or any other goods, be sold to a VAT-registered business in the EU, then providing the buyer's VAT registration number is quoted on the invoice, and there is evidence that the horse has been dispatched from the UK within three months of the date of the sale, then it can be treated as a zero-rated supply.

The sale to another EU business is known as a 'dispatch' and will need to be recorded on the VAT return as an EU sale. Once EU sales of goods commence there is also a requirement to complete quarterly EC Sales Lists and these should be sent to automatically once the business has declared a sale of goods within box 8 of the VAT return. The more complex Intrastat declarations for the statistical recording of EU sales will not be triggered unless the value of the sale of goods exceeds £233,000 within a calendar year.

The above assumes that the horse is within the UK when it is sold – if the horse is already in another EU Member State then it may be necessary to register for VAT in that Member State as any VAT liability will crystallise there.

Example

A horse is moved to France for show or competition and, as a temporary movement, this will not create any liabilities. However, a local French buyer makes a substantial offer for the horse and you decide to sell it whilst it is in France. As the horse is physically located outside of the UK, the sale should be reported on the UK VAT return as an 'own movement' of goods within the EU and a French VAT registration will be required in order to account for local French VAT as an acquisition. The French buyer would then have to be charged French VAT on the purchase although it may be applicable to use the French margin scheme. Note that in some EU States there are simplification measures that can be used to avoid the necessity of registering but this must be checked in advance and cleared with the local VAT authorities. It is also worth noting that in many EU States there is no VAT registration threshold so that a single sale could crystallise a registration requirement.

Acquisitions (or purchases)

17.15 The purchase of a horse or goods from another EU supplier will result in no local VAT being charged as long as the business quotes its UK VAT registration number and the horse is removed from the EU Member State of purchase. In the case of a purchase from an EU individual obviously there will be no VAT as the supplier is not VAT registered.

However, in the case of the purchase of the horse from an EU business this will need to be treated as an acquisition in the UK. On the arrival of the horse in the UK it will be necessary to self-account for UK VAT by making a declaration in box 9 and box 2 of the VAT return. This simply means that the value of the horse, in sterling, is recorded and an amount of VAT, being 17.5% of the value, is declared as acquisition VAT in box 2. This acquisition VAT can then be recovered as input VAT on the same return providing that the goods are to be used for business purposes.

For purchases from private individuals or for goods bought under the margin scheme there is no need to declare acquisition VAT, although the purchase value of the goods should still be recorded on the VAT return. When purchasing horses or any second-hand goods from an EU vendor check whether the supplier is using the margin scheme as this will affect the VAT treatment when goods are then sold.

Non-EU exports and imports

Exports (or sales)

17.16 The sale of horses from the UK to a non-EU buyer can be treated as a zero-rated sale providing that the buyer is not established in the EU and that the horse is exported from the EU within three months of the date of the supply. Export evidence and evidence of the buyer's status will need to be retained to ensure that the zero-rating is supported.

Imports (or purchases)

17.17 The importation of horses into the UK from outside the EU will trigger a requirement to pay import VAT. This VAT is calculated on the value of the goods being imported and will include insurance, shipping and handling charges. Due to the high level of care needed in transit, these costs could lead to a significant increase in the amount of VAT payable. VAT at 17.5% will be charged on the importation of horses but this will be recoverable if the importer is VAT registered and will be using the horse for business purposes. Normally the import VAT will have to be paid to Customs prior to the release of the horse into 'free circulation' but there are special reliefs that allow for the immediate release providing security and guarantees are given.

The temporary importation of goods into the UK can be made without payment of import VAT by the completion of a TI (temporary importation) document. This allows for the horse to be brought to the UK for a period of up to two years but, in special circumstances, this period can be extended on application to Customs. The TI procedure requires a security or guarantee to be made to Customs but this is still a better option than the payment of full VAT on the horse's arrival in the UK. Should the horse be sold whilst in the UK then Customs need to be informed immediately and VAT will become payable on the value paid by the purchaser.

Overseas trade – services

17.18 Anything which is not deemed to be a supply of goods is treated as a supply of services. The VAT place of supply rules for services differ from those of goods and care must be taken to ensure that the correct VAT treatment is applied.

The sale of a horse will be a supply of goods, whereas the sale of a share in a horse will be a supply of services. The basic place of supply rule for services is that determined by where the supplier belongs. For UK businesses it is therefore likely that services provided through their horses will be subject to UK VAT, irrespective of the customer's status. Supplies of services within the bloodstock industry are considered at **17.19** below.

Bloodstock services

Breeding

17.19 Customs will allow a Breeder to register for VAT prior to the making of any taxable supplies (sales or leasing of the foals or yearlings). This is known as an intending trader registration. However, Customs must be satisfied that the breeding is a genuine commercial activity and they will require evidence to demonstrate this. As a mare will not produce a foal each year, Customs normally expect the breeder to have more than one mare in order that the 'commerciality' test is met. If the intention is to breed with only one mare then a good business case is needed to support the application for VAT. The sponsorship rules that apply to the registration scheme for racehorse owners do not apply to owner breeders.

Syndications – supplies of shares

17.20 Colts which are to become stallions are often syndicated into shares. These shares will be sold to owners giving them an interest in the stallion and/or the right to a nomination during the breeding season. It is important to identify whether the share is for a nomination or for an interest in the stallion (or for both) as the VAT treatment will vary.

The sale of both types of share is treated as a supply of services, rather than a supply of goods.

For *shares of interest,* a UK VAT registered breeder will have to account for VAT whether the purchaser is an UK or non-UK resident.

The purchaser of the share will be entitled to VAT recovery only if he is VAT registered and will be using the 'share' for business purposes. If input VAT is recovered then the onward supply by the owner of his share will also need to be standard rated for VAT purposes. This assumes, of course, that the owner is established within the UK.

Should the owners come together to sell all the shares in the stallion then this will be a supply of goods and Customs will accept that the normal VAT rules should be applied to determine the VAT liability of the sale. In these circumstances, the individual sale of the shares is normally ignored for VAT purposes when the stallion is sold to a purchaser outside the UK.

The *supply of a nomination* is normally deemed to take place in the country where the covering takes place. This means that if the stallion is within the UK then the nomination will be subject to 17.5% UK VAT. If the covering occurs in another EU Member State then local EU VAT may be charged.

There are two exceptions to this general rule:

- if a mare is temporarily imported from outside the EU for nomination then the supply can be zero-rated providing that the mare is then exported once the nomination is complete. Customs accept that completion of the nomination is normally the end of the covering season being the middle of July;
- if a mare is brought temporarily into the UK by an EU VAT registered business, then the place of supply of the nomination will shift to the EU Member State of the business. Under these circumstances, the supply will not be liable to UK VAT but the EU business must declare local VAT on the supply under its own VAT registration. This 'reverse charge' procedure also applies to UK businesses that buy in the services of non-UK suppliers. If a UK mare is sent to France for nomination, French VAT will be charged unless the owner is UK VAT registered. If a UK VAT registration is held then French VAT will not apply, but the UK business must declare 17.5% VAT on the value of the supply as output VAT in its UK VAT return. This output VAT can be recovered as input VAT on the same VAT return providing that the services are incurred for business purposes.

If a mare is sent outside the EU to be nominated by a stallion then the supply is outside the scope of EU VAT. If a stallion is sent to another EU country then the supply of a nomination of a UK VAT registered stud is outside the scope of UK VAT but, as the supply takes place where the nomination occurs, the UK stud could be liable for a VAT registration in that Member State. It should be borne in mind that most of the EC Member States have no VAT threshold for non-resident businesses.

Syndicates

17.21 Normally a syndicate will be formed to control and manage the transfer of the shares of interest and nominations. As this syndicate is also responsible for the upkeep of the stallion, the owners will contribute to the syndicate who disburses this income to the stable. The syndicate may also sell nominations over and above that of the 'share' entitlement of the owners. This income is used to offset the stabling and veterinary costs incurred. With effect from November 2000, Customs accept that a syndicate making supplies of these surplus nominations is making a business supply. It must therefore register for VAT if this income exceeds the VAT-registration limit. The registration can either be in the name of the syndicate, as a partnership of its members, or the syndicate secretary can register as an agent for the entire membership.

The syndicate can consider a voluntary registration if the value of its taxable supplies are below the VAT-registration limit. This should, however, be considered carefully as the level of administration will increase and value of syndicate input VAT may not justify the VAT obligations.

There is an agreement between Customs and the Thoroughbred Breeders Association called 'Keeping of Stallions at Stud'. This agreement can be found on Customs' website at www.hmce.gov.uk under publications, Notice 700/57 section 22, and includes fairly comprehensive information on the valuation and VAT treatment of stallion nominations including those provided free of charge.

Supplies of additional services

17.22 When nomination services are supplied there will often be additional services supplied as ancillary to the nomination. These may include veterinary services, blacksmiths services and consultancy and breeding advice. Providing that these services are ancillary to the nomination, and are not separately invoiced or supplied, the VAT liability of the nomination service will also apply to the additional services.

In cases where separate supplies are made the following rules apply:

- consultancy, advertising, marketing and advisory services can be treated as outside the scope of UK VAT when supplied to a non-EU owner or to an EU VAT registered business;
- stable rental and services relating to land are supplied where the land is situated. Generally, bare stabling is exempt from VAT unless the stable owner has 'opted to tax'. Where there is a high level of care (which there usually is with the nominations and mares in foal) then the services are not treated as land-related and will remain taxable;
- the vast majority of other services, such as veterinary and blacksmiths' services, are supplied where the supplier belongs and will therefore be taxable at 17.5% if these are invoiced by UK suppliers.

Equestrian activities

Livery services

17.23 Customs always held the view that the livery services provided by stables to horse owners were taxable at the standard rate. The only exception to this was the single supply of grazing rights (being zero-rated) or the letting of a bare stable or field which was accepted as exempt unless the option to tax had been made (see **17.27** below for further information on the option to tax).

However, this view was slowly being eroded by the way in which stables continue to diversify in order to raise further sources of income. In particular, they are now far more flexible about the level of services offered and there is a continued growing trend for all landowners to be more aware of 'tax planning' incentives and to take advantage of ways in which their services can be provided at a better value than a competitors.

The ruling in the VAT tribunal case of *John Window [2001] V & DR 252* confirmed that the stabling of horses should remain exempt from VAT unless the option to tax has been made. However, it then ruled that where livery services are provided as an incidental part of that stabling then the whole supply should also be exempt. It does not become a wholly standard-rated supply and nor should an apportionment of the supply be made between the taxable and exempt elements.

The *John Window* case was the lead case of several other cases and although the principles of the 'single supply' rule were established well before this hearing, the decision opened the door for many liveries to save VAT and for the horse owner to pay less for the services received.

However, care should be taken in determining the VAT liability as the nature of the supplies made will vary from owner to owner – some owners may only require DIY livery services (clearly exempt subject to the option to tax) whereas others will request full livery such that the level of care becomes the most predominant part of the supply and therefore makes the whole charge standard-rated.

The higher the level of care required by the owner then the more likelihood there is that the entire supply will remain standard-rated. Indeed, the level of care given by racehorse trainers, stud farms and breaking-in schools are such that Customs will not accept that the exemption can be applied.

For those liveries that might have opted to tax, the availability of exemption is removed entirely although it is hoped that the majority of stable and land owners have not taken this route.

The ability to exempt livery is, as mentioned, very dependent upon the level of care offered. For the DIY livery or one where the owner is offered simple turning out, mucking out and feeding services then probably the exemption would apply. When exercising and grooming is added to the package then the predominant supply is becoming one of care. There can be a very fine line between the VAT liabilities and it is essential that any contracts, written or verbal agreements and what actually happens in practice is structured to ensure that there can be no future arguments with Customs concerning the VAT liability.

For those liveries that feel they have been incorrectly charging VAT on their supplies then they have the opportunity to revisit their VAT treatment and to make a 'voluntary disclosure' to Customs for VAT overpaid. However, it should be remembered that whilst the exemption gives rise to opportunity for keeping the charges at a competitive level, the businesses will lose the ability to recover VAT on costs relating to the exempt supply. Any refund of VAT by Customs will need to take into account the repayment of input VAT that might have been made on livery expenses. Customs have also stated that they will not repay output VAT unless this was previously suffered out of profits, ie not separately charged to horse owners. This stance is variable from VAT office to VAT office but persistence should usually result in a refund.

It is also notable that some horse owners have demanded a refund of VAT from their liveries and it is suggested that if such demands are met, then any refunds should take into account the cost of irrecoverable VAT and reasonable expenses in seeking the refund from Customs (including any professional fees incurred!).

Tuition

17.24 Commercial supplies of horse riding lessons and tuition are considered to be educational and are normally standard-rated. However, when provided by a partner, sole proprietor or non-profit making organisation, the VAT liability becomes exempt. Corporate entities should treat the supplies as standard-rated unless they are also non-profit making and plough any 'profit' from this educational activity back into the furtherance of those activities.

A sole proprietor or partnership offering tuition should be aware that the exemption does not extend to services offered by employees of the business. Thus if a partnership employs three other tutors, only the partners' teaching services will be exempt – the services of the three staff remain taxable. This might be enough to ensure that the level of taxable income remains beneath the VAT threshold but care still needs to be taken to ensure that the turnover levels are monitored.

Unless hacking and trekking services can be linked to an educational supply, these will remain standard-rated whoever they are supplied by.

With the increasing exemptions available for both stabling and educational tuition the business will need to consider the benefits of structuring such activities to maximise its VAT position. Whilst exemption will bring savings to the end consumer, the business should consider the loss of VAT on related and overhead costs very carefully.

Partial exemption – the basics

17.25 Legislation governing the application of partial exemption can be found in the Value Added Tax Regulations 1995 (SI 1995/2518) and Customs' interpretation of this in Notice 706.

When a business makes a mixture of exempt supplies it does not have to charge its customer any VAT on the sale value. This can mean that the pricing structure becomes more competitive or that the business can make a little more profit as it can still undercut the price of suppliers who may have to charge VAT. However, the business needs to be aware that the cost of exempt supplies is the inability to recover input VAT incurred in making those supplies. This restriction is known as partial exemption. VAT relating to these supplies can only be recovered if it falls beneath a de minimis limit.

Any business making a mixture of exempt and taxable supplies should carefully consider the impact of partial exemption so that it can determine how much VAT is likely to be lost as a result of making these supplies – or what planning can be put in place to ensure that any loss is mitigated.

The first step for a business making exempt supplies is to attribute all input VAT incurred either directly to a taxable supply, directly to an exempt supply or to an overhead cost (such as professional and running costs). Having identified the amount of overhead VAT, this must be apportioned so that only the proportion relating to taxable supplies is recovered. Any costs directly relating to an exempt supply and the exempt proportion of the overhead cost are added together and are known as exempt input VAT. If the total amount of this exempt VAT is less than the de minimis limit (£625 per month and less than 50% of all input VAT) then all VAT is recoverable. If this limit is exceeded then none of the exempt VAT can be claimed in the VAT period.

The method used to apportion the overhead VAT needs to be determined very carefully. The 'standard method' is the most common method and does not need the prior permission of Customs. It is the method that must be used if no other method is requested or granted. The amount of overhead VAT that can be recovered is determined by the percentage that taxable supplies bear to total (taxable plus exempt) supplies. This percentage is rounded to the next whole number. An example of the standard method is given below.

Example

A stud business has taxable sales of nominations, some training, sale of foals and yearlings. It also has stabling which is let to other horse owners on a DIY basis (exempt from VAT).

(a) Identify all input VAT wholly attributable to taxable (ie standard-rated, lower rate and zero rate) supplies – say, £15,000 in connection with veterinary fees, feeds, stabling costs of the stud and feeds.
(b) Identify all input VAT wholly attributable to exempt supplies – say, £1,000 on repairs to the stables let for DIY use.
(c) Identify the overhead VAT being attributable to both taxable and exempt supplies – say, £5,000 on professional and accountancy fees, telephones, computer purchases and general office and farmhouse costs.

The amount of input VAT that may be recoverable under (c) can be calculated by reference to the percentage of taxable supplies to total supplies in the period concerned.

Taxable supplies	£135,000
Exempt supplies	£5,000
	£140,000

Amount of overhead VAT recoverable under (c) is therefore 97% (£4,850) and the amount of VAT which is therefore deemed to be attributable to exempt supplies is 3% (£150).

The total amount of exempt VAT in the period is therefore £1,000 plus £150, a total of £1,150. The VAT recoverable in the period is £15,000 plus £4,850, a total of £19,850.

The business should then check whether the value of exempt VAT is beneath the de minimis limit – if it is, all the VAT can be recovered.

In our example £1,150 is below £625 per month on average (£1,875 per quarter) and below 50% of all input VAT. As both tests are met then all of the exempt VAT can be recovered in this period.

However, at the end of the year (usually March, April or May dependent upon the VAT-return periods that the business is on) an annual adjustment is carried out and the quarterly calculation is repeated but using the year's figures. This may give the opportunity to recover exempt VAT which might have been irrecoverable in a previous VAT return, as the de minimis limit is multiplied to a threshold of £7,500 and less than 50% of all input VAT.

Of course, as, in our example, we have recovered all of the exempt VAT in the current quarter, the effect could be that, over the year, we should not have recovered the exempt input VAT and the business may have to repay this to Customs.

Alternative Methods

17.26 If the standard method does not produce a fair and reasonable result, a business can apply in writing to Customs for approval to use a special method. Once accepted, the special method can be applied to the start of the current partial exemption year or from the start of the next year.

A special method can take any form – the business needs to consider which is the most fair and reasonable and whether the business has all the information to be able to calculate the figures each period.

Land and property

17.27 The VAT treatment of land and property transactions can be extremely complex and it is recommended that the sale or purchase of property is always checked for VAT purposes to ensure that the business can plan or at least be aware of the VAT impact.

Residential properties

17.28 In summary, the sale of a brand new residential building is zero-rated whilst the sale of an existing residential property will be exempt. Repairs, maintenance work, annexes and extensions to existing properties will be standard-rated but there are reliefs for works of approved alterations to listed dwellings. This relief enables structural work to be zero-rated providing that the work required and received listed planning consent.

It is also possible to benefit from a reduced rate of 5% when works are carried out to convert a non-residential building to residential use and to modernise a dwelling that has not been occupied for three years. In these cases, the builder carrying out the work should only charge VAT at 5% and not at 17.5%. If the property is listed, the zero-rating will take precedence.

The rental of residential property is always exempt and the owner cannot choose to 'opt to tax' (see **17.29** below). The only exception to this is the rental of holiday accommodation which is automatically standard-rated.

Commercial property

17.29 The sale of a new commercial property is standard-rated but, unlike a residential property, 'new' for commercial properties means within three years from the date of construction completion. All other commercial property sales will be exempt from VAT unless the owner has 'opted to tax'.

The option to tax is a mechanism that allows a VAT-registered person to choose to charge standard-rated VAT on the supplies of commercial property. The option is made on a property by property basis so that a business can choose to opt to tax one building and leave another 'united'. Once the option has been made it is largely irrevocable until a period of 20 years has elapsed. Great care must therefore be given before the option is made. The option can be made on any commercial property or on land so it is possible that an owner could opt to tax stables, pasture land and/or commercial buildings. It is unusual for equestrian land and buildings to be opted as most owners choose to keep their buildings VAT-free in order to keep fees low for their clients, but this point should always be checked.

Once the option has been made, all disposals, leases and lets must be taxed at the standard rate unless the lessee or purchaser is to use the site for charitable purposes or for residential use. Under these circumstances the option is misapplied for those transactions and will become exempt.

Works to commercial properties will be standard-rated and it is irrelevant whether the work is to a listed building or whether it is an extension, repair or refurbishment.

If an equestrian business incurs VAT on a commercial property construction, repair or lease then it will be entitled to recover this VAT providing that the cost has been incurred for wholly taxable business purposes. There will be no need to opt to tax to recover this VAT unless the business intends to sell or let the property for what would otherwise be an exempt supply.

Agreement with the BHB and racehorse owner

17.30 Agreement with the British Horseracing Board about the revised arrangements under which racehorse owners may register for VAT and the procedures that must be followed (January 1998).

1 The terms of the previous memorandum of 16 March 1993 between the Thoroughbred Horseracing and Breeding Industry and HM Customs and Excise will continue to apply for those owners who were registered for VAT before 1 January 1998.

Background

2 The VAT Registration Scheme for Racehorse Owners, 'the Scheme', was introduced on 16 March 1993 following representations from all sections of the Racing Industry. In particular, new proposals put forward by the Jockey Club in connection with sponsorship, appearance money and prize money enabled Customs to recognise that persons racing horses are intending to make taxable supplies and are subject to VAT registration.

3 The Scheme was introduced on the understanding it would be reviewed in its fourth year of operation. That review has now been completed and it is agreed. The Scheme will continue but with some modifications to be effective from 1 January 1998.

New arrangements

4 The new arrangements, effective from 1 January 1998, are:

(a) Owners applying for registration must have a sponsorship agreement registered at Weatherbys, or be able to demonstrate they have received business income, and will continue to do so from their horseracing activities, eg appearance money, sponsored number cloths (SNCs). The effective date of registration will normally be the date the declaration on Form D1/D2 is received at Weatherbys.

(b) The sponsorship agreement may be either one payment for participation in one or more races or represent payments over a period of time.

(c) Upon expiry of a sponsorship agreement an owner will be able to remain registered provided they can demonstrate they are actively seeking sponsorship.

(d) If a sponsorship agreement does not cover all an owner's racehorses they will nevertheless be allowed to include those racehorses not covered within the Scheme registration provided the owner can demonstrate they are actively seeking sponsorship for them.

(e) Owners holding less than 50% share in a racehorse must register for VAT as a partnership, club etc.

5 With the exception of 4(e) above the new arrangements for registration will not apply to those owners registered for VAT before 1 January 1998 and who hold a sponsorship agreement or can show they are continuing actively to seek sponsorship. However, if an owner fails to meet these requirements their registration may be cancelled.

Breeders

6 Customs will continue to require or allow VAT registration where a business of breeding horses for sale exists. Customs accept that where breeders engage in racing activities with the purpose of enhancing the value of their stock and/or their business, these activities are by way of business. For these purposes stock means colts, fillies and home-bred geldings.

7 Breeders who meet these conditions will be able to claim all tax incurred as input tax in accordance with the normal rules. Output tax will become due on the full amount realised on the sale of all stock. However, no output tax will be due on the transfer of stock to training if the transferor is registered for VAT.

8 Breeders who own racehorses on their own account, or with others, for racing purposes only may not recover tax incurred under the above. However, they may qualify to do so under the arrangements for owners outlined in paragraphs 4, 16, 17, 18 and 19.

Trainers

9 Customs will continue to require or allow VAT registration where a business exists of providing training services to owners. Where racehorses are owned by the trainer and also trained by him, and providing the number are not disproportionate to the training activity, any related costs will be regarded as business expenditure for VAT purposes.

10 Trainers who own racehorses on their own account, or with others, and which are not trained by them may not recover tax incurred under the above. However, they may qualify to do so under the arrangements for owners outlined in paragraphs 4, 16, 17, 18 and 19.

Dealers

11 Persons engaged in the purchase and sale of horses in the course and furtherance of a business will continue to be regarded as liable or eligible for VAT registration. The racing, for business purposes, of racehorses held as trading stock by a VAT registered dealer, is accepted as part of the trading activity whilst the stock remains available for sale, and any tax incurred can be claimed as input tax in accordance with the normal rules.

12 Dealers who purchase racehorses on their own account, or with others for racing purposes only, may not recover tax incurred under the above. However, they may qualify to do so under the arrangements for owners outlined in paragraphs 4, 16, 17, 18 and 19.

Company owners

13 Customs will continue to examine the claims by company owners that racehorses have been purchased for advertising their own businesses against a number of criteria. If they are satisfied that there is a business use and purpose any tax incurred may be recovered as input tax in accordance with the normal rules.

14 Companies that own racehorses on their own account for racing purposes only may not recover tax incurred under the above. However, they may qualify to do so under the arrangements for owners outlined in paragraphs 4, 16, 17, 18 and 19.

15 Companies that are racing companies set up specifically to acquire racehorses fall to be treated under the arrangements outlined in Notice 700/67.

The Scheme conditions

16 Owners will have to complete a declaration confirming they meet the conditions for VAT registration as set out in paragraph 4 above. The declaration will be certified by Weatherbys to confirm the applicant is registered under the Orders and Rules of Racing as an owner, and has in place a sponsorship agreement. On receipt of the declaration and VAT registration application form (VAT 1) Customs will register the owner subject only to normal checks on status and completeness. Where a sponsorship agreement is not held but the owner is requesting registration because they have received business (taxable) income, eg appearance money, sponsored number cloths (SNCs) from their horseracing activities, full details should be sent with the application form (VAT 1).

17 Owners whose application for registration has been accepted, and those whose racing activities are included within an existing registration, will be subject to the normal rules that apply to new registrations.

18 Owners will be entitled to recover as input tax the tax incurred on supplies used for the purposes of their business activities subject to the normal rules. Output tax will be due on income received from sponsorship, appearance money, prize money (excluding sweepstake element) and the sale of racehorses. Output tax will also become payable on racehorses diverted to non-business use when the tax should be calculated on the current market value.

19 Owners registered under the Scheme will be subject to normal periodic visits for VAT control purposes and will have to show they meet the conditions of the Scheme. If at any time this is not the case, repayment of input tax claimed may be required, and action taken to cancel the registration. Owners will be able to appeal any such decision to the independent VAT Tribunals.

Scheme review

20 Customs will review the operation of the Scheme in consultation with the British Horseracing Board and other trade bodies during 2001/02 to access whether the levels of business income available to owners justifies them continuing to recover in full the VAT incurred on their racehorse purchases and training and general up-keep expenses. If it transpires the Scheme is to be withdrawn all registrations accepted under its terms will be cancelled from a date no earlier than three months thereafter. Any other significant changes to the Scheme will be implemented from a date to be agreed between the parties to this memorandum.

21 If the Scheme is withdrawn Customs will not require a refund of input tax claimed unless, in the case of particular owners, it is clear that reasonable efforts were not made to seek business income from sponsorship. Also no output tax will be due on stock and assets held at the date of de-registration.

22 In the event of the Scheme being discontinued individual owners who consider that they have carried on their activities, and will continue to do so, in a businesslike way may ask to retain their registration. In this respect the normal rules will require each registration, and application for registration, to be decided on its own merits with owners having to demonstrate individually that they have a business intention.

Other Equestrian Businesses and Tax Issues 18

Types of livery agreements

18.1 A thorough understanding of the type of livery arrangement in use in an equine business will be central to the tax adviser's ability to give useful assistance to his client. Since the *John Window ((2001) Decision 17186)* VAT tribunal, do-it-yourself liveries have been classified as exempt supplies for VAT. In effect, the owner is regarded as renting their own stable. Clearly this could have adverse tax considerations if it were to result in the business income being assessed under Schedule A and therefore treated as unearned income! The VAT angle is dealt with at **17.23** above.

Two specimen agreements are for *full livery* and an agreement for *DIY livery*. These sample agreements and commentary on current new schemes can be obtained from the British Horse Society's (BHS) website. These give a clear indication of the volume of paperwork that can be required and the extent of the problems which may be encountered. This aspect may influence the choice of trading vehicle chosen by the owner and/or the livery yard proprietor which in turn, will, of course, influence the tax treatment of the income.

Livery refers to the arrangements under which one person provides facilities and/or care for a horse(s) that belong to another person, in return for payment. There is an almost infinite number of different possible arrangements under the broad heading of livery.

The aim of this section is to give the reader an understanding of the need to think of all the problems and preparation required for livery agreements prior to visiting a solicitor to have the agreement drafted and to highlight just how much information can be obtained through organisations such as the BHS.

Only 'working livery' arrangements fall within the Riding Establishments Acts 1964 and 1970, under which the appropriate local authority must license the establishment.

Precedents IV and V can be obtained from the BHS. They cover the two 'extremes' of full and DIY livery to show the respective obligations of the parties.

Precedent IV, for full livery, assumes that the livery operator will be responsible for all aspects of the care and supervision of the horse, and even for preparing the horse for the horse owner to ride. At the other end of the scale, the DIY livery agreement (Precedent IV) imposes no obligation whatsoever on the livery owner for the care of the horse. It essentially provides a simple licence to the horse owner for the use of a particular stable and facilities. These two agreements may be adapted to meet many intermediate types of livery.

A 'grass livery' will commonly follow a similar pattern to the DIY agreement.

Whatever the proposed form of livery, it is essential that the agreement clearly identifies who is responsible for the following:

- watering, feeding and bedding;
- worming, teeth inspection and inoculations;
- attendance by veterinary surgeon and farrier (including the position in an emergency);
- grooming and exercising;
- provision, cleaning and security of tack; and
- insurance.

The Livery yard

18.2 Whilst livery agreements are arguably not formal licence arrangements (as set out at **18.1**), the advisable paperwork and related documentation is set out below as nowadays clients commonly expect accountants and tax advisers to include this type of added value facility. In addition, there are many yards that have come to livery as part of the farm diversification process or from previously casual arrangements, and who may not be aware of the potential problems which can arise.

The author is aware that opinion among members of the equestrian industry is currently split on the issue of diversifying farmers entering the livery field in numbers. Whilst this does perhaps lead to the growth of better facilities and, perhaps, previously unexplored aspects of the business may be developed, there are also those who do not welcome the increased 'competition' with the inevitable pressure this may put on existing well-run livery yards as well as the possibility of overcapacity in the market, ie too many new facilities, too few horses. The proposed hunting ban may introduce yet another pressure if it results in a shortage of clients. The commercial livery yard operator already has to compete with a number of 'casual livery' arrangements operating at low prices, whose operators almost certainly do not declare their 'cash in hand' profits to the Inland Revenue.

Horses are expensive to keep, labour costs are high and good labour is hard to find, so commercially, it is essential that every equestrian establishment prepares a proper business plan with profit projections and cash flows. Horse owners are notoriously difficult customers , and frequently slow to pay. The problems of insurance, legal liability and business rates etc (see **18.15** below) have already been identified and although organisations such as the BHS and the BEVA lobby hard on behalf of the industry it is not always easy to make a profit.

The riding school

18.3 The Inland Revenue is commonly perceived to have a long-standing and deep-seated mistrust of 'mainly cash' carried on by the self-employed individual, among whom are riding schools and self-employed riding instructors. These are probably quite high up the Inspectors' list of priority cases of 'enquiry'. This inevitably means that a higher proportion of such clients can expect to face an enquiry than in some other sectors. Experience suggests that where enquiries are carried out on such businesses they nearly always bring some success for the Inland Revenue, mainly because the proprietor(s) did not keep adequate records.

In view of the problems of cash transactions and potential trauma and costs of an Inland Revenue enquiry the gross profit percentage should be kept under annual review and variations and unexplained trends investigated by the adviser before returns are submitted to the Inland Revenue. Normally, the following will be charged as direct costs before calculating the gross profit rate:

- purchases of feed, bedding and supplements;
- shoeing, farrier costs, purchases of replacement tack and tack repairs;
- staff wages;
- veterinary and medicine costs.

After charging these expenses, the gross profit rate should typically be between 55% and 65%, less if accommodation and food are provided for riding holidays. Gross profit percentages do, however, vary considerably especially if there is an element of horse dealing or sales of the riding school horses. These could, perhaps, be identified as a separate profit and loss source so as to clarify this particular issue.

The competition yard

18.4 The competition yard may operate as an extension of the activities of a professional horseman or even one or two such professionals. It may also be an extension of a livery yard. Competition yards and livery yards can be very complementary activities both commercially and as regards horse care etc. The business may include some, or all, or a mix of disciplines such as polo, eventing, dressage, show jumping, endurance riding, showing etc.

A lot of competition yards provide livery facilities for amateur competitors who take instruction from the professional.

The professional horseman will often buy and sell horses in order to supplement their income. Bringing on young horses will require a yard to keep and develop these animals.

The income of such yards may include a variety of sources such as tuition fees, prize money, sponsorship money, sale proceeds of horses, livery income and breeding income. This variety of income will mean that the VAT of such a varied and multiple activity yard can be complex (see further **CHAPTER 17: PLANNING FOR VAT**).

Where the yard does include this variety of activities it may well be effective from a VAT viewpoint to separate the business into its component parts with different members of a family running distinct profit units, some of which will be VAT registered and some not. This can give clarity as to the division of the income and the allocation of expenses and may also help reduce exposure. Care (and advice) must, however, be taken to ensure that the proprietors do not fall foul of the strict rules on disaggregation which is now enforced so enthusiastically by HM Customs and Excise.

Where a yard includes breeding activities the tax advantages accruing from the fact that a stud farm is regarded as 'farming' by the Inland Revenue should be protected as far as possible (see further **CHAPTER 7: TAX PLANNING FOR STUD FARMS**).

In summary, the main benefits are the availability of farmers averaging, agricultural property relief from inheritance tax, and the potential facility to use the herd basis election.

Ideally, tax computations for the competition yard should be divided between farming and non-farming income and the expenses apportioned appropriately. The close relationship between the 11-year loss relief rule for stud farms and the distinction between 'hobby or farming' and a bona fide commercial business (see **CHAPTER 3**) will also need to be kept closely in view.

The main tax issues for the competition yard are similar to those issues covered elsewhere in this book, but in summary they will be:

- *Gifts from owners*

  It is likely that a yard will have house competition horses whose owners enjoy seeing them ridden in competition by either the professional in the yard or the yard proprietor. Such owners will be charged fees for this. In effect, this is an extension of livery income.

  When a horse is successful in competition the owner might like to reward the yard with a gift for the success. This must be regarded as taxable income for the business.
- *Business divisionalisation?*

  As mentioned previously, a competition yard might divide its business into different segments which can have VAT advantages. However, client and adviser alike need to be cognisant of Customs and Excise's fairly negative attitude towards 'business splitting' where the sole aim is to reduce the need to charge VAT etc. There might also be business splitting between taxable and non-taxable elements of the yard and the Inland Revenue will be very mindful of the need to ensure that there is a correct division.
- *Personal horses*

  Clearly horses kept by the yard proprietors purely for their own pleasure should not be included in the business accounts and any expenses associated with them ought to be charged to drawings. However, when horses are being used in competitions, the distinction may not always be clear-cut. Historically, some equestrian yards have, on occasion, tried to argue that horses which are about to be sold for a large profit have suddenly become suitable only for personal use. They are then drawn out of the business at a lower market value and then, a relatively short time afterwards, sold privately. Clearly, this is open to challenge by the Inland Revenue and such transactions should be approached with extreme caution.

  One of the key issues here is consistency. A yard should establish a policy for competition horses. There should be a clear division of treatment between those which are personal and those which are regarded as business assets and this policy should be applied consistently and be capable of being evidenced in the firm's books and records.
- *Plant and machinery*

  CHAPTER **10:** OVERVIEW OF EQUINE BUSINESS TAXATION deals with the availability of 40% first-year allowances where appropriate and also the key issue of tax relief for repairs rather than improvement expenditures. The Inland Revenue's Inspector's Manual does say that show jumpers can be treated as plant, but it is rare in practice to have competition horses treated as plant and machinery. Whilst there is a clear tax advantage available from a 40% first year allowance, policies must be applied consistently and, with so many horses always potentially up for sale, the reality is that most horses are included in stock.

The competition yard is a trading business for tax purposes so its assets should normally qualify for capital gains tax rollover relief and business asset taper relief (see **CHAPTER 13: BUYING AND SELLING EQUESTRIAN PROPERTY – TAX PLANNING**). Similarly, the equestrian property should also qualify for the inheritance tax reliefs associated with business and agricultural assets.

The farrier

18.5 The tax planning and compliance issues for farriers are very similar to those faced by any small business.

The initial requirement for the newly qualified farrier will be to register as self-employed with the Inland Revenue by completing form CWF1. The farrier may consider incorporation but there are many practical advantages from starting as a sole trader and moving on to incorporation once established.

Whilst there are distinct advantages to operating via a limited company, even for quite small businesses, starting as a sole trader gives the small-scale farrier an opportunity to learn about running his own business before attempting to deal with the rigours of a limited company. **CHAPTER 9** deals with business structure. A farrier whose business grows and becomes profitable is a classic example of a sole trader who can move on to either partnership or limited company.

The farrier will eventually have to consider VAT registration. A lot of farriers will be working for private individuals who are not VAT registered so that VAT registration can impact directly on profitability. As mentioned previously, there has been a move away from the larger riding school to small livery yards and individuals who have their own stables and their own paddock and it is also likely that these customers would prefer their farrier not to be VAT registered.

Input VAT in relation to shoeing costs are likely to be minimal, covering things such as the cost of the metal or possibly the cost of ready-made shoes. Other input claims will arise from expenses such as the commercial vehicle used by the farrier, for example, a van or similar on which input VAT can be claimed. Many farriers, particularly in rural locations, operate via a very simple business structure dealing with mainly private customers and generally keeping turnover below the £56,000 currently required for VAT registration – thus avoiding the need to complete quarterly VAT returns.

Prior to April 2003, many sole trader farriers incorporated their businesses in order to take advantage of the last days of capital gains tax

(CGT) retirement relief by capitalising goodwill and then selling it to limited company.

It is generally considered that a farrier's business can generate a goodwill valuation in the form of a loyal customer base which may be sold to an incoming farrier at a later stage. Incorporation of the sole trader farrier's business may, therefore, enable the proprietor to take advantage of the currently beneficial regime for business asset taper relief (BATR) by capitalising the goodwill. This can mean an effective 10% rate of capital gains tax (75% taper relief assuming a 40% top rate of tax) and, although any capital gains tax liability arising will have to be paid on the 31 January following the tax year in which the business is incorporated, the corollary will be the creation of a loan account balance (from the sale proceeds owing by the company), which can then be drawn down with no tax implications.

Many farriers' businesses are husband and wife partnerships with the farrier doing the physical work of shoeing and the administration being dealt with by his or her partner/spouse. Paperwork would involve organising the diary, booking appointments, arranging the sequence of visits, sorting out customer problems and dealing with all other queries etc. The business can therefore be structured either as a partnership which has the advantage of an income stream being passed to both partners or spouses or a limited company, where the family members are involved in share ownership as well as administration. Care will have to be taken with regard to the settlement provisions of ICTA s 660A.

The job of a farrier is a physically demanding one and many farriers have to retire early due to ill health. Consideration will normally have to be given to ensuring protection through cover for injury and illness along with some pension planning.

Qualifying as a farrier also involves a structured training programme for apprentices.

The veterinary practice

18.6 Historically, veterinary practices are run as partnerships working from a suitably placed surgery with the facility to take in schoolers and to carry out operations and operate effective animal hospital facilities.

Whilst the small animal practices, particularly in urban locations, tend to generate the highest profits, whilst more rural general practices which deal with the traditional mix of domestic pets, farm animals and equine clients, has suffered with the recent decline in the farming industry. The economics of modern farming have led to reduced visits from the vet with some livestock farmers being forced to let animals die rather than afford the veterinary expenses of healing them in extreme cases!

There are many practices which specialise in equine work and thus they often spring up close to the horse training centres. Almost all veterinary practices other than those which are purely small animal and town-based will deal with some equine work of a routine nature, such as inoculations, and their role is likely to grow with the introduction of the horse passport (see **5.4** above).

Dedicated equine practices normally have stabling and an extensive operating theatre and related facilities. Key veterinary work is associated with stud farms, for example, ensuring that the mares are 'keen' before they visit a stallion. Mares often have a large number of scans especially as the equine stud industry generally works on the basis of 'no foal, no fee'.

As with all equine businesses, there is a great deal of variation among equine veterinary practices and income is generated from a large variety of different sources. The facilities required can be very expensive so that investment decisions on plant and equipment can involve considerable pre-planning issues in order to maximise capital allowances, particularly when some of the improvements are to buildings rather than on actual equipment (see **CHAPTER 10**).

The traditional structure of the veterinary practice has been a partnership which owns its own freehold property, although again, there has recently been a move towards incorporation. A large number of veterinary practices incorporated prior to 5 April 2003 to try and take advantage of retirement relief and there is still scope for incorporation.

In order to have the necessary workforce to be able to offer the equine client the full range of specialist skills, there are often a large number of partners in a vets practice. In this instance a limited company can be particularly useful as variations in the size of shareholding and shareholders agreement can be easier to operate than a complex partnership arrangement with changes in profit-sharing ratios.

One particular problem with incorporating a veterinary practice can be the appropriate treatment of cars and business vehicles. Veterinary surgeons frequently travel a large number of business miles on visits to clients premises, race meetings and competitions etc. These call-outs may also be to attend animal emergencies so the veterinary surgeons requires a fast and reliable car to ensure that they can quickly get to the horse with colic or with problems foaling. The vet will also need a large car to carry all the medicines and equipment they may be needed on site. These requirements can bring tax issues, in particular, involving exposure to tax charges on high benefit in kind charges on the veterinary motor vehicle. Care should therefore be taken over the choice of vehicle.

As mentioned, most veterinary practices own their own freehold property. They may need a lot of specialist work carried out with regard to the adaptation of buildings and installation of equipment. This may impact on capital allowances claims.

Where a veterinary practice is incorporated, close attention will need to be paid to whether or not the property goes into the company's balance sheet. Company property does not attract business asset taper relief so the partners may prefer to retain the property personally and charge the company a rent. However, this may raise awkward inheritance tax issues. Although this can have logistical advantages (ie some members of the practice may not wish to be exposed to the problems of property ownership), it can also reduce eligibility for inheritance tax and business property relief which is only available to controlling shareholders.

As with the farrier, a veterinary practice may have goodwill and incorporation can offer some useful tax planning possibilities on capitalising goodwill via a director's current accounts with the ability to draw the resulting balance down tax-free.

Many modern veterinary practices now use electronic communications to remind clients of such matters as vaccination dates, regular worming and regular health checks. With the 100% first-year allowance on ICT equipment being extended to 31 March 2004, this has made IT improvements very attractive to the veterinary practice.

Another advantage of the limited company, perceived by some in veterinary practice, is that it provides the facility to 'promote' junior surgeons to the role of director without having to give an equity share until the time is right.

Where a large number of veterinary surgeons are involved in the practice, the decision on whether or not to incorporate can be very complicated and in the same way that the partnership would need a very strong comprehensive partnership agreement, so too will the limited company need a very complex shareholders' agreement which would cover issues such as the purchase of shares on death or retirement and other important matters.

The riding club

British riding clubs to benefit from tax changes

18.7 Following lobbying by the British Horse Society (BHS), BHS affiliated riding clubs, along with other community amateur sports clubs, can now benefit from new government legislation to ease tax bills. If clubs register with the Inland Revenue they can benefit from:

- tax exemption on fundraising income up to £15,000;
- tax exemption on income from interest;
- tax exemption on rental income up to £10,000;
- disposals assets exempt from capital gains tax;

- gift aid on individual donations;
- inheritance tax relief on gifts;
- gifts of assets on 'no gain, no loss' basis for capital gains;
- business relief on gifts of trading stock.

Riding clubs are eligible for these reliefs if they are open to the whole community, are organised on an amateur basis and have as their main purpose, provision of facilities for, and promoting participation, in horse riding.

Further information for riding clubs and how to register is available on the Inland Revenue website at www.inlandrevenue.gov.uk.

The betting industry

18.8 It would be impossible to write a book on equine tax (which includes an emphasis on bloodstock and racing) without looking at the subject of gambling.

Although gambling, ie placing bets on anything, particularly horses, is not regarded by the tax authorities as trading (because most people who gamble make losses not profits!), an organised activity to make profit from the gambling public will normally amount to trading, ie the activity of book-making or running a gambling establishment.

When is gambling a trade?

18.9 In *Partridge v Mallandaine (1886) 2 TC 179* a professional bookmaker systematically attended race courses for the purpose of carrying on that activity; although he could not legally recover amounts due to him, he was held to be carrying on a vocation and hence assessable under Schedule D Case II.

Bookmakers' pitches are a new category of property for inheritance tax (Inland Revenue *Tax Bulletin* 43, October 1999). This arises from a change in the administration of on-course betting, introduced with effect from 8 October 1998, with a change of bookmaker control. Control of racecourse betting rings are now held by the National Trust Pitch Council (NJPC), which is run by the Horserace Betting Levy Board (HBLB). This has resulted in the change that bookmakers giving up their pitch on the racecourse may auction their seniority amongst bookmakers wishing to take over that pitch. The Revenue now regard the right to occupy a pitch as property to which the deceased is beneficially entitled within IHTA 1984 s 5(1). This property might qualify for 100% BPR provided conditions apply (see **10.14** above). The right to occupy a pitch is regarded by the Revenue as an asset for CGT disposal. Disposal will therefore involve standard CGT planning criteria, for example annual exemptions, BATR, rollover relief, etc.

'There is no tax on a habit' – Graham v Green

18.10 In *Graham v Green (1925) 9 TC 309*, a case which concerned a man whose sole means of livelihood came from betting on horses at starting prices, Rowlatt J says at 313:

> 'Now we come to betting, pure and simple ... It has been settled that a bookmaker carries on a taxable vocation. What is the bookmaker's system? He knows that there are a great many people who are willing to back horses and that they will back horses with anyone who holds himself out to give reasonable odds as a bookmaker. By calculating the odds in the case of various horses over a long period of time and quoting them so that on the whole the aggregate odds are in his favour, he makes a profit. That seems to me to be organising an effort in the same way that a person organises and effort if he sets out to buy himself things with a view to secure a profit by the difference in what I may call their capital value in individual cases.
>
> Now we come to the other side, the man who bets with the bookmaker, and that is this case. These are mere bets. Each time he puts on his money, at whatever may be the starting price. I do not think he could be said to organise his effort in the same way as the bookmaker organises his. I do not think the subject matter from his point of view is susceptible of it. In effect all he is doing is just what a man does who is a skilful player at cards, who plays every day. He plays today and he plays tomorrow and he plays the next day and he is skilful on each of the three days, more skilful on the whole than the people with whom he plays, and he wins. But I do not think that you can find, in his case, any conception arising in which his individual operations can be said to be merged in the way that particular operations are merged in the conception of a trade. I think all you can say of that man ... is that he is addicted to betting. ... There is no tax on a habit. I do not think "habitual" or even "systematic" fully describes what is essential in the phrase 'trade, adventure, profession or vocation.'

The principle in this case was followed in *Down v Compston [1937] 2 All ER 475, (1937) 21 TC 60* where a professional golfer attached to a golf club habitually engaged in private games of golf for varying amounts and won substantial amounts. He was found not to be liable under Case II on the basis that the bets did not arise from the playing services and that there was no organisation to support the view that he was carrying on the business of betting on the games of golf. It is possible, however, that the courts might take a different view if this came to court today.

Betting by professional bookmakers

18.11 Betting by professional bookmakers is assessable even if carried on in an unlawful way (*Southern v AB Ltd (1933) 18 TC 59*) (see **18.14** below). Private betting is not assessable, however habitual. Its profits, if any, are also exempt from CGT (TCGA 1992, s 51(1)). Receipts from newspaper articles based on a betting system were, however, held to be assessable to income tax in *Graham v Arnott (1941) 24 TC 157.*

Lottery run by a club

18.12 Lotteries and football pools promotion constitutes trading in the hands of the organisers unless run by a registered charity which is subject to special tax rules, and where a pool or small lottery is run by a supporters club or other society on the terms that a specified part of the cost of the ticket is to be donated to a club or body within the purposes of the Lotteries and Amusements Act 1976 s 5(1), the donation element is not treated as a trading receipt (see Inland Revenue pamphlet IR 131, C1).

Gambling – the practical concerns

18.13 The racing world involves a large amount of gambling at all levels. In practice, if the Inland Revenue tried to assess the 'winners' to tax there would be a deluge of loss claims. The cautious tax practitioner should advise clients to keep a record of their winnings in case evidence is required at a later stage. The Inland Revenue always like to verify sources of income and windfalls in an enquiry situation so it is important to keep records to avoid any future problems over the identification of any capital introduced into a business. The money laundering provisions also have a large potential impact for tax advisers, their clients and illustrate the need for information of gambling activities to be provided by the taxpayer to the tax adviser.

The betting exchanges

18.14 One of the current growth industries in the UK is that of the betting exchanges. These are termed betting intermediaries by the Minister for Sport and Culture and they have been the subject of a lot of discussion between bookmakers and the Government. These discussions have involved several leading organisations in the sports world in general.

For the tax adviser, these organisations also involve a number of serious considerations. In the broadest of terms, historically, the bookmaker has been a taxable trade or vocation. This was established in the early case of *Partridge v Mallandaine (1986) 2 TC 179*. As set out at **18.11** above, it has also been held that betting by professional bookmakers is assessable even if it is carried on in an unlawful way. See *Southern v AB Ltd (1933) 18 TC 59* where it was held that there is no tax on a habit. It was been considered that the words 'habitual' or even 'systematic' do not fully describe what is a trade, adventure or professional vocation.

The professional gambler has always been something of an awkward problem for the Inland Revenue. In some cases it can be shown that all the badges of trade are present in what the gambler does and also a clear profit motive. There have apparently been some cases when their activity has been treated as taxable although there are no reported cases in this area. The professional bookmaker is trading; the compulsive casual gambler is not. Care should be taken with the affairs of the client who is a professional gambler or who perhaps falls somewhere between these two extremes. They should be advised to keep detailed records wherever possible or at least this advice should be properly documented to protect the adviser. Betting is exempt from capital gains tax under TCGA 1992 s 51(1).

It is generally accepted that an organised activity to 'make profit from the gambling public' will normally amount to trading.

2003 has seen the first formal betting exchange shop open in Scotland, much to the annoyance of many connected in the gambling industry.

It could be argued that the betting exchanges turn a person who is potentially a gambler into a small and individual bookmaker. The betting exchanges work by allowing individuals to offer betting and invite other gamblers to make bets. Modern IT facilities make this a facility which is now easy to operate. The organisers of the betting exchanges are not exposed themselves to much commercial risk as they effectively determine the maximum amount which can be paid out as winnings.

If this innovation were to be deemed to constitute the carrying on of a trade by the Inland Revenue would there be a multitude of loss claims submitted on Tax Returns? This is such a major issue for the

Government that the Minister for Sports and Culture has said that at this stage they will not redefine the expression 'bookmaker'. It was important enough to be included in the Finance Act 2003.This resulted in the Betting and Gaming Duties Act 1981 being amended to provide for a new charge to general betting duty on the amounts that parties to a bet are charged for using the facilities of a betting exchange. The Finance Act 2003 also provided for a restriction of the definition of 'on-course bet'.

While the entrepreneur behind the betting exchanges, the bookmaking industry and the Government fight out this particular issue, the tax adviser must be careful to ensure that their clients are declaring all these activities and assessing each case on its merits. If the badges of trade are present then they will need to consider whether these activities should be notified as a trade and whether a disclosure should be made to the Inland Revenue.

Equine business rates

Introduction

18.15 This section has been introduced by 'popular demand' to offer some very basic principles to help guide the equestrian business towards the ability to seek more information. It appears that the most universal problem encountered by equestrian businesses (other than employing staff, making a profit, surviving paperwork etc) is that of rates.

Agriculture

18.16 The House of Lords in *Whitsbury Farm and Stud Ltd v Hemens (Valuation Officer) [1988] AC 601, [1988] 1 All ER 72* held that horses not used in farming were not livestock, and so their stable and stud buildings were not agricultural buildings, and were therefore liable to full business rates. The land on which they grazed was, however, exempt agricultural land.

There is a special relief available for stud buildings. The rateable value is reduced by an amount specified by the Secretary of State. At present (2003), this figure is £3,000. To qualify for the relief, the buildings must be:

- used for the breeding and/or rearing of horses or ponies; and
- occupied together with any agricultural land or agricultural building.

For the purpose of the relief, 'agricultural land' must be agricultural land of more than two hectares, which is not used exclusively for the pasturing of horses or ponies.

It is to be noted that only buildings used for breeding or rearing horses, not just for keeping them, qualify for this special relief. Riding and livery stables, which are not used for breeding, continue to be rated in full.

Uniform business rate

18.17 Rating continues for non-domestic property, and on some domestic property, which is used partly for business purposes. The business rate remains a qualifying deduction in calculating income tax profits, and where premises such as farmhouses are used partly for business purposes and partly for residential purposes, the business rate is deductible to the extent that the part of the premises on which they are paid is, in fact, used for business purposes.

The old rule for valuing property and for calculating its rateability remains in force for business rates. In general, the rateable value is:

> 'An amount equal to the rent at which it is estimated the hereditament might reasonably be expected to be let from year to year, if the tenant undertook to pay all usual tenant's rates and taxes and to bear the cost of repairs and insurance and the other expenses (if any) necessary to maintain the hereditament in a state to command that rent.'

[Local Government Finance Act 1988 Sch 6 para 2(1)].

Profitability

18.18 Whether or not a business makes profits is largely irrelevant to the rating process. The liability to pay rates rests on the physical use of a building, and not on the nature or level of profitability of the business. Business rates are levied on all non-domestic property. Although they are commonly described as business rates, this is actually a misnomer. So, even if a stable is owned 'just down the road' and used only by a child, this will be liable to rates. The only circumstances in which rates might be avoided are if the stables are relatively small (say, four, or possibly six, boxes), they are in close proximity to a dwelling and are in the personal use of the occupiers of that dwelling. In such a case, the rating authorities are likely to regard the stables as being part of the curtilage of the dwelling, akin to an outbuilding or garage, and as such the stables will be reflected in the council tax valuation band for the dwelling.

Grazing

18.19 It should be remembered that the above only applies to buildings used as stables. So far as grazing is concerned; land used only for grazing by horses is regarded as being agricultural, and therefore is exempt from rates. Nevertheless, caution is necessary here. Once again the agricultural exemption is available only where the land is used solely for agricultural purposes. So, for instance, if the grazing land is also used for training, tuition or jumping of horses, then the agricultural exemption may be lost.

Change of use

18.20 Although there is no duty to inform the local authority of a change of use which gives rise to a liability to rates, there is power for the authority to backdate rates to when they first should have been paid, in theory going back as far as 1992. In practice, the farthest that local authorities seem to go back is 1995 (the date of the last rating list), and some may not go back as far as this.

Obtaining planning permission

18.21 Planning permission is not relevant to the liability to pay rates. For instance, it is sometimes thought that, if planning permission were obtained several years ago, the planning department at the local authority ought to have informed the rating department. In fact, in practice, there seem to be no channel of communication of this nature between departments in most local authorities. Unfortunately, this will not help the owner to resist a claim for backdated charges should rates subsequently be imposed. Equally, the absence of planning permission does not affect the liability to pay rates, although this may be used as an argument for a lower rateable value.

Who is liable?

18.22 Is the person liable to business rates the 'occupier' for rateable purposes? If land buildings are let out on a tenancy, then, clearly, the occupier will be the tenant. If, however, stables are 'let' for livery (even if DIY livery), it is likely that the owner will still be held to be in occupation for rating purposes, and therefore liable to pay the rates. In the absence of prior agreement, the owner will not be able to recover any contribution to rates from those in livery. There is generally no liability for rates on vacant property.

Rateable value

18.23 Rates are currently payable at just under 50% of the rateable value. The rateable value (or 'RV') is the annual rent at which the tenant and the tenant paying the rates might let the stables on a hypothetical tenancy with full insuring and repairing covenants.

For stables, which, in practice, may never be let separately from the surrounding land or house, this can be very difficult to establish, as the tenancy would be very hypothetical indeed. But, equally, this uncertainty may work to the advantage of the ratepayer.

The fact that stables are not run on a commercial basis is not strictly relevant, although, of course, this may be evidence that there is no ready market for livery, and therefore grounds for a lower rateable value. The local authority can ask to see books or accounts, and the ratepayer can require the local authority to disclose details of comparables relied upon.

Rural areas

18.24 Since the Local Government and Rating Act 1997, local authorities have had the discretion to grant up to 100% relief for the business in rural areas with a rateable value of less than £10,000. Nevertheless, the granting of the relief has to be shown in the interest of the local community. In practice, it is unlikely this discretion would be exercised in favour of an equine establishment, except in a very special case, perhaps where an establishment has been set up specifically for charitable purposes, eg the very young, underprivileged, or the disabled.

Point to Point

18.25 Land used as a racecourse is not agricultural and is therefore rateable, unless the use is de minimis. In *Hayes (Valuation Officer) v Lloyd [1985] 2 All ER 313,* the House of Lords held that grazing land was rateable, where a Point to Point racing event was held only once a year. However, in that case, a circuit had been laid out with some permanent fences and rails, and the annual event was large and commercially profitable. Not all such events would result in land, which would otherwise qualify for agricultural exemption, being rateable.

Gallops

18.26 Meadows or pastureland used for existing horses can continue to be exempt from rates as agricultural land (*Jarvis v Cambridgeshire*

Rural Assessment Area Assessment Committee [1938] 4 All ER 186). Whether it remains exempt depends on the extent to which it is used as gallops. In *Foster v Simpson (Valuation Officer) [1984] RA 85*, land from which the farmer produced a hay crop but which was also used as gallops for training racehorses was held rateable. The Lands Tribunal held that the land was not used just as arable, meadow or pasture ground, and therefore not exempt as agricultural land, because it was used for business purposes (the training of racehorses) to an extent that could not be disregarded as de minimis.

Rating list and backdating of rates

18.27 It is the responsibility of the local valuation officer of the Inland Revenue to enter property in the local rating list. There is no obligation on a ratepayer to initiate an entry in the list in respect of a hereditament, which is liable to rates. However, where an entry is made in the current rating list, liability to rates can be backdated to the date the activity commenced. Liability for back rates on an activity will only be avoided after the first anniversary of the date on which the next rating list is compiled.

The present rating list dates to 1 April 2000 and is based on rental values at 1 April 1998, which means that any new entry on the list could only now be backdated to the April 2000. The next rating list will commence on 1 April 2005.

When a new entry is made in the list, the valuation officer has to send the ratepayer a notice giving details of the entry. The ratepayer has six months from the date of that notice to appeal; such appeals must be in writing and must contain the following certain basic information to be valid:

1 the name and address of the person making it, and the capacity in which he does so;
2 identification of the property to which it relates;
3 identification of the manner in which it is proposed the list be altered; and
4 include:
   - a statement of the reasons for believing the list to be incorrect;
   - if it is believed there has been a material change of circumstances, a statement of the nature of the change, and of the date on which the person making the proposal believes the change occurred;
   - if the proposal disputes the accuracy of an alteration made by the valuation officer, the day on which the valuation officer issued the relevant notice under the regulations;
   - if the proposal disputes the day from which such an alteration should have effect, the day proposed in its place.

Appeals

18.28 Appeal forms, called Proposal to Alter the Rating List, are obtainable from Valuation Offices. If an appeal is not resolved by negotiation, it is referred to a Valuation Tribunal and a hearing held. Whilst an appeal is outstanding the ratepayer is liable to pay the rates assessed. Where that liability is subsequently reduced, any over-payment will be refunded with interest.

If the valuation officer is to use any documentation at a hearing, such as evidence of comparables, not less than two weeks prior to the heading he must serve notice on every other party to the proceedings specifying the information to be used and the hereditament(s) to which it relates. Any such party on whom notice is served may on giving at least 24 hours' notice inspect and take extracts from the documents.

Proposal to alter the rating list

18.29 A ratepayer may also make a Proposal to Alter the Rating List on the basis that there has been material change of circumstances. This is defined in the Local Government Finance Act (LGFA) 1988 Sch 6 para 2(7) and includes;

- matters affecting the physical state or physical enjoyment of the hereditament;
- the mode or category of occupation of the hereditament;
- matters affecting the physical state of the locality in which the hereditament is situated or which, though not affecting the physical state of locality, are nonetheless physically manifest there; and
- the use or occupation of other premises situated in the locality of the hereditament.

The above procedures apply in like form to such a proposal, including the requirement to make the proposal within six months of the day on which the change took place. A recent example of the application of this ground is businesses adversely affected by the impact of the 2001 outbreak of Foot and Mouth Disease (there can be difficulty in cases of this nature in establishing exactly when the change took place, and therefore from when the six-month time limit runs).

Unoccupied property

18.30 Unoccupied non-domestic hereditaments on a rating list are rateable with a 50% reduction, but the Secretary of State can make regulations prescribing exemptions (LGFA 1988 ss 45 and 46). The exempt categories are to be found in the Non-Domestic Rating (Unoccupied Property) Regulations 1989 (SI 1989/2261) as amended by SI 1995/549. These include:

- the first three months of unoccupation;
- properties with rateable value of less than £1,900;
- certain industrial premises, namely those used for manufacturing, repairing or adapting goods or materials, storage, the working or processing of minerals, and the generation of electricity, provided none of the buildings are for the retail provisions of goods or services;
- where the owner is prohibited by law from occupying the hereditament;
- where the building is 'listed' and unoccupied;
- where the hereditament is included in the Schedule of Monuments compiled under the Ancient Monuments and Archaeological Areas Act 1979 s 1.

There is also a notice procedure for establishing when unoccupied newly erected buildings are to be deemed to be completed for rating purposes: see LGFA 1988 s 46A, so as to prevent deliberate delays in completion in order to avoid attracting rating liability.

Charities

18.31 There is a mandatory 80% rating relief for hereditaments of charities wholly or mainly used for charitable purposes. Charging authorities have discretion to increase the relief up to 100% (LGFA 1988 ss 47 and 48).

Discretionary relief for recreational clubs etc

18.32 In addition, local authorities have discretion to reduce or eliminate the rates payable by non-profit making organisations including recreational, philanthropic, religious, educational, scientific, welfare, literary and artistic organisations (LGFA 1988 ss 47 and 48). This will be of importance to riding clubs etc.

Mixed uses of agricultural land

18.33 Where land normally used as arable, meadow or pasture ground is occasionally used for a non-agricultural purpose it should be noted that the word 'only' occurs in para (a) of the definition. This is a narrower definition than the other paragraphs, and the de minimis rule will apply to land more strictly.

This was exemplified in *Hayes (Valuation Officer) v Lloyd [1985] 2 All ER 313*, where the House of Lords held that some land for grazing except for one Point to Point meeting a year was rateable as 'land used for a racecourse', because it was laid out with permanent rails, jumps and other sophisticated racecourse facilities and the annual event was big and commercially profitable. On the facts of the case the racing was not to be ignored as de minimis. The court explained that in different circumstances the racing activity might be so little or informal as not to make the land rateable.

The VOA seems to accept that some activities held for a few days in a year may be disregarded (eg a field occasionally used for amateur cricket and football matches or as a car park in connection with such occasional events), but only where it is clearly a use that ceases to exist before the end of the day and does not resume again without an intervening agricultural use. Ultimately each case will judged on its own facts, having regard to the size, scale and duration of such as event.

Agricultural Buildings

18.34 The LGFA 1988 defines agricultural buildings exempt from rating. By Sch 5, para 3:

> 'A building is an agricultural building if it is not a dwelling and:
>
> (a) it is occupied together with agricultural land and is used solely in connection with agricultural operations on the land; or
>
> (b) it is or forms part of a market garden, and is used solely in connection with agricultural operations at the market garden.'

In interpreting the word 'solely' no account shall be taken of any time during which a building 'is used in any other way, if that time does not amount to a substantial part of the time during which the building is used' (LGFA 1988 Sch 5, para 8(3)). It appears that this is judged in temporal terms, rather than on the basis of intensity of use, hence distinguishing itself from the de minimis test, which will still be applied to minimal ongoing users.

In summary, for a building to come within the agricultural exemption: first the agricultural land must be identified, then it must be determined what the agricultural operations carried on upon that land are, and finally it must be decided whether the buildings are used solely in connection with those agricultural operations.

Livestock buildings

18.35 Even if not 'used solely in connection with agricultural operations' on the agricultural land as stated in the definitions of 'agricultural building', a building for keeping or feeding livestock is an agricultural building exempt from rating provided it is:

- solely for that purpose; or
- occupied with agricultural land and its sole use is in connection with agricultural operations on that land and keeping or breeding livestock; and
- surrounded by or contiguous to an area of agricultural land, which amounts to not less than two hectares.

This is a slight simplification of the rather complex provisions to be found in of the LGFA 1988 Sch 5 para 5.

'Livestock' defined in the LGFA 1988 is stated to 'include' any mammal or bird kept for the production of food or wool or for the purpose of its use in the farming land. Rating exemption does not therefore extend to buildings for keeping animals in wildlife parks or zoos.

Horses

18.36 As set out at **18.16** above, horses are not agriculture. The House of Lords in *Whitsbury Farm & Stud Ltd v Hemens (Valuation Officer) [1988] AC 601, [1988] 1 All ER 72*, held that buildings for breeding and keeping riding horses were not exempt from rating, but the land on which the horses grazed was exempt agricultural land.

This contradicts the IHT rule. IHTA 1984 s 115(4) allows the breeding and rearing of horses in a stud farm and the grazing of horses in connection of such breeding and rearing to be taken to be agriculture. This IHT position is dealt with at **1.2**, **2.2** and **CHAPTER 7** above.

Following this decision the Government was persuaded by *inter alia* the Country Landowners and Business Association (CLA) to give a measure of exemption of buildings for rearing and keeping horses and ponies, where it was a minor activity on farms. Currently, the first £3,000 of rateable value is exempt from rating assessment (see the Non-Domestic Rating (Stud Farms) (England) Order 2001 (SI 2001/2586).

Special rural rate reliefs

18.37 The Rating (Former Agricultural Premises and Rural Shops) Act 2001 introduced a new and special relief for farm diversifications. The key points of this relief are as follows.

- The Act provides for a 50% mandatory rate relief for land and buildings used non-agricultural purposes on what has been agricultural land or agricultural buildings for at least 183 days during the year prior to the date in which the provisions come into force (15 August 2001 in England).
- Local authorities have a discretionary power to increase the relief to up to 100% where they feel that the change use will be of benefit to the rural community and that the cost to the council taxpayer is justified.
- Both the mandatory and discretionary relief are initially be limited to a maximum of five years from the date of commencement of the Act, with a provision for this to be extended by order. However, premises that had already benefited from the relief prior to any extension will only receive relief for a maximum of five years from the date the original premises first qualified for the relief.
- This rate relief will only apply to hereditaments with a rateable value less then the prescribed amount, which is currently £6,000 in England: the Non-Domestic Rating (Former Agricultural Premises) (England) Order 2001 (SI 2001/2585).

In addition, under the Local Government and Rating Act (LGRA) 1997, local authorities have had the discretion to grant up to 100% relief for businesses in rural areas with a rateable value of less £12,000. However, in exercising this discretion, the local authority has to be satisfied that that the business is of benefit to the rural community and the cost to the council taxpayer is justified (the council bears 25% of the cost of such reliefs). Therefore, a special case would have to be shown, for instance because the activity was targeted at children or the handicapped, or created local employment.

Under the LGRA 1997, there is also mandatory relief for sole post offices and general stores in rural areas with a rateable value of £6,000 or less, with a discretion to grant relief for as much again. The 2001 Act extends this to all village shops that mainly sell food for human consumption.

Rates on sporting rights

18.38 Following lobbying by the CLA, rates on sporting rights, where there were enjoyed separately from the land over which they existed, were abolished by virtue of the LGRA 1997 s 2 with effect from 1 April 1997.

Property on which council tax is payable

18.39 Council tax is payable in respect of any dwelling, unless it is exempt. Composite hereditaments (ie hereditaments part of which is used for domestic purposes and part for business) are also dwellings for the purposes of council tax. A property or part thereof used wholly or mainly in the course of a business for short-stay accommodation falls to be rated as a non-domestic hereditament.

Certain descriptions of property cannot in themselves constitute dwellings for council tax, despite their domestic use, unless they form part of a larger property which is a dwelling, namely a yard, garden, outhouse, private garage, private storage used wholly or mainly for the storage of articles of domestic use. Therefore if any of these types of property exist or are located separate from a dwelling, they will be liable to rates. This can lead to anomalous results. For instance, a small number of stables close to and contiguous with a dwelling and in the personal use of the residents at that dwelling will form part of the council tax assessment of that dwelling, and will not be liable to separate assessment; by contrast, if those stables are located 'down the road' from the dwelling, they will be liable to rates, because they cannot come within the council tax treatment of the dwelling (the fact that they are not in business use makes no difference – as reiterated above, rates are imposed on non-domestic property, and are not business rates). The same might apply to a garage, which was not contiguous with the dwelling with which it was enjoyed.

Persons liable to pay the council tax

18.40 The general rule is that liability depends upon residence of a dwelling. In order of priority, it falls as follows:

- a resident freeholder;
- a resident leaseholder (including a tenant holding under an assured tenancy) whose interest is not inferior to another such interest held by another such resident;
- a resident statutory or secure tenant;
- a resident who has a contractual licence to occupy the whole or any part of the dwelling;
- a resident;
- the owner of the dwelling.

Liability will only fall on one of the above categories of people. Where there is no person answering the description in the first category, liability falls to the person in the next category and so on. Where two or more persons fall into the applicable category, they are jointly and severally liable to pay the council tax in respect of the dwelling. Council tax is calculated on a daily basis.

The owner of a caravan or boat, which constitutes a dwelling, is liable to council tax except in respect of those days when a person other than the owner is resident and so becomes liable for those days.

Racing clubs

18.41 A racing club can be organised by a trainer or other individuals/companies. The club can open up the ownership of racehorses to a wider range of members. Members pay a subscription for a combination of a share in the ownership of a horse, a contribution towards training fees together with the enjoyment of the hospitality at the racecourse.

Equine hospitality providers

18.42 In view of the harsh approach taken by the Tax Acts to business entertainment expenses and the large element of entertainment involved in the equine world (especially racing), hospitality businesses have evolved to deal with this element of the business.

As mentioned in **CHAPTER 8**, the charging of a fee for a subscription can be tax allowable.

Bloodstock agents

18.43 Bloodstock agents operate in different countries and there is a need to ensure that the VAT and income tax compliance issues are dealt with correctly.

Agents receive income from a number of sources:

- the sale of a horse as 'principal';
- commission on sale;
- valuation services;
- general consultancy services.

There can be a need to register for VAT in more than one country which can be extremely complex. The VAT liability on general consultancy services depends on the location of the customer. If an agent acts in the sale of a horse in, say, France or Ireland, then the commission will be subject to French or Irish VAT. If the agent's customer is VAT registered somewhere in the EU and provides their VAT number to the agent then the supply is deemed to have taken place in the country of residence.

The VAT planning and compliance issues on sales of horses are possibly the most complex and frequently asked questions.

The horse sold by an agent on behalf of a non-VAT registered owner can become subject to VAT when the agent invoices the sale. Planning in connection with the purchase and disposal of horses can be more VAT than tax driven.

Some vendors try to give 'gifts' (sometimes known as 'kickbacks') to agents who purchase horses. Likewise, happy owners will give gifts to agents and, as with jockeys and trainers, these gifts will be taxable.

Other Legal Issues 19

Transportation

19.1 The Welfare of Animals (Transport) Order 1997 (SI 1997/1480) details requirements for the transport of animals – these include fitness to travel, conditions of transport, maximum journey times, rest, feed and water intervals, the duties of the transporters (and the documentation required). It is an offence under the Order to cause any animal unnecessary suffering or injury. Certain exemptions apply if the transport is not of a commercial nature, if the animal is an individual animal accompanied by a person having responsibility for the animal during its transport or if it is a pet accompanied by its owner on a private journey.

The Animal Health Act 1981 s 37 contains provisions for the prevention of suffering, and section 38 of the same Act contains provisions concerning the supply of food and water for animals being transported. (Both the 1997 Order and 1981 Act includes horses amongst the animals to which they relate.)

Cruelty

19.2 Although they have been amended over the years, the 'core' statutory provisions dealing with the matter of cruelty to animals are contained in the Protection of Animals Act 1911. Section 1(1)(a) of the 1911 Act sets out the offences of cruelty – the list is extensive and include, amongst other things:

- beating, kicking, ill-treating, over-loading, torturing, infuriating or terrifying an animal;
- administering to an animal a poisonous drug or substance;

- subjecting an animal to an operation which is performed 'without due care and humanity' and tethering 'under such conditions as to cause the animal unnecessary suffering'.

The offence of cruelty is deemed to include not only cruel acts but also cruel acts of omission, and a horse owner can be deemed to have permitted cruelty if he did not apply reasonable care and supervision in protecting the animal from cruelty.

Subject to one exception, in prosecuting a cruelty offence the prosecution only need prove that pain and suffering were caused amounting to cruelty, and not that the horse owner caused that pain and suffering deliberately.

A horse owner convicted of cruelty can expect a fine and/or imprisonment (not exceeding six months). Furthermore, the magistrates' court can make orders for compensation, removing ownership of the horse or for the horse to be destroyed – and on a second conviction, to order that the offender is prohibited from keeping any animal.

The Abandonment of Animals Act 1960 s 1 makes it an offence of cruelty for an owner (or essentially a keeper of the animal) to abandon (whether on a temporary or permanent basis) an animal without reasonable cause or excuse in circumstances likely to cause suffering to the animal.

It is worth noting also that the Farriers (Registration) Act 1975 and Farriers Registration (Amendment) Act 1977 make it an offence for anyone who is not a registered farrier to carry out farriery. (The definition of what constitutes farriery does not extend to include trimming a hoof if there is no intention of immediately fitting a shoe.)

Diseases

19.3 The Department for Environment Food and Rural Affairs (DEFRA) has provided in the Infectious Diseases of Horses Order 1987 (SI 1987/790) and the Equine Viral Arteritis Order 1995 (SI 1995/1755) those diseases horse owners have a legal obligation to report if the relevant symptoms are exhibited by their horse.

Notifiable diseases are:

- African Horse Sickness;
- Anthrax;
- Contagious Equine Metritis;
- Dourine;
- Epizootic Lymphangitis;
- Equine Infectious Anaemia;
- Equine Viral Arteritis;

- Equine Viral Encephalomyelitis;
- Glanders;
- Rabies; and
- Vesicular Stomatitis.

Noxious weeds

19.4 Noxious weeds, and in particular ragwort, are the bane of many horse owners' lives. The Weeds Act 1959 permits DEFRA to serve notice on an occupier of land to take action to prevent the spread of noxious weeds (which for the purposes of the Act are spear thistle, creeping thistle, curled dock, broad leaved dock and ragwort). If the occupier unreasonably fails to comply with the notice he commits an offence.

A landowner whose neighbour fails to control the spread of noxious weeds from his land, may consider a civil action for an injunction against his neighbour, if the landowner can establish his neighbour is committing a private nuisance which unreasonably interferes with the landowner's use and enjoyment of his own land. (Note that the landowner may seek compensation where he has suffered damage or loss.)

Rider obligations

Riding on public highways

19.5 The Highway Authority has a duty to provide special margins for the safety of ridden horses alongside dangerous roads (Highways Act 1980 s 71). Technically, highway margins are usually part of the public highway and therefore should be available to all users for free passage (there may be exceptions where the margin is common land or manorial waste), however, prudent riders, in practice, will exercise their discretion in which margins they ride over, because of hidden hazards on poorly maintained margins in particular. However, under the Highways Act 1835 s 72, it is an offence to ride, drive or lead a horse on a footpath by the side of the road which is for the use of pedestrians only. A rider on a public highway must keep his horse to the left hand side, and avoid obstructing anyone who wishes to pass (Highways Act 1875).

Those who enjoy pub rides or Boxing Day meets should also note that it is an offence to be drunk in charge of a horse on a highway or other public place (Licensing Act 1872 s 12).

Protective headgear

19.6 The Horses (Protective Headgear for Young Riders) Act 1990 makes it compulsory for anyone under the age of 14 to wear protective headgear when riding on a road (other than a bridleway or footpath that is not associated with a carriageway). The person responsible for the child, as well as the owner (or person who has custody or possession of the horse or pony being ridden), are liable if the child does not wear protective headgear.

Planning Through Financial Services 20

Andrew Miles
Head of Research for Thomson's Group plc

Introduction

20.1 Financial advisers are often depicted as commission-hungry life assurance salesmen. This is a misleading picture as the vast majority of firms are staffed by professional advisers with the requisite knowledge and experience to provide innovative and effective solutions to potential problems faced by equine businesses and individuals involved with horses in almost any capacity.

Most professional firms are happy to discuss their remuneration in detail and, if required, agree a fee in advance for any work carried out. Financial advisers work closely with other professional advisers and most accountants and solicitors are usually able to recommend a reputable firm.

The objective of this chapter is to illustrate some of the financial services strategies worthy of consideration and how they may be best employed. In particular, the following subjects have been concentrated on:

- the need for financial planning;
- financial planning for businesses;
  - stakeholder pensions and employers;
  - self-invested pensions;
  - business protection;
  - employee benefits;
- financial planning for individuals;
  - house purchase and mortgages;

— pensions and divorce;
- Pensions Green Paper.

The need for financial planning

20.2 The term 'financial planning' covers a wide spectrum of products and services from mortgages to advanced tax mitigation, interpretation of intricate pension legislation and the complex interaction of life assurance and trusts. A glance through the personal finance supplements of the quality Sunday newspapers provides an indication of the mind-boggling array of products available in a very competitive market. An independent adviser is crucial to provide an impartial guide through the planning maze and help sort the 'wheat from the chaff'.

For many of us, horses form part of a relaxing and enjoyable pastime and, in many cases, a vocation – but one that is not without danger. In its simplest form, financial planning through life assurance provides valuable financial protection for the family in the unfortunate event of death or a debilitating accident. For those involved in equestrian businesses, executive financial planning can assist in compliance with the law regarding the provision of stakeholder pensions for employees, business protection and the delivery of employee benefit packages, all of which can prove crucial in attracting and retaining quality staff.

Specialist advice can also assist individuals from professional jockeys to stable lads to ensure that their financial circumstances are best matched with their future aspirations through purchasing their own home to managing their savings and investments in a tax-efficient manner.

Financial planning for businesses

20.3 Financial services professionals can assist business owners and managers of equine ventures at every stage from start-up to mature businesses. A detailed understanding of the taxation and interaction of the various pension regimes can be invaluable in assisting the principals of a business in profit extraction. Basis year pension planning has an important bearing in the salary versus dividend debate whilst National Insurance increases have reinforced the attractiveness of salary and bonus sacrifice strategies.

Other applications of note are the use of different types of self-invested pension schemes which themselves may be used to invest in the business or commercial property, business protection strategies for key employees and executives, the provision of employee benefit schemes and investing business assets.

Stakeholder pensions

20.4 Stakeholder pensions were introduced in April 2001 with immediate implications for companies. If a business employs five or more people, it is likely that it is required to offer employees access to a stakeholder pension scheme in accordance with the Welfare Reform and Pensions Act 1999 (WRPA 1999). There are limited exemptions from these requirements, notably where employers offer access to an occupational pension scheme or offer to pay a minimum employer contribution of 3% of salary per annum on behalf of their employees to a group personal pension scheme.

Non-exempt businesses must comply with the stakeholder pension legislation or face a fine of £50,000 from the Occupational Pensions Regulatory Authority (OPRA). Broadly speaking, stakeholder pension schemes are personal pension contracts which meet government stipulated standards for charges, access and terms.

Employers' responsibilities

20.5 WRPA 1999 s 3(2) sets out the obligations for non-exempt employers, who must:

- designate (formally choose) a stakeholder pension scheme;
- discuss the choice of scheme with their employees or any body which represents them such as a trade union;
- supply 'relevant employees' with the name and address of the designated scheme;
- deduct stakeholder pension contributions directly from an employee's salary and pay it across to the stakeholder pension scheme provider within 19 days of the end of the month in which the payment is due;
- offer scheme access to new employees within three months of joining.

'Relevant employees' can broadly be described as those with earnings above the lower earnings limit with more than three months' continuous service. For example, if a riding school that normally employs three people takes on two temporary employees in summer, they will have to offer access to a stakeholder pension to all employees after three months.

Directors and spouses of directors who are employed within the business and paid more than the lower earnings limit will count towards the total of five employees.

Basis year planning

20.6 The stakeholder pension legislation within WRPA 1999 introduced the concept of basis year planning, which has particular relevance for profit extraction.

The dividend versus salary debate is one that almost all company directors periodically have with their accountants. Dividend remuneration has a number of attractions – however, one major disadvantage has been the restriction that this places on the director's ability to fund an approved pension scheme.

Under the basis year rules pension contributions for stakeholder and personal pensions, a year may be chosen (the basis year) to set the earnings used to calculate maximum pension contributions. The basis year may be any of the previous five tax years. It is, therefore, possible for company executives to be paid a high bonus in one tax year and a lower salary for the next five years whilst maintaining personal pension contributions based upon the higher earnings. In theory this may then be repeated every six years until retirement, when, due to the cessation year rule, pension contributions may be maintained for a further five years.

This strategy may also be used by company directors who employ their spouses within the business, with earnings reduced below the lower earnings limit during the intervening years to minimise the effect of tax and National Insurance.

The cessation year rule works in a slightly different way in that, when an individual ceases working they may continue to fund their pension for a further five years based upon their salary in the year of cessation, or the highest salary in any of the previous five years. Therefore, in practice, it is possible to continue pension funding in retirement based upon a salary earned 11 years earlier.

Self-invested pensions

20.7 The term 'self-invested pensions' applies to Small Self-Administered Schemes (SSASs) and Self-Invested Personal Pensions (SIPPs). Both schemes allow considerable flexibility over the investment of pension assets within the scheme, including self-investment in the business (notably by SSASs) and the purchase of commercial property.

Care must be exercised where property is being considered as a pension scheme investment, as it is an illiquid asset. It is often appropriate to consider investments of this nature in terms of the proposed life span of the pension scheme itself and succession planning for the business. An example of this could be the use of the pension scheme of a racehorse trainer to purchase additional land and develop gallops. This would not necessarily be in the trainer's best interest if he/she were approaching retirement and funds would need to be found to bring the asset back into the business. Where clear succession planning exists, perhaps with other generations involved in the business and the pension scheme, the property could remain as a pension scheme asset for their future benefit, and so on.

In the twenty-first century, as pension provision becomes ever more complex, those ignoring pension planning run the risk of missing out on some valuable and effective tax allowances and solutions.

Small Self Administered Schemes (SSASs)

20.8 A Small Self Administered Scheme or SSAS is a type of occupational pension scheme aimed at shareholding directors of limited companies. These schemes offer a greater degree of control of investments and the opportunity to utilise the pension fund within the business itself. To qualify, a SSAS must fulfill the following requirements:

- less than 12 members;
- at least one of the members must be connected with another member, a trustee or the employer;
- a proportion of the schemes assets must be invested other than in insured assets, eg in unit trusts, company shares or property;
- one of the trustees must be a pensioner trustee.

The pensioner trustee is usually appointed by the company which is chosen to operate the scheme and must be a party to all scheme bank accounts and transactions. A scheme may be set up for one member but more usually is established for shareholding directors and their families.

Self-investment is permitted and defined as an investment where there is a direct connection with, and usually a benefit to, the employer. This may be a loan to the employer, purchase of shares in the employer's company or purchase of commercial property which is occupied by the company.

Contributions to occupational pension schemes by both employers and members attract tax relief and funds within a scheme grow largely without liability to UK tax on either income or capital gains. Employer contributions on behalf of a member are not regarded as benefits in kind and there is no National Insurance liability.

SSAS Investments

20.9 SSAS schemes may invest in a wide range of investments such as:

- quoted stocks and shares;
- unit trusts/open ended investment companies (OEICS);
- insurance policies;
- deposits (bank or building society);
- property;
- self-investment.

Note that self-investment is a general term used to describe a loan by the trustees to the employer participating in the scheme, or the purchase of the employer's premises by the trustees (the premises are then leased to the employer at a commercial rent).

The main specific restrictions on investments are as follows:

- the scheme trustees cannot directly or indirectly buy sell (unless the asset was acquired by the scheme prior to 15 July 1991) or lease investments to or from a member of the scheme including any individual, partnership or company that is connected with a scheme member;
- investment in 'pride in possession' assets are not allowed, eg jewellery, classic cars, art, etc;
- the scheme cannot purchase assets that have been owned by a scheme member or connected person within the previous three years. Employers that participate in a scheme, and companies associated to these employers, are not connected parties for this purpose.

Loans to the employer are permitted and must be for a specific purpose, eg the purchase of additional stock. 'Cashflow' is not deemed an acceptable purchase. There is no set term for the loan which must be constructed at a market rate, the rule being that the term should generally match the purpose of the loan. Thus, a one-year term may be suitable for the purchase of equipment, whilst a loan to purchase land could be structured over five or ten years.

Property investments are restricted to commercial property, with a few exceptions such as a shop with a flat above. Investment in farmland or forestry land is acceptable, however, care is required as the restrictions on investing in residential property will usually disqualify property, which includes a farmhouse. The Inland Revenue will usually expect there to be no amenity rights, such as hunting or fishing rights, attached to the land from which the scheme member could benefit.

In principle, the Inland Revenue will allow the purchase of premises, for example, for riding stables, livery or gallops, again providing there is no residential element to the purchase. The Inland Revenue is, however, concerned that members may benefit from these facilities and will judge each case on its merits.

The pension scheme may make purchases jointly with the employer, another pension scheme or a third party. The scheme trustees may borrow money, subject to a limit of three times the ordinary annual pension scheme contribution (calculated over the last three complete scheme years) plus 45% of the scheme assets. The trustees usually borrow from a commercial source such as a bank or building society. Borrowing from other sources is permitted provided the borrowing is on commercial terms.

A pension scheme may also purchase shares in the employer's company, whether listed or not. In practice, the restriction on the purchase and sale of scheme assets to connected parties greatly restricts these investments.

Self-Invested Personal Pensions

20.10 Self-Invested Personal Pensions (SIPPs) were introduced in 1989 to widen the flexibility and appeal of personal pension provision. SIPPs are written under personal pension legislation and subject to most of the same limits and controls.

Contributions attract income tax relief at the marginal rate and accrue in a favourable tax environment. Under current legislation, benefits can be taken from age 50 and up to 25% of the fund may be paid out as a tax-free cash lump sum.

There are many ways in which benefits may be taken at retirement, indeed, it is not even necessary to actually retire in order to take benefits.

SIPPs work in exactly the same way as normal Personal Pension Plans (PPPs). Regular or single personal contributions can be made as well as employer contributions or pension transfers (including from retirement annuities). Contributions, excluding transfers, must not exceed the relevant percentage of net relevant earnings in any one tax year, as follows.

Age attained (as at 6 April)	*Maximum contribution as a percentage of earnings*
Up to 35	17.5%
35 to 45	20%
46 to 50	25%
51 to 55	30%
56 to 60	35%
61 to 74	40%

The pension funds themselves are invested in accordance with the member's specific instructions into allowable investments and not restricted to those provided by any single insurance company or investment house.

Under current legislation, the member can take the benefits at any age between 50 and 75. The SIPP offers the facilities of 'phased' retirement by means of multiple policies, and 'pension fund income withdrawal'.

SIPP investments

20.11 Joint Office Memorandum (JOM) 101, issued in October 1989, provided the basic rules for allowable investments. The list has since been kept under review and was updated by the Personal Pension Schemes (Restriction on Discretion to Approve) (Permitted Investments) Regulations 2001 (SI 2001/117). Allowable investments currently include:

- stocks and shares quoted on the UK Stock Exchange (including securities traded on the unlisted securities market);
- stocks and shares traded on a recognised overseas stock exchange;
- Unit Trusts and Investment Trusts;
- insurance company managed funds and unit linked funds;
- deposit accounts;
- property.

As with an SSAS, property investments are limited to freehold or leasehold commercial property where the interest is not acquired from a connected person. The SIPP may lease a property to the employer but it is important to note that unlike an SSAS, a SIPP may not purchase a property from the scheme member's business or any associated companies. Similarly, it is not possible for a SIPP to make any loans from the scheme.

The borrowing restrictions for a SIPP are more relaxed than that of a SSAS. Borrowings, in relation to the purchase of a freehold or leasehold commercial property or towards the development of such property, are limited to 75% of the purchase price and must be secured upon that property.

The installation of a SIPP is also simpler, lacking the individual approval from the Inland Revenue that is required for a SSAS, thus scheme costs are usually less expensive.

Property purchase via pension schemes – conclusion

20.12 Property purchase via a pension scheme can release valuable cash into the balance sheet making development capital available for the business. In the case of an SSAS this may be made available directly. There is no loss of control over the property asset which is simply transferred into the pension fund for the future benefit of the owner/managers. The pension fund benefits from both future capital appreciation on the value of the property and current rental income, as well as being an acknowledged 'safe haven' investment strategy. By structuring the scheme in this way, the expenses to the tax exempt pension scheme are reduced as the company can pay the management fees for the future pension administration.

Business protection

20.13 Equestrian businesses take care to insure the horses, buildings and vehicles, but will rarely have protected themselves from the financial consequences of losing, arguably, one of their most valuable assets – their people.

Business protection can provide valuable assistance to a company when it is needed most, at the time of a death or incapacitating injury to an owner, manager or other key employees.

Key person protection

20.14 Most equestrian business owners and managers will be able to easily identify the individuals who play a key role in the success and profitability of the operation. Often it is the owners and managers themselves, but key people may also be found amongst jockeys or head lads. It is these individuals whose death or inability to work through illness which could cause problems for the business, such as a loss or fall in morale or customer loyalty and, subsequently, profits. For small businesses such as riding or livery stables, the loss may be keener still. These operations often have a small number of employees and the cost involved in recruiting an experienced temporary replacement could be high.

Whether run as a company or a partnership, key person life assurance could provide a vital cash injection to the business, especially where the venture has bank borrowings. Where the key employees identified are jockeys, especially jump jockeys, it may not be possible to obtain income replacement (permanent health) insurance or life assurance from traditional product providers or the cost may be prohibitive. In these instances, specialist advice should be sought.

It is not always easy to place a cash value on the monetary contribution an individual employee makes to a business. The amount of cover required is usually calculated as a multiple of salary, profit or from the following calculation designed to determine the contribution to profitability:

$$\frac{\text{Key persons' salary}}{\text{Total salary bill}} \times \text{Average gross profits} \times \text{Anticipated recovery period}$$

The tax treatment of key person assurance cover is largely based upon a statement made in the House of Commons in 1944 by the then Chancellor, Sir John Anderson. He stated that the decision regarding the taxation of key person policies rests with the local Inspector of Taxes but that, in general, tax relief would be allowed on premiums and the proceeds taxed as a trading receipt if:

- the sole relationship is that of employer and employee;
- the insurance is provided to meet a loss to the business resulting from the loss of services of the employee;
- it is an annual or short term assurance.

Best practice is to obtain confirmation from the local Inspector of Taxes.

Partnership protection

20.15 Under the Partnership Act 1890, a partnership is defined as 'the relationship which exists between persons carrying on a business in common with a view to profit', other than by forming a limited company.

Example

Consider the situation where two individuals, Mrs Golden and Miss Miller, operate a successful riding stable. After many profitable years in business, Mrs Golden is taken ill and dies.

If no formal partnership agreement exists then the provision of the Partnership Act 1890 applies and the partnership will dissolve automatically with Mrs Golden's share of the dissolution proceeds passing to her widower.

Mr Golden lacks the necessary skills or interest to make a viable contribution to the business and approaches Miss Miller with an offer to buy out the share of the business. Miss Miller has a mortgage on her home and is forced to approach the bank and borrow against her share of the business, which itself is under further strain as she has been forced to hire a full-time manager.

One possible solution to the above example is partnership protection cover. This provides the surviving partner or partners with a lump sum to ensure that they can purchase the deceased's share of the business, minimising any financial strain and ensuring that the deceased's family is adequately provided for.

Partnership protection may be effected at the same time as a buy and sell agreement which binds the deceased partner's estate to sell the share of the business to the surviving partner. However, as this is a binding agreement, Business Property Relief (BPR) is lost for Inheritance Tax (IHT) purposes.

In many circumstances, a double option (or cross option) agreement may be more suitable. This provides the deceased's estate with the *option* to sell the share of the business to the surviving partners, at the same time providing the surviving partners with the *option* to buy the share of the business from the deceased's estate. This is not a binding contract as neither party is obliged to exercise their option and, for IHT purposes, BPR is retained. If, however, one party does decide to exercise their option, the other is obliged to comply.

Each partner arranges life assurance in trust with the remaining partners as both trustees and beneficiaries. This is usually provided by way of a term assurance policy written to the expected retirement age of the relevant partner. Alternatively, in the case of more mature partnerships, whole of life cover may be more suitable as this provides a retiring partner with the option to use the cover for alternative purposes. In either instance, critical illness cover may be included and the cover integrated with the arrangements of individual partners.

The partners usually pay premiums themselves from taxed income. If paid directly by the partnership they are treated as advanced drawings of a partner's profit entitlement and assessed to income tax and National Insurance. As the policies are effected as part of a commercial arrangement and under a suitable trust, the death benefits of the plan are excluded from the deceased partner's estate for IHT calculations.

Shareholder protection

20.16 Cover in the form of shareholder protection is relevant for limited companies, as illustrated in the following example.

> *Example*
> The shares of a racing stable, National Hunt Training Limited, are primarily owned by the Managing Director, Mr Red, and the Racing Director, Mr Rum, with a minority shared amongst the senior staff.
> Following a prolonged period of illness, Mr Rum dies. His shares pass to his estate, and in turn to his son, Mr Rum Jnr who is invited to join the board of National Hunt Training Limited. Mr Rum Jnr

quickly demonstrates that he lacks the requisite knowledge and application to significantly contribute to the business and, realising this, approaches Mr Red to purchase his shares at an inflated price. Mr Red is unable to do so without incurring significant expensive bank borrowings and Mr Rum Jnr subsequently approaches a local competitor with a view to selling his shareholding.

This is perhaps an extreme and somewhat melodramatic example, but illustrates the type of situation which may be avoided by the use of a shareholder protection plan.

Again, life assurance policies are utilised to provide surviving directors with the necessary funds to purchase the shareholding of a deceased colleague. As with a partnership, cover is often combined with a double option agreement. Whilst the company's articles of association may contain provisions for dealing with the death of a director, a separate agreement is usually advisable to prevent a deadlock situation arising. The double option agreement will usually also include a clause stipulating the method of valuing the shareholding.

Life assurance cover is provided on a 'life of another' basis or by each director on their own lives in trust to the other directors. The directors may also wish to consider critical illness cover, which is usually available as an option to a plan. In the case of our example, critical illness proceeds may have been available when Mr Rum fell ill, providing him with the means to retire and recuperate on the benefits of the sale to Mr Red.

As with partnership protection, shareholding directors will usually pay the premiums themselves out of taxed income. If the company pays contributions on their behalf, the premium is treated as extra salary and subject to income tax and employee National Insurance contributions. There will also be a liability to employer National Insurance contributions but this is a deductible business expense.

Business loan protection

20.17 Many equine businesses require bank borrowings of some means, often operating significant business overdrafts to aid cashflow. Business lending is almost always conditional upon the key people within the business being protected by life assurance and, increasingly, by critical illness cover. This ensures that, from the perspective of the lending bank, borrowings are protected in the event of a death or critical illness to a principal, causing disruption to the business.

In many cases, the performance of a business will be heavily dependant on one or more individuals, examples of this could be a talented trainer or the principals of a relatively young business which is growing strongly.

The bank will often arrange life assurance cover for the relevant parties. However, to a degree they have a captive market and the rates offered can be amongst the most expensive. Re-broking cover with an alternative product provider will often lead to considerable savings for the business.

For limited companies, the policyholder is usually the company, whereas sole traders should effect cover on their own lives, and for partnerships, a joint life policy may be suitable. However, this is usually restricted to two lives assured.

Premiums to a term assurance policy are unlikely to qualify as a deduction from profits. For limited companies, the tax position of proceeds is usually determined by the principle that, if tax relief is not allowed on premiums then the proceeds will avoid taxation. Best practice is to seek clarification on the tax treatment of premiums at outset from the company's Inspector of Taxes.

One area which may be considered is structuring borrowing through a Self-Invested Personal Pension (SIPP) or Small Self-Administered Pension Scheme (SSAS) where borrowings are being considered to fund the purchase of new commercial property.

Employee benefits

20.18 Employee benefit packages can be invaluable in recruiting, retaining and motivating staff. Equine businesses rely on the family atmosphere generated within the yard more than almost any other type of enterprise. Staff loyalty is often such that it is never brought into question, but by its very nature, the equine world is competitive, and an attractive and equitable benefits package can provide an edge in recruitment.

The communication of employee benefits can be crucial to their success and to the main benefit derived from such arrangements – enhancing employer/employee relations.

Choice is an important part of a benefits package and scheme details should be communicated in such a way that staff understand the benefits to them in detail.

A realistic timetable for implementation should be set, so as to provide time for employees to consider the benefits without the initiative being lost.

Unlike most businesses, equine enterprises often provide staff with accommodation, itself a valuable employee benefit. The following measures are also worthy of consideration.

Group pension scheme

20.19 The legislative requirements of the stakeholder pension legislation are dealt with at **20.4** above, and, with few exceptions, apply to all businesses.

Increasingly, employees have come to expect their employer to provide a scheme which offers benefits in retirement. The basic State pension can only ever provide minimum benefits and successive governments have increasingly turned to employers to supplement these.

There has been much debate as to the relative merits of defined benefit (or final salary) pension schemes versus defined contribution (or money purchase) pension schemes. Defined benefit schemes can provide employees with greater security as the level of pension is anticipated in advance, being calculated as a percentage of final salary. For schemes of this nature, it is the employer that carries the investment risk. These schemes have become less attractive over recent years partly as a result of the introduction of Financial Reporting Standard 17 (FRS17), which compels employers to include pension scheme assets and liabilities in their accounts. The incidence of new final salary pension schemes is very small, especially for companies with less than, say, 500 staff.

Defined contribution schemes give the employer control of cost, but no certainty is provided to employees as to the benefits they will receive at retirement. These are accrued on a money purchase basis and will potentially vary according to the level of contributions made, annuity rates and the performance of a member's individual 'pot' of pension assets which will fluctuate in value in line with investment markets.

The introduction of stakeholder pensions with costs effectively capped at a maximum of 1% per annum has had a revolutionary effect on pension scheme design. The cost of defined contribution pension schemes has been driven down and these now offer very good value for money.

Group life insurance

20.20 Often referred to as 'death in service' cover, group life assurance plans provide security for employees that their relatives, families or partner will be provided for in the event of their death during the term of their employment.

Cover is often expressed as a multiple of salary and written under a central trust so that benefits are normally paid free of inheritance tax. Members usually complete a 'nomination of beneficiaries' form instructing the trustees of the scheme to whom they would like benefits paid. Policies are arranged on a group basis and cover is often available cheaper than if it had been arranged on an individual basis. The premiums are treated as business expense.

Group permanent health insurance

20.21 Permanent health insurance is often referred to as income protection, insuring against the loss of earnings during a prolonged period of incapacity through accident or illness. Protection of this type is potentially advantageous to both employer and employee. It can be an attractive perk for the employee whilst providing a solution to the employer about how to deal with and remunerate a member of staff unable to work for a long period.

The employer's liability for a percentage of salary, National Insurance and even pension contributions may be insured. From the employees' perspective, they will continue to receive income payments as a continuation of salary, or a percentage thereof, until they are able to return to work gainfully. Premiums are treated as a business expense whilst the benefits are taxed.

Where the riding of horses forms an integral part of the job function, it is likely that the cost of this protection will be higher, although different categories of employee may be included within one scheme. For professional jockeys, cover may be difficult to place and professional specialist advice should be sought.

Group private medical insurance

20.22 Private medical insurance (PMI), from providers such as BUPA, is viewed by employees as a very valuable benefit, especially when cover is extended to include the family of an employee. There are a myriad of options and scales of benefits which may be incorporated and cover can be provided to suit all budgets.

In the event of a claim, it is often possible for the member to choose the hospital and consultant of their choice. Private hospitals are often available, as are private wards within NHS hospitals.

In cases of routine hospitalisation, the queue for a hospital bed can be long and this could lead to a large amount of time away from work. A private medical scheme will usually be able to facilitate treatment much faster resulting in less disruption to the business.

Policies are renewable each year and are taxed as a benefit in kind to the employee.

Group critical illness

20.23 As the name suggests, group critical illness plans provide employees with a cash lump sum in the event that they are diagnosed as having a serious illness. Conditions and treatments covered usually include heart attack, stroke, cancer, coronary artery bypass, major organ transplant, and multiple sclerosis. This list is by no means exhaustive and cover also usually incorporates a number of less common conditions.

Advances in medical science are such that many individuals who are diagnosed with a critical illness such as cancer or who suffer a heart attack, recover and survive for many years. It is likely, however, that the illness will have had a dramatic effect on their lifestyle and finances, especially if a prolonged absence from work is required.

Employees are five times more likely to suffer a critical illness than they are to die before reaching retirement age, and critical illness cover demonstrates an employer's willingness to provide assistance at the time that it is arguably needed most.

Premiums are treated as a business expense and taxed as a benefit in kind to the employee.

Financial planning for individuals

20.24 In the twenty-first century, few people would question the need for financial advice. Dealing with financial products such as mortgages, bank accounts and credit cards is a daily occurrence for many people.

The world of personal finance is complex enough when one contemplates the array of investment schemes, pension plans and protection contracts available. When considered in conjunction with personal and corporate taxes and further complicated by the interaction of trusts and financial planning, independent advice is a must.

Circumstances and finances rarely remain constant and marriages, births, changing careers and inheritances all have an effect, both in the short term and on aspirations for the future. Financial planning can assist in identifying and prioritising needs and ensuring that as much preparation as possible is achieved for all eventualities.

Mortgages

20.25 For many, house purchase without the assistance of a mortgage is simply not a viable option. Mortgages form part of our everyday lives and may be sourced via High Street lenders, specialist mortgage brokers or even on the internet.

The nature of equine businesses is such that accommodation is often provided on site and many who work with horses, such as stable lads, do not own property of their own. In recent years, we have witnessed a boom in house prices, arguably more so in rural areas where prices have, to a degree, been forced up by the demand for rural property from former town and city residents seeking a more pleasant environment in which to live.

It is now quite common for first-time buyers in rural areas to be forced to look further afield for property than they would like, due to the prohibitive cost of housing. Of course, if accommodation is provided at the stables this is not necessarily a problem but one must consider that there is no longer such a thing as a job, and by extension a cottage or other accommodation, for life.

Equine business owners have already felt the impact of the introduction of the minimum wage as stable lads are as much compensated by the fringe benefits associated with the career, such as subsidised or provided accommodation, as they are by salary.

It is, however, prudent for stable lads to consider that there may come a time when accommodation will not be provided for them. As already stated, the salary of a stable employee may not be sufficient to raise a mortgage to purchase property in the area that they would like. However, with the housing market there is little advantage to be gained from a 'wait and see' attitude.

One potential solution may be shared mortgages. Groups of two or more friends can apply for a joint mortgage, although finding a willing lender may be less easy.

For those with the means, specialist 'buy to let' mortgages are available, although with rural accommodation it is normally advisable to conduct research in the locality to gauge the demand for rental accommodation. If there is no intention of living in the property at any time, purchasing in another area may be possible, however, the pros and cons of property as an investment should be considered no differently than any other asset class. Capital gains tax is payable on the sale of property which has been let and does not serve as the owner's main residence.

Pensions and divorce

20.26 When divorce proceedings have begun or are about to begin, one might be forgiven for not immediately contacting a financial adviser. However, much of the mechanics of a divorce concern the division of assets, and although not always immediately apparent, pension scheme assets often form a significant proportion of total wealth.

There are three ways main strategies for dealing with pension rights at the time of divorce:

- offsetting;
- earmarking/attachment; and
- pension sharing.

Offsetting

20.27 By far the easiest way in which pension scheme assets may be taken into account in any settlement is offsetting. This is a 'clean break' option whereby other assets are used to offset the share of the pension benefits which the ex-spouse would ordinarily have been entitled to.

Earmarking/attachment

20.28 The Pension Act 1995 s 166 introduced the concept of earmarking. Following an earmarking order, pension assets are allocated to the former spouse and become payable to them on the death or retirement of the member. In these circumstances, the benefits payable to an ex-spouse remain to a degree dependant on the member's circumstances. The member may, for example, dictate the timing of the payment of benefits.

Pension sharing

20.29 Pension sharing is a further clean break option introduced by WRPA 1999 where a divorce petition is filed on or after 1 December 2000. Pension sharing provides the ex-spouse with a share of the pension assets, which are deemed to belong to them and effectively split off for their benefit.

> *Example*
> Mr Arkle has substantial accumulated funds within an SSAS. Mr Arkle's entire fund is deemed to be a matrimonial asset irrespective of whether or not it was accumulated in the duration of the marriage (under Scottish law only pension benefits accrued during the term of the marriage are considered), and the court subsequently issues a pension sharing order. The former Mrs Arkle then receives a share of the pension fund, known as a pension credit. She can remain a member of the scheme in her own right. However, the trustees have the right to impose a transfer to an alternative pension arrangement of the former Mrs Arkle's choosing if they wish.

The Pensions Green Paper

20.30 In December 2002, the Government released the long-awaited Pensions Green Paper detailing plans for the future of pension provision in the UK. The paper was accompanied by a further consultation document produced by the Inland Revenue dealing with the issue of simplifying the taxation of pensions.

The paper contains radical recommendations for changes to the current pension system including replacing the eight current pension structures in favour of one flexible tax regime. This new regime will then apply to all individuals. It is proposed that contribution limits be relaxed and existing maxima replaced with an overall annual restriction on funding of £200,000 per annum. Personal contributions will be restricted to the greater of £3,600 and 100% of earnings.

An overall lifetime limit on pension funds is to be introduced, initially at £1.4m, with a punitive tax charge on benefits accrued in excess of this amount. By way of example, for a higher rate taxpayer, the effective tax charge would be nearly 60%. For those with accumulated funds in excess of £1.4m, the fund value will be 'certified' at the date the new rules come into force ('A day') and this 'certified' value, increased in line with an as yet unspecified index, will replace the overall limit. However, the rate of increase is likely to be small and may quickly be outstripped by the increase in the value of pension assets.

One particular proposal of note is the removal of the earlier retirement age for individuals with personal pensions in 'recognised occupations'. These currently include flat racing jockeys who may retire at age 45 or later and national hunt jockeys for whom the retirement age is 35 or older. A similar restriction will also apply to occupational pension schemes.

Other Green Paper proposals include:

- the concept of a 'normal retirement age' will be removed (not least as it appears to contravene European age discrimination laws) and the minimum age at which retirement benefits may be taken will be increased from age 50 to 55 by 2010;
- flexibility in retirement will be increased as the rules preventing occupational scheme members from taking retirement benefits and continuing to work will be dropped.

The nature of a Green Paper is such that it raises almost as many questions as it answers. One clear message is that individual pension provision is essential and that any delay in funding should be avoided. Whilst we are sure that the devil will be in the detail, the Green Paper provides confirmation that income tax relief on contributions will remain at an individual's marginal rate.

There is little to be gained from a 'wait and see' attitude. In the majority of cases significant advantages can be gained by maximising contributions within the existing pensions regime.

Racecourse League Table **A**

In order of racecourses' percentage contributions to overall prize money.

Figures relate to prize money for the 12-month period: 1 January to 31 December 2002.

Racecourse league table

Location	*Racecourse Exec + sponsors* £	*% of Total*	*Levy Board* £	*% of Total*	*Owners* £	*% of Total*	*Div. Fund* £	*% of Total*	*Total* £	*2000/01* %	*Up/ down*
Aintree	1,312,265	71.4	329,790	18	194,735	10.6	0	0	1,836,790	67	Up
Cheltenham	2,378,910	59.8	961,190	24.1	640,720	16.1	0	0	3,980,820	50.4	Up
Ascot	4,433,456	56.2	1,612,355	20.5	1,836,900	23.3	0	0	7,882,711	56.9	Down
York	2,141,835	55.8	855,450	22.3	840,741	21.9	0	0	3,838,026	56.6	Down
Goodwood	1,665,517	54	982,023	31.9	434,565	14.1	0	0	3,082,105	56.8	Down
Chester	669,440	52.4	493,330	38.6	103,990	8.1	10,000	0.8	1,276,760	53.6	Down
Epsom Downs	1,619,205	52.1	528,250	17	9,627.45	31	0	0	3,110,200	51.2	Up
Sandown Park	1,550,325	49.4	1,182,330	37.7	398,177	12.7	6000	0.2	3,136,832	48.7	Up
Newmarket	2,882,890	46.9	1,925,270	31.3	1,331,015	21.6	14,200	0.2	6,153,375	44.2	Up
Newbury	1,552,250	45.1	1,362,800	39.6	488,929	14.2	3,700	1.1	3,440,979	47.2	Down
Doncaster	1,474,360	40.8	1,255,050	34.7	856,150	23.7	31,000	0.9	3,616,560	37.3	Up
Kempton Park	871,648	40	1,097,940	50.4	199,988	9.2	8,500	0.4	2,178,076	43.6	Down
Haydock Park	859,905	37	1,189,120	51.1	259,825	11.2	17,500	0.8	2,326,350	39.2	Down
Pontefract	326,050	33.3	546,450	55.8	86,596	8.8	20,000	2	979,096	25.1	Up
Stratford-on-Avon	218,540	32.4	393,660	58.4	48,822	7.2	13,000	1.9	674,022	17.6	Up

Towcester	94,260	32.1	173,260	59.1	21,170	7.2	4,700	1.6	29,3390	20.2	Up
Windsor	386,760	32.1	652,400	54.1	129,991	10.8	37,200	3.1	1,206,351	34.6	Down
Perth	168,040	30.3	342,960	61.9	38,020	6.9	5,000	0.9	554,020	25.9	Up
Newcastle	420,430	30.1	850,750	60.9	110,041	7.9	15,250	1.1	1,396,471	31.2	Down
Hamilton Park	224,027	30	450,973	60.4	67,475	9	4,000	0.5	746,475	26.2	Up
Wincanton	245,225	29.7	497,860	60.4	66,876	8.1	14,800	1.8	824,761	29.2	Up
Thirsk	202,490	29.5	392,520	57.2	82,685	12	9,000	1.3	686,695	22.8	Up
Ayr	447,135	29.4	893,235	58.8	179,212	11.8	0	0	1,519,632	27.9	Up
Salisbury	276,050	29.4	526,450	56.1	90,828	9.7	45,250	4.8	938,578	27.5	Up
Uttoxeter	303,505	27.8	702,760	64.3	75,107	6.9	12,000	1.1	1,093,372	17.4	Up
Ripon	198,990	26.8	466,800	62.8	71,394	9.6	6,000	0.8	743,184	24.4	Up
Wetherby	183,350	26.4	458,650	66.1	52,248	7.5	0	0	694,248	22.9	Up
Musselburgh	235,060	26	574,890	63.7	69,700	7.7	23,000	2.5	902,650	20.3	Up
Warwick	277,280	25.5	684,470	62.9	112,072	10.3	14,100	1.3	1,087,922	19	Up
Chepstow	290,395	24.8	782,910	66.9	75,232	6.4	22,400	1.9	1,170,937	32.1	Down
Beverley	211,070	24.3	538,920	62	105,130	12.1	13,900	1.6	869,020	24.4	Down
Fontwell Park	152,120	24.3	419,680	67	48,040	7.7	6,300	1	626,140	22	Up
Cartmel	40,320	23.7	116,580	68.5	13,215	7.8	0	0	170,115	25.5	Down
Kelso	118,250	22.7	371,250	71.1	32,415	6.2	0	0	521,915	15.4	Up

Racecourse league table

Location	*Racecourse Exec + sponsors* £	*% of Total*	*Levy Board* £	*% of Total*	*Owners* £	*% of Total*	*Div. Fund* £	*% of Total*	*Total* £	*2000/01* %	*Up/ down*
Leicester	276,840	22.5	788,060	64.1	119,300	9.7	44,700	3.6	1,228,900	15.5	Up
Huntingdon	134,030	21.8	432,600	70.3	38,690	6.3	10,300	1.7	615,620	18.7	Up
Bath	140,943	21.6	461,157	70.8	40,537	6.2	8,600	1.3	651,237	19.8	Up
Brighton	144,299	21.3	469,201	69.2	48,130	7.1	16,400	2.4	678,030	17.5	Up
Newton Abbot	119,310	20.9	425,390	74.4	26,913	4.7	0	0	571,613	19.8	Up
Yarmouth	157,480	20.2	558,620	71.6	46,688	6	1,700	2.2	779,788	19	Up
Exeter	95,280	19.3	341,770	69.2	48,933	9.9	7,900	1.6	493,883	14	Up
Lingfield Park	541,087	18.9	1,796,213	62.8	214,857	7.5	306,650	10.7	2,858,807	15.7	Up
Carlisle	126,995	18.4	467,805	67.6	74,747	10.8	22,200	3.2	691,747	19.1	Down
Market Rasen	148,991	17.8	616,515	73.7	64,916	7.8	6,000	0.7	836,422	19.9	Down
Ludlow	93,160	17.6	395,475	74.6	37,905	7.1	3,600	0.7	530,140	13.3	Up
Redcar	133,110	17.2	405,590	52.5	227,992	29.5	5,500	0.7	772,192	15.5	Up
Worcester	82,230	16.7	369,520	74.9	32,492	6.6	9,050	1.8	493,292	20.4	Down
Fakenham	52,165	16.1	256,035	79.1	15,444	4.8	0	0	323,644	14.6	Up
Bangor-on-Dee	80,880	15.9	377,420	74.1	47,221	9.3	4,000	0.8	509,521	17.3	Down

Catterick Bridge	116,540	15.5	522,460	69.5	81,695	10.9	31,500	4.2	752,195	12.4	Up
Nottingham	114,370	14.9	514,580	67	99,307	12.9	39,300	5.1	767,557	13.3	Up
Hexham	46,125	12.8	279,225	77.5	32,440	9	2,400	0.7	360,190	10	Up
Hereford	67,260	12	437,545	78.1	52,230	9.3	3,500	0.6	560,535	10.5	Up
Folkstone	66,255	11.5	446,045	77.5	48,547	8.4	15,000	2.6	575,848	11.6	Down
Wolverhampton	253,720	11.5	1,654,130	75.3	122,503	5.6	167,150	7.6	2,197,503	17.9	Down
Taunton	52,310	11.2	345,740	74	44,796	9.6	24,300	5.2	467,146	14.7	Down
Sedgefield	71,450	11.1	531,625	82.6	30,375	4.7	10,000	1.6	643,450	8.4	Up
Plumpton	46,250	9.7	394,150	82.6	36,655	7.7	0	0	477,055	11.9	Down
Southwell	19,245	1.1	1,517,055	83.9	112,910	6.2	159,100	8.8	1,808,310	6.2	Down
TOTAL	31,611,678	37.5	39,416,302	46.8	11,870,973	14.1	1,304,250	1.5	84,203,203	37	Up

Racing Review – The Racing Product

B

The BHB have introduced the Racing Review Part 1 – The Racing Product. The details set out below were presented at the IOD (Institute of Directors) on 28 April 2003.

Summary of the recommendations

Fixtures

- Expand the fixture list.
- Separate the additional races for lowly rated flat horses into separate fixtures.
- Create 3-tier racing.
- Introduce regional racing in 2004 on a test basis.
- Appoint a recruitment and training director.
- A review of jockeys' working hours. Supervise turf management more strictly.

Race planning

- Place all flat races into one of five Classes.
- Make no change to the way in which responsibility for deciding the race programme of each fixture is exercised.
- Continue the expansion of the programme for better quality fillies and mares.
- Introduce more races, especially handicaps, confined to three-year-olds only.

- Allow all horses bought at major overseas sales to be eligible for maiden auctions.
- Expand all classified stakes to have a 5lb band.
- Reduce races with small fields to no more than 10% of the race programme.
- Place more emphasis on merit when eliminating horses from oversubscribed races.
- Enable racecourses to programme a number of 'consumer interest' races.
- Enable more people to participate in the claiming process for claiming races by allowing telephone bids.

Handicaps

- All flat handicaps for three-year-olds and up rated 46 and higher, other than Heritage Handicaps, should be run as narrow-band handicaps with a 10–15lbs weight range in Classes 1–4.
- There should be banded stakes rather than flat handicaps.
- A limited number of high profile, traditional long-band handicaps, to be called Heritage Handicaps, should continue to be run, providing they fulfil certain criteria.
- The change to a system of narrow-band handicaps should be carried out over a two-year period to enable a smooth transition.
- All horses with a handicap mark within or below the rating range of the handicap band should be entitled to run in that handicap.
- The title 'Rated Stakes' should be dropped and all narrow-band handicaps renamed 'Handicaps' with 'Heritage Handicaps' distinguishing long band from narrow-band handicaps.
- Flat ratings should be published in the Racing Calendar putting the rating into the appropriate column marked Class 1, 2, 3, 4 or the band letter (A, B, C, D) into Class 5.
- Narrow-band handicaps appear to be unsuitable for Jumping at the present time.
- Narrow-band handicaps should not be introduced for two-year-olds racing at this time.
- Once-raced winners should be allowed to run in all handicaps other than Heritage Handicaps and handicaps with a value of more than £25,000.
- All horses, other than two-year-olds prior to 1 September, should only be eligible for a handicap mark after their third or subsequent run if they finish in the first six in any of their first four runs.

Prize money

- There should be a substantial differentiation between prize money for each race class in order to create an improved meritocracy system where owners and trainers seek promotion for their horses.
- Prize money should be paid to placings according to the level of the Class with most placings being paid in the highest class.
- Prize money should be divided between placings and connections in a more simplified way.
- Flat races for amateurs, ladies and apprentices should be programmed in the appropriate class with the appropriate level of prize money for that class rather than downgraded as at present.

Appearance money

- Appearance money for the flat should only be paid to horses rated no more than one class below the race class in which the horse is running, instead of to all flat horses rated 45 or above.
- Appearance money regulations for Jumping should be changed to discourage abuse of the system.
- Appearance money should not be paid for regional racing.
- Racecourses should be encouraged to pay appearance money.
- Appearance money should be paid to all mares running in steeplechases.

Race entry and declaration

- The race entry system for five-day entries should remain unchanged for both flat and Jumping following the changes made in November 2002.
- Racecourses should be encouraged to pay appearance money as a means of reducing the unacceptably high number of races with less than eight runners.
- A committee sub-group, which has already been set up, should review the current early closing entry systems for pattern and sales races.
- Specific goals should be set to reduce entry fees as a percentage of the total prize fund.
- Racecourses should show all prize money for a race as 'Total Prize Fund' rather than 'Added to Stakes'.
- In the interests of transparency, the amount contributed to each fixture's prize fund from HBLB, owners and racecourses respectively should be identified.

- There should be a gradual extension of 48-hour declarations providing the benefits of changing from 24-hour declarations can be clearly identified.
- Heritage Handicaps and all group races for the flat as well as major Jumping handicaps should be converted to 48-hour declarations in 2004.
- All premier race meetings should have 48-hour declarations if introduced in 2005.
- Racing should be willing to switch to more general 48-hour declarations upon evidence of significant signed contracts between Attheraces and foreign bookmakers with a pre-condition to closing that British Racing switch to 48-hour declarations.
- Reserves should be allowed for Heritage Handicaps.

National Hunt Racing

- Recommendations should be structured according to five objectives for Jumping.
- Provide British-bred jumpers of all ages with 25% owners' premiums in addition to the prize money.
- Provide British-bred jumping fillies and mares of all ages with 50% owners' premiums.
- Maintain existing race values for 0–75 rated jumpers by *not* introducing Regional Racing for jumpers.
- Develop a strategy and a programme to build the physical and mental durability of jumpers, thus enabling them to become a part of Jumping at an earlier age.
- Introduce a special end of season appearance money scheme for chasers rated 140 and above, which have run at least five times.
- Appearance money should be paid to all mares in steeplechases.
- Racing should programme provisional flat all-weather fixtures at the five-day entry stage where the weather forecast gives reason to believe that already programmed fixtures may be abandoned.
- Ensure that field sizes for Jumping progress towards matching those of the all-weather.
- Introduce a winter triple crown and grand slam.
- Introduce an International Invitational Race in early December.
- Build at least two more weekend jumping festivals in addition to the two existing Cheltenham Festivals in November and March.
- Convert an appropriate proportion of novice chases to beginners chases.
- Maintain existing long handicap bands for all NH handicaps for the present.
- Novices should run at least three times in a chase before being eligible for a Class A or B handicap chase.

- Increase the number of mares' races.
- The Jockey Club should carry out a further review of the efficacy and safety of re-introducing Jumping on all-weather tracks.
- Bumpers for British-bred horses should be removed from the race programme.
- Develop closer ties with Point to Pointing.

British breeding industry

- Introduce an owners' premium scheme for British-bred horses in 2004.
- Continue the breeders' prize scheme.
- Continue to improve the number of races for quality fillies and mares.

Other recommendations

- Encourage the development of all-weather racing.
- Develop a British Racing Hall of Fame.
- Introduce the weighing of all horses at the racecourse prior to a race.
- Encourage racecourses to introduce sectional timing.
- Make no changes to the start and finish of the racing seasons.
- Introduce floodlights on more racecourses.

Racing review – the business plan

Any accountant involved in looking at a business review for any equine business must be aware of the impact of the Racing Review.

Points raised in **CHAPTER 2** should also be considered, eg the horse population could increase by 2,300 over the next five years. The current 'fight' for improving the conditions for stable staff is of great relevance to the trainer. How will the increase be funded?

Points of interest in the Racing Review that would impact on the business plan are the review of jockey's working hours, the appearance money proposed to be paid by racecourses and the owners' premium scheme for British-bred horses.

It could be argued that trainers focus on finding the 'right race' for a horse and their own tally of winners. Some trainers could focus on a higher yield of prize money and appearance money for their owners rather than increasing their tally thus trying to make the racehorse more 'economically viable' and encourage owners to stay.

An Example of Chattel Leasing C

CHATTEL LEASING

PARTIES

1 The parents namely ...
2 The children namely ...

BACKGROUND

(A) The children are beneficial owners of the chattels set out in the schedule below ('chattels').
(B) The children wish to allow the parents the use and enjoyment of the chattels on the basis of full consideration payable by the parents.

AGREEMENT

1 Bailment
The children grant a lease of the chattels to the parents for the following term and generally on the terms and conditions following:

2 The term
The term of lease shall be equal to the joint lives and life of the survivor of the parents, terminable earlier:

2.1 Upon six months written notice given by either party.
2.2 Immediately upon default of any obligations contained in clause 9.
2.3 Immediately upon both the parents or the survivor of them becoming mentally incapable within the meaning of section 94(2) of the Mental Health Act 1983.

3 Ownership

3.1 The children retain the ownership of the chattels.
3.2 The children reserve the right to fix any planting or other means of identification to chattels or any of them.
3.3 The parents covenant not (nor take steps) to sell, deal, charge or part with the chattels in any other way contrary to the ownership of the children.
3.4 The parents will immediately pay any sum required to remove any lien, which may arise over the chattels.

4 Enjoyments and housing

4.1 The children covenant with the parents (provided the parents pay the rent and perform the parents' covenants) that the parents shall peaceably hold and enjoy the chattels during the term without any interruption by the children or any other person rightfully claiming under or in trust for any of them.
4.2 The chattels shall be housed at ... [Name of property] ... or at other locations from time to time agreed between parents and the children.

5 Rental

5.1 The initial annual rental for the chattels shall be £ ... per annum (which is agreed by the children and the parents to reflect ... % of the current open market value of the chattels).
5.2 The rental shall be paid annually; the first year's rental is due on the signing of this agreement (and the children's acknowledgement receipt of it); further annual rental payments shall be due on the anniversaries of this agreement. Such adjustments as is necessary on the termination of the agreement by the death of the survivor of the parents shall be made as is required; otherwise there shall be no adjustment.
5.3 The rental shall be reviewable by agreement at three-yearly intervals from the date of this agreement to ensure that the parents give full consideration for the use and enjoyment of the chattels. In default of agreement the reviewed rent shall be determined by a valuer appointed by the president for the time being of the Incorporated Society of Values and Auctioneers acting as expert and not an arbitrator; either party shall be at liberty to request the president to make such an appointment.

6 Insurance

6.1 The parents will insure the chattels for their full replacement cost comprehensively against all risk with the interest of the children noted on the policy and will duly and punctually pay all premiums and on request will promptly produce the insurance policy and proof of payment of premiums to the children. All claims under such insurance policy will be dealt with in accordance with the written direction of the children. The parents in trust shall hold all claims and moneys received by the parents under such insurance policy for the children.

7 Preservation and repair

7.1 The parents undertake to preserve the chattels.

7.2 The parents undertake to keep the chattels clean and in good and substantial repair and will bear the cost of any repairs not covered by the insurance.

7.3 The parents will permit the children and any other person authorised by them at any reasonable hour to view or survey the state and condition of the chattels.

7.4 The parents will forthwith after being required to do so by the children make good any repair to the chattels.

PROVIDED that nothing in this clause shall require the parents to maintain the chattels in anything other than their current condition or require the parents to improve or put the chattels into first rate condition.

8 Security

8.1 The parents undertake to put in place, maintain and bear the cost of such security arrangements as are from time to time agreed between the parents and the children or as are responsibly stipulated by the children to reflect the requirements of any relevant insurance company, advice from the police or advice otherwise specifically received from a specialist security company engaged for the purpose.

9 Default

If the parents default in the punctual payment of any of the instalments of rent provided for, or default in the payment of the insurance premiums as provided for, or default in the performance of any of the terms and conditions of this agreement, the children may immediately retake possession of the chattels, without notice to the parents, with or without legal process, and the parents by this agreement authorise and empower the children to enter the premises or other places where the chattels may be found and to take and carry away the chattels. All moneys due under this agreement shall become immediately due and payable plus all reasonable costs of repossession.

EXECUTED on … 200(3)
Signed by …

Note to the precedent

(A) The initial rent should be arrived at preferably by written negotiation between two competent valuers aware of the terms of the lease, the value and condition of the chattels, cost of insurance and security etc.
(B) The agreement is said to be a chattel lease as that is the common understanding. Strictly it is a bailment agreement though nothing turns on that.

In the case of property, which is an interest in land, any occupation by the donor of the whole or any part of the land is disregarded for the purposes of above if:

(i) It results from a change in circumstances of the donor since the time of the gift, being a change which was unforeseen at that time and was not brought about by the donor to receive the benefit of this provision; and
(ii) It occurs at a time when the donor has become unable to maintain himself through old age, infirmity or otherwise; and
(iii) It represents a reasonable provision by the done for the care and maintenance of the donor.

Inspector's Manual for Late Loss Claims

D

IM3357 – Trading losses: late claims

(The following extract is reproduced from the Inland Revenue's Inspector's Manual)

Although, as IM3357 says, there is no explicit provision in the Taxes Acts to allow late loss relief claims, the Board is prepared in certain circumstances to exercise its general powers of care and management under TMA 1970 s 1 to give the relief which would have been due had the claim been made in time. In practice, late claims are admitted only where the taxpayer had effectively been prevented from making an in-date claim for reasons beyond their and their agent's control AND the claim was made within a reasonable period thereafter.

Applying this principle, and subject to the caveats below and in IM3359, Inspectors should accept late loss relief claims in circumstances which follow. In explaining that a late claim may be admitted Inspectors should mention the general approach set out in the first sub-paragraph above and say in which of the circumstances described below the claim falls.

(a) Where illness of the taxpayer, a close relation or an agent caused or substantially contributed to the failure to claim in time, unless someone else could reasonably have been expected to step into their shoes. We would expect alternative arrangements to be made as soon as it became apparent that an illness would not be short (say lasting less than three months). Claims should have been made within three months of the earlier of such alternative arrangements being made, or recovery from the illness. Claims admitted under this sub-head should not normally therefore be made more than six months late.

(b) Where information was waited from a third party. The information must have been needed before it was possible to establish that a loss had been sustained in the relevant year, and reasonable and persistent efforts must have been made to obtain it in good time. This sub-head does not apply where the existence of a loss for tax purposes in the relevant year (albeit unquantifiable) was, or should have been, clearly known to the taxpayer or agent even without the outstanding information.

(c) Where an informal notification within the terms of IM3354 (second sub-paragraph) was given by the taxpayer or agent within the time limit but he or she was not invited to make a formal claim. The taxpayer or agent must reasonably have believed that an acceptable claim had been made and thought that nothing more was needed. The aim is to protect the taxpayers who would otherwise be prejudiced by the Revenue failure. Conversely, where an agent advised only an intention to claim and it is clear that there was no misapprehension that this formed a valid claim, the claim should be refused.

(d) Where, at the date of expiry of the time limit, the taxpayer or agent was unaware of income against which the loss might be set. A late claim may be admitted if it is presented within a reasonable period of the taxpayer or agent becoming aware of the income. Cases where the taxpayer or agent is aware of the income, but that income has not been assessed, do not fall within this sub-head.

(e) Where the emergence of a profit or loss depended on discussions with the Inspector, which were uncompleted when the time limit expired and the delay in agreeing figures is not wholly the fault of the taxpayer or agent. A late claim may be admitted if it is presented within a reasonable period of the relevant figures being agreed. This sub-head does not apply where the accounts themselves were not submitted until the time limit had expired or was about to expire, or where a claim could have been made on the basis or the original computations.

For the purposes of this instruction and IM3359, a reasonable period should be taken as three months or any shorter period specified in the Inspector's letter.

Useful Websites E

www.abi.org.uk	**Association of British Insurers** Provides information for customers and companies, including information about the ABI, news items, consumer advice, industry advice and a database of members.
www.amateurjockeys.co.uk	**Amateur Jockeys Association** Information on how to join the Association, a list of amateur riders races; the latest copy of the Association newsletter appears on these pages.
www.architecture.com	**Royal Institute of British Architects (RIBA)** An extensive website outlining the work undertaken by members of the association and their current policy on agriculture in general.

www.beva.org.uk	**British Equine Veterinary Association** This site contains news and membership information on the association. It also contains guides on how to best care for your horse.
www.bhb.co.uk	**The British Horse Racing Board** A website filled with useful information on racing, ownership, training and useful links.
www.bhs.org.uk	**British Horse Society** This website is a thorough guide to all equine information. It includes details of riding clubs, instructor registration, careers and trade and equine directories.
www.bhtb.co.uk	**British Horseracing Training Board** With company profile, education information and lots of useful links this is a really good website for all equine needs.
www.butler-co.co.uk	**Butler & Co** An introduction to the firm of chartered accountants and the services it provides. The author, Julie Butler, is managing partner.
www.cla.org.uk	**The Country Land and Business Association (CLA)** A website that gives a further viewpoint on the rural economy and looks at ways to diversify. Model form of agreements, such as share farming and grazing agreements.

www.comeracing.co.uk	**The Racecourse Association** Information on fixtures and racecourse locations.
www.cpre.org.uk	**The Council for the Protection of Rural England (CPRE)** This website looks at the rural economy as a whole and includes sections on the latest planning thinking, as well as campaigns. CPRE exists to promote the beauty, tranquillity and diversity of rural England by encouraging the sustainable use of land and other natural resources in town and country.
www.defra.gov.uk	**Department of Environment, Food and Rural Affairs (DEFRA)** This website includes the current thinking of the government on the farming industry and the rural economy. It contains sections on sustainable farming and food and rural development. It can be used to ensure that any diversification fits in with current thinking, which will enable it to be accepted quicker.
www.hblb.org.uk	**Horserace Betting Levy Board** Information on the Board's policies, levy scheme and plans for improvement of horseracing.

www.hmce.gov.uk	**HM Customs and Excise** Similar to the Inland Revenue website but not as clear.
www.hdc.org.uk	**Horticultural Development Council** From this site you can search through all HDC funded research projects, publications, HDC News articles and events.
www.inlandrevenue.gov.uk	**HM Inland Revenue** The latest Revenue interpretations can be found on this website together with copies of all the Revenue's manuals, some copies of all the Revenue's manuals, some of which are quoted in this book. Fairly easy to use.
www.ilph.co.uk	**International League for the Protection of Horses** Information on correct care of your horse. Also able to make a donation online.
www.jagb.co.uk/mainsite.htm	**Jockeys Association of Great Britain** Jockey profiles and related news.
www.mfha.co.uk	**Masters of Foxhounds Association** Find out more about your local hunt and foxhunting in general. What it is – Where it happens – How you can take part or have a look.

www.njpc-ltd.co.uk	**National Joint Pitch Council** Information on Application to the Bookmakers Lists, Qualification to Bet, Authorised Bookmakers, Advance Booking System and Allocation of Pitches, List Positions, Attendance in the Betting Ring, Nominated Officers, Authorised Representatives, Bookmakers Assistants, Authorisation Badges.
www.nfu.org.uk	**National Farmers' Union** The National Farmers' Union is the democratic organisation for farmers and growers in England and Wales; their website has all sorts of useful information for farmers.
www.planning.odpm.gov.uk	**The Office of the Deputy Prime Minister** This website includes details of all the current planning policies of the Government, including copies of all the PPG statements.
www.pvprojects.com	**Pro Vision Planning and Design** An emerging website with a practice outline, introduction to the company and contact details.
www.rics.org.uk	**Royal Institute of Chartered Surveyors (RICS)** An introduction to the work undertaken by members and the policy and views of the Institute.

www.racehorseowners.net	**Racehorse Owners Association** This website is packed with the latest news and information on the racing industry.
www.racingpost.co.uk	**Racing Post** A detailed guide to races past, present and future, including tips and reports.
www.riba.org/go/RIBA/Home.html	**Royal Institute of British Architects** Information on the Institute and how to become a member.
www.rspca.org.uk	**Royal Society For Prevention of Cruelty To Animals** Visit this site for RSPCA news, information on current campaigns and your local RSPCA.
www.smmt.co.uk	**The Society of Motor Manufacturers and Traders Ltd (SMMT)** Useful for CO_2 emission details.
www.thebritishthoroughbred.co.uk	**The British Thoroughbred** A website for news and information on racehorses, from breeding to ownership.
www.thejockeyclub.co.uk	**The Jockey Club** Responsible for the conduct of racing, safety and welfare, licensing of racecourse and individuals, compiling and applying the orders and rules of racing.
www.thevatconsultancy.com	**The VAT Consultancy** A guide to the services provided by the firm and to all VAT matters and concerns.

www.thompsons.com	**Thompson's Group plc** An introduction to the firm and its breadth of private and corporate client financial planning services.
www.thoroughbredbreeders association.co.uk	**Thoroughbred Breeders Association** The voice of the British Breeder with information on government issues relating to horse breeding and information on upcoming events.
www.ukonline.gov.uk	**Open Government** With links to all national and local government department websites.
www.vcacarfueldata.org.uk	**Vehicle Certification Agency (VCA)** Details of CO_2 emissions are available on this site.
www.withers.co.uk	**Withers** A comprehensive guide to the services that are provided by the firm.
www.weatherbys-group.com	**Weatherbys Group** Use this website to learn more about Weatherbys and to access statistics.
www.wandb.co.uk	**White and Bowker** Mark Charter, a contributor to this book, is a partner in this firm. The site gives a guide to the services provided.

Index